DATE DUE

JAMES J. KILPATRICK

JAMES J.
KILPATRICK

SALESMAN FOR SEGREGATION

WILLIAM P. HUSTWIT

THE UNIVERSITY OF NORTH CAROLINA PRESS | CHAPEL HILL

© 2013 THE UNIVERSITY OF NORTH CAROLINA PRESS

All rights reserved   Manufactured in the United States of America
Designed by Sally Fry   Set in Charter and Ultra by codeMantra

Library of Congress Cataloging-in-Publication Data
Hustwit, William P.
James J. Kilpatrick : salesman for segregation / William P. Hustwit.
pages cm
Includes bibliographical references and index.
ISBN 978-1-4696-0213-4 (hardback)
1. Kilpatrick, James Jackson, 1920–2010 2. Television journalists—United States—
Biography 3. Journalists—United States—Biography 4. Editors—United States—
Biography 5. Segregation—Political aspects—Southern States—History—
20th century 6. Government, Resistance to—Southern States—History—
20th century I. Title.
PN4874.K5355H87 2013
070′.92′4—dc23
[B]
2012037477

17 16 15 14 13   5 4 3 2 1

For Mom and Dad

I think of [Kilpatrick] as the primary editorialist on our side of the fence dating back so many years. In fact, I sometimes jocularly refer to him as "Number One." —WILLIAM F. BUCKLEY JR.

Know your audience. —KILPATRICK, *Fine Print*

CONTENTS

A section of illustrations begins on page 197

ACKNOWLEDGMENTS

My debts are many to Charles W. Eagles for generously reading the manuscript during various drafts, suggesting improvements, and running over a few of my puppies; to Ted Ownby and Bob Haws for their encouragement; to Joe Ward for arranging research support; to William A. Link and Nancy MacLean for offering sensible advice; to Jeff Roche for conversations and friendship; to Peter Rutkoff and Will Scott at Kenyon College for inspiring me; to the anonymous readers at the University of North Carolina Press; to the faculty and staff of the history department at the University of Mississippi; to the librarians and staff at the Library of Virginia and the Virginia Historical Society; to the wonderful people at the University of Virginia Special Collections; to J. L. and Diane Holloway for their generous gift; to Charles Reagan Wilson for introducing me to Charles Grench, a patient and smart editor; to the staff at the University of North Carolina Press, especially Sara Jo Cohen and Mary Caviness; to my friend Andy Douglas; and to Brenda Eagles for her support and proofreading.

I regret that two special people in my life did not live to see the publication of this book. My brave brother-in-law, Jack Tate, and Cora Minor Jordan, a veteran civil rights activist and my dear friend, both hoped to see the finished product. Both are missed daily.

Finally, I appreciate the endless support of my family: Ron and Barb Hustwit, Holly Tate, Ron and Heather Hustwit, and, of course, my nephew, Liam, and niece, Molly.

INTRODUCTION

In 1960 or "thereabouts," James J. Kilpatrick vaguely, unhappily remembered, two black journalists came to his office in Richmond to report on the city's response to the 1954 *Brown v. Board of Education* ruling and asked for his opinion as editor of the *Richmond News Leader*. Forty-two years later, in 2002, Kilpatrick noted the reporters as about his age, attractive, and intelligent. Despite their engaging conversation in his office about the city's reactions to the desegregation decision, Kilpatrick had not extended invitations to them for dinner or drinks. His reasoning could not have been simpler: they were black; Negroes and whites were not equals or friends. Raised in the Jim Crow South, Kilpatrick had been "nurtured on the mother's milk of segregation," which formed "the natural order of mankind." He went to bed ashamed and slept terribly, but snubbing his black visitors was "an epiphany of sorts," he later recalled. During the decade after his awakening, Kilpatrick claimed to edge toward edification on racial matters. By 1970, he had recognized the "terrible evils" of "state-sponsored racism." The story of Kilpatrick's retreat from espousing segregation also involves conservatism and the South's long entanglement with white supremacy. For more than four decades in public life—first as an influential editor defending Jim Crow in Virginia, then as a major syndicated political columnist—Kilpatrick captured how support of segregation could segue into conservatism as the civil rights era faded and gave a lot of fumbling, apprehensive people ways out of a predicament beyond their control.[1]

Kilpatrick's apology was wrapped up in his career, and his life chronicles the emergence of modern American conservatism and the collapse of segregation. Though not at first recognized as a sentinel segregationist, he led a campaign at the *News Leader* against school desegregation and the Supreme Court based on a resuscitation of states' rights to defend "the southern way of life" from an intrusive and expansive federal government. Kilpatrick pitched segregation to white southern resisters and a national audience alike, and his work at the newspaper earned him a reputation as the fire-breathing editor-intellectual of massive resistance. Behind that notoriety, however, hid a more complex man with a strategic ability to change over time into an underappreciated yet significant figure on the political right. For Kilpatrick, massive resistance served as a springboard to larger venues and a wider purview and acted as an early conduit between his region's conservatives and their ideological counterparts beyond the South. He refused, however, to let racial malice blind him to positions the right found more tenable over the long term.

The fight against the *Brown* decision consecrated a marriage between Kilpatrick's segregationist thought and political and intellectual conservatism that challenged the civil rights movement and its progeny. Working with William F. Buckley's *National Review*, David Lawrence's *U.S. News & World Report*, Henry Regnery's press, and Barry Goldwater's presidential campaign swept Kilpatrick into a clique within the conservative movement where the high priests of the right set the parameters for orthodox beliefs and the linkage between states' rights and civil rights became a thoroughly domesticated issue. Already by the late 1950s, in the view of historian George H. Nash, James Kilpatrick had emerged as the "more or less 'official'" conservative spokesman on constitutional issues and civil rights. Southern, western, and national conservatism speedily teamed up in the postwar years, and Kilpatrick's attacks on civil rights, based mostly on constitutional grounds and enshrined in the 1964 Republican presidential platform, meant that his racial beliefs were in league with national trends and attitudes.[2]

During the late 1960s and 1970s, Kilpatrick contested federal affirmative action and school busing programs and popularized the notion of "reverse racism" even as he admitted that legal segregation was wrong. In post-1965 America, his approach actually furthered a broader conservative opposition to race-conscious policies. As America's foremost syndicated political columnist and a well-known network television personality, he emphasized freedom of association as he tried to foil government intervention that proposed remedies for public and private forms of discrimination. In the process, Kilpatrick erased the troublesome issue of impolitic racial bigotry and deprived civil rights leaders and liberals of the very arguments that they had monopolized for almost a generation. His rhetorically race-neutral rejection of minority rights engineered on themes of strict constitutionalism, civil libertarianism, organic community, opposition to social uplift programs, and equality of opportunity suggested a deeply racial current in both southern and American conservatism. By the 1970s, Kilpatrick's columns and television spots were lodestones for the right and showed how compatible indifference to or uneasiness with black equality was with conservatism. During and after the 1980s, Ronald Reagan's attitudinal revolution in politics also helped germinate Kilpatrick's racial narrative as more Americans embraced the language of individual merit and turned away from government antidotes.

In important ways, Kilpatrick's story is a revisionist statement to the history of conservatism and segregationists. Aspects of the white South's struggle with the end of Jim Crow and the politics of race have previously been told. The move away from segregation and massive resistance, and even a distinctive southern conservatism not purely race-based, has become a mantra for understanding the American conservative movement. The passing of the old racial order, however, did not relegate the South's regional identity and all massive resisters to irrelevance and ignominy. As did thousands of white southerners, James Kilpatrick opposed the black freedom struggle, but the contours of his struggle in Virginia and elsewhere bore little resemblance to the fate of many defeated segregationist leaders. During the heyday of civil rights victories, segregationist survival became the name of the game; Kilpatrick survived.[3]

Kilpatrick's racial politics deserve attention because they challenge a historiography of conservatism that focuses on either the movement's populist activism or the mandarins who built the modern Republican Party. While the scholarly literature on the right has debated whether grassroots fomenters or political and intellectual elites played the most important role in the development of conservatism, it was journalists, such as Kilpatrick, who held critical positions as mediums and opinion makers and who gave the right an effective political vocabulary. Though historians of modern American conservatism have almost all recognized the appeal of Buckley, Goldwater, Nixon, and Reagan, few have explored the intermediary figures who expressed and articulated the ideas of the right. Kilpatrick was a link between two groups that may at first seem diametrically opposed: the conservative elite and those marginalized by the dominant culture and liberalism. As conservatives organized from above and below and fought for political power in America, they found an ally in Kilpatrick and his adept ability to redefine the racial and political landscape. With access to state and national leaders and a knack for responding to the concerns of the public and powerful alike, Kilpatrick found new authority as an alternative voice of authentic conservative views.[4]

This book is an effort to correct rather than to reverse directions or altogether reject other interpretations, though readers familiar with the scholarly debates about conservatism may not be inclined to see it that way. One striking shortcoming in some current literature is the tendency to assume that the white South lost any distinguishing regional features after the civil rights movement. Whether historians describe the modern South as the "Sun Belt South" or the "suburban South," such labels rob the region of idiosyncrasies and betray discomfort with the Americanization of the South. Historians would do well to recall that regions can be different and exceptional at the same time and that the Americanization of the South and the "Southernization of America," to borrow journalist John Egerton's term, occurred simultaneously. Kilpatrick illustrated that complicated process in his profession and his life. His thick, Tidewater Virginia accent on television and his paeans to the South's traditional, organic community in syndication contributed to his rise to national prominence and even added charm to his appeal.[5]

Kilpatrick's beliefs and story point to political and regional continuity within the nation's transitory, partisan politics. His life spanned, almost precisely, the ascent of conservatism as a coherent political movement. He came of age during the Depression and the New Deal when liberalism and conservatism took on their contemporary, conflicting meanings. He died in August 2010, nearly two years after the election of Barack Obama, the nation's first black president. But his life was more than a mere chronological link between pre- and postwar conservatism: white southerners like Kilpatrick had a consciousness of history and their unique place within it. His ancestors fought in the Civil War; his mentors revered the South's statesmen and the Confederacy's generals; his successor at the *Richmond News Leader* continued the fight against racial reform. He chose to take a stand against civil rights when racism became the defining issue of the day, but that is not the same as a right turn in Kilpatrick's politics or the South's. Kilpatrick's political priorities, like those of his peers and the region, had moved very little. Party labels and partisan allegiances mattered less to him and many other white southerners than their fundamental politics and seemingly ubiquitous, nearly inexhaustible conservatism.[6]

Ingrained into Kilpatrick's conservatism was the omphalos of race, even in muted and so-called color-blind forms. While this study focuses on the trajectory of Kilpatrick the segregationist, in important respects, he was also typical of how opposition to civil rights and equality adapted in the South and in America, which reveals the disturbing continuities between race and conservatism's popular causes in the 1960s and 1970s. Rather than compartmentalizing or stripping divisive issues, like taxes, social programs, the free market, property rights, and law and order, of their relationship to race, Kilpatrick recognized them as wrapped up with minority rights and egalitarianism. The affinity for such politicized topics among conservatives and the mainstream, he understood early on, had everything to do with race and whites' desires to protect their material interests from black advancements and the government.[7]

Salesman for Segregation analyzes Kilpatrick within the greater context of the confluence of race, politics, economics, and the media in postwar America. It examines him as a prophetic and emblematic figure linked to two interwoven trends that have shaped modern America: the ever-present—even when dismissed and disorganized—constellation of political and economic ideas known as conservatism and the ramification of civil rights on whites. As the political climate in the 1970s and 1980s tilted starboard, Kilpatrick took his place as a dean of conservatism, especially its southern strand. In the wake of segregation, the South's right found a new, heavyweight spokesman with national exposure in syndicated columns, in alliance with the Goldwater campaign, in Buckley's *National Review*, and on network television. An awareness of his arguments and defiance helps uncover the racial problem in the white mind that the Swedish economist Gunnar Myrdal called attention to in 1944.[8]

What follows is not a traditional biography. This book explains much of Kilpatrick's life, far beyond his well-known role in massive resistance, but through an assessment of a particular variety of conservatism. Racial conservatives such as James J. Kilpatrick played a vital role in southern and American political discourse. Simple racism, however, will not divulge the drives, needs, ambitions, and ideational forces that shaped Kilpatrick's worldview. As historian Winthrop Jordan remarked in 1966, "To understand people's attitudes about race, you have to understand their attitudes about everything." Since basically every successful public figure in the South was a segregationist in the 1950s and early 1960s, little may be gleaned by concentrating only on segregationism. Comprehending opponents of the civil rights movement has entailed unraveling the political, economic, and cultural dimensions of southern white society to explain how and why a man like Kilpatrick held the racial attitudes he did. When scrutinized, his opinions surface as far more complicated than the candid race-baiting of Lester Maddox, George Wallace, and other demagogues. Born in segregated Oklahoma City and raised by conservative parents during the Great Depression, Kilpatrick experienced a setting and family background that prepared him for his defense of white supremacy. He persisted in preventing advancements for blacks while succeeding as a professional editor and columnist. Sometimes his words and deeds encouraged prejudice. At other times, he worked to pacify racial hate and demagoguery. The complexity of his character was often hidden behind his public persona.[9]

James Kilpatrick's career and writings provide an excellent opportunity to probe one white southern conservative's changing racial language as the race question drew increasing attention in the South and the nation. A dissection of the progression of his thought also helps to explain the thinking of other conservatives and illuminate larger developments in southern race relations. The editor confronted many of the racial problems of his time and created a few, too. Rooted in his beliefs and yet aware of the inevitability of change, he searched for order amid the tide of civil rights victories. For nearly thirty years he continually reconsidered, revised, and refined strategies to deal with black-white relations and African American rights. Relentlessly, he objected to racial equality and advocated laws meant to keep blacks as second-class citizens.

After the civil rights movement, Kilpatrick publicly repented for advocating racial discrimination but remained dissatisfied with the legacies of the black freedom struggle. The tug-of-war between his professional success and racial thinking paralleled transformations in southern and national race relations. He lived and practiced his line of work in the mainstream of southern and American life. It was in the columns and editorials of conservative writers like him that thousands of Americans first found a recognizable expression of their own longings for traditional, local communities and individual freedom from state interference without confronting the controversial history of race.

Limited to an account of Kilpatrick's racial beliefs, this study does not attempt to explain the entirety of the postwar conservative and civil rights movements. An examination of him instead provides insight into the forces that collided over equal rights in America and the dilemma of the race problem in the white mind. The tragedy of his life was not any kind of economic or political failure but rather his personal inability to recognize the equality of nonwhites and his unwillingness to fight for black justice. His stubborn racial bias, his fears, and his opportunistic desire for respectability—pathologies that plagued too many Americans of all classes and from across the nation—belong in the mainstream history of the years before and up to the last days of the civil rights movement.[10]

ONE

Into the Byrd Cage

When James J. Kilpatrick went to Richmond in 1941, he had a limited understanding of writing for a professional newspaper, even less knowledge of Virginia, and only a nascent political philosophy. But that Kilpatrick was an authentic conservative in the making there could be no doubt. Although he did not come from aristocratic Virginia bloodlines or from a powerful political family, Kilpatrick was imbued from his childhood with the ideals of genteel southern conservatism tempered by individualism and the realities of capitalist imperatives. In perhaps unconventional ways, a sense of place, family background, and eventually acceptance of Richmond's old-line high society added ingredients to a life that started in Oklahoma.

Rising from the Plains

Concerning Oklahoma's identity in the early twentieth century, there was pure flux and only a shared consciousness of being "new." If nothing else, Oklahomans understood that their Plains State, admitted in 1907, had little sense of a past and was hundreds of settlers, businessmen, opportunists, and the nation's largest concentration of American Indians. In terms of cultural landscape, Oklahoma had entered a liminal zone, a threshold between the New West and the Old South. Tucked between two political cultures, the region soon fell under the South's gravitational influence. The white voters of Oklahoma imported a Democratic power bloc in state politics and immediately established the southern way of life in race relations to control the hundreds of thousands of blacks who accompanied it from the South. Oklahoma may have looked western with its dry prairies and homesteads, but it felt southern in its proscriptions against racially integrated schools, transportation, and marriages. The insistence that a hierarchy of white over black differentiated the races and a premium placed on the natural orders of the world, particularly the idea that individuals stood free from impersonal institutions and government, shaped Kilpatrick's upbringing.[1]

The Kilpatrick family's settlement in Oklahoma was the culmination of moves dating back nearly two hundred years. The Kilpatricks originated in lowland Scotland. Driven off their land in the wake of the eighteenth-century Jacobite uprisings, the failed rebellions by Catholic Scots to put a Stuart king on the throne, they first went to Ireland. According to family lore, there the Kilpatrick clan acquired its temperament and its coat of arms when a remote ancestor—a county sheriff—chased a murderer into a church, stabbed him despite the sanctuary, and emerged onto the church steps with his dagger dripping blood. "I make sure," the ancient Kilpatrick frankly stated, and the motto, which appears on the family crest along with a depiction of a hand clutching a blood-spattered blade, came to define the family spirit. After the Reformation, the Kilpatrick clan divided into Catholics and Protestants, relocating in Dublin and Belfast accordingly.[2]

Around the end of the eighteenth century, W. W. Kilpatrick, representative of the Protestant branch, arrived in New Orleans and became a lumber dealer. His son, Douglas Mitchell Kilpatrick, grew up in a merchant's household, worked as a store clerk before the Civil War, and married a local girl named Alice Sedette Filleul, whose family descended from France. In the Civil War, Douglas Kilpatrick joined the city's prestigious Washington Artillery and fought as a captain in the Army of Northern Virginia. In 1886, he named his newborn son James Jackson Kilpatrick in honor of the Confederate general Thomas Jonathan "Stonewall" Jackson. By then, Douglas Kilpatrick had already built a lucrative retail business supplying food and provisions to ship captains in the Crescent City.[3]

In late-nineteenth-century New Orleans, the Kilpatricks were a prominent merchant family and members of the local gentry. Douglas Kilpatrick participated in civic life as president of the city's Chamber of Commerce and even played a role imposing order on and restoring racial hierarchy in postwar New Orleans. Family history maintains that he suppressed an 1890s insurrection by African Americans. In reality, despite the fabled account, Douglas Kilpatrick was a ringleader of the paramilitary Crescent White League's 1874 coup against the federally backed Reconstruction government that endorsed interracial democracy in Louisiana. Kilpatrick's young, inexperienced volunteers, eager to emulate their older Confederate heroes, charged metropolitan police and federal soldiers armed with howitzers and Gatling guns in downtown New Orleans. The 1,500 White Leaguers routed the opposition and sacked the statehouse, customhouse, and arsenal. For years, Liberty Monument, an obelisk at the foot of Canal Street, commemorated the incident in which twenty-one White Leaguers died.[4]

Mainly, Douglas Kilpatrick concentrated on his supply trade and not on punitive illegalities. Over time, he passed on his business knowledge to his son. James Kilpatrick, dour even as a young man and beset with a large brow, solid jaw, and fearsome mustache, also learned to sell goods to sea captains but decided to break away from his parents after he graduated in 1910 from Tulane University. In the first of several unexpected decisions, the maverick son migrated that same year from the Lower South to Oklahoma City and started in the lumber business.[5]

Joining a host of new timbermen, James Kilpatrick cruised Oklahoma's virgin forests for cordwood, shingles, telegraph poles, mining timber, and construction lumber, estimated their worth, and bid on them. Kilpatrick's timber company catered to the railroad corporations and farmers. The firm sold three items crucial to building the state's transportation infrastructure and to separating parcels of new land: railway ties, bridge timbers, and fence posts. Business flourished, and he, able to support a family, looked for a bride.[6]

In 1914, Kilpatrick met and soon married Alma Hawley, a tender, striking, and intelligent woman and a native of Oklahoma City. Alma Hawley's people drew a lineage back to Virginia and Kentucky and worked their way north and west throughout the nineteenth century. Her father, Franklin Hawley, a medical doctor, born in 1864 in Wisconsin and raised in Minnesota, relocated the family to Oklahoma. Before him, the Hawleys had put down roots across the country from Maine to Kansas. The story was told with reverence of Franklin Hawley's choice to risk life and uncertainty and participate in the 1889 Oklahoma land rush, part of the proud "Great Run" boomer generation. Alma, born in 1894, grew up in the raucous atmosphere of territorial Oklahoma. What the Hawleys lacked in southern heritage, they made up for by being one of Oklahoma's founding families. James Kilpatrick Jr., or "Jack," a shortened version of his middle name, born on November 1, 1920, became the second of Alma and James Sr.'s three children. Daughter Blanche, born almost four years before, and son Hawley, three years later, made the Kilpatricks a family of five.[7]

Early on, James Sr. and Alma groomed their oldest son to be a writer, not a timber cruiser. Alma Hawley initiated James Kilpatrick Jr.'s love of writing and concluded that Jack should spend his life in some sort of literary endeavor. He drew his southern cultural coordinates from the Kilpatrick side of the family, but the Hawleys determined his career. The education of James Kilpatrick began in the crib, or so his mother later told him, with reading labels on cans of Ammen's talcum powder and bottles of baby oil and then on to Mother Goose stories, Aesop's fables, and the Grimm Brothers' fairy tales. Alma Hawley's father composed amateur adventure novels about pioneer life in the north woods of Minnesota and Wisconsin that she read to her son for entertainment as well. She also taught him composition and the poet's discipline of rhyme and meter. Doting on her son, she typed his prose and poetry efforts into a notebook for display.[8]

Kilpatrick was an attentive child around his mother. Reading enthralled him, and he took in everything she put in front of him. At age five, Kilpatrick plunged into Giovanni Boccaccio's *Decameron* and finished 612 of the *One Thousand and One Nights*. In the same year, he published a commentary about his first-grade marble tournament. The next year, an essay heralding the recent transatlantic flight of Charles Lindbergh reached a children's magazine. "I had lost my amateur status," Kilpatrick later celebrated. "Then came a copy of the magazine itself. Byline! It was a thrill that comes once in a life time." From then on, the precocious boy craved a life in print.[9]

Frequent research trips to the Carnegie Library in downtown Oklahoma City fine-tuned Kilpatrick's compositions. The ample library introduced him to a realm of ideas that he otherwise could only have guessed at, and he felt completely at ease among books. "I lived [in the library] almost as much as I lived at home," Kilpatrick remarked. From a young age, he had a voracious reading appetite that continued throughout his life. Jack Kilpatrick loved epics and poems the most, especially the works of Robert Louis Stevenson, Henry Wadsworth Longfellow, Rudyard Kipling, T. S. Eliot, A. E. Housman, and Edgar Allan Poe. He and his siblings spent hours quoting lines of poetry to each other. In the Depression years, reading served as an escape from the problems of society for him. It also filled the void left from being a physically unimpressive and often sickly child who suffered from asthma.[10]

His formal education progressed, too. Homework included preparing for spelling bees; writing themes, plays, book reviews, and verse; memorizing poetry and drama, and reciting words to improve pronunciation. At Taft Junior High School and Classen High School, several years of Latin helped him master the foundation of much of the English language. Kilpatrick enjoyed sentence diagramming more than any other writing exercise. It taught him respect for the language and ordered it in definite terms.[11]

Even as a teenager, Jack Kilpatrick needed a position, a place in an organization where he could find an outlet for his fascination with writing. Without such an association, he might drift without purpose. At thirteen, after becoming friendly with the son of the *Oklahoma City Times*'s editor,

Kilpatrick worked as a copy boy at the evening newspaper. Walter M. Harrison, the manager of the paper and famous newsman in the Southwest, trained dozens of journalists and carried a commanding nickname, "The Skipper." The experience in print journalism gave Kilpatrick the chance to apprentice under a top-notch editor.[12]

Work at the city paper spilled over into school, where Kilpatrick's skills in setting type by hand and running the proof press led to his editorial direction of both the junior and senior high school papers. The mere scent of printer's ink enraptured Jack, and "writing, writing, writing" consumed his spare time. In junior high, he briefly forayed into independent journalism. Unhappy with the school's paper and its banal stories, he created a rogue periodical, "The Weekly Keyhole," free from adult supervision, to cover adolescent gossip and fights. One particularly large student who disliked Kilpatrick's reporting took him "outside the confectionary and beat the living s[hit] out of me," Kilpatrick remembered. The principal then intervened and declared that either the independent paper should close or Kilpatrick should leave school. Rarely a risk-taker like his father, he played by the rules and instead became editor of the student newspaper, whose faculty adviser, George Sturm, stoked Kilpatrick's newspapering bug. While growing as a writer, he sharpened his sense of place and an inchoate political agenda.[13]

Much of James J. Kilpatrick Jr.'s conservative education developed from his experiences within this Great Plains setting. His Oklahoma was a product of the Deep South transplanted west and the twin local traditions of individualism and free market economics. The core of that cultural geography began with small, productive family farms and ranches in the late nineteenth century but transformed into the petroleum industry in the early twentieth century. In the late 1920s, oil and Oklahoma became synonymous. The discovery and development of the Oklahoma oil fields only reinforced the bias of Oklahomans toward using nature for profit, and like the farming and ranching it replaced, the oil business relied on landownership.

Oklahoma City soon gushed with oil when drillers tapped a major deposit inside city limits. Roughnecks swarmed into the capital and pumped 60,000 barrels daily from the first well. By the mid-1930s, oil workers dug 1,300 wells in backyards and nearly on top of buildings. Throbbing pumps and spidery derricks crowded the southeastern quarter of the city and the homes that were wedged between them. Kilpatrick recalled that the arthritic steel oil towers near the houses conjured "scenes from Dante: gas flares, billows of black smoke, figures in the gloom."[14]

The wildcat oil drilling frenzy that swept the state had generated a get-rich-quick mentality. Petroleum seemed everywhere, even underneath the state capitol, where an oil tower rose on its grounds. Oilmen loomed as iconic figures operating outside government controls and corporate hierarchies. Wildcatters bet everything on the next big strike, and their families made and lost fortunes suddenly. Kilpatrick listened to the sad "dry hole" stories told by oilmen's children about ruined businesses when they drilled holes and found nothing. They supposedly then sold the cavities as ready-made postholes. Life in Oklahoma could be unpredictable, Kilpatrick learned, and one's family often proved to be the only reliable source for stability and guidance.[15]

Amid the struggling roughnecks on the vanishing frontier, the Kilpatricks became the primary educators for Jack's emergent conservative philosophy and self-identity. Both parents were staunchly conservative people, but Jack drew particularly on the views of his father, a man of deified bearing. Standing in the presence of "Father," Kilpatrick reflected nearly fifty years later, was like "climbing Olympus with God." At the center of this seemingly mythical man's ideology was individual freedom. In other words, government should not seek to regulate behavior and should impose only the bare minimum of restrictions on society needed to prevent total chaos.[16]

Informal instruction commenced with Kilpatrick and son packed into the family's maroon Studebaker coupe in search of wood for fence poles along the roads of Oklahoma, Arkansas, and North Louisiana. If the two came across a pile of ties near a railway track, Kilpatrick Sr. stopped the automobile and inspected the lumber to make sure his brand (a capital *K* in a circle) and not a competitor's label marked them. His business travels revealed the man beneath the suit. Rebelling against the federal government's Prohibition amendment, on the way home Kilpatrick Sr. stuffed the car with Mason jars full of Arkansas corn whiskey. His contraband activity lasted beyond the national government's repeal of Prohibition. Although Oklahoma law kept the state dry, James Kilpatrick Sr. would not comply with a statute that defied social custom. Nor would he change his drinking habits as he, along with thousands of other Oklahomans, continued to bootleg liquor and beer. One family story recounted the time that he turned the household bathtub into a home brewery. Alma Kilpatrick complained while young Jack bottled the beer.[17]

The illegal activity planted irreverence for certain institutions in Kilpatrick, and he studied his father's violation of the law with keen interest. Society, not government, determined the rules. "The government," Jack

Kilpatrick realized, "made feeble efforts to enforce the law, but this was a law that couldn't be enforced. Some things governments just can't do." Kilpatrick Sr. indoctrinated his first son with what amounted to a tutorial in marketplace economics, the limitations of government, and respect for social custom. "Not all economic education lies in textbooks," noted the younger Kilpatrick. "A man can learn something of venture capitalism and something of profit and loss in the middle of nowhere."[18]

Reinforcing both Kilpatrick's antistatist perspective and his identification as a conservative was his father's electoral politics. Favoring politicians—including Republicans—who championed right-leaning ideas passed from father to son. Kilpatrick Sr. supported any candidates who pledged devotion to private wealth and laissez-faire economics. In the 1924 presidential election, he broke with his Louisiana family's preference for Democrat John W. Davis and voted for the Republican Calvin Coolidge. For much of the twentieth century, a white southerner voting Republican bordered on a cruel joke. Political scientist V. O. Key called the Republican presence in the South so minimal that it "scarcely deserves the name of party. It wavers somewhat between an esoteric cult on the order of a lodge and a conspiracy for plunder." When his father chose Coolidge, Kilpatrick Jr. believed that his grandfather, the former Confederate officer, "was down in Louisiana spinning in his grave." Kilpatrick Sr. could have agreed with Coolidge's maxim that "the chief business of the American people is business." He may even have appreciated the candidate's small-town conservatism or his endorsement of limited government, or he may have disliked Davis's Wall Street lawyer background. Oklahoma's townspeople and businessmen, additionally, liked Republicans because the state party often allied with the Ku Klux Klan on moral reform issues and support for Chambers of Commerce. Jack Kilpatrick found that "southern" and "Democrat" were not synonymous, and he observed his father's willingness to tout politicians who struck others as unusual choices.[19]

In state politics, the Kilpatricks backed William Henry Davis Murray. The man Oklahomans called "Alfalfa Bill" Murray represented the beliefs already active within the Kilpatrick family. Murray towered over Oklahoma as a ferocious, bull-voiced, and abusive man who chomped cigars under his thick mustache. Born in 1869, the legendary farmer-politician lived through Reconstruction to the 1950s presidency of Dwight D. Eisenhower. A Democrat, he served as the state's first Speaker of the House and later as governor during the early years of the Depression. For Murray, who helped articulate the conservatism of the people who settled the state, the only real

Americans were strong-willed farmers, the yeomen descendants of Thomas Jefferson's nation of freeholders. From central Texas, where he grew up, Alfalfa Bill Murray brought both his conservative, agrarian views and his disdain for urban, industrial America and distant centralized government with him to Oklahoma. According to Murray, preserving the family farm and individual property rights promised the redemption of America and captured the essence of Oklahoma political culture. Jack Kilpatrick venerated the governor for his rugged individualism and colorful personality. (In adulthood, Kilpatrick had Murray's portrait hanging behind his writing desk at home.) James Kilpatrick Sr. introduced his son to Murray to strengthen conservative ideals, but sometimes their father-son activities had unintended consequences.[20]

James Kilpatrick's study of Oklahoma society occasionally led him down eccentric and accidental paths. Raised an agnostic in a family mostly indifferent to religion, Kilpatrick rummaged for meaning in the secular, natural world rather than in church. He found spiritual order in two unrelated sources: the Constitution and baseball. As substitutes for churchgoing, they became his first two civil religions, and each required devotion, faith, ritual practices, and love. As did religion, sports and the Constitution structured people's lives and mandated codes of conduct. They became incubators for Kilpatrick's sense of individual freedom, respect for rules, and drive for perfection. For Jack, to love the Constitution and baseball entailed a celebration of their magic and majesty, and the founding fathers and ballplayers alike assumed a nearly sacred aura.[21]

Kilpatrick learned to interpret the Constitution in the southern tradition of states' rights. In the Kilpatrick house, James Sr. instructed the children that Congress could not act before finding authority in the Constitution. The individual states, on the other hand, only needed to ask whether the Constitution prohibited a state's action. Kilpatrick thought the Constitution afforded Americans the best means of living within the nation as a collection of individuals. Its austere and uncomplicated language provided the kind of order that Jack revered. No confusing abstractions or moral laws superseded it in governing men. He later told a confidante to ignore natural law and that "men must be governed in their public and political affairs by the established law which related to political and governmental matters."[22]

If the Constitution commanded respect for ordering public life, then baseball inspired admiration for individual talent. With lifetime passes secured because Kilpatrick Sr. contributed timber for the municipal ballpark, father and son rarely missed an Oklahoma City minor league game.

The son kept statistics and observed the cadence of innings while his father talked business. A random amusement for other people served for young Kilpatrick as an object lesson in the natural patterns of life. In some ways, the discipline of the sport resembled the Constitution's careful checks and balances. Umpires acted like the judiciary, lone batters under pressure were the executive, and the fielders worked together to counteract the hitters, much like Congress kept the power of the president in check. The athletes also functioned like the independent states. Players performed actions consecutively rather than collectively and consented to limited cooperation in their mutual interest—an association of individuals. Baseball depended on a proper balance of power among people. The contest focused on the showdown between pitcher and batter, and at some point in the game, every man batted alone.[23]

The game also involved earning small, tactical points over a slow period of time. "A part of the charm of baseball," Kilpatrick later observed, "is that time plays no part in the rules; in theory a game could go on forever, inning after endless inning, the score always tied." At a young age, he took from baseball a method of dealing with problems through attrition. Incremental victories over a long period would wear down adversaries; in baseball, the defense had the ball.[24]

Baseball was as characteristic of Kilpatrick's conservative thinking as a hierarchical white/black caste system. A fixed racial separation remained the accepted order of the day, and whites sometimes used barbaric customs to subjugate black Oklahomans. In June 1921, when Kilpatrick was an infant, one of the worst race riots in American history occurred when whites flattened the Negro section of Tulsa, burned churches and homes, and murdered scores. Kilpatrick's embrace of Oklahoma's racial structure was neither calculated nor ideological but routine and a result of a culture that treated Negroes as second-class citizens and often as subhumans. He learned early that "the acceptance of racial separation begins in the cradle." His home provided the first arena for his racial education. Behind the Kilpatrick house, above the garage, lived Lizzie, the family's black domestic worker, whose servant status was indisputable evidence of the divide between the two races. Kilpatrick was already raised to believe in the inferiority of blacks, so his childhood education in segregated public schools solidified an expectation for racially unmixed classrooms and social relations.[25]

Even before his youth had ended, Kilpatrick strained to begin work. By his teenage years, he was clearly ready to move forward and put childhood behind him. Kilpatrick knew no higher ambition than to report for the *New*

York Times or some other prestigious newspaper. Ability and education could lessen the distance from boomtown Oklahoma City to cosmopolitan New York City. The realization of his ambition began with the University of Missouri in Columbia, which housed one of the best journalism schools in the nation. The program's "Journalist's Creed" told incoming students that they should be "stoutly independent, unmoved by pride of opinion or greed of power, constructive, tolerant but never careless, self-controlled, patient [and] unswayed by the appeal of privilege or the clamor of the mob." Kilpatrick wanted just such an education. Impatient, he graduated high school two years early in 1937 at age sixteen and headed to Missouri.[26]

For Kilpatrick, the work in Columbia brought him closer to the East and the South and provided an invaluable introduction to journalism. Though he found most of his classes uninspiring, one stood out. In Roscoe B. Ellard's required course, the History and Principles of Journalism, the professor stuttered but made up for it in showmanship. Nothing pleased Ellard more than warding off uncertain students with warnings. He stumbled through one famous line at the start of each semester: "Going into newspapering is like g-g-getting married. Don't do it if you p-p-possibly can help it." Some students trembled, and still others giggled at the advice. Few comprehended the point of Ellard's remark. Kilpatrick did. To him, Ellard spoke about loving writing as much as living.[27]

Ellard possessed no practical experience as a journalist, but he charmed and beguiled students throughout the term by testing their endurance and teaching them to love the written language. More than anything, Ellard encouraged Kilpatrick to love facts, to organize facts, and to represent facts accurately. From Ellard he learned that every good journalist should recognize when a crucial fact hid from a story and that the soul of a newspaper rested in facts. Compiling endless lists of evidence and figures to shove down opponents' throats became a trademark Kilpatrick device. Ellard also pushed students to diversify their knowledge. He challenged students to take classes in history, literature, and the law. Kilpatrick minored in history. No other teacher matched the ability and skill of Roscoe Ellard, who dominated Kilpatrick's attention at Missouri. "The rest of college washed over me like the tides," Kilpatrick recalled, "but some Ellardian residue remained. [Ellard] planted in me a critical sense of the unattainable, a hunger for perfection, a reverence toward the mother tongue." Only nature and Kilpatrick's father stood in his way.[28]

In the fall of 1937, the Great Depression and a family scandal nearly ruined Kilpatrick's education and dreams. It started with the destruction of his home. The world's largest grassland turned into a suffocating waste-land of dirt that blotted out the sky as the southern Plains experienced one of the most destructive natural disasters of twentieth-century America. In that year, 134 dust storms, more than had occurred in any other year on the Plains, deposited layers of grit on farms and choked crops. The farmers lacked money for fence posts after the winds and powdery dirt destroyed their land. As the railroads failed, too, they quit laying new track. Worse, bridge construction switched from the big four-by-sixes that James Kil-patrick Sr. mongered to new, concrete floors. The natural disaster and the change in bridge design broke him.[29]

The earth betrayed the timber trade, and then James Kilpatrick Sr. de-serted his wife and children after disclosing an affair with his secretary. He pulled out of town and joined over 300,000 other Oklahomans in an exodus to California. James and Alma Kilpatrick soon divorced. Kilpatrick Sr. eventually relocated to California's Central Valley and married the sec-retary. The infidelity severed the emotional bond between father and son, and Jack Kilpatrick never saw his father again. The elder Kilpatrick's adul-tery caused a triple public humiliation—an affair, a dissolved marriage, and the collapse of the family business. His abandonment remained a sub-ject of terrible sadness throughout Jack Kilpatrick's life and the most trau-matic event of his youth.

Later, in the 1950s, when the father established sporadic correspondence with his oldest son, usually to ask for money to treat a number of afflictions and a stroke, he received a chilly response. Jack Kilpatrick offered neither prayers nor money. Kilpatrick Sr.'s choice "to break clean" with the family, an embittered Jack wrote his father's second wife, was "Father's decision, not ours." In Kilpatrick's mind, he owed his father nothing and notified him to cease attempts to reestablish a relationship that only injured Jack and his brother and sister. Reconciliation never occurred. In 1960, James Sr. died in Fresno.[30]

The remaining Kilpatricks nearly capitulated to the Depression. Kilpat-rick's mother became the sole support of the children. She worked at a local bookstore earning twenty-five cents an hour and became the proxi-mate foundation to whom Jack and his siblings could cling to in times of distress. He sometimes referred to her as his "sainted mother." Jack Kilpat-rick also began to wrestle with the economic and emotional debilitation caused by his father. As he struggled to find meaning in his anguish, he grew more conscious of the social and political repercussions of his per-sonal loss.[31]

The Great Depression tested Kilpatrick and proved formative. The severity of the 1930s taught people who survived it that dark times might never end. The cauldron of events brewing in the Kilpatrick household provided life lessons that stressed self-reliance born out of hardship and displacement. In Jack, the Kilpatrick family trauma brought about a "feeling for the individual in distress." His highly attuned sense of individualism was more than naked self-interest, however. Kilpatrick packed self-sufficiency into his conception of individualism. Perseverance and achievement followed only from a strong work ethic, responsibility, and individual enterprise, not from the assistance of others. Kilpatrick's stress on empowerment for the imperiled individual ignored African Americans, the poor, and those who were guaranteed help through government largesse. His future conservative writings idealized the redemptive force of private initiative and one's character rather than the messy pottage of government reform and dependency.[32]

James Kilpatrick Sr.'s departure also embedded in his son a deep concern for financial stability. To combat the effects of financial ruin and to finish his degree, Kilpatrick worked a variety of jobs in school. Left on his own, he quickly handled multiple jobs at once. The challenging work ethic he enjoyed as a child mushroomed into an unrelenting pursuit for good jobs as an adult. In the summers, he still worked at the *Oklahoma City Times*, but during the academic year, gainful employment around the university remained scarce. Kilpatrick became a photographer at Stephens College, the neighboring women's school in Columbia. He also tutored American history, waited tables, edited students' papers, and composed freelance articles. To save money, Kilpatrick moved out of his fraternity's basement and into a boardinghouse. When he could, Kilpatrick relaxed with other journalism students, and his good friends truncated his last name to "Kilpo," a nickname that stuck for life.[33]

During his senior year, Kilpatrick focused almost exclusively on finding employment. By February 1941, after he completed a baccalaureate, the need to earn a living tugged at him. Kilpatrick expected to work in a newsroom and never considered any other occupation. The reputation of Missouri's journalism program made it reasonable for him to aspire toward a big city paper. Before graduation, he applied to the afternoon dailies in New Orleans, Louisville, Atlanta, and Richmond. To impress potential employers and assure them of his maturity despite his youth, he lied whitely in his job-inquiry letters that he "knew the streets of Paris as well as he knew the streets of Philadelphia." Charles Henry Hamilton, city editor at the

Richmond News Leader, responded first with an inquisitive telegram about the salary the recent graduate anticipated and indicated the paper could pay $35 a week. "Will report Monday," an eager Kilpatrick replied on the same day. Five days later, on March 30, 1941, before Hamilton could make an official job offer, Kilpatrick took a train to Richmond. He walked up the street from the railroad station to the *News Leader* offices and proclaimed himself ready for work.[34]

Kilpatrick would not have made an intimidating first impression. His best suit, a three-piece brown herringbone tweed, hung on his small frame. At age twenty, he weighed 130 pounds and his ears stuck out slightly from his boyish, round face. He looked at his employers with large, baby-blue eyes that gazed frankly from below his slicked-back, thinning dark hair. Little in his outward appearance indicated his tenacity and drive. Hamilton stood dumbfounded and grumbled about not having hired him but decided to take a chance on the young man. He directed Kilpatrick to a battered desk with a telephone and a worn Underwood typewriter and then informed the cub reporter that he would oversee the rewrite desk and clean up copy from the morning newspaper to make it look new. Kilpatrick's journalism career did not seem to be on a meteoric course, but he never flinched. "Fifteen years after I had pronounced to an indifferent world a five-year-old's determination to become a newspaperman," Kilpatrick remembered of his first day on the job, "[I] drew a delirious breath. The phone rang. 'Rewrite,' I said. 'Kilpatrick.'"[35]

The Virginia Way

When Kilpatrick arrived in Richmond, the Virginia town was over two hundred years old. Though the site of Richmond had seen explorers and occasional settlers shortly after the English arrived in North America, eighteenth-century planter William Byrd II's purchase and donation of land permitted the town's settlement. Located on the fall line of the James River, Richmond was incorporated in 1737. The town sat at the edge of the rising hills of the piedmont to its west and the flat, humid tidewater to its east. By the early nineteenth century, it was the commercial and industrial center of Virginia. Richmond served as a slave market, as the place where upcountry farmers unloaded their tobacco and wheat crops, and as home to the South's largest ironworks and flour mills. During the Civil War, Richmond was the Confederacy's capital and its most important military depot with its armory, ironworks, and factories. In 1865, Confederate sympathizers burned parts of the city before Federal forces came. Despite the war's turmoil, Richmond remained the seat of political power and Virginia's principal city.[36]

In the early 1940s, Richmond seemed to some an unusually pleasing and attractive southern community, especially for the city's white, patrician leaders, whose families often traced ancestors back to the seventeenth century and the founding of America. In an essay titled "Spirit of Virginia," one newspaperman observed "a deliberate cult of the past" in Richmond and that all "eastern Virginians are Shintoists under the skin. Genealogy makes history personal to them in terms of family. Kinship to the eighth degree usually is recognized. There are classes within castes." To Richmond's elite crowd, looking with satisfaction at the city's bloodlines, good-old-boy networks, private schools, garden and dining clubs, churches, and many businesses, the status quo must have been ideal. The community pointed with pride to the town's traditions and history. An entire municipal thoroughfare announced the history of the Commonwealth of Virginia to automobile drivers. On Monument Avenue, a statue of Robert E. Lee sat astride his horse, Traveller, which faced south to enliven the spirit of southerners, while James Ewell Brown ("Jeb") Stuart's equestrian monument looked north to oppose potential outside threats. Other bronze statues celebrated the lives of Jefferson Davis and Stonewall Jackson. Downtown, next to the capitol, which Thomas Jefferson designed to replicate a Roman temple in Nimes, France, stood the former White House of the Confederacy.[37]

The customs and gentrification of the privileged class appealed to many whites but held little fascination for Richmond's African Americans. Intricate, informal standards forced blacks to concede their inferiority. Although attitudes toward segregation varied among Negroes, depending on the situation and the issue, blacks generally conformed. By and large, they rarely questioned their status in public, and whites believed that they lived in a harmonious civilization and treated Negroes with dignity. White Virginians referred to their condescending, genteel paternalism that prevented violence and amalgamation as the "Virginia Way," a living tradition and euphemism for segregation. Racial disturbances occurred without much press, and Virginia acquired a reputation as a model for good, southern race relations. In the mid-twentieth century, the state recorded only two lynchings of African Americans, and the General Assembly, in a rare act, outlawed the offense. Because of the peaceful image they cultivated, white Virginians viewed other southerners as practitioners of a more severe variety of racial oppression that tolerated vigilantism and virulent

racism. "Rabble-rousing and Negro baiting capacities, which in Georgia or Mississippi would be a great political asset," remarked an onlooker, "simply mark a person as one not to the manner born" in Virginia. Style, more than substance, differentiated Virginians from their southern cousins. Despite their massive self-deception about equanimity between the races, the commonwealth's southern counties, in particular, were a bastion of white supremacy that abhorred race-mixing and could turn into, noted one white newspaperman, a "prairie fire of racist fanaticism."[38]

Part of the southern counties' reputation for hotheaded segregation derived from its political economy. Virginia in the 1940s remained largely rural, with most of its power flowing from below the James River rather than from above it. Richmond's strategic location near the lucrative tobacco counties and coastal shipyards in the southeastern Tidewater, or Southside, ensured the city's place as the seat of power. Most of the major state politicians came from the agricultural communities of the Southside or Black Belt, an area comprised of nearly thirty-one adjoining counties with a total Negro population in excess of 40 percent, twice the percentage of blacks (22 percent) residing in the state as a whole. The parity between white and black made the social menace of integration more real there, and the Southside was intensely segregationist to suppress the numerical threat of African Americans. For eastern and Southside Virginians, the defense of the racial caste system trumped all other concerns. They liked laws that neatly divided society into black and white because it fit their rigid mindset, and they barred black Virginians from state politics. The insistence on Negro inferiority propped up their understanding of the world because otherwise, they feared, Virginia would collapse into social disorder and racial miscegenation. Calling this area the Black Belt also reminded Virginians of the Old South; the name suggested a way of life as much as a demographic marker. Nineteenth-century habits held a grip on the state, and guarding Virginia's race laws and limiting the power of minorities depended on the political group that made all the rules for the commonwealth.[39]

In 1949, the renowned political commentator V. O. Key traveled the South gathering insights on local politics. "Of all the American states," wrote Key, "Virginia can lay claim to the most thorough control by an oligarchy. Political power has been closely held by a small group of leaders who, themselves and their predecessors, have subverted democratic institutions and deprived most Virginians of a voice in their government. . . . It is a political museum piece." Virginians obeyed the wishes of their homegrown kingpin, Democratic senator Harry F. Byrd, and his political outfit, the Byrd "machine," to its enemies, or "organization," to its supporters. Byrd's power pyramid resembled that of a nineteenth-century, Gilded Age political machine, but he added a dose of eighteenth-century gentility and deference to his patronage that suited the Old Dominion's aristocratic pretensions. Born in 1887, Byrd, a direct descendent of the founder of Richmond, became governor in 1925, and then in 1933 won a U.S. Senate seat. A man who never graduated high school emerged as the mastermind behind the South's most unified and unassailable political network. His Republican opponents could barely mount a campaign against the organization until the 1950s. Even from Washington, D.C., he exerted considerable influence on almost every election within Virginia, and his stalwarts worked ceaselessly to retain control.[40]

Byrd articulated a platform that kept state expenditures to a minimum, encouraged big business growth, checked racial liberalism, and scorned outside interference from labor unions and the federal government. Rural Virginians, concentrated either in Byrd's home district of the Shenandoah Valley or in the Southside, provided the senator and his people in the General Assembly with home bases. The voters and the organization shared a belief in the separation of the races, limited government, and low taxes, and they cared little about public infrastructure, health, or education.[41]

In addition to having the electoral advantage, Byrd stood at the apex of power through structural advantages. Virginians voted overwhelmingly Democratic, but from a local point of view that kept Republicans and blacks out of office. The Byrd machine's myriad lords and their various vassals controlled important state appointive offices, like circuit court judges and county clerks. A poll tax and disfranchisement ensured low voter participation. A smaller proportion of Virginia's potential electorate voted in gubernatorial races than did that of any other southern state. From the 1920s through the mid-1960s, the organization only needed to persuade the 8 to 11 percent of eligible voters to support them. Throughout the forties and fifties, Virginia's election turnout ranked just ahead of that in the Deep South states but behind that in Texas, North Carolina, Florida, Tennessee, and the Border states. Voting restrictions in the Old Dominion made the state about as democratic as the Soviet Union.[42]

Byrd's power partially depended on the backing of the Virginia press. The senator enjoyed the cooperation of several newspapers, but two tribunes in particular, the *Winchester Evening Star,* run by his son, Harry Byrd Jr., and the Bryan family's Richmond dailies, defended the Byrd machine. The Bryans, one of Richmond's elite families, owned the city's morning and afternoon papers, the *Richmond Times-Dispatch* and the *Richmond News Leader*, respectively. In 1870, Joseph Bryan moved to Richmond, bought and married his way into the town's influential circles, prospered, and got into the newspaper business. As a former Confederate cavalryman, he combined the romance of the Old South with a New South businessman's contempt for organized labor. After gaining control of the Richmond press in 1908, he faced down union-affiliated printers who planned to strike and shut down the paper. The tough, uncompromising veteran threatened them that he had survived on rotten meat during the war and would take all necessary measures to thwart the union and protect his family's interests. Joseph Bryan reigned over his tight-knit clan until his death.[43]

Under Joseph's son, John Stewart Bryan, a former president of the College of William and Mary and a rector at the University of Virginia, the newspapers shifted from family oversight to professional supervision. By the time James Kilpatrick joined the *News Leader*, Bryan had already cultivated two distinct personalities at his papers, especially in the editorial sections, and encouraged competition between the two staffs. He allowed the editorial pages to follow independent courses, and, as a result, they earned praise for their professionalism. The integrity of the editors, Douglas Southall Freeman, who assumed the position at the *News Leader* in 1915, and Virginius Dabney, who won a Pulitzer Prize for editing at the *Times-Dispatch*, attracted talented journalists and solidified the reputations of the papers, especially among local political animals.[44]

Richmond was a city of people obsessed with politics. The *News Leader* offered them an afternoon installment of the latest political news and acted as a rubber stamp for the Byrd outfit. State and local politicos who wanted to know how news earlier in the day broke to the public in the evening read the newspaper religiously. Conservatives took the paper's editorials as literal truth and expected unequivocal and unabashed commentary on all the events of the day. The tribune also gave Richmond a sense of place, and the Bryans were an unusual sort of publisher who shaped their city's personality and instilled a consciousness of class and caste through coverage of the news. The newspaper earned the trust of Richmond's upper crust because of the patriarchal and genteel disposition of its editor. According to Douglas Southall Freeman, the *News Leader* should set the tone for the town's tastes and "strive, of course, rightly to lead the community, but never in dogmatism and never so far ahead that its effort is wasted."[45]

During his tenure from the 1920s to the 1940s, Freeman became a respected newspaperman and one of the nation's top scholars of the Civil

War. Born in 1886 in Lynchburg, Virginia, the same year as James J. Kilpatrick Sr., Freeman accompanied his family to Richmond, where his father ran an insurance business. Freeman grew up with Lost Cause pageantry and legends and watched former Confederate officers walk the streets. He later earned a doctorate in economics at Johns Hopkins University and in 1909 began writing editorials for the Bryans.[46]

The editor possessed a cool, austere personality and, according to Kilpatrick, looked like a cross between an archbishop and an accountant. The office staff affectionately called him "Doc" behind his back and "Dr. Freeman" to his face, but never "Douglas." Colleagues adored and admired the prolific writer for his scholarship and work regimen as he pursued four simultaneous careers—editor, historian, educator, and broadcaster. From 1934 to 1941, Freeman commuted to New York to teach journalism at Columbia University. In the early twentieth century, he was the country's ranking military historian of the Civil War and served as a president of the Southern Historical Association. The story around the office was that he stopped and saluted the statue of Robert E. Lee on his drive to work every day. His biographies of Lee and George Washington both won Pulitzer Prizes. Freeman spent nineteen years researching and writing his tome on Lee, and his final project, *Lee's Lieutenants*, garnered national attention. In the 1920s and 1930s, he attended to Richmond's spiritual needs as the popular radio host of *Lessons in Living* for local Baptists. Freeman's only recreation was work. He once told a reporter what it took to succeed: "There's only one way to get a job done—just shove your belly up against it and *do* it." He even quit smoking because he calculated that the addiction wasted eight hours a week. "Time alone is irreplaceable. Waste it not," read a misspelled motto in Freeman's office. Languor was foreign to the *News Leader* offices.[47]

Hired as a junior reporter, James Kilpatrick adjusted to the rhythms of the newspaper and worked to impress Freeman and the *News Leader*'s bureaucracy. He started rewriting obituaries from the *Times-Dispatch* for the afternoon paper, and his first two months passed uneventfully until the peacetime military draft took effect. Several journalists reported for duty, including Kilpatrick, who tried to enlist in the Army Air Corps but received a deferment because of chronic bronchial asthma. May 1941 launched him into more responsibilities in the office and sporadic assignments as he filled in for sick or absent columnists. As World War II escalated, more senior reporters left for the armed services. Kilpatrick stayed in the understaffed newsroom and became a regular contributor, which opened opportunities for him. Editor Charles Hamilton relied on the remaining writers ineligible for military service to work a variety of jobs. Kilpatrick covered nearly every beat, including business, outdoors, features, and drama. He also reported on military servicemen, fires, concerts, city hall, and criminal courts. Because of Richmond's size—the entire metropolitan area had fewer than 250,000 residents—a newcomer like Kilpatrick could attend to several stories at once and acquaint himself with the people and their perspectives.[48]

In 1943, James Kilpatrick's limitless reporting earned him the job of chief of staff, in charge of the state's political beat. Covering the courts, however, won James Kilpatrick's affection, and he learned Virginia's legal labyrinth. In addition to the state courts, a court of chancery, two hustings courts, two courts of law and equity, and the Fourth U.S. Circuit Court of Appeals, one of two circuit courts serving the South, heard cases in Richmond. Keeping to a habit from his youth, Kilpatrick sought out mentors to assist in his transition to the study of the law and to counsel him on his career. John J. Parker, the eminent Republican appellate judge from North Carolina on the federal circuit court, often invited Kilpatrick into his chambers to discuss the day's rulings and lent the young reporter his constitutional law books. At home, Kilpatrick read histories of the Supreme Court and the biographies of former justices John Marshall and Oliver Wendell Holmes. On many afternoons, Israel Steingold, a lawyer with a respected federal practice, prepared Kilpatrick in the ways attorneys presented cases. Kilpatrick came to love the law as much as writing. "[I]f I had it all to do over," he commented a few years after starting his coverage of the courts, "I expect I would study law instead of technical journalism. There is something in the study of law—the pure cerebration required in the examination of a changing set of circumstances as it relates to a fixed and immutable statue—that sets red corpuscles to churning in your brain cells." The way the law ordered society through reason and precedent and without emotion or moralizing piqued Kilpatrick's sense of propriety.[49]

One equity court judge provided the most important lesson for Kilpatrick about the law when he remarked, "[T]he law is one thing. Equity is often something else." The law and the natural rights of man were separate issues, and a sound legal ruling should never rely on moral judgments. If Kilpatrick doubted him, the harsh verdicts pronounced in cases involving blacks proved otherwise. Richmond's police court judge often convicted African Americans on thin evidence and usually ordered them to leave town as a punishment. Justice and the law were sometimes as separate and unequal as blacks and whites.[50]

Just as Kilpatrick adjusted to his responsibilities with the courts, he turned to experienced politicians to coach him in Virginia politics. He had a rare gift in young men: the ability to learn from one's elders and to seek their direction. Because of the *News Leader*'s prominence and its affection for Senator Harry Byrd, Kilpatrick wove tightly into the inner circles of the Byrd machine. In 1943, he met Byrd, who welcomed him into his sanctum and the staid world of the Old Dominion's political elite. One of Kilpatrick's earliest mentors was Senator Carter Glass, a former newspaper editor born in 1858 and a well-known eugenicist who designed the poll tax to restrict Negro voting in the 1902 Virginia state constitution. Both Glass and Byrd probably felt more at home in the nineteenth century than in the twentieth; they also opposed the New Deal and built their reputations on the defense of states' rights, segregation, and fiscal restraint. With introductions from Glass and Byrd, Kilpatrick made his way further up the mighty Byrd ziggurat by befriending William ("Bill") Tuck, a powerful Southside politician and the senator's No. 2 man. Kilpatrick even accompanied Tuck to national political conventions and rallies, where they discussed their shared contempt for labor unions and fear that the national Democratic Party would abandon segregation. When he assessed Bill Tuck's governorship for the *News Leader*, Kilpatrick heaped accolades on the Southsider for his country charm and attacks on liberals: "Bill Tuck never pussy-footed or equivocated or covered up. If he loved turnip greens and mountain music, if he liked to put his feet on the desk and chew tobacco, if he reveled in politics and played the game with a shrewd and canny hand—that simply was Bill Tuck, and there was no affection about him. And if he loved to dish it out against such targets as Harold Ickes, Jonathan Daniels, and visiting do-gooders from California, he was perfectly ready to take it."[51]

James Kilpatrick learned to distinguish the Byrd brethren from adversaries, and he began to replicate the senator's approach to national politics. He supported political candidates like any good Byrd Democrat and abandoned the Democratic ticket in national elections to back Republicans and conservatives. In 1948, he abandoned both major political parties because neither organization denounced civil rights reforms. He instead voted for the states' rights Democrats and their candidate Governor Strom Thurmond of South Carolina to protect the South's racial customs from federal interference. His *News Leader* columns often captured white southerners' resentment toward liberal Democrats and the growing split in the Democratic Party. "It has been apparent for more than two years now," he wrote in 1949, that there are not two major political parties in the nation, but three. Labels have become badly scrambled. Mr. Truman most certainly is not a "Democrat," as Virginians understand the word, nor is Senator Byrd a "Democrat" as Mr. Truman understands it. Sooner or later this fiction will give way. Mr. Truman and his southpaw friends will become the Spendthrift Party or the Fair Deal Party or the Left Fielders, and Southerners will become the Conservatives, or the Conservative Democrats, or something else. But such a realignment of labels . . . is likely to come later rather than sooner. The *New Republic* simply will have to bear up bravely under the fact that Southerners were Democrats long before Mr. Truman was born, and will remain Democrats long after he is dead, and they are not likely to sell their political souls just to sit in the *New Republic*'s bleachers down by third base.[52]

Kilpatrick preferred traditional, and even antiquated, societies like the South to the postwar drift toward liberalism, and one of Byrd's friends encouraged his bias. Colgate W. Darden, governor of Virginia from 1942 to 1946 and later president of the University of Virginia, taught the young journalist to enjoy the Roman and Greek classics and the writings of historian Edward Gibbon, particularly *The Decline and Fall of the Roman Empire*. Gibbon warned about the ancient Romans' centralization and extravagance, pointing out that reckless governments collapse slowly from corruption and complacence. Kilpatrick was convinced that the federal government, like imperial Rome, would eventually grow less powerful and expose itself to internal and external threats. Darden also prompted Kilpatrick to read Plato, who disliked societies without natural aristocracies. The Greek philosopher wanted the elite to rule and to control people's thoughts to prevent disorder and to limit democracy. Kilpatrick tried to replicate that Platonic ideal in his private life as well.[53]

Appended to the hereditary elite of Virginia and sharing its lifestyle to the degree they could were members of a deferential, professional class who did not challenge the aristocracy because they aspired to join it. As one of the professional-class retainers in Richmond's broad gentry, James Kilpatrick lived as a cultured gentleman. He even found a wife attuned to the city's high society. In 1941, he married a short, slender woman named Marie Louise Pietri, who became the mother of their three sons, Michael, Christopher, and Kevin. Marie Pietri, born in Wilson, North Carolina, in June 1920, to Ben and Mary Pietri, second-generation Italian immigrants, grew up in Virginia. Marie took after her father and worked as an accomplished sculptor. Despite the Italian surname, Kilpatrick regarded Marie Pietri as "pure Virginia" because of her family's roots in the commonwealth and her social cachet with Richmond's art community and urbane elite. The two met on a Tuesday and married that Friday. "It was just one of those things," Kilpatrick said brightly. It may have been love at first sight, but he was also probably aided in his decision to wed her after only a few days of courtship because of her talent and refinement. Diligent, educated, and intelligent like her husband, Marie encouraged a love of high culture in her spouse that he channeled into hobbies ranging from raising camellias in their garden to attending Richmond Symphony Orchestra concerts. Music, like baseball and writing, had beauty based on order, rhythm, and pace. To confirm their status as fixtures among the city's privileged few, the Kilpatricks moved to the "little Georgetown," or Fan, district near Richmond's fashionable West End and refurbished an old Edwardian townhouse on Hanover Street.[54]

In spite of his marriage to a local artist and his budding political connections, Kilpatrick never reached the full standing of a Richmond aristocrat because he attended the University of Missouri rather than "Mr. Jefferson's" University in Charlottesville, which mattered to people in Virginia. To compensate, he aspired to the town's upper-class lifestyle by surrounding himself with physical reminders of Virginia's rich history, especially the state's founding fathers. For his family's new home, he constructed a brick wall in their backyard from the razed manor of Spencer Roane, the early-nineteenth-century states' rights judge on the Virginia Supreme Court and son-in-law of the revolutionary Patrick Henry. What Kilpatrick lacked in pedigree, he made up for with his willingness to work hard for the *News Leader*'s editor.[55]

Kilpatrick learned the newspaper trade in Virginia from the "didactic, Lee-worshiping" Douglas Southall Freeman. The edifying Freeman, "the first genius" Kilpatrick claimed to have ever met, became the young man's new model newspaperman. By the late 1940s, however, editing the *News Leader* held less appeal for Freeman. In fall 1948, after thirty-three years of a tireless work routine, he wanted to retire and concentrate on his history books rather than his editorial page. Freeman compared writing editorials to "writing on sand." He began to mull over potential successors but wanted one who put as much energy and dedication into the job as he did. James J. Kilpatrick fit the profile. From the moment he arrived, people knew Kilpatrick would be an asset to the newspaper. Young, skillful, assertive, foreign to Virginia, and dedicated, he stood out from the crowd. When Freeman entered the office at 4:15 each morning, Kilpatrick was often still at his desk finishing copy, which had impressed the older newspaperman. Freeman also admired Kilpatrick for befriending more people and politicians in Richmond in five years than many natives had in four decades. "Simply as a matter of record and a comforting thought for the future," Freeman told Tennant Bryan, John Stewart Bryan's son, in November 1948, "I would like to say that as of the present time, much the promising young man around these parts for my assistant and perhaps ultimately for my successor is Kilpatrick."[56]

In January 1949, twenty-eight-year-old Kilpatrick assumed the position of associate editor and apprenticed under Freeman, now sixty-three. He was the youngest editorial page editor of a large daily paper in the country. Kilpatrick moved from the city room upstairs to the editorial offices and took on random news assignments until the paper promoted him to editor of the editorial page. On 1 July 1950, Bryan named Kilpatrick editor, and Freeman quietly withdrew from the paper. Freeman died of a heart attack in June 1953, the same day he finished his last book. In a letter to a friend, Kilpatrick worried about his ability to follow Freeman: "With Doc's death, it seems to me that a vacuum has been created that none of us is competent to fill. God knows I am no Mentor—I am the youngest Telemachus of them all." With Freeman gone, all eyes turned to James Kilpatrick.[57]

Freeman's death ended an era at the newspaper. His editorial style relied on intellect, restraint, and appeasement, which mirrored his gentility. A new tone at the paper, however, showed the influence of the Bryan family's conservative publisher. Born in 1897, John Dana ("Jack") Wise, the lean, hawk-nosed general manager of the *News Leader* and *Times-Dispatch*, worked as an advertising man at several South Carolina papers before he went to Richmond in 1936 to direct the Bryans' newspapers. The *News Leader*'s ownership approved of the conservative ideology that Wise introduced.[58]

In 1944, following his father's death, David Tennant Bryan, then serving in the navy, inherited the paper but still relied on Jack Wise to run it during the Second World War. After the war, Bryan served as president of the newspapers for the next three decades and guided them toward strict conservatism and away from the moderation of his father and the level-headedness of Freeman. He also expanded his newspaper holdings, acquiring tribunes in Tampa, Winston-Salem, and New Jersey, which made the Bryans the largest media group in Virginia and one of the most important ones on the East Coast. Given the opportunity in the late 1940s after Freeman's retirement, Tennant Bryan decided to make the *News Leader* the mouthpiece for his press empire and encouraged aggressive conservative thought. "I don't think necessarily that you have to offend people to get your page read," he explained, "but sometimes people need offending." He also found a willing partner in John Dana Wise. Demanding, confident, and intolerant of weakness and unorthodox views, Wise held considerable power at the newspapers and helped to shape the personality of the editorial pages.[59]

Unlike most publishers, who focused on sales, John Dana Wise pushed a political agenda. When possible, he manipulated the newspapers' staffs to infuse a conservative slant into their writing. Before Tennant Bryan settled on Kilpatrick as his editor, for instance, he lunched with Harry Ashmore, the editor of Little Rock's *Arkansas Gazette*. Wise also met with Ashmore, but the editor detected a "yawning void" between Ashmore's ideology and that of the two Richmond newsmen. Wise could not bear Ashmore's liberal sentiments and after the interview said, "I thought so—we've never had any luck with these Tarheels." Ashmore squirmed throughout the job talk and wondered how Virginius Dabney, who recommended him to Bryan, survived under publishing executives who detested an independent style. Wise and Bryan wanted an uncompromising and contentious editor to solicit their politics. Dabney struggled with Bryan, but he conceded "that the owner of a newspaper has the final say as to policy; and that on critical issues he determines the paper's editorial stand."[60]

Known around the office as a forceful coworker because of his strong opinions, Kilpatrick found traction with his bosses when he expressed conservative principles. His youth and impressionability also made him malleable to the designs of Wise and Bryan, and they loved their disciple's eagerness to please. Though most newspaper readers would remember Kilpatrick as a progenitor of anti-liberal reaction, he had been relatively apolitical as an undergraduate. In college, he maintained no affiliations with political groups or causes on campus and focused on work. Missouri's journalism program had also encouraged students to rise above partisan politics and to report without bias. Some of Kilpatrick's colleagues at the newspaper, however, confused his professionalism with liberalism. Upon his arrival in Richmond, Kilpatrick appeared "rather on the liberal side," recalled Mike Houston, a *News Leader* columnist, who noted a conspicuous absence of political ardor in the Oklahoman. "But he found out we were conservative," Houston continued, "and learned quickly which side the bread was buttered on." The *News Leader* editor soon fell under Wise's partisan persuasion. "Every time I let a liberal impulse escape into print," Kilpatrick recalled, "he summoned me into his office." Wise would lean in closely and drawl, "Now, how could you have written that sentence?" When Kilpatrick expressed his desire to retain liberal columnists for the editorial page, Wise also objected. Such confrontations harried Kilpatrick into submission. By 1954, Kilpatrick dropped both Walter Lippmann, the nation's foremost syndicated columnist, and Drew Pearson, a liberal writer for the *Washington Post*, from the editorial section. Their endorsement of New Deal programs, government spending plans, and civil rights laws diverged from the ideology of the *News Leader*. Kilpatrick replaced them with conservative columnists David Lawrence and George Sokolsky.[61]

Kilpatrick mostly approved of Wise's views, anyway. He began to tell readers who complained about the cancellation of Lippmann and Pearson that he would not surrender control of the editorial page "to a syndicated columnist one hundred miles away, who so often propagandizes for causes that we believe to be wholly unwise." He preferred to take cues from Wise, who stood only a few feet away. The decision to remove liberal columnists from the newspaper coincided with a policy of hiring conservative writers to assist with editorials. Kilpatrick informed one man interested in the associate editor job that the *News Leader* would only employ someone who was against low-income housing and business and farm subsidies and for fiscal restraint, balanced budgets, and keeping the government out of individuals' business.[62]

Wise was a man whom Kilpatrick could trust for advice and guidance in his new environment. His friendship with the elder publisher also intensified into a political education. Wise schooled the editor in the central books of Western conservatism. Beginning in the forties and into the early fifties, the South Carolinian introduced him to the political literati of the late Enlightenment period—Jean-Jacques Rousseau, John Locke, Alexis de Tocqueville, and Edmund Burke. Kilpatrick's intellectual awakening accelerated after studying Russell Kirk.

Kirk, whose ideas resembled the beliefs of an eighteenth-century English Tory, thrilled Kilpatrick most of all. He read Kirk's books several times and concluded that he "comes closer to a thoughtful analysis of my sort of conservatism than anyone I have read." Kirk encouraged conservatives to study the past and to preserve institutions, and his writings on Edmund Burke, the Anglo-Irish apologist for the rule of law, refined Kilpatrick's appreciation for innate orders, tradition, and natural inequalities. For Burke, a balanced society was one where liberty survives through compromise, order, and virtue. Obedience to the law and civility guaranteed a free society and served the common good. Burke also emphasized "natural law," but to postwar American conservatives, that term meant respect for inherited law and not for inalienable rights—a reinterpretation that downplayed the perceived "invention" of freedoms for minorities. Might, American conservatives argued, made right. Following Burke, traditionalists in the United States stressed the fixed nature of man, or the idea that man must obey society's laws and prescriptive values. Burke, additionally, warned against moral relativism, democracy, revolution, and apostasy and had something to teach Kilpatrick about the pace and direction of change. The Burkean notion said that social change unfolded best when it was the unplanned, incremental result of sensible actions and concrete realities, rather than imposed sweepingly from afar on the basis of ideology and lofty abstractions.[63]

John Dana Wise augmented the readings on classical and European conservatives with Americans who derided state centralization. The writings of South Carolina's mid-nineteenth-century statesman John C. Calhoun, the father of nullification and states' rights philosopher, and John Randolph of Roanoke, Virginia's premier champion of individualism and aristocracy, appeared on Kilpatrick's reading lists as well. "I am an aristocrat," affirmed Randolph. "I love liberty; I hate equality," he declared in a summary of his philosophy—and that of Wise and Kilpatrick. Thomas Jefferson, Burke's ideological archenemy, crept into Kilpatrick's thinking as well. Kilpatrick was no Jeffersonian democrat, but he backed the sage of Monticello's advocacy of individual liberties and states' rights against corruption by the central government and his insistence that people accept their born status and accept the rule of their social and political superiors. Kilpatrick, additionally, studied the observations of the aristocratic Tocqueville, the traveling French critic who came to America in the early nineteenth century. Tocqueville predicted that an unrestrained democracy in the United States would create despotism, but Kilpatrick believed that the new tyranny of twentieth-century America would arise from the central state becoming "more expansive and more mild" as it "would degrade men without tormenting them." The national government's subtle corruption bore the gifts of funding, equality, and services but left dependency in its wake. Twentieth-century liberalism teemed with danger. Kilpatrick accepted Wise's certainty that New Deal gigantism threatened the nation and capitalism with prolabor and welfare policies and that Franklin Roosevelt and Harry Truman's programs concealed totalitarian designs.[64]

Wise inspired Kilpatrick to revere southern strongmen from the past and present who ruled an orderly society. Harry Byrd and Thomas Jefferson embraced small government, free markets, prudent public finance, and individual liberties. Kilpatrick's respect for state sovereignty and the strict construction of the Constitution and his racial views came with him from Oklahoma, but his growing conservatism could best be contextualized in contrast to his understanding of liberalism. Kilpatrick preferred variety to what he saw as liberalism's insistence on uniformity. He thought liberals treated society as a faceless mass; conservatives, on the other hand, appreciated individualism and the diverse nature and needs of humanity. The young editor advocated freedom and private decision-making, while liberals favored compulsion and government mandates. "My old-fashioned view is that there is far too much 'authority' exerted by government fiat over the lives of free Americans," he told a correspondent. "The libertarian ideal, which is the vision I happen to cherish, cannot be served by extension of 'authority,' but only by a more steadfast devotion to those peculiarly American doctrines of individual liberty which are most dear to me." His most frequent definition of a "conservative" was more Burkean than libertarian, however: someone who defended "the status quo who, when change becomes necessary in tested institutions or practices, prefers that it come slowly, and in moderation."[65]

When choosing a national political party, Kilpatrick usually sided with the Republicans but distanced himself from official party labels. He often described his political views as that of an "eighteenth-century liberal" rather than as a conservative. He believed the liberal and moderate wings of the Grand Old Party had adulterated the principles of conservatism. A true conservative would never support federal subsidies and spending programs the way some Republicans did. Like others on the right at the time, Kilpatrick struggled to come up with a name for his particular opposition to liberalism. The editor eventually called himself a Whig to avoid troublesome party affiliations and retain a semblance of journalistic independence. Despite his efforts to appear above party tags, he endorsed every Republican presidential candidate from Eisenhower on, and *News Leader* editorials made his partisanship clear.[66]

Kilpatrick introduced a shrill and pugnacious style to the *News Leader* editorial page. Though of similar mind in regard to hard work, he and Freeman had quite different personalities and style. Freeman wrote conversational pieces, but the new editor read like an H. L. Mencken aesthete debunking the idea of the common man and smashing doctrines he deemed backward and wrong-headed. Earlier in the twentieth century, Mencken, as editor of Baltimore's *American Mercury*, chastised southerners for the disappearance of an aristocratic tradition that let the region slip into lawlessness and cultural and intellectual atrophy by the end of the nineteenth century. Mencken's scathing critiques gained the admiration of many young southern journalists.[67]

Kilpatrick had regarded Mencken as a role model for years. The Baltimore editor's questioning of people's intelligence and rationality appealed to Kilpatrick and guided his approach to editorial writing. Without strong editorial opinions and constant attacks on odious views, they both believed, society might recede into stagnation. Kilpatrick thought of himself as a "critic of ideas" and styled his often angry editorials after Mencken, who, according to Kilpatrick, "went at his targets with shillelaghs, fungo bats, and bung starters; he had a way of honing his carving knife with a couple of extra licks, just for dramatic effect, before he began slicing some suckling pig."[68]

A caustic approach to newspaper writing immediately differentiated Kilpatrick from Freeman. Kilpatrick avoided the middle ground and saw issues in terms of right and wrong, black and white. Conversely, when Freeman backed a political idea, he offered it to his readers as an option. In the 1948 presidential election, for example, the *News Leader* endorsed the segregationist Dixiecrats, but Freeman did not force the paper's position on people; he merely noted the historical splits in the Democratic Party dating back to 1860 and asked readers how they would vote. On other occasions, however, Kilpatrick did not trust his readers and forced issues on them. In one 1950 editorial, he warned voters about a potential Republican gubernatorial candidate who advocated the construction of a publicly owned hydroelectric plant, a position that showed that the congressman could "succumb . . . abjectly to socialistic theories." Kilpatrick even goaded people to fight with him about mundane topics. A defiant editorial about farm subsidy programs, "Let's All Get Mad About It!," foretold Kilpatrick's leadership and attitude at the paper.[69]

Kilpatrick's polemics erupted from solid, clear writing, and he actually wrote the way that he spoke, with purpose and determination. "We have a lot of fun on our [editorial] page," he explained, "but we try never to be wishy-washy or fence-straddly; we want to run a strong, lively, provocative, opinionated, outspoken, sometimes outrageous page, calculated to stir up the animals and keep the adrenals flowing." In 10,000 words weekly and over half a million annually, Kilpatrick tackled every subject that came his way and unabashedly expressed himself. His daily routine started in the morning with a grudge about some event from the previous day, and on his way downtown, he gradually awoke by cursing the negligence of city government or denouncing a bill in Congress. "Thus equipped for the day's labors," Kilpatrick chirped, "I go refreshed and purified to my typewriter and the day's damnations begin."[70]

Kilpatrick's *News Leader* editorial page aimed at a posture somewhere between reactive and stodgy, and he presented a general conservative philosophy in a number of fields, from free market capitalism to anti-Communism to states' rights. His writing was masculine and aggressive but showed variations. Sometimes he wrote from his instincts and attacked opponents head-on. In his first editorial, he projected the elite Richmond view of the Ku Klux Klan, calling members of the organization variously "po' white trash that hide beneath their pillow slips [who] might crawl out of the garbage," "cowards," "lip-twiddling little bullies," and "cockroaches in the American home." Other editorials could be less offensive but no less sarcastic. On welfare, he nudged liberals: "Onward and upward to the welfare state! Away with the shadow of national bankruptcy! The new Utopia lies ahead!" More than a few columns appealed to white Virginians' romanticism for the Old South and renewed their attachment to the Confederacy as the centennial anniversary of the war approached. The Confederate flag was not only a defiant reminder of the "War for Southern Independence" but served as a symbol in "a new war for individual independence from the massive socialist state." Kilpatrick could also keep his prickly comments in check and produce serious, intellectual editorials meant for an educated audience. "The Declaration [of Independence] states merely that men are created equal," he instructed readers, for example, "and the whole basis of the American philosophy is that thereafter men are not equal at all—that they are free to rise to whatever unequal heights their initiative and ambition can reach. The equality of man, indeed, is the very opposite of the American doctrine."[71]

Growing confident in his new job and conservative stances, Kilpatrick sometimes turned dogmatic, and he began to look for any opportunities to damn the political left. In a speech before journalism students in 1951, he twisted an address on freedom of the press into a diatribe against liberal Democrats and galloping socialism: "To achieve the tinkered, jerry-built utopia of the planners, we must take a bulldozer to American heritage; we must level off the high and shining places and fill up the valleys of individual inadequacies, and replace initiative with contrived security and liberty with the opiate, poppy-seed controls of the transcendent state." Men may be equal at birth, but the left's demands for their equality thereafter was a halfway house toward socialism and stagnation. Even radical action taken against the national government could justifiably preserve individual freedom. "The more I meditate upon the bloated thing our federal government has become," Kilpatrick complained, "the more convinced I am that only drastic surgery will save us." His comments made him sound like a beleaguered curmudgeon, and he cultivated his role as a biblical pariah shouting warnings to an errant people. "The Elijahs had a bad time of it," Kilpatrick consoled one supporter. "Prophets usually do. Abused and discredited, they wandered in a wilderness for 20 years, and meanwhile the fantastic structure [federal government] grew." Kilpatrick and his patrons at the *News Leader* steadied themselves to defend individualism, but not everyone at the newspapers shared their zeal.[72]

The *News Leader*'s intolerance of liberalism furthered a breach between the paper's bureaucracy and the editor of the *Times-Dispatch*, Virginius Dabney. John Dana Wise and Tennant Bryan failed to control Dabney, who often winced at their maneuvering of editorials in reactionary directions. Dabney, born in 1901 and named after his grandfather and the commonwealth, was from an old, established Virginia family. On his mother's side, he descended from Thomas Jefferson, and his father taught history at the University of Virginia. Dabney came from bloodlines and status that Kilpatrick could only wish for, but he could be progressive in spite of his genteel roots. In editorials, he supported unions and treated African Americans courteously. In 1948 he won a Pulitzer for an editorial denouncing lynching. Dabney's columns attempted to address the needs and concerns of the black community, calling for better educational resources and facilities for people of color and approving of desegregation in Richmond's public transportation system. Despite his progressive streak, Dabney's racial beliefs remained essentially paternalistic. He told one liberal newsman that as much as he deplored deficiencies in the Virginia way of life, he believed that it would be disastrous for Negroes to push for civil rights without white supervision. "I cannot believe that these matters are going to be righted by anybody who insists on an over-night reversal," he wrote. Even though Dabney maintained the separate-but-equal position, his willingness to point out injustices toward African Americans and to scold Virginia's political rulers risked opprobrium. Wise accused Dabney of injuring the newspaper's reputation with his independent style. Dabney often resented the publisher's interference and insisted that Wise hated anyone "to the left of Calvin Coolidge" and had tried to purge him from the newspaper for years.[73]

In the 1940s, Dabney's racial ideas qualified him as a moderate. The simple act of opposing racial violence broke the South's silence on lynching and established Dabney as someone sensitive to the plight of blacks. James Kilpatrick, unlike Dabney, raised few questions about the racial order. The *News Leader* usually treated blacks with civility but also with paternalism. Kilpatrick believed that African Americans were content with southern race relations, something he accused northern critics of failing to recognize, and preferred life in the South to any other region. Like many white southerners, he refused to acknowledge serious racial problems. Kilpatrick eagerly defended Virginia's segregated way of life to his audience. Negroes had an "essentially happy nature," which allowed them "a vast and enviable enjoyment of life under almost any circumstances," he calmed *News Leader* subscribers.[74]

Kilpatrick remained a staunch segregationist and reminded readers that white Virginians would never tolerate efforts to end racially segregated schools. Other southern states might admit qualified blacks to public schools as undergraduates and graduates, but Virginia would stop funding higher education in the event of integration. He found the idea of desegregation "distasteful." If African Americans wanted reforms, they should work amicably with whites and never demand change or divide the community. When the Richmond chapter of the NAACP organized a boycott of all segregated public performances and gatherings in the winter of 1951, Kilpatrick commented, "[S]urely they will gain more support from the public as a whole by a cheerful cooperation in civic gatherings and by participation in Richmond affairs than by deliberately walling themselves off." He worried about the federal government's interference in race relations as well. After President Truman proposed to strengthen the Fair Employment Practices Commission in late 1951, Kilpatrick saw it as an infraction of states' rights and the beginnings of a new federal despotism bent on reshaping the customs not only of the South but of the nation without regard to the law and precedents. He exhorted,

[W]hat the advocates of the Administration's "civil rights" bills refuse to recognize or to accept is that ours is a society based upon law—*constitutional law*. And under the Constitution, only limited powers are granted to the Federal government or denied to the States, and all other powers are specifically reserved to the States or *to the people*. . . . Government derives from the consent of the governed. Destroy this basic principle and something priceless will have been lost. New super-state tyrannies, new compulsions and controls over the lives and habits and customs of individuals, would breed resentment and provoke contempt for law. We have been immensely successful in our own region, thank God, in putting down old seeds of bitterness. But in dark political cellars, a new germination stirs.[75]

But constitutional arguments against "civil rights" reform—Kilpatrick routinely put the phrase in quotes to suggest illegitimacy—were sometimes insufficient to raise public concern about challenges to the racial order. Kilpatrick occasionally resorted to coarse descriptions of blacks as ignorant and prone to criminal behavior. Between April and June 1953, he ran a series titled "Crime in the Deep South" in which he attributed violence in the South to Negroes and rejected the argument that segregation and poor employment opportunities led blacks to break the law. He insisted that African Americans had a predisposition toward criminal activity. He also published statistics on the number of crimes committed each year by blacks but never examined the social and economic factors that produced increases in criminality, nor did he distinguish between Negroes accused of a crimes and those convicted or offer comparative white crime rates. When a few readers confronted him about his unwillingness to explore why blacks committed crimes, Kilpatrick assured them that segregation and racial discrimination were not the root causes since they did not explain "the violence *wrought by Negroes on each other*." For Kilpatrick, it was unacceptable to suggest sociological and economic explanations for problems in the black community.[76]

Kilpatrick usually focused on racial stereotypes and published columns that ignored unequal facilities and limited opportunities for African Americans. John Dana Wise instructed his pupil not to deny the circumstances that plagued the Negro community, however. If the white South neglected all the burdens of blacks, it risked drawing outside interference into the region's affairs. Wise also cautioned him against relying on too many abstract arguments about protecting individual freedoms from creeping socialism in his editorials. "A shield and a sword and a lance are honorable weapons," Wise warned Kilpatrick, "but they are not very effective against a Sherman tank. If we are to preserve our freedoms in a changing world, we must adapt ourselves to changing weapons and to changing tactics in the struggle. I do not propose to win a battle, and to lose the war." Whites must occasionally fix problems in the racial order and meet some of the black community's expectations to preserve segregation. Black southerners, in return, must be patient and defer to whites for help.[77]

When Kilpatrick addressed the need for improvement in Negro schools, he called on African Americans' forbearance and time for the Richmond school board to fund improvements for black education. He hoped this would lead to a "more pleasant racial harmony" rather than an "atmosphere of threats and recriminations." Kilpatrick's response to the demands of Richmond's blacks was that the only solution for them was to wait, for however many decades it required, that, together, Negroes' infinite patience and whites' latent civility would somehow work out grievances. To act more assertively, he warned, invited the heavy-handedness of social engineering and federal bullying.[78]

Even a segregationist like Kilpatrick could not ignore the racial bias engrained in Virginia's legal system, which led to the one instance that he editorialized on behalf of blacks. The murder charge brought against twenty-one-year-old Silas Rogers, an African American shoe-shiner, in 1944 briefly turned Kilpatrick into a crusader for black rights. Virginia's Supreme Court found Rogers guilty of murdering a police officer after dismissing substantial evidence that authorities beat him for a confession. Kilpatrick heard of the case in the winter of 1950–51 while covering the courts, and as editor he investigated the trial. Two factors shaped Kilpatrick's interest in Rogers: his paternalism toward Negroes and his suspicion that the court issued its sentence first and looked at facts later. Always a hound for details, he independently interviewed witnesses and uncovered inconsistencies in the prosecution's case and police misconduct. Kilpatrick bombarded Governor John S. Battle with over fifty letters to convince him of the prisoner's innocence. "John," he wrote the governor, "there is something wrong here some place." A "simple colored boy" like Rogers could not have committed such a malicious crime, Kilpatrick contended, and the evidence against him looked like a "tissue of lies."[79]

Kilpatrick also ran a series called "The Curious Case of Silas Rogers." The columns specifically avoided sensationalist reporting that might capture the same kind of attention the racially and politically charged 1930 Scottsboro affair did. In that case, the Communist Party helped appeal the conviction of nine black youths accused of rape in Alabama. He instead stuck to the facts. Kilpatrick insisted on Rogers's innocence and pled with readers: "Silas Rogers is imprisoned for life—*for a crime he never committed.*" The NAACP looked into the conviction as well and revealed that one witness misidentified Rogers. In 1953, after two years of gathering evidence and Kilpatrick's examination of witness testimonies, Battle pardoned Silas Rogers after he served nearly ten years in prison. Kilpatrick won some national recognition when *Time* magazine praised his campaign to save Rogers. With justice rendered, Kilpatrick commented, "It is, for this newspaper,

the end of a long trail—a trail at once heart-warming and heart-breaking."
The *Richmond Afro-American*, the town's black newspaper, placed the editor on their honor roll in appreciation.[80]

Not that Kilpatrick aspired to be a racial liberal. In a photograph that appeared in *Time*, Kilpatrick posed on the court steps with the freed man. To maintain racial decorum, they stood a few feet apart on separate steps and exchanged no handshake. Rogers, in a blue suit he made in prison, smiles with relief that his ordeal has ended. Kilpatrick looks almost like he was trying to back out of the camera's lens. In the next two years, he would become much better known as an archsegregationist than as the hard-digging reporter who gave Rogers a second chance at life. His experience with Rogers embittered Kilpatrick about taking risks for African Americans. Just three years after his release from prison, Rogers raped a woman in New Jersey and went back to prison. Blacks, many whites murmured, squandered even the most basic freedoms and opportunities. "Sometimes you have to learn lessons the hard way," a chagrined Kilpatrick wrote.[81]

In Richmond, James Jackson Kilpatrick thought and acted like an elite Virginian. The Byrd machine and his employers continued the education that his father began about the evils of liberalism, centralized government, and racial equality, and fashioned him into a formidable weapon for their causes through the pages of the *News Leader*. The approaching racial turmoil of the 1950s and 1960s would demonstrate his allegiance to Virginia's conservative principles and intensify his opposition to the federal government and social reform. In spite of, and because of, the revolution going on in southern race relations, he committed himself to maintaining the dominance of whites in the racial caste system.

Though ambitious and talented, the young segregationist conservative might have remained an obscure editor of a provincial newspaper had not history placed Kilpatrick in a central role in the civil rights era. Less than five years into his editorship, Virginia found itself engaged in the greatest social movement of the twentieth century. Perched in the trenches of his downtown office, James J. Kilpatrick Jr. would not be a vicarious player in the upcoming battles. In newsprint and more, he shaped the language of massive resistance that embroiled the South in the most serious political clash with the federal government since the Civil War. Sifting through old states' rights creeds, he would hone a lingua franca for the segregationist South's conservative political discourse.[82]

TWO

Jim Cronyism

By Christmas 1955, James Kilpatrick was one of the loudest voices of intransigence toward civil rights reform and a budding star in the segregationist South and the conservative intellectual movement. In a series of columns, beginning in late November 1955 and ending in early February 1956, the *News Leader* editor revived the states' rights philosophy of James Madison, Thomas Jefferson, and John C. Calhoun from the annals of American history and resurrected the wizened doctrine of interposition to halt the effects of the *Brown* decision handed down on 17 May 1954 by the U.S. Supreme Court and Chief Justice Earl Warren. To Kilpatrick, *Brown* was an egregious example of judicial activism that breached the Constitution's separation of powers by allowing the Court rather than Congress to make a law. States affected by the ruling could, accordingly, protest the Court's decree and base their resistance on a defense of the constitutional order. Kilpatrick asserted that a state could "interpose" its authority between the people and the central state if the federal government stripped an individual state of its power. The appeal of state sovereignty had not diminished among many southern conservatives, even if the glory of the Old South had been eclipsed.

For James Kilpatrick, Robert E. Lee's surrender at Appomattox Courthouse almost ninety years earlier had not altered the relationship between the respective states and the federal government; the war only eliminated secession as an option. Reinstating interposition as a redoubt against the spread of federal power also satisfied Kilpatrick's desire to hinder twentieth-century liberalism and to prevent changes in the southern racial order. His dream of returning to late-eighteenth-century and early-nineteenth-century federalism—an insistence on the separation between the federal government and the authority of the states—went beyond a rejection of racial equality and the liberal state, however. Kilpatrick began to present the Southland as more than a bridge to an earlier era but a stronghold of conservatism and interposition as a tool to unify the white South and find allies within the broader conservative movement.

Through the language of individual freedom and protection of the local community, Kilpatrick voiced white southern disgust with integration. Instead of racial demagoguery, he offered southern conservatives a political ideology with a genealogy back to the founders of the republic. While some defenders of Jim Crow made racial spats the centerpiece of their opposition to *Brown* and the civil rights movement, Kilpatrick concentrated on the role of government and the separation of powers. As a means of halting *Brown* and civil rights reform, interposition knew limitations. The federal courts denounced it, many white southerners refused to rally to it, and the will of African Americans to end state-sanctioned segregation overwhelmed it. Interposition also tried to deny African Americans their civil rights, and it reflected Kilpatrick's devotion to segregated public schools and a racial caste system. Though he believed that Negroes were his social and intellectual inferiors, he also understood conservatism as a defense against the central state. In a contribution to twentieth-century American conservatism, Kilpatrick mixed opposition to racial progress with rhetoric about the excesses of the federal government. He restructured traditional southern views for more mainstream consumption.

By focusing on states' rights and federalism, Kilpatrick provided segregationists with an impassioned first response against court-ordered desegregation that refrained from racial arguments. Interposition sent a message that the white South would not accept the demands of the Court, and many civil rights reformers learned the hard way. Rather than allow desegregation, a few southern state governments closed their public schools, and many waged a cold war with civil rights activists by establishing private academies and resisting court-sanctioned integration into the 1970s.

Contesting the Court

For a few months in the spring and summer of 1954, the shock of the *Brown* decision numbed subversion of and compliance with the new desegregation ruling and created an uneasy standoff between the South and the federal government. Ineffective federal supervision of the edict by the executive and judicial branches also eased tensions. The Court provided weak leadership and waited a year before implementing its verdict. President Dwight D. Eisenhower, who appointed Warren, remained pessimistic about *Brown* and reluctant to enforce it. Congress split on the school issue with only a minority of congressmen committed to African American civil rights.[1]

The South found itself almost alone with the problem of desegregation. Some white southerners even hoped that *Brown* would only affect the five communities named in the decision. For the people of Prince Edward County, Virginia, one of the original litigants, *Brown* would be a local issue. J. Barrye Wall, editor of the *Farmville Herald* in Prince Edward, asserted, "The problem is ours, we must solve it."[2]

Moderation was the initial response to the decision in Virginia. Governor Thomas B. Stanley told constituents that *Brown* called for "cool heads, calm study, and sound judgment." J. Lindsay Almond Jr., Virginia's attorney general and a defense lawyer in the *Brown* case, felt confident that white Virginians would accept the Court's decree and deal with desegregation "realistically and endeavor to work out some rational adjustment." Temperate voices could be heard at the Richmond newspapers as well. Virginius Dabney asked for peace and thoughtfulness even though he disliked the prospect of mixed classrooms and felt pressured to attack the Court. John Dana Wise demanded that Dabney run an article by a conservative columnist who advocated withholding tax appropriations from public schools if local parents opposed desegregation. Dabney refused. Neither of the Bryan family's papers boldly rejected *Brown*, although such a troubling Court ruling seemed inevitable to at least one of their editors for years.[3]

James Kilpatrick predicted a confrontation between the South and the Supreme Court over civil rights before Earl Warren's nomination as chief justice. In 1953, Kilpatrick criticized his appointment: "[A] Supreme Court justice must stand aloof from political wars, detached from the dust and noise of convention floors, clean of the smell of smoke-filled rooms." He wanted an experienced judge, not one of Eisenhower's political appointees, and his condemnation proved apocryphal considering Warren's later ruling. The day after *Brown*, however, Kilpatrick urged patience. To readers stunned by the decision, he cautioned, "This is not a time for rebellion. It is no time for a weak surrender either. It is a time to sit tight, to think, to unite in a proposal that would win the Supreme Court's approval." He also offered a practical solution and hoped the Court would grant the South a ten-year trial period to integrate 10 percent of the public schools. He told an assembly at the University of Richmond that *Brown* "so far as it goes, and it goes a good deal further than I like, is now the law of the land, and as good citizens we must accept it as such."[4]

From the beginning, Kilpatrick counseled readers to stay united and trust their political leaders to find an answer to the Court's mandate. He also wanted a peaceful implementation of the ruling that would preserve public education and leave wide discretion for local communities to interpret the order. In a letter to Harry Byrd Sr., he recommended that the state "permit segregated schools to be maintained where particular localities desire to maintain them, without doing violence to the Supreme Court or to the Constitution." Localities with large black populations, like the Southside, simply would not accept desegregation, and Kilpatrick thought a system of private schools could augment public education for parents who disliked *Brown*. In contrast to Wise, who proposed that the state withdraw funds for public schools, Kilpatrick stood by public education. "We are not about to return to some dark, medieval night of tutors and private schools for the well-to-do, and illiteracy for everyone else," he wrote.[5]

Waiting for a constructive solution to the desegregation crisis left Kilpatrick's readers unsatisfied. Many of the *News Leader*'s faithful demanded that he take a position. Some letter writers hated the idea of compromising with the Court while others welcomed a negotiated settlement. In a letter to the editor, June Purcell Guild, lawyer and expert on Virginia race law, wrote that he expected Kilpatrick to "lead in emphasizing respect for law, order, and the Constitution" through dignified editorials, which would not stir up illegal and bad behavior among southern whites. Two years later, Kilpatrick claimed that *Brown* had bewildered him into inaction, which accounted for his moderate-sounding editorials in May 1954. "I think all of us in the South were intensely conscious at that moment that the whole country was looking at us, so in some excess of gentility, we were determined to be on our best behavior. Nobody likes to cry in front of strangers," he explained.[6]

Kilpatrick's conciliatory tone contradicted the hostility he felt for the *Brown* decision. His private correspondence during the summer of 1954 indicated that he quickly absorbed the threat of desegregation and perished the thought. Initially, *News Leader* editorials called for Negro leaders' patience and the Court to give the white South time to adjust to the ruling, but Kilpatrick soon deviated from moderation and hinted at more extreme plans for resistance. "I am not about to advocate that Virginia secede from the Union," he confided to his friend Harry Byrd Jr., but "I would toss an old battle-cry back to the NAACP: Hell, we have only begun to fight."[7]

Virginia's state officials also began to line up against *Brown*. Governor Tom Stanley felt intense popular pressure to resist *Brown*, and the public inundated his office with letters urging him to stand up against the federal government and prevent race mixing. The governor greeted the Warren Court's verdict with circumspection but drew flak from Byrd machine

insiders shortly after the ruling when he invited five of the commonwealth's most prominent African Americans to discuss a resolution to the
school situation. They refused, which embarrassed Stanley. Opposition to
his attempts at appeasement intensified when a group of Southsiders pronounced themselves "unalterably opposed" to integration, which meant
the bastion of white supremacy in Virginia and Byrd's power base would
fight *Brown*. Kilpatrick also watched Stanley's actions carefully. Although
the *News Leader* generally supported the governor, its editor distrusted
him. A year earlier, Kilpatrick wrote Harry Byrd Sr. that Stanley had "no
imagination, no stature, no drive. . . . He has been wishy-washy, mealy-
mouthed, half-hearted, [and] equivocal," adding that he "isn't an asset,
he's a liability." To prove his credentials and retain the confidence of the
Byrd organization, Stanley decided to harden his stance, and in June 1954
he announced, "I shall use every legal means at my command to continue
segregated schools in Virginia."[8]

Stanley's embrace of a tougher position on desegregation encouraged
Kilpatrick. He wrote his old friend William Tuck, now a Southside congressman, "I just hope this doesn't turn out to be one of those things like the
weather where everybody talks about it, but nobody does anything about
it." Kilpatrick, like most other influential figures in the state, had few ideas
about fixing the situation and gave Stanley room to consider his options.
"Lord knows I have no pat solution to propose," he admitted to Barrye Wall.
"I don't think there is one. But I do know that the mill wheels of the courts
grind exceedingly slow, and we can litigate a long, long time before mixed
schools ever become a reality in eastern Virginia," Kilpatrick wrote confidently. He believed that Virginia's leaders had time to save segregation.[9]

In August 1954, Stanley gathered state politicians to find a legal solution
to the Court's order. Comprised mainly of Black Belt Virginia legislators
and headed by state senator Garland Gray, the Gray Commission searched
for a legislative response. Publicly, Kilpatrick praised the Gray Commission
and expected it to suggest that counties and towns oversee desegregation.
Throughout the fall, he promised segregationist stalwarts that Virginia's
leaders would never let the federal government force an unacceptable ruling on the South. In late September, he told readers, "We will resist this
judgment of the court; we will resist it quietly, honorably, lawfully, but
we will resist it with the strength of a tradition that has resisted tyranny
before."[10]

The longer it took the Court to decide on an implementation ruling, the
more perturbed James Kilpatrick became. "The sooner the court acts, the

sooner the South can lay its plans," he wrote in an editorial titled "Is This Delay Necessary?" He grew so upset that some of his editorials showed less restraint: they conveyed fears about miscegenation, warned that admitting blacks to public schools would retard white children's education, and documented the deleterious effects of desegregation. "I am going to keep hammering away," he wrote Lindsay Almond.

> I have in mind for the next few weeks, if I can get all of the facts together, doing a display on venereal diseases, divorce rates, by race, by county and city, as a follow-up to the table we ran a week ago on [black] illegitimacy. Also, I have obtained from the State Department of Education some most remarkable statistics on the results of educational testing among all of the eighth grade students, white and negro alike, throughout the State. The results should be enough to make even the most pro-integration person pause for a second look. . . . The Supreme Court may have held that segregation is unconstitutional on the grounds of race, but this Court would have to go further afield than even its members have gone in order to say that the 14th Amendment would prohibit the grouping of children according to mental age, or reading aptitude or I.Q. . . . [I]t occurs to me that sort of a tool might be devised from the tests, to use along with such other tools as gerrymandering or school districts.[11]

While Kilpatrick raised concerns about desegregation, members of the Gray Commission designed a solution to the *Brown* decision that would simultaneously recognize local authority and the Supreme Court. The most outspoken and determined opposition to extreme solutions came from within the commission. Although state legislators officially supervised the Gray Commission, David John Mays, a respected Richmond corporate and banking lawyer, soon dominated the commission. Mays joined the committee in January 1955 as an ad hoc counselor. He never advocated outright resistance to Warren's ruling and, because of his legal training, worried about the fallout from a rejection of the Court's authority. He believed that some measure of integration was certain, that white Virginians would not tolerate school closures to subvert *Brown*, and that the commission must find ways to soften desegregation at the local level while passing general guidelines at the state level. He recognized the power of the Court "while destroying its effect, at least at present, in the counties having heavy Negro populations." According to his plan, the cities and counties would face *Brown* one at a time, which fit with the idea of Virginia as a commonwealth—a collection of independent local entities. Prior to the Court's implementation ruling, Mays gained considerable influence within the commission and convinced many members not to flout the Court and to abandon their belief that segregation would last forever. His strategy to create a unified response that respected the Court immediately faced challenges.[12]

The first problem the Gray Commission encountered resulted from political infighting and power struggles within the Byrd machine. "Involved in the whole segregation affair," Mays recorded in early November 1954, "is a backstage fight over the next governorship. Peck [Garland Gray] and his friends . . . are busily trying to undermine the Atty-Genl. [Lindsay Almond], who has gained considerable ground in the past four months." Gray and Almond both hoped to use the commission's success as a vehicle to the governorship, and the school segregation question became the key to the next gubernatorial race. Gray wanted his name attached to the school solution, and Mays often frustrated him by not steering a more radical course of resistance that would win the approval of Virginia's segregationist electoral power base in the Black Belt. Almond, conversely, who as attorney general would be negotiating the implementation of *Brown* with the Court, saw the Gray plan as an obstacle to his legal work within the court system.[13]

Governor Stanley's inept direction led to further disputes among his potential successors. He repeatedly passed up Almond's legal advice and at one point refused to consult him about when to call the state legislature to deal with school desegregation. If the state failed to take swift action to resolve the problem, Almond fretted, it might give the Court an excuse to force immediate desegregation. Stanley also excluded Gray from important deliberations, and the lead commissioner nearly resigned and spearheaded a separate course of outright resistance to the Court.[14]

The 31 May 1955, *Brown II* opinion put additional pressure on the Gray commissioners and other Virginia white supremacists. The Court ruled that local school districts must desegregate with "all deliberate speed" and gave the federal district courts jurisdiction over implementation. Put into a managerial role, federal judges refused to set a schedule for the beginning and end of school integration. The slowness of the federal courts to intervene should have encouraged segregationists. Even though the Court granted all of Kilpatrick's wishes after the first *Brown* case, including breathing room for the South, preservation of good race relations, and grounds for states and local school districts to oversee desegregation, he and others like him either would not or could not tolerate the implementation decision. Time seemed to be running out on them.[15]

The ruling heightened Kilpatrick's discomfort and roused him to new outbursts on the editorial page. After the second *Brown* decision, he shed any notions of moderation and unleashed his antipathy. The double impact of changing race relations and interfering with the states' control of public education, the latter guaranteed in the Tenth Amendment's provision that all powers not delegated to the federal government or prohibited to the states by the Constitution were reserved to the states, or to the people, proved more than he could bear. On 1 June, Kilpatrick's editorial threatened the Court with increased litigation, noncooperation, and indefinite delay. Virginians could "now . . . formulate some orderly systematic counter-moves," he smoldered, adding, "And if it be said that the court's opinion was conciliatory, we would reply that the South is no more of a mind to conciliate on Wednesday than it was on Tuesday. When the court proposes that its social revolution be imposed upon the South 'as soon as practicable,' there are those of us who would respond that 'as soon as practicable' means never at all." Foreseeing decades of obstruction to *Brown*, he chastised the errant Court: "If it be said now that the South is flouting the law, let it be said to the high court, *You taught us how*."[16]

For the next several months, Kilpatrick waited for the Gray Commission to finish its work and provide a way around the implementation decision. In November 1955, the commission's report suggested locally based pupil assignment plans and tuition grants for private education to parents who did not want to send their children to desegregated schools. The Gray plan left wiggle room for the state to continue segregation without denouncing the entire program of school desegregation. Convincing the public to accept the proposals lay ahead.[17]

Kilpatrick liked both of the Gray Commission's recommendations. He favored local solutions to problems and, back in June 1954, had proposed a similar tuition grant package that would allow determined resisters to keep their children out of public schools. The Gray plan's tuition incentives could potentially eliminate public education in areas of white supremacy. Kilpatrick explained to readers that the demise of public schools would not be catastrophic. "We have made a fetish of 'public education' to the point that education under the auspices of the state has come to be considered the only education," he assured anxious parents. "It is not, and ought not to be."[18]

To authorize the use of state funds for private schools, Virginians had to amend the commonwealth's constitution, which banned publicly financed private education. The Gray Commission suggested that the citizens vote for a special assembly of the state legislature to write a constitutional amendment. Governor Stanley summoned state legislators to an emergency meeting to begin the emending procedures, and they set a date for a referendum vote on 9 January 1956. On 18 December, Harry Byrd approved of the vote for a constitutional convention, and it looked like Virginia would follow a path of limited integration for school districts that had small black populations and private academies for whites who opposed the *Brown* decisions. While Virginians argued about the approaching vote, Kilpatrick already decided on a radical course of opposition to *Brown*.[19]

As the Gray plan emerged, at a meeting called in the first week of November 1955, Kilpatrick, Wise, Bryan, and other editors at the paper discussed ways to keep white Virginians united against desegregation during the coming months. They also debated the merits and liabilities of noncompliance with the Supreme Court. The idea of rebellion held some appeal except for possible secession from the federal union—an unpleasant reminder of the past and one the nation would never permit. Kilpatrick left the talks disappointed and without answers. "I confess," he told his friend Tom Waring at the *Charleston News and Courier*, "I have no suggestions to offer on how best to acquaint the rest of the Republic with the many reasons and considerations that have led southerners to believe they are pursuing a right and proper course."[20]

Kilpatrick soon stumbled onto a solution when he read a pamphlet by William ("Wild Bill") Olds, an alcoholic country lawyer from Chesterfield County, Virginia. The twenty-eight page booklet suggested legislation to declare *Brown* an improper amendment of the Constitution and to enable the state to withdraw its funding from public schools. It called for interposition based on Madison's and Jefferson's Kentucky and Virginia resolutions—tracts that validated states' rights and interposition as defenses against despotic national laws—to thwart the Court orders. The booklet also summoned a long history of successful resistance in several states against the Court, and it avoided racial language, which made it ideal for selling the South's program to the rest of the republic. The pamphlet became the blueprint for Kilpatrick.[21]

A copy of Olds's work reached Kilpatrick's desk in summer 1955, but he put it in his growing pile of material on desegregation, where it lay until November. After reading it, he walked straight to the Richmond library and checked out books on Madison, Jefferson, and the constitutional period. Kilpatrick also gravitated toward and relied on the thought of John C.

Calhoun—the preeminent nineteenth-century states' sovereignty philosopher and proponent of nullifying unjust federal laws, even if it meant seceding. The editor then gave Olds's pamphlet to Bryan and Wise and scheduled an editorial meeting to review the subject. They met with several local attorneys to discuss the doctrine and also pitched the idea of interposition to ten members of the General Assembly. Bryan told the congressmen that he intended to use his paper to develop "as much unanimity as possible among the white people of Virginia" and to halt implementation of the *Brown* decision. After consultations in subsequent meetings, lawyers counseled Bryan and Kilpatrick that interposition rested on an unsound legal position made irrelevant by the death of states' rights in the Civil War. Objections notwithstanding, the idea of no compromise and no integration appealed to the attorneys and the *News Leader*'s management.[22]

Kilpatrick had no prior understanding of nullification and interposition and therefore was often more eloquent than accurate when he shared his amateur knowledge of the Constitution. In his editorials on the subject, he stayed just ahead of his reading. A few weeks before, John Calhoun, James Madison, and Thomas Jefferson were luminaries he discussed at dinner parties or with John Dana Wise, not people he read with great attention. Once he swung into action on an issue, however, he was nearly impossible to redirect, and he impulsively plunged ahead. While everyone else waited, Kilpatrick acted. Two weeks after reading Olds's booklet, Kilpatrick pounded out his first interposition editorial, and the dusty doctrine permeated the editorial pages for the next three months.[23]

On 21 November, readers of the *News Leader* opened their daily to find a sophisticated and serious editorial section titled "Fundamental Principles," including long passages of the Kentucky and Virginia Resolves next to portraits of Madison and Jefferson. Kilpatrick outlined the doctrine of interposition as the way to suspend the operation of an unconstitutional federal encroachment and to protect state sovereignty. He also argued that the relationship between the states and the federal government was the "transcendent issue" in the Court's *Brown* ruling and that the matters of race and desegregation were secondary problems. Virginians must turn to "certain historical documents that shed light upon evils of today that were prophetically seen long ago," he asserted. The founding fathers predicted such a clash between state sovereignty and federal authority more than 157 years before *Brown* and called on the states to defend themselves: "Jefferson and Madison did prophesy a time when the Federal government might usurp powers not granted it. And in such an emergency, these great men asserted, the States may declare their inherent right—inherent in the nature of our Union—to judge for themselves not merely of the infraction, but 'of the mode and measure of redress.' This is the right of interposition."[24]

Without states' rights, Kilpatrick persisted, individuals' rights would "be swept away by judicial encroachment, and the States reduced to the status of mere counties." Couching the school segregation issue in terms of the protection of the local community made the debate appear racially neutral and appealed to traditionalists' distrust of big government. Kilpatrick retrieved the Burkean perspective that said far away actors must not engender social changes based on abstractions. The right of interposition protected the Union from Court and federal authority. The central state would metastasize into a "single mass, monolithic . . . creature more powerful than its creator" if not for states' rights, cried Kilpatrick.[25]

Kilpatrick insisted that when the states decided to form a compact and created the Union in the late eighteenth century, the central state existed at the behest of the separate states, which granted the federal government certain powers but retained others not explicitly given to the national government. The states' essential sovereignty, therefore, never diminished, and they made all final decisions on changes to the U.S. Constitution. "If our strength be in union," Kilpatrick asserted, "it lies first in apartness." He believed the states, as sovereign bodies, still had the responsibility and the power to counteract extreme actions by the federal government, or to "interpose" themselves between the national government and the local level on behalf of the people's liberty. Interposition acted as a check against the central government by allowing states to protest grievances and protect their citizens from tyranny.[26]

From November 1955 through February 1956, Kilpatrick inundated editorial pages with arguments designed to couple many Virginians' and southerners' familiarity with resisting the federal government with their love of debating constitutional issues. "I was on a horse and the pen was a lance," he later wrote. Sitting behind a banged-up typewriter, he reached for law books and histories that helped him explain states' rights. When he needed a statistic to prove a point, his fingers danced over yellow file folders containing research material that he kept next to his desk. To excite readers, he reissued entire speeches and essays from Madison, Jefferson, Calhoun, Tocqueville, and others and included portraits of them. In one editorial, he reprinted former Virginia governor John Floyd's 1833 address on interposition in which Floyd denounced unfair federal laws and told the General Assembly that "interposition is the true remedy for violations of the Constitution"; it will "enable society here to defend itself, and punish those disturbers of the peace of the Commonwealth." Kilpatrick worked to keep the attention of the public, and when he wrote, he tried to picture them, their vocabulary, and their history, and then pulled them in close.[27]

Kilpatrick even changed the syntax of the newspaper to attract readers to his states' rights arguments. He abandoned the words "nation" and "national" to downplay the centrality of the federal government and instead talked about "States" and their rights. The designation "United States," additionally, never referenced a single entity because Kilpatrick, in all instances, paired it with the plural form of the verb. Thanks to Kilpatrick, the word "interposition," which southerners had not spoken since the nineteenth century, was in common usage throughout the commonwealth. The *Southern School News*, a moderate periodical that documented the school desegregation process, claimed that "after six weeks and fifty-thousand words in the *News Leader*, the strange new word 'interposition' had entered the vocabulary of most adult Virginians and of politicians all across the South."[28]

The interposition editorials touched a powerful nerve in the commonwealth that Kilpatrick hardly needed to reawaken. Interposition "was not an idea that had to be planted," he boasted. "That was an idea that grew like dandelions and crab grass." Kilpatrick's ideas set many whites' imaginations aflame, and he republished only positive letters to the editor for weeks after the initial interposition editorials. What remained absent from the flurry of discussion over *Brown* were letters to the editor that embraced white supremacy. While many readers surely submitted rabidly racist diatribes, Kilpatrick included only letters by writers who decentered race in their arguments. "More power to you in your valiant fight," declared reader William Olds, for example. Another supporter wrote, "You have gone, and are going, far beyond the details and arguments of the present perplexing problems, and you are opening up an entirely new vista which may well have a marked effect." Some respondents even demanded that the General Assembly oppose the Court's ruling. R. A. Ricks urged Kilpatrick to pressure the legislature to pass a resolution "to the effect that the state of Virginia respectfully declines to honor its segregation ruling." The old political philosophy of states' rights reassured Virginians that resistance formed a continuum with the defiance of their forefathers. It was now the twentieth-century Old Dominion's job to defend the constitutional order from the Supreme Court. Despotism seemed synonymous with the Warren Court.[29]

The *Brown* decision convinced Kilpatrick and other segregationists that the Supreme Court amended the Constitution. The editor was so conservative in his view of the Constitution that he regarded each amendment since the Thirteenth Amendment to end slavery as unnecessary. He remained contemptuous of democratic alterations to the Constitution after its ratification, especially when modifications built a framework for later reform. In 1954, according to Kilpatrick, Warren and the associate justices ignored the power of states to run their educational systems and misinterpreted the Fourteenth Amendment to give states' citizens the freedom to attend desegregated schools. Even worse, the Court acted without legal foundation as a moral arbiter that insisted on the inherent wrongness of racial separation, partly because of the psychological injury it inflicted on black children. Cases dating back to the 1875 *Slaughterhouse* cases and the 1896 *Plessy v. Ferguson* decision protected the South's legal right to segregate, but the Court negated the precedents. Nine justices, ex nihilo, replaced years of legal protections for segregation with their personal view that a separated school system "generates a feeling of inferiority . . . that may affect their [black children's] hearts and minds in a way unlikely ever to be undone." To Kilpatrick, morality and the law should function separately. With *Brown*, however, the Court confused law with politics. Kilpatrick detested judicial activism and an insistence on equality of results between blacks and whites. The "discretion of the judge," he quoted from Edward Gibbon, "is the first engine to tyranny." Kilpatrick saw the court ruling as a crude attempt to please people outside the South, and it made him cringe. "In matters of taste and intelligence," he once commented, "public opinion is often worth next to nothing." The Court's verdict was more intolerable than a bad opinion. Kilpatrick dubbed it "a revolutionary act by a judicial junta which simply seized power, and thus far has managed to get away with its act of usurpation." The purpose of the law was to harness government to restrain it from stripping the people of their individual rights. Government run by the emotions of a few men, who misconstrued or ignored legal precedents, Kilpatrick charged, violated the will of the people and threatened the constitutional order that placed ultimate power in the hands of "We the People."[30]

Kilpatrick refused to be coerced into accepting an unwarranted ruling, which ended segregation and established new privileges for the Supreme Court, and he tarred the Warren Court for its "rape of the Constitution." The Court's reliance on the Fourteenth Amendment troubled him because he, like many conservative southerners, regarded that amendment as illegitimate legislation passed during federal occupation of the southern states that placed the power to enforce powers of the law in the hands of the central government. Rather than deny the power of the Court to hear cases in law and equity, he proposed that the states reserved the power to object to judicial interpretations. The idea of interposition arose in part as an attempt to restore order to an errant state and to reassert the separation of powers between the judicial and legislative branches. The doctrine of interposition, Kilpatrick hoped, supplied the missing link for an effective check on a Court that acted like a legislature. The proper role of the Court was to review the law, not make it. Warren reversed that tradition. "Who," Kilpatrick queried Harry Byrd, "is to watch the watchman?"[31]

Federalism was Kilpatrick's remedy. The states, according to the theory of interposition, still had the power to hold Court rulings null and void until the matter could be resolved by a constitutional amendment. Only the creators of the national government—the states—could determine the authority of the central state. Was it "reasonable to believe that the States, like Frankenstein, have created an agency superior to themselves," the editor asked, "and that they are powerless to contest their own destruction." Kilpatrick even discussed the prospect of the states appointing a review board to assess the actions of the national government. Each state could interpose its sovereignty if the central government overstepped its authority. Fifty independent state committees approving the legality of the federal government's decisions seemed like anarchy to some, but Kilpatrick preferred it to tyranny and the violation of the Constitution.[32]

Kilpatrick's interpretation of government powers looked more like the one agreed upon in the eighteenth-century Articles of Confederation than the one guiding twentieth-century America. His view of state sovereignty disregarded the judicial nationalism of John Marshall in the 1800s and the federal government's war against the states during and after the Civil War. Kilpatrick returned to the days before the constitutional convention of 1787 and the Virginia and Kentucky Resolutions of 1798 and hoped others would too. If the Civil War ended states' rights, argued Kilpatrick, then "this fact surely would have been spelled out for us to read in the Constitution today." Interposition, as Kilpatrick described it, assumed that the states remained in the Union and accepted terms they approved and jettisoned the rest. It stopped short of secession, however. Kilpatrick protested the Court's actions but never declared a new civil war. He privately retained the belief that the states reserved the power to secede, telling the *Tampa Tribune*'s editor, James A. Clendinen, "Now I, myself, am willing to go the whole way with Mr. Calhoun. As a matter of fact, I am willing to go a bow-shot beyond him, and insist that the right of secession still exists." Regrettably for him, the war dashed secession, and Kilpatrick had little inclination for meaningless pursuits. He wrote another correspondent, "Life is short, honest to God it is, and life is too short to waste it in vain and abortive causes that offer no conceivable hope of advantage anywhere. I don't mind taking up lost causes—it is the fate of every Southerner—but I want to be a little selective in the lost causes I take up."[33]

Although John Calhoun was principally responsible for implementing interposition during the 1830s tariff crisis in South Carolina, Kilpatrick associated it with Jefferson and Madison more often because their names reminded Americans of the birth of the nation and patriotism. Many people tied Calhoun, conversely, to the sectionalism of the nineteenth century that bred divisions and later secession and war. Historian Garry Wills has pointed out that conservatives tend to revere the anti-Federalists and enemies of the Constitution more often than the framers and nationalists. Kilpatrick preferred the jumbled, decentralized confederation of states that the anti-Federalists tried to hand the United States. He lionized the losers in American history, Calhoun, John Randolph, and the Confederates, rather than the winners, Alexander Hamilton, John Marshall, and Abraham Lincoln. Kilpatrick loved to style himself as one of the underdogs besieged by the scourge of liberalism and made plans for an upset victory.[34]

For Kilpatrick, interposition would serve several purposes. He often intoned that his states' rights campaign diminished racial tension and avoided violence by focusing white southerners on constitutional issues. His contrived peacemaking was misleading. Raising questions about the legality of the Court's opinion would buy time for segregationists to develop more plans of resistance. Kilpatrick remembered the lessons of the failed Prohibition laws that his father subverted. Sustained rebellion against an intolerable law might force the Court to withdraw its demands, as was the case when Congress repealed its ban on alcohol. "When these changes are produced from below out of the depths of public conscience and the deep waters of subtle attitudes," he reminded an audience at the University of Richmond, "they can win peaceful acceptance. But they must come from below; they cannot successfully be imposed from above." If the South could survive a few years of federal interference, popular support for desegregation might dwindle as well. He also contemplated a national amendment to ban segregation that would never clear the necessary thirty-six states because the southern states would reject it. Once it failed, the South could argue that the country rejected the *Brown* decision.[35]

Kilpatrick also hoped interposition would gain political support and, in time, diminish support for school desegregation. Kilpatrick wanted interposition to draw Virginians together in strong, unified opposition to the federal government and to summon assistance from other areas of the nation among traditionalists and conservatives displeased with the central government and judicial activism. "Think upon these things Virginians! Whether one opposed racial integration, as we do, or supports integration... is beside the point. All Virginians, liberal and conservative alike . . . are united in devotion to the Constitution." From late 1955 through 1956, interposition served primarily as a rallying point for the white South. "Our thought here," he told one North Carolina supporter, "is that if six or seven—or hopefully, nine of 10—Southern States should unite in a common front, all of them undertaking to nullify the Court's mandate, and all of them appealing to their sister States to resolve a question of contested power, the Supreme Court would be faced with a truly formidable problem in enforcing its orders."[36]

Kilpatrick believed that as a national procedure, interposition might win "many converts in the North, even among those who don't understand our position on race." In editorial headlines, he presented the case for interposition as a national struggle and referenced examples of resistance to federal authority with captions like "New England" and "Wisconsin Proclaimed the Right" or "Iowa Successfully Challenged." One student of Virginia's struggle against *Brown* pointed out that Kilpatrick designed a respectable rhetoric that relied on the beliefs of the founding fathers more than racial bigotry to win over potential outside allies. The doctrine of interposition could elevate the desegregation struggle "above the sometimes sordid level of race and segregation," the editor explained to one correspondent. "[S]chool segregation, however critical a problem it may be right now, is not the overriding problem," he assured readers publicly. "The transcendent issue lies in finding some effective check upon the encroachments by the Federal judiciary upon the reserve powers of the States."[37]

Draping interposition in constitutional language allowed Kilpatrick to reclaim the high ground in the desegregation controversy. Linking his beliefs to the founding fathers accomplished the same objective. Many segregationists turned to Thomas Jefferson in particular as an authority on government, liberty, and race relations. He gave their beleaguered cause authenticity and a cover of respectability. Jefferson enjoyed popularity as a pillar of the American republic, author of the Declaration of Independence, and Enlightenment thinker. Though liberals claimed him as their inspiration for the defense of liberty and equality, the *News Leader* editor argued, he knew the "real" views of Jefferson on state powers and race relations. As much as some Americans might dislike it, Jefferson was a conservative in many respects, and Kilpatrick was not incorrect in his understanding of the founding father. Jefferson owned slaves, enjoyed the status of a patrician, and preferred local over centralized government. When he wrote the Declaration of Independence, he never intended that "all men" were equal, but only white men of property. Kilpatrick believed that if Jefferson had lived in the 1950s, he would have rushed to the aid of embattled southern defenders of the racial hierarchy and would have found *Brown* to be a despotic and heinous ruling. Jefferson provided segregationists with a direct tie to the foundations of the republic. Kilpatrick identified with the sage of Monticello as a kindred spirit and used his writings to justify interposition. From a psychological standpoint, claiming a shared heritage with a revered American must have also comforted the young editor and other white southerners and given them a sense of security and aplomb in their time of crisis.[38]

With the centennial of the Civil War approaching and states' rights in the air, a local crowd expected the *News Leader* editor to explicate the southern way of life and the Old Dominion's heritage and to defend the honor of the South. Colleagues at the paper wondered if Kilpatrick's desire to obstruct the Supreme Court was partially due to peer pressure. Richard Whalen, one of Kilpatrick's associate editorial writers, thought his boss reacted to personal convictions but also satisfied the paper's bureaucracy and Virginia's elites. Racial concerns primarily motivated Kilpatrick, but by advocating interposition, he figured out a way to fulfill his ambitions and solidify his place among the Richmond elite. "Jack was not a native Virginian, and he succeeded Freeman, an institution in the South," Whalen commented; "[he] felt obliged to uphold the ideology of the Old South and the Lost Cause." Kilpatrick, however, was not merely a hired gun. He did not chafe under impositions by Bryan, Wise, or Byrd. The editor fanned the flames of resistance and then watched as much of the South responded with alacrity.[39]

The *News Leader* struggled to keep pace with fan mail and requests for copies of Kilpatrick's interposition columns. The demand for his editorials grew so large that the newspaper reprinted the series as a booklet to distribute across the South to inspire people. Before the pamphlet finished publication, the public placed 1,000 advance orders. By Christmas 1955, more than 13,000 copies sold. Kilpatrick also sent the booklet to the governors of North Carolina, Texas, Louisiana, Arkansas, and possibly others. One judge on the North Carolina Supreme Court received six copies with a note from Kilpatrick to pass them out to the other members of the bench. In Connecticut, Senator Prescott S. Bush, father and grandfather to two future presidents, received a handful of interposition editorials in the mail from a Gray commissioner. Interposition's tremors reverberated across the land and provided a label for policies of resistance already awakening among many opponents of desegregation.[40]

In the segregationist press community, interposition became a cornerstone. Three days after the first interposition editorial, Tom Waring followed Kilpatrick's lead by staying clear of the race issue and focusing on the defense of the Constitution and the founders. If "southerners are looking into the past for fundamental principles," Waring asked, "where better should they look than to . . . Thomas Jefferson, author of the Declaration of Independence, architect of American liberty and one of the great political thinkers of all time? Is Jefferson out of date? If so, the American Republic is dead." The *Jackson Daily News* in Mississippi asked readers if "there is any higher ground upon which [southerners] could stand than the asserted sovereignty of their state," and answered, "No. They would be in company of people like Jefferson and Madison, and that is concededly good company." The Mississippi-based anti-integrationist Citizens' Council dedicated most of its December 1955 journal to the praise of interposition as well. Even some western conservatives approved of interposition. Eugene C. Pulliam, the influential Arizona media mogul, pushed Kilpatrick's ideas in his daily newspapers in Phoenix and Indianapolis.[41]

At home, the interposition campaign had Harry Byrd's blessing, as well as the power of his Southside constituency, which remained hostile to any desegregation efforts and sensitive about the Tidewater's large black population. Byrd congratulated Kilpatrick for his editorials: "You certainly stirred up something when you brought out the interposition approach. I only wish we could have gotten started on this sooner." Kilpatrick provided Byrd with the intellectual and political foundation for state action against the Court edicts without crossing the line into racial demagoguery, a taboo in Virginia politics. The senator believed wholeheartedly in the legality of the interposition gambit. "Look who drafted the [Virginia] Resolution," Byrd assured a fellow Virginian. "It's got to be right." He felt obligated to honor Jefferson and Madison and role-played as a modern-day Robert E. Lee, outnumbered and encircled by federal forces. Only the Gray plan stood in Byrd's path to fighting another historic battle.[42]

By December 1955, Virginia's leaders faced a choice between the earlier recommendations of the Gray Commission and the obstructionism of interposition. The commonwealth's response to *Brown* might shift from cooperation, which the Gray plan offered, to defiance. Kilpatrick saw an opportunity to sideline the Gray proposals and replace them with a formal rejection of the *Brown* decision based on interposition and privately derided the commission's work as a "hodge-podge of expediency and compromise." Byrd, however, convinced the *News Leader* editor to keep his objections out of the public debate until voters could approve the statewide referendum. The senator worried that Kilpatrick's insistence on interposition instead of the Gray plan and an influential voice like the *News Leader* battering the commission's suggestions might convince the Virginia electorate to stay home rather than approve the constitutional convention. "The difficulty that finally caused us to put it [interposition] off until January," Kilpatrick explained, "was our fear that many persons, whose votes we need in a State Referendum in January, would feel that 'interposition' had solved everything, and would stay away from the polls." Preserving the appearance of unity in the state's top levels meant that Kilpatrick had to remain silent on the Gray recommendations before the January vote. His objections to the Gray Commission, however, did not mean that Kilpatrick rejected legislative solutions.[43]

Kilpatrick intended his interposition strategy to work alongside the state legislative efforts. Interposition, he told Tom Waring, "never was thought by any of us [as] a substitute for the legislative program laid down by our Gray commission; it is only an addition to that program, and works very well with it." The special assembly suggested by the Gray Commission could legitimate resistance by formalizing Virginia's opposition to the Warren Court, something that interposition editorials could not do. Interposition offered one of many tactics that politicians could use to wreck *Brown*, and Kilpatrick often told people that it could take many different forms, ranging from the merely symbolic to an official protest. Its primary purpose was the interstate unification of the white South and the support of nonsoutherners, but it also embraced anything from mild protests in state legislatures to nullification of federal actions. In addition to state assemblies, governors and state judges could, theoretically, invoke interposition as well. Although its implementation and articulation could differ from state to state and newspaper to newspaper, interposition translated into folksy, southern, even western, vernacular. The West Texas rancher-activist J. Evetts Haley outlined the doctrine to his radio listeners. "If you look over a menu and order ham and eggs for breakfast, you have made a contract," he said. "If Brussells sprouts and beans are brought to you instead, you, as a partner in that contract, interpose your objections, and refuse to eat and pay for them. . . . Interposition, in spite of all the political mumbo-jumbo, is just as . . . Constitutional as ham and eggs." Despite its applicability and flexibility, Kilpatrick knew interposition's limitations.[44]

Kilpatrick's basic optimism about the rightness of interposition did not allay all of his concerns. Interposition supplied segregationists with a slogan and the bold stand southerners expected from their leaders, but it stood on shaky legal ground. Kilpatrick knew it. Rather than create a legal solution to thwarting *Brown*, he believed interposition enlivened "the spirit of the [Virginia] resolution of 1798, in that it is intended to excite public opinion, and not to have any binding legal effect." The federal judicial and executive branches still had the power to deny the South its attempts at subversion. Despite his commitment to interposition, Kilpatrick admitted that it was only a theory—albeit a correct one—and that the force of the federal government trumped any theory or idea. "[W]hile we hope earnestly that interposition will void the Supreme Court's decisions, we cannot say, as matter of certainty, that that will be the effect. I imagine it will depend entirely upon how much force the Supreme Court is able to exert in carrying out its mandates," he wrote Harry Byrd. "If Eisenhower should send troops in to enforce the court's decisions," Kilpatrick added, "I believe we would find that [interposition] had not actually 'voided' these decisions at all."[45]

Without the law on their side, segregationists in Virginia needed a miracle to prevent desegregation. The decision to proceed with resistance instead of the Gray plan now rested with the voters of the state. On 9 January 1956, the electorate approved the Gray Commission's recommendation of convening a special assembly of the state legislature to legalize tuition grants for private schools. As far as voters knew, Virginia would enact the Gray proposals as the way to deal with *Brown*.[46]

Interposition involved more than proximity to power; it exerted political muscle in the state. Behind the scenes, Byrd and his men scotched the commission's course of action and replaced it with interposition. The day after the referendum, Kilpatrick announced in the *News Leader* that Virginians had voted not for a constitutional convention but, "with a perfect, intuitive clarity," to oppose the Supreme Court. Three days later, Byrd gathered his top lieutenants in Washington to discuss his desire to torpedo the Gray plan in favor of outright resistance to *Brown*. He believed that allowing even token integration betrayed the trust of white Virginians and preferred to coordinate a stand with the southern states. Governor Stanley and other Byrd men also endorsed the total resistance package.[47]

One of the few prominent Virginians to oppose interposition from the beginning was David Mays, the architect of the Gray plan. In late November, Kilpatrick met with Mays to convince the lawyer of interposition's legitimacy and had hoped the January referendum would spontaneously create momentum for the adoption of an interposition bill. Kilpatrick's editorials already had won over many members of the Gray Commission, but Mays objected to the illegality of a position that declared *Brown* null and void. He also resented the mounting pressure that Byrd applied to Gray commissioners to forget about their recommendations. As Mays watched the Byrd machine barrel toward the precipice of an interposition resolution and away from his proposals, he grew furious. "Continuing with a moderate course of action, one pleasing to neither set of extremists," he wrote, "is the only way to cushion the shock of integration and give people time to work out the problem. Looking back upon today, historians will pronounce extreme integration[ists] to be great statesmen and moderate people as pygmies." Ignored by Byrd, Mays could not abort Virginia's stampede toward radicalism.[48]

Most of Virginia's elite raised few questions about the rationality of Kilpatrick's thinking. Any dissent occurred politely and privately to keep the public uninformed and to preserve the semblance of a naturally harmonious aristocracy. To insult an opponent publicly would have been considered bad form in Virginia politics, and civic leaders never turned a disagreement into a public brouhaha. The patrician and secretive Commonwealth Club in downtown Richmond was where the state's privileged class settled contentious issues. Despite the apparent consensus on interposition, some whites did demur. At a symposium held at the club on 16 January 1956, head of the Richmond school board, local lawyer, and future U.S. Supreme Court justice Lewis F. Powell Jr. debated Kilpatrick about the validity of interposition. Powell thought interposition would injure the state by scaring away businesses and reviving an idea rendered moot by the Civil War. He argued that interposition respected neither the Court, the Constitution, nor the public school system. Kilpatrick lost the contest when Powell exposed the shoddy legal ground that supported interposition. The next day, Kilpatrick told an associate, "Good God, did I get chewed up last night!"[49]

Unswayed, Kilpatrick continued to write an interposition resolution that called the *Brown* ruling null and void, which he had worked on since late December. He intended to give Virginia and each southern state the power to act as its own supreme court without deference to the federal government. Within days of his debate with Powell, however, the "null and void" language of Kilpatrick's original interposition resolution disappeared. A new draft, stopping short of proposing nullification but promising opposition, met with more approval from Virginia's upper crust and would soon appear before the General Assembly.[50]

Kilpatrick prodded Virginia's legislature to create an interposition resolution to protest the Supreme Court's desegregation order. On 10 January, he reminded the General Assembly of its duty to obey the "unmistakable voice" of the people and interpose the state's power. A 23 January *News Leader* editorial titled "Time to Fight It Out" accused the Virginia solons contemplating giving in to the more moderate Gray plan of cowardice. He harangued them, "[Q]uerulous little voices piping on Richmond's Capital Hill . . . [c]omplaining that, oh, the Supreme Court's decision in the school cases was dead wrong, but what would Chief Justice Warren say about 'interposition' must recognize that *the hour has come to stand up and be counted. . . . God, give us men*! We resist now, or we resist never. We surrender to the court effective control over our reserved powers, or we make a fight to preserve these powers. We lie down, piteous and pusillanimous, or we make a stand." Few legislators ran afoul of Kilpatrick, but one of his longtime adversaries, Republican delegate Robert Whitehead, during the floor debate on interposition in the House, depicted Kilpatrick's plan as a nightmare scenario: "[T]he editor had a vision and dreamed a great dream. He saw the New Jerusalem—a land of 48 sovereign states, each separate and independent, composing what therefore had been called the United States of America, and operating under a league or confederation like the one of old on the Balkan peninsula; and each judged for itself what was the law of the land; and he was pleased with the disorder of things, and solemnly resolved to call it home." Whitehead's comments notwithstanding, with Kilpatrick and Byrd virtually unchallenged and bent on interposition, the rest of the Byrd organization and much of the white South lined up behind them.[51]

After steering Virginia toward total resistance by stalling the Gray plan, Byrd and Kilpatrick contacted other powerful leaders and tried to formulate a pansouthern position. On 24 January, politicians from across the South traveled to Richmond and agreed to pass interposition resolutions, but the nature of such declarations varied from state to state. A monolithic reaction never materialized across the states. The Virginians decided against pushing further than a bill that condemned the Court's ruling. Georgia governor

Marvin Griffin announced his state's willingness to nullify *Brown* and close their schools. Governor George Bell Timmerman of South Carolina pledged a firm protest but not nullification. Governor Luther Hodges of North Carolina, on the other hand, made no commitments to interposition. J. P. Coleman, Mississippi's governor, also guaranteed nothing from his state and said he would not subscribe to nullification because it did not solve the problem of desegregation. Nullification implied force and would be "treason and we wouldn't win anyway," he dissented. Ultimately, the gathering, except North Carolina, expressed outrage at the Court, protested the *Brown* decision, and asserted that the Fourteenth Amendment never applied to school desegregation.[52]

Not all the southern states needed Virginia's provocation to "interpose" their authority. Alabama had passed an interposition resolution before the Virginians approved their special assembly. On 1 February 1956, Virginia's General Assembly followed Alabama and also enacted a resolution that vowed to resist *Brown*. Kilpatrick wrote the resolution after consulting with attorneys, who recommended he use "legally, honorably, and constitutionally" to describe how Virginia would oppose *Brown*. The resolution committed Virginia to enacting "all appropriate measures, legally and constitutionally available to us, to resist this illegal encroachment upon our sovereign powers and to urge upon our sister states . . . their prompt and deliberate efforts to check this and further encroachment by the Supreme Court . . . upon the reserve powers of the states." Virginia claimed the right to decide where sovereignty ultimately resided. More states followed suit.[53]

Throughout 1956 and 1957, interposition had an immediate impact on the South's response to *Brown* and the civil rights movement. In the aftermath of Virginia's and Alabama's resolutions, Georgia, Louisiana, Mississippi, and South Carolina passed interposition resolutions. Alabama, Georgia, Mississippi, and Florida even declared *Brown* null and void, and the Mississippi legislature forbade public employees from complying with desegregation orders. U.S. representative John Bell Williams of Mississippi summarized the Magnolia State's position: "If the states are to preserve their sovereignties, if they are to preserve the Constitution, they must interpose and declare the Black Monday decisions [the *Brown* rulings] to be illegal and invalid and of no force and effect." By mid-1957, eight states enacted interposition measures, and North Carolina and Tennessee passed resolutions that ridiculed the Court order to desegregate.[54]

Across the region, the interposition resolutions carried much of the same protest theme and borrowed from the wording of the Virginia draft, which paraphrased from Madison's Virginia Resolution of 1798. The documents reminded citizens that the states were sovereign entities, that the Tenth Amendment guaranteed the states' control of schools, and that the Fourteenth Amendment never prevented states from segregating public facilities. The states also maintained the right to interpose their authority between the local community and the federal government and deemed the *Brown* decision an unconstitutional amendment. Most of the resolutions followed Virginia's recommendation to call state constitutional conventions to ratify or reject *Brown*, "to settle the issue of contested power here asserted," and to clarify states' rights.[55]

After the initiation of the legislative resolutions, an entire movement, known as "massive resistance," arose to identify and police opponents of segregation and unify the white South. In late February 1956, Harry Byrd Sr. told reporters, "If we can organize the Southern states for massive resistance to this order [*Brown*] I think that in time the rest of the country will realize integration is not going to be accepted in the South. In interposition, the South has a perfectly legal means of appeal from the Supreme Court order." During the next year, southern states cracked down on internal dissent and among them created 106 anti-integration laws. The legislation often gave private school teachers publicly financed benefits, allowed public schools to lease property to private, all-white academies, and banned NAACP members from government employment and organizing. While restricting internal opposition, southern congressmen wrote the March 1956 "Southern Manifesto" to deprecate the Court's reckless subversion of the constitutional order and to force southern politicians to demonstrate their loyalty to segregation by approving the statement.[56]

Virginia lawmakers decided to enforce their interposition resolution with new statutes designed to prevent the implementation of the *Brown* ruling. In August and September 1956, the General Assembly met and passed thirteen anti-integration bills. Twelve of the laws ratified parts of the original Gray plan and permitted the future use of tuition grants. The most controversial bill allowed the state to seize control of any local school district ordered to desegregate and the governor to close its schools. The state government would also interpose its sovereignty against the federal courts. Private lawsuits, additionally, must be directed at the state itself, and the state declined the ability to be sued as stipulated under the Eleventh Amendment. Any school system that desegregated without a court mandate would face a cutoff of state funds as well. William Tuck's indelicate nature produced a curt assessment about the state's power to resist court orders to desegregate: "Goddammit, the only thing to do is tell the courts that there will be no integration."[57]

None of these vibrations surprised Kilpatrick. Enjoying his role, he remarked, "There is a feeling that knits together the Georgian, the Virginian, the Carolinian, the Louisianan. All of us stand figuratively on the ramparts together, facing a common foe; and for the first time in years, we enjoy that wonderful camaraderie of brothers in arms." Kilpatrick more than reviled the Court's decision. He hoped his editorials would mobilize white southerners to stand fast against desegregation. Support for massive resistance, however, was conditional for large numbers of whites, even among Kilpatrick's colleagues.[58]

Despite the editor's best efforts to present a united segregationist front, critics of interposition emerged from inside the southern press. From the outset, Virginius Dabney, across the hall from Kilpatrick, found defiance of the Court onerous. As a person with deep ties to the state, Dabney feared any actions that might embarrass Virginia. At first, he accepted interposition but with the understanding that it would not replace the Gray plan. When Kilpatrick won the ear of Byrd and the newspapers' bureaucracy, Dabney knew that he faced a choice between remaining loyal to the Bryans and maintaining his professional independence. Rather than agree to interposition and massive resistance, he almost resigned. In true Virginia fashion, however, he kept his displeasure private and allowed the *Times-Dispatch* editorial pages to promote interposition through his conservative associate editor, K. V. Hoffman. Throughout the massive resistance period, the twin newspapers endorsed interposition and states' rights. Dabney stayed out of the matter and took no official position lest he divide Virginia further.[59]

Other southern newsmen and politicians publicly condemned interposition. Alabama's populist governor Jim Folsom called interposition "just a bunch of hogwash" and compared it to "a hound dog baying at the moon." Lenoir Chambers, moderate editor of Norfolk's *Virginian-Pilot*, bucked the Byrd machine and derided Kilpatrick's legal ideas as a "fantasy." Editors in Charlottesville, Roanoke, and Lynchburg either joined in Chambers's denouncement or criticized the dismissal of the Gray Commission's solution. Raleigh's Jonathan Daniels and Louisville's Mark Ethridge maligned interposition. Home on vacation from the University of Texas, Willie Morris, the young editor of the *Daily Texan*, first heard of Kilpatrick and interposition at his Mississippi town's initial Citizens' Council meeting. Interposition "sounded, to the bearer of adolescent loins, obliquely sexual," Morris recalled. Despite such reservations and outbursts, most southern editors and politicians supported Kilpatrick, especially in the Deep South. In the Upper South, only Virginia stayed committed to interposition, and the *News Leader* remained a formidable influence and daily reading for Virginia's state officials and legislators. Kilpatrick's success in Virginia expanded his goals for interposition.[60]

Courting the Conservatives

Winning regional support for interposition formed the initial step in Kilpatrick's plan to stop *Brown*. After most southern states passed interposition resolutions and corralled internal dissent, Kilpatrick pursued a complementary campaign to attract nonsoutherners and conservatives nationwide. By late 1956 and early 1957, he turned his attention north. Using interposition to rise above the issue of race could create a national retinue. "Virginia, by the adoption of [interposition]," Kilpatrick speculated in one editorial, "might succeed in elevating this controversy from the regional field of segregation to the transcendent, national field of State sovereignty. There is a tactical advantage in higher ground, and we would do well to seek it." He wrote a supporter in March 1957, "I don't think it is a 'wild idea' at all that we should stimulate pressure by the voters in such areas as New York, Chicago, and Detroit, in behalf of the southern position. Indeed, it seems to me the only sane political approach to the problem." He continued, "The most important task before the South right now . . . is to foster this very sort of opposition among conservative groups in the North, middle West, and far West. To the extent that they can be aligned with the Southern cause, we will begin making headway."[61]

Kilpatrick's optimism led to his first serious effort to convince America's conservatives of the rightness of the southern way of life. To achieve such a goal, he reiterated using states' rights as a defense of limited government to remove the miasma of race from the South's position, which might repulse some nonsoutherners. In general terms, Kilpatrick banked the success of his arguments on the distaste that conservatives shared for the far-reaching powers of the federal government. "What the whole States' rights movement needs most of all is the support of the people . . . who have no emotional feeling one way or the other on the segregation issue," he explained to one correspondent, "but are capable of looking beyond that to the broader and more important questions of State and Federal relationships." He assured another ally, "I am persuaded that if we can only hold out long enough here in the South, until the Supreme Court trods as heavily upon the rights and privileges of some other major section of the country, we may be able to come out of this yet." His tactic required patience, and it lacked a massive following until the courts made more liberal rulings in the 1960s and proposed school busing programs in the 1970s. Kilpatrick decided, for now, that only a book-length study could clarify his ideas for people unfamiliar with the states' rights philosophy.[62]

Over a period of several months in 1956 and 1957, Kilpatrick researched during spare time to formalize his interposition argument and attract a wider reading public. "We have needed, all along, some publication that would put forward our point of view," he told a fellow conservative journalist, "and one of the things that has hurt us most has been our inability to put in the hands of Northern supporters some tangible, concrete material which they could use in spreading the gospel up there." Kilpatrick worked feverishly to prepare a book before the opening of state legislatures in 1957 in the hope that congressmen would draw on his work to draft new laws to protect states' rights. The book appealed to a nonsouthern audience by raising awareness about the federal government's long train of abuses against the states and was also a genuine manifestation of his ideas. For years, he regarded it as the finest account of his beliefs.[63]

Kilpatrick settled on a title, *The Sovereign States*, and it became his tribute to the proper relationship between the states and the federal government. Divided into four sections, the manuscript discussed the motley usages of interposition in America, covered the history of the federal government's erosion of states' rights, and attacked judicial activism and state centralization. In his introduction, Kilpatrick notified readers that "the political heirs of Alexander Hamilton and John Marshall will not care much for [this book]." He rehearsed Madison's and Jefferson's Virginia and Kentucky Resolves and Calhoun's nullification campaign. Kilpatrick also documented instances throughout the nineteenth century in which nonsoutherners invoked states' rights, like at the Hartford Convention, and then called attention to the corruption of individual states' powers under the New Deal and twentieth-century liberalism that culminated in *Brown*. The fourth part of *The Sovereign States* focused on the *Brown* decision and the Court's reliance on flawed psychological studies and misguided legal thought.[64]

In 1957, the most respected conservative publisher in America, Henry Regnery, released *The Sovereign States*. Since 1948, the Regnery house operated in Chicago as one of the nation's few conservative publishing companies and reached out to traditionalists and conservatives in the heartland of America. His press produced some of the best books of the conservative intellectual movement, including William F. Buckley's *God and Man at Yale* (1951) and Russell Kirk's *The Conservative Mind* (1953). Regnery learned about Kilpatrick after reading a 1955 article he wrote against desegregation for the scrappy Washington, D.C.–based conservative newsletter *Human Events*. The most striking feature of Kilpatrick's arguments lay in his ability to present the South's position without delving much into the supposed racial inferiority of Negroes. The Chicago publisher wrote the young man from Richmond and encouraged him to turn his ideas on federalism into a book. Between Regnery's support and the enthusiasm generated among southern segregationists, Kilpatrick decided to finish his manuscript on interposition.[65]

When Regnery received Kilpatrick's chapters in mid-1956, he saw it as a great opportunity to promote states' rights. "I was so convinced by the lucidity and persuasiveness of your argument that I fully expected to see the 14th Amendment repealed momentarily and the Doctrine of Interposition recognized by the Supreme Court," he told Kilpatrick. He believed Kilpatrick's thesis addressed the essence of postwar American conservatism—the defense of local communities against big government. Regnery promoted *The Sovereign States* as the southern version of conservatism's respect for traditional institutions and values and its rejection of outside forces that threatened them.[66]

Protecting southern values and traditions served one purpose of *The Sovereign States*, but it also became the book's drawback. Although the published version of *The Sovereign States* came closer to diminishing race as a factor in the school controversy than the original draft, it made the kind of racial arguments that hampered the South's case with the rest of the country. Initially, Kilpatrick intended to present a case for the South in the last section of *The Sovereign States*. He portrayed southerners as a people with sophisticated constitutional ideas, but he also devoted seventeen pages to the deficiencies of Negroes as a race. In the final adaptation, only two pages mentioned the inferiority of African Americans. One of Regnery's editors, Charles Lee, convinced Kilpatrick to reduce statistics on blacks' illegitimate births, illiteracy, and venereal diseases. The original manuscript contained a chapter called "On the Merits" that introduced a number of sociological, psychological, and anthropological arguments against blacks as well. Regnery's staff seemed more racially sensitive than Kilpatrick, and the content on African Americans nearly disappeared from the book.[67]

Toward the end of the published edition, Kilpatrick addressed the subject of race. He described a region torn into two worlds: white and black. The separation resulted from characteristics intrinsic to each race. "The experience of generations has demonstrated that in the South (whatever may be true of the Negro in urban areas of the North and West) the Negro race, as a race, has palpably different social, moral, and behavioral standards from those which obtain among the white race," he scoffed. African Americans corroded civilization through their venereal diseases, marital infidelity, and ignorance, which could hinder white children's educations in mixed schools. In the last chapter of his book, Kilpatrick also tackled the issue of desegregation and insisted that the school integration controversy erupted from centuries of disputes over the authority of state and federal governments. *Brown* reinterpreted the Constitution, misused the Fourteenth Amendment, and violated a sacred trust that permitted states to oversee their educational institutions.[68]

In his quest to protect state sovereignty, Kilpatrick could not resist asserting the inferiority of African Americans. The defect in his argument exposed the weakness of states' rights as a cover for racial prejudice. Throughout its history, states' rights had always been a philosophy invoked for the self-interest of groups, states, or regions. White southerners invoked states' rights to conceal their dependence on slavery before the Civil War. For Kilpatrick, the states' rights argument served as a genteel alternative to expressing gross racial bias. The infusion of race into states' rights, however, dogged the interposition campaign from its beginning. The General Assembly's commissioned study of the history of the interposition resolution based its findings on white supremacy and statistics on black crime and illegitimacy. Kilpatrick tried to prevent his opponents from accusing him of racism by defending segregation through constitutional arguments. Because *The Sovereign States* was his first synthesized attempt to transcend race as an issue of contention, it lacked the refinement that would come in his later work.[69]

In private with fellow travelers, Kilpatrick revealed his true racial views. He mentioned to one confidant that "the Negro race has never been able to build a civilization of its own, and it has debased every society in which its blood has been heavily mixed." Sometimes Kilpatrick dropped his arguments about the corruption of the central government and confessed the real issue behind his states' rights philosophy. He explained to prominent conservative essayist Frank Chodorov, for example, that "Southerners will abandon their cherished schools with the deepest, most poignant regret, and for one reason only: To avoid what they regard as the greater catastrophe of a mixed society and an intimate social mingling with the Negro race." Employing states' rights defended the founders and the Constitution on a meta-legal plane but also supported racial segregation.[70]

In spite of his insistence on a rational approach to *Brown*, Kilpatrick willingly deviated into making disparaging remarks about blacks. A number of factors could have led him to include race-based arguments despite the costs. He may have felt the challenge of the civil rights movement even more keenly than his peers in Richmond, which made him more desperate to resist desegregation at any price. Racial change scared him, and it stalked him from his youth. In his freshman year at Missouri, the NAACP won a court case to integrate the university. Virginians, by contrast, he deplored, "had pondered the matter [of school desegregation] scarcely at all. The earlier admission of a few Negro college students in Missouri, Oklahoma, and Texas was something that had happened to some other fellow in some other place, a long way away." Perhaps the editor also did not understand the harm his racial ideas would have on his constitutional arguments or was blindsided by the negative image the rest of the nation had of the segregationist South. "I simply do not understand the antipathy to the South that seems to be held so widely across the nation as a whole," Kilpatrick wrote a correspondent. "Assuming that every lie about the 'treatment of the Negro' is true, could considerations of race relations alone be responsible?"[71]

Kilpatrick might have depicted Negroes as immoral and ignorant because Thomas Jefferson, his role model for the interposition campaign, made similar comments in his *Notes on the State of Virginia* (1784). Jefferson and Kilpatrick both believed in white supremacy, and the editor probably felt vindicated by the fact that such a venerated founder of America shared his view of blacks. "Comparing [blacks] by their faculties of memory, reason, and imagination," Jefferson wrote, "it appears to me, that in memory they are equal to the whites; in reason much inferior . . . and that in imagination they are dull, tasteless, and anomalous." Many segregationists during the civil rights struggle accepted Jefferson's view of African Americans. Fancying himself Jefferson's heir, Kilpatrick subtitled *The Sovereign States*, *Notes of a Citizen of Virginia* to honor his illustrious predecessor and to claim solidarity with him.[72]

Despite the respectability of Jefferson and Kilpatrick's positions within Virginia, *The Sovereign States* found a less enthusiastic reception outside the South. The *New York Times*, the *Wall Street Journal*, and the *Washington Post* reviewed the book, but *Harper's*, *Atlantic*, *Saturday Review*, *Time*, and the *New York Herald Tribune* all snubbed it. Inside legal circles, Kilpatrick's resurrection of Calhoun, Madison, and Jefferson met with sharp criticism. The *Harvard Law Review* called *The Sovereign States* "ill-intentioned nonsense."[73]

The most severe diatribe came from Walter Murphy, a professor of politics at Princeton. Kilpatrick's fundamental argument posited that the Tenth Amendment provided the foundation for the entire Constitution, and, thus, the states reserved all powers not specifically abridged by the federal government. Murphy accused him of ignoring the amendment's legislative history and the ability of the Federalists, the eighteenth-century proponents of a national constitution, to retain the concept of implied powers in the federal government despite repeated anti-Federalist objections. Kilpatrick also misinterpreted Madison and Jefferson, according to Murphy. Madison abandoned the concept of interposition in the 1830s and defended the power of the Court to arbitrate national disputes, and Jefferson never resisted federal authority when Congress handed him the presidency in the 1800 election. Kilpatrick, additionally, botched Calhoun by ignoring the South Carolinian's long record as a nationalist.[74]

Kilpatrick knew that he omitted the intellectual evolution of the founders and other statesmen but told a fellow southern editor, "I will take the Mr. Madison when he was closest to the Constitution; you can take him as an old man in 1830." More importantly, Kilpatrick failed to acknowledge that by submitting to and depending on the judgment of other states in a nullification or interposition crisis, he sacrificed the sovereignty of his state to the will and cooperation of outsiders. Kilpatrick also argued that the Civil War did not settle the question of state sovereignty because only force of arms allowed the federal government to assert dominion over the states. The southern states' resort to military aggression in 1861 combined with the opposition of the majority of the states to secession cancelled the South's legitimate claims to states' rights, however. If the South won the war, based on Kilpatrick's own reasoning, it would only have proven its superiority on the battlefield, not its right to secede. His historical and legal thinking often seemed to rely more on rhetorical appeal than logical thought.[75]

In James Kilpatrick's mind, because the Court grounded its *Brown* ruling in political motives, southerners could rely on political language to fight it. His view of the law and politics suffered from a serious deficiency as a result and made him sound hypocritical. He interpreted the law as a political tool used by the Supreme Court through *Brown* to correct immorality. States' rights, he hoped, could lift the debate above the passions of the Court and race-baiters. The Constitution and state sovereignty went beyond the politics of the law and, accordingly, should be unadulterated. Kilpatrick's states' rights arguments fell victim to the exact criticisms he espoused because of his attempt to mandate the kind of society he wanted. The Court, similarly, manipulated the law to implement societal changes that it deemed proper. Interposition replicated the same legal realism and the same approach to fixing contemporary society that he accused the Court of dictating. Circumstance and context mattered in both accounts.

Flaws aside, Kilpatrick's book came at a pivotal moment in the history of postwar conservatism. During the mid- to late 1950s, a number of conservatives from across the country began to see that they had new and unforeseen common bonds. In foreign affairs, the threat of Soviet aggression created widespread anti-Communism and united Americans against a common foe. Domestically, conservatives felt besieged by the Supreme Court and increasingly saw states' rights as a legitimate defense against the judiciary's encroachments. Many conservatives condemned the 1955 decision in *Pennsylvania v. Nelson* where the Court affirmed a reversal of a sedition conviction, which they considered a violation of the states' right to prosecute suspected Communists. Businessmen also feared the Warren Court for its pro-labor stance and unwillingness to uphold anti-union right-to-work laws. North and South, conservatives and libertarians understood liberty as the key to maintaining American institutions and defended private property rights, employers, and the states as protections against the central government and its perceived socialist reforms.[76]

Conservative opinions on race relations often reflected Kilpatrick's antipathy for the goals of the civil rights movement. Some traditionalists challenged black activism because it might undermine the natural order. Granting African Americans equality could pave the road toward socialism. Egalitarianism, warned Russell Kirk, bred "mediocrity [that] may trample underfoot every just elevation of mind and character." Others believed Negro advancement would drag down Western civilization. "The Negro had shown that his tendency, when he was released from all constraining forces," argued Richard Weaver, an apologist for southern civilization, "was downward rather than upward." Willmoore Kendall, spokesman for America's heartland, worried about liberal activists and their "egalitarian principle [of] one-man one-equal-vote."[77]

Many conservatives reacted favorably to Kilpatrick's denunciation of civil rights and black life. He felt at home with his conservative brethren, who found unity in their fight for tradition and order. Kilpatrick claimed

David Lawrence, publisher and editor of the *U.S. News & World Report*, which became conservatives' favorite newsweekly in the 1950s, and William F. Buckley Jr., founder of the *National Review*, as two of his most ardent northern supporters. Other conservative heavyweights who welcomed Kilpatrick's arguments included Barry Goldwater, Frank Chodorov, Frank Meyer at the *National Review*, and Felix Morley, a libertarian columnist and founder of *Human Events*. In 1959, Morley used Kilpatrick's research to give intellectual ballast to his book *Freedom and Federalism*. Kilpatrick's book also came on the heels of the creation of the nation's new conservative journals: Kirk's *Modern Age* and Buckley's *National Review*.[78]

The late 1950s proved an exciting time for young conservatives, and no one embodied that Renaissance more than William F. Buckley. Born in 1925 to a Texas oil millionaire, classically educated, and raised in upper-class Sharon, Connecticut, Buckley was a prodigy on the right. His one-man undergraduate rebellion against liberalism at Yale University and his book *God and Man at Yale*, which called on academics to be pious and patriotic, catapulted him into celebrity. His self-confidence, wit, grace, eloquence, and sincere devotion to Catholicism and tradition made him irresistible to many conservatives. Belonging to his inner circle meant being part of a battle against the egalitarianism, humanism, and utopianism of liberal reformism. A self-described revolutionary, Buckley once told interviewer Mike Wallace that he advocated a "counterrevolution [that] would aim at overturning the revised view of society pretty well brought in by FDR." Since late 1955 and the debut of the *National Review*, the articulate Buckley worked tirelessly to unite the diverse camps of American conservatism under one tent and to urge them to join in his embattled political revolution against twentieth-century liberalism. Kilpatrick's bold ideas soon caught his attention.[79]

Buckley probably heard of Kilpatrick before the publication of *The Sovereign States*, but in late 1956 Regnery sent him a copy of the forthcoming book and introduced Kilpatrick as one of the new leaders in southern conservatism and states' rights. The editor's ideas meshed well with the *National Review*'s self-image as the custodian of Western civilization and opponent of state regimentation. In a review of his book for the *National Review*, libertarian Frank Meyer approved of Kilpatrick's "simple, rational, and moral truth that the Constitution is a compact between the states." Obviously, not all conservatives or *National Review* contributors advocated denying blacks their civil rights, but the journal routinely backed Kilpatrick's views on the subject.[80]

In March 1956, the *National Review* denounced the first *Brown* decision on constitutional, not racial, grounds as "an act of judicial usurpation" that was "shoddy and illegal in analysis, and invalid as sociology." The magazine's line on race relations, at least in the mid- to late fifties, called for the protection of traditional values against an unpredictable and increasingly impatient black population. In August 1957, Buckley made the *National Review*'s position on the civil rights movement clear with an editorial titled "Why the South Must Prevail" that discounted African Americans as full members of society. He questioned Negroes' contributions to Western culture and democracy and claimed that because southern whites offered the superior civilization they could impose their cultural mores and political system of exclusion on blacks. The South seemed like a racial utopia, a haven of order, and a reliable bastion of tradition. Posing a rhetorical question to readers about whether southerners had legitimate grounds to discriminate against blacks, Buckley answered, "Yes—the White community is so entitled because, for the time being, it is the advanced race." Beneath Buckley's approval of white resistance to civil rights lay his concern that race might undermine the movement he wanted to build. The magazine regarded race as potentially divisive in that unified front and considered the white South an ally in the fight against the growth of the post–New Deal superstate. In 1958, *National Review* columnist Anthony Harrigan applauded the South's "essential conservatism" for acting as a "built-in power brake" against reform and change. Instead of providing an alternative path for African Americans to pursue civil rights, Buckley's magazine became a rallying point for opponents of equality.[81]

Eager to embrace and unite conservatives from around the country, Buckley sought bright young minds in the South, and the *National Review* tapped Kilpatrick, a man only five years older than Buckley, as a rising star in the conservative movement. They soon anointed him as the journal's authority on the civil rights movement and the Constitution. In his articles for the journal, Kilpatrick commented on southern affairs and made states' rights philosophy and segregation palatable to conservative intellectuals. Because of him, "states' rights" and strict "constitutionalism" became common vernacular in conservative discussions about desegregation. The staff at the *National Review* loved Kilpatrick's new book and interposition campaign and asked the *News Leader* editor to contribute regularly to the magazine. The positive reception at the *National Review* elevated Kilpatrick's standing on the right, and by 1958, he helped formulate policies for conservatives to win national elections. His ties to segregationist groups also provided Buckley with an outlet to sell his magazine in the South. In 1958, Buckley contacted Mississippian William J. Simmons, the courtly head of the Citizens' Council in Jackson and acquaintance of Kilpatrick, to secure its mailing list of 65,000 members. Buckley assured Simmons, "Our position on states' rights is the same as your own."[82]

As important as Buckley's patronage of Kilpatrick was the support of David Lawrence, a distinguished conservative columnist and media mandarin. Lawrence began *U.S. News & World Report* in 1948 to criticize the changes in national government initiated by the New Deal and to oppose the spread of liberalism, which he saw as the forerunner of socialism. On racial issues, Lawrence emerged as an opponent of the civil rights movement. Many of his editorials supported states' rights, and he even advocated a court of chief justices chosen by the states that could override the U.S. Supreme Court. In his nationally syndicated column, he often questioned the wisdom of the *Brown* ruling and interracial education. Lawrence wanted slow advancement for blacks, depicted African Americans' demonstrations as violent mobs, and urged Negroes to earn equality through responsible action only. Beginning in 1956, Kilpatrick wrote several articles for Lawrence that reflected the publisher's views and abstained from racial bigotry.[83]

Thanks to Lawrence and Buckley, the interposition campaign, and *The Sovereign States*, Kilpatrick garnered attention from various other conservatives and reactionaries. Some sought him out for comments on the white South's position on race relations and others expressed respect for his ideas. His essays showed up in *Human Events*, Frank Hanighen's periodical with 50,000 subscribers, where his writings on desegregated education and limited government complemented the magazine's stances. His push for interposition also fit perfectly with the message of the *Citizen*, Bill Simmons's journal, because Simmons and Kilpatrick both promised to halt government regulations, race mixing, and social equality by returning control over communities to the people of the southern states. The interposition campaign gave resistance against federal interference sustenance at the local level and "our people . . . a sense of their own power," one *Citizen* writer declared. Richard Weaver, University of Chicago English professor and defender of traditionalist conservatism, loved *The Sovereign States* but complained that Kilpatrick appeared too modest in praising the South. Donald Davidson, the Nashville Agrarian at Vanderbilt, questioned the logic of *Brown* and cited Kilpatrick's work as evidence of "what has happened to the bench and bar in what is supposed to be the United States, plural." Clarence

("Dean") Manion, conservative host of the popular weekly radio show *For America* and a John Birch Society national council member, called Kilpatrick's interposition drive a "courageous stand" and "thrilling" and wanted states' rights to thwart all kinds of advances by the central government. Asking his listeners to consider the legitimacy of Kilpatrick's ideas, he proclaimed interposition "the current answer" to the "federal invasion of the long standing constitutional prerogative" of the states. *The Sovereign States* even received mention on the floor of the U.S. Senate when South Carolina's Strom Thurmond read Kilpatrick's book aloud as part of his filibuster of the 1957 Civil Rights Act. In two years, the young editor rose from a provincial newsman to a national standard-bearer for states' rights.[84]

Although many conservatives supported interposition, its unconstitutionality diminished its ultimate viability. Despite his best efforts, Kilpatrick failed to convince opponents that the school controversy should be addressed on an exclusively constitutional basis. They not only challenged the doctrine's legality but insisted that the desegregation issue remained bound to race. Interposition never completely transcended either problem.

The limitations of his quixotic arguments aside, Kilpatrick's work on interposition had a significant impact on the postwar South. He rallied segments of the white South to fight the federal government more immediately than John C. Calhoun, who only managed to lure South Carolina into the nullification crisis. Civil rights advocates understood that without the influence of writers like Kilpatrick, white southerners would have been less likely to refuse *Brown*. Roy Wilkins, head of the NAACP, believed that "groups of so-called respectable people" animated ordinary southerners. In 1993, reflecting on white resistance to the *Brown* decision, Thurgood Marshall, lead attorney of the NAACP's legal defense team, attested to the damage Kilpatrick inflicted: "[W]e put some trust in the decency of man. . . . I'm afraid we assumed that after a short period of time of one to five years the states would give in. We did not, however, give enough credence to the two Richmond newspapers, the *Richmond Times-Dispatch* and the other one [the *News Leader*] . . . who were determined that they would build up the type of opposition that would prevent the states from voluntarily going along." Martin Luther King Jr. also decried the malicious effects of interposition. In 1963, he dreamed that the governors of the South, "lips dripping with the words of interposition and nullification," would one day see blacks as their brothers and sisters.[85]

In the aftermath of the *Brown* decisions, many white southerners' determination to defy the Court rather than acquiesce inspired and encouraged bold, often reckless, insolence among some southern leaders and undergirded and prolonged massive resistance. Compliments of James Kilpatrick, the segregationist South used states' rights arguments steeped in the region's history of defiance to the federal government, linked to the founders' beliefs, and nearly free from all references to race. Although the doctrine of interposition failed to redraw the boundaries between federal and state sovereignty, it created the language of massive resistance and offered southerners a conceptual shield to conceal their racist views. It also removed the South's segregationist politicians from ties to actions by the Ku Klux Klan and other violent white supremacist groups and instead called on southern leaders to seek a sophisticated solution to *Brown*. Not all situations concluded peacefully.[86]

Some scholars have suggested that Kilpatrick's ideas inspired the Little Rock school crisis of 1957. James Johnson, an energetic Arkansas lawyer, tried to transform the state's Democratic Party into an interpositionist party after reading Kilpatrick's editorials. Johnson campaigned to the right of Orval Faubus in the 1956 gubernatorial race and forced him to endorse interposition to win. After losing, Johnson advised Faubus to resist the federal court order to integrate Little Rock's Central High School. When Faubus invoked the doctrine of interposition as the justification for sending state troops to block the school's integration, William J. Smith, his personal attorney, had been reading Kilpatrick's book and may have encouraged the governor's actions.[87]

The rhetoric that led to massive resistance and school closures also made alternative proposals look modest. In the late fifties and sixties, many southerners turned to token integration as an acceptable substitute for school segregation. Tokenism translated to little to no desegregation, which fit with white southerners' expectations. By fall 1960, less than two-tenths of one percent of all black students in public schools in the former Confederate states enrolled in integrated schools. Many of the South's schools remained segregated until the 1970s. Token integration provided white southerners with the kind of resistance that made violence unnecessary to prevent change.[88]

In the long term, interposition could not keep public schools segregated. From 1959 to the early 1970s, efforts to hide segregation behind constitutional arguments fizzled as the federal courts desegregated Jim Crow schools. In Kilpatrick's hands, however, interposition attempted more than the preservation of racially segregated education. Kilpatrick used a states' rights philosophy to bolster the South's confidence and tapped into a defense of local communities that resonated with southern and nonsouthern conservatives alike. As a first try at elevating the level of public debate beyond race and drawing external support, interposition proved to be flexible and attractive. It also introduced Kilpatrick to the inner web of the postwar conservative intellectual movement, and he demonstrated the South's relevance. Southerners had retaliated against the forces of liberalism with any resources, short of military action, that they could muster.

In future clashes, Kilpatrick would alter his arguments to remove stark racial prejudice from his public campaigns against civil rights. As black activism picked up, he contended that the civil rights issue was not primarily a matter of justice or institutional racism. The more important concerns, he insisted, were individual rights, social disorder, the power of the federal government, and liberalism's destructive effect on the Constitution. As the courts handed segregationists defeats, he reexamined old ways in light of new realities and imagined opportunities. Interposition opened the salvo in the war against desegregation. In the violent and turbulent squall that the South was caught in, Kilpatrick intensified the discontent.

THREE

If at First You Don't Secede

In the summer and fall of 1957, James J. Kilpatrick's work at the *Richmond News Leader* consumed at least fourteen hours of each day, and the preservation of segregation dominated much of his thought. The man most responsible for making interposition a reality and stirring portions of the white South to protest the Supreme Court's *Brown* decision was once again under duress. Massive resistance in Virginia showed signs of crumbling when federal courts began to hear cases about the desegregation of public schools in Norfolk, Charlottesville, and the suburbs of Washington, D.C. Kilpatrick wrote to his friend William J. Simmons, "Things are moving toward a showdown here in Virginia, and between us girls, I am rather gloomy about what is likely to happen." Virginia's options looked bleak, but outright defiance could work still, and the editor remained optimistic. "If the will of the people were stronger everybody would simply say 'no' and wait for the marshals to show up with writs of contempt. We have our backs to the wall in this fight now, but maybe that's not so bad a place to fight from. At least, they can't goose us from the rear," he joked.[1]

One week after writing Simmons, Kilpatrick's humor turned into anguish. Charlotte, Greensboro, and Winston-Salem, North Carolina, desegregated their schools. Virginia now had fewer allies in the South. He commented to Simmons, "That means that eight States no longer are standing firm. We are only seven now, and I doubt that Florida will hold out much longer. With North Carolina cracked, the pressure will turn harder than ever on Virginia, and unhappily, I doubt that our people have guts enough to stand up against it." By August, the situation soured. The first civil rights bill approved by Congress since 1875 set up a Commission on Civil Rights to document interference with the right to vote and a Civil Rights Division within the Justice Department to prosecute offenders. Describing his mental exhaustion from defending segregation and unhappiness about the new law, Kilpatrick told his acquaintance Don Shoemaker, editor of the *Southern School News*,

As one old friend to another, I confess I am so sick of the whole business of school segregation I try most of the time not to read about it, think about it or even to write about it. Most of the Southside Virginia counties, I expect, will abandon their school systems before they will integrate. Over the rest of the State, the people probably will accept mongrelization, a little at first, then a lot. I expect the word offends you. It used to offend me. The longer we fight, though, the more intransigent each side becomes, and the more bitter becomes the emotional involvement. I'll never yield. I have no idea that the Afro-American will either. Where does that leave us?[2]

The Second Lost Cause

As James Kilpatrick groped for answers, trouble loomed for the future of segregation. Other southern states also felt the pressure of the federal courts. In the fall of 1957, the Supreme Court ordered Arkansas governor Orval Faubus to admit black students to Little Rock's Central High School. When Faubus refused, President Eisenhower authorized the use of federal troops to guarantee African American enrollment. Until that point, few white southerners thought the national government would force desegregation. A year earlier, Kilpatrick assured a supporter, "All we have to do is to say, we will have public schools, and we will not integrate, and stick by it. In a show down, I do not believe the Federal government would attempt to use force or troops against us." After Little Rock, however, interposition seemed increasingly like a doomed cause. For the *News Leader* staff, the desegregation of the city's schools was utter shuck. One reporter wept when he heard the news. A despondent Kilpatrick regretted, "It looks mostly as if Reconstruction days are here again."[3]

Negative press coverage of white intransigence further frustrated southern segregationists. At Little Rock, the entire nation witnessed the brutality of southern bigotry when television networks broadcast images of students maligned and journalists assaulted by white mobs. After Eisenhower rushed the 101st Airborne to Little Rock, the three television networks interrupted daytime programming to report the developments. In Richmond, Kilpatrick watched the crisis with a sense of revulsion and feared its impact. "All day long, these brighteyed commentators came on the screen, to assert in the most unequivocal tones that Governor Faubus had 'defied' the court, and that his sole intention was to 'block integration.' These things were said not as questions, but as facts. That sort of repeated statement is bound to have an almost hypnotic effect," he lamented. In a letter to Tom Waring, Kilpatrick admitted that the segregationist South had lost an important public relations battle because its inarticulate rationale could not compete with the arguments of civil rights leaders. "All of the Negro sources talk like Oxford dons," he complained, "while all of the white people talk like Southern white people." The Little Rock crisis dealt a fatal blow to interposition and highlighted the South's misconception that it could legally and respectably escape desegregation.[4]

Kilpatrick skewered Eisenhower in editorials and magazine articles. He labeled federal troops the "imperial forces" of tyranny and summoned the other states to stand up for Arkansas. Only together could the states defend themselves from federal power. "The political philosophy urged by the South ought never to be regarded as a regional philosophy only," Kilpatrick testified. "That way lies certain defeat. Old Glory is as much our flag as it is Maine's; the pledge of allegiance to one indivisible Nation is our pledge, as it is Ohio's; the anthem of a great Republic is our anthem, too." In the *National Review*, Kilpatrick blasted Eisenhower and the courts for stealing power from the states to invent new rights for blacks. The federal government had violated the rights of the white community to make laws and protect itself from "tumult and lawlessness." "This is sort of a community right," he went on, "a societal right, one retained not by the individual alone, but 'by the people.'"[5]

With the desegregation of Central High School, Kilpatrick resorted to less polite language. He redbaited and denounced the federal courts as the forerunners of Communism and forced equality. The Supreme Court's "Marxian philosophy," he charged, "embraces a dull and plainless mediocrity, in which the shiftless and incompetent are rewarded, and the industrious and thrifty are penalized." Kilpatrick also recruited sympathizers to link the national government and Eisenhower to socialism. One of the early postwar conservative columnists favored on Kilpatrick's editorial page, Holmes Alexander, pontificated that what Eisenhower accomplished in Little Rock "may not be Communism in name but it is undoubtedly Communism by nature. The thing which the President inadvertently enforced at Little Rock, and to which he is now unhappily tied, is the force for overturning the established ways of the Western World and of American life."[6]

Some white Virginians trusted that the Arkansas crisis would never disturb the commonwealth. To its segregationists, Virginia basked in the defiant glow of smooth opposition to civil rights reform. It claimed few acts of civil disobedience by protesters and little, or at least unreported, violent retribution by whites. The Old Dominion had also avoided any direct clashes with federal authorities, unlike Faubus, and had instead chosen a path of resisting the Supreme Court through legislative channels rather than rejecting federal judicial rulings outright. The lack of civil rights momentum in the state since the interposition crusade convinced many whites that they had invalidated the *Brown* decision and stymied the federal judiciary. The courts had not yet tested the governor's authority to shut schools and deny funds to desegregated school systems. Few Virginians questioned the commonwealth's power to interpose itself between local school districts and the federal government. A post–Little Rock poll showed that two out of three white Virginians would rather eliminate their public schools than integrate them. In his inaugural address, written by Kilpatrick, Governor Lindsay Almond declared that Virginia "must marshal a massive resistance" in similar circumstances.[7]

The informal rules that kept the races separate in Virginia applied not just to schools but to many aspects of life, including religion. Virginia's massive resisters demanded total conformity in their fight against integration and tolerated no dissent from religious authorities, no matter how marginal the threat. Few ecclesiastical voices in Virginia dared to question the massive resisters. In early July 1958, when the Charlottesville office of the Anti-Defamation League (ADL) distributed pro-integration literature at an NAACP workshop, they drew Kilpatrick's ire. Because southerners often conflated Judaism with an outside, alien presence in their mostly evangelical Protestant region, Jews sometimes invited suspicion that added to their vulnerability as a minority group. Kilpatrick's 7 July editorial, titled "Anti-Semitism in the South," was a subtle warning to Jews who interfered in civil rights matters. "By deliberately involving itself in the controversy over school segregation," announced the *News Leader*, "this branch of B'nai B'rith is identifying all Jewry with the advocacy of compulsory integration." What benefit, asked Kilpatrick, could southern Jews find "in a Jewish organization that foments hostility toward Jews?" Although he did not threaten Jews with violence, the editorial hinted at the repercussions for Jewish support for civil rights.[8]

Kilpatrick's remarks circulated widely among Jews. The director of the Atlanta branch of the ADL read a copy of his editorial, as did Jewish officials in Nashville, New York, and Washington, D.C. Responses to the editorial reflected Kilpatrick's power to shape thought within the region and divided southern Jews. The anti-Israel American Council for Judaism, led by Clarence Coleman, hailed the *News Leader*'s stance. Charles Bloch, the Jewish segregationist attorney from Macon, Georgia, and author of *States' Rights: The Law of the Land*, agreed with the editor too. He pushed Kilpatrick to write another editorial that pummeled groups like the American Jewish Committee and the American Jewish Congress. Kilpatrick merely passed Bloch's letter along to Richmond's Jewish leaders.[9]

The controversial editorial spiraled into an embarrassing ordeal. Jews swamped the Virginia ADL with letters demanding that officials desist in supporting desegregation, a cause that distracted the ADL from its larger mission of ending anti-Semitism. Local ADL representatives hastily assembled to discuss their reply to Kilpatrick's editorial and decided to confer with the editor. In a congenial meeting, they assured Kilpatrick that the ADL sought an interfaith dialogue and not integration. The editor considered the matter closed, thanked them for their overture, and handed them segregationist materials that dealt with the race issue. Apologizing for any problems they created, the ADL leaders backed off the subject of desegregation and published a resolution, stating, "[In] accordance with the religious principles of Judaism, the Anti-Defamation League of B'nai B'rith in the Commonwealth of Virginia affirms that its basic philosophies are to combat anti-Semitism and improve interfaith relations." The ADL never again implicated itself in the storm of desegregation. Kilpatrick's rumblings about the ADL quickly yielded to more contentious matters that he could not so easily tamp down.[10]

In fall 1958, soon after the ADL controversy, the federal courts ordered the desegregation of Virginia public schools in Norfolk, Charlottesville, and Warren County. In response, Governor Almond shut down one school in Warren County, two in Charlottesville, and six in Norfolk. Hard-line segregationists celebrated. Parents, however, scrambled to find alternative schools, including private academies for whites. In other cases, their children simply did not attend school. In Virginia's Southside, the Prince Edward County School Board closed its public school system until 1964 and set up a private academy for white students. For the next twenty years, Kilpatrick advocated the creation of private schools to prevent desegregation and used his newspaper to raise funds for the maintenance of Prince Edward Academy. He also contributed personal funds and secured over 10,000 books for the academy's library, named in his honor, including his own first edition copy of Edmund Burke's *Reflections on the Revolution in France*, to make it a model for other private schools. Faced with an uncertain future for their children's education, white Virginians inconsistently resisted desegregation.[11]

Once implemented, the school closures revealed some Virginians' reservations about prolonged defiance. The disposition of many whites changed from rebellion against the federal government into a revolt against state officials. Moderate groups like the Parents' Committee for Emergency Schooling, which wanted immediate education for children displaced by the closings, and the 25,000-member Virginian Committee for Public Schools joined with a few state politicians to demand an end to massive resistance. In October and November 1958, most of Virginia's press also turned against the school shutdown. Former accomplices became bitter opponents of the Byrd oligarchy's policies. The Lynchburg newspapers, Norfolk's *Ledger-Dispatch*, and the *Charlottesville Daily Progress* all renounced their previous support for massive resistance.[12]

Displeasure with the governor also emerged from within the Richmond newspaper offices. Virginius Dabney maintained a vow of silence about the closings, but privately he contemplated the idea of leaving Virginia for a career elsewhere because of his discomfort with massive resistance. Even Kilpatrick's former associate editor, John A. Hamilton, son of the *News Leader*'s managing editor, broke with his idol Kilpatrick. Hamilton, like so many other Virginians, began to realize that their children's future might be jeopardized by the Byrd organization. "Poor kids," he thought to himself. "Suppose they were my kids? Is this something we should be doing?"[13]

Not even the prestigious Forum Club could console massive resisters. At the 15 September meeting of the group, David Mays, a member of the Gray Commission, startled an assemblage of concerned segregationists when he called Virginia's political leaders "bankrupt" and pointed out the endgame of their massive resistance laws. Kilpatrick sat next to Mays with a solemn, blank stare. Mays regretted that Virginians had undertaken such a flawed and fated course. They had dishonored themselves and past generations. "Our grandfathers faced a tougher problem during Reconstruction and with few resources, but they knew how to master it. We of this generation should be ashamed of ourselves," he jotted in his diary. A lot of segregationists grasped for anything noble, durable, or wise about the second Lost Cause.[14]

Desperate to preserve massive resistance, Kilpatrick wanted the state's leaders to take extreme measures, including closing public schools, to prevent the mixing of the races. His desertion of public education diverged from his initial position in the months immediately following the first *Brown* decision. In 1955, he told an assembly, "I cannot imagine the South will be so suicidally foolhardy as to abandon public education, though it may come to this in some areas if the South is pushed suddenly in the wrong way." Throughout the early fall of 1958, Kilpatrick insisted that if the courts desegregated the schools, Governor Lindsay Almond should seek arrest and imprisonment to dramatize the South's situation. The editor advised Almond to follow a Pickett's Charge course of "contemptuous defiance" to create a national incident to display states' rights and to orchestrate a collision between Virginia and federal power. Taking bold action, Harry Byrd comforted Almond, could also elicit more public support because "the people will lionize you." Almond and others in state office had no desire for a salamandrine visage, however. Many segregationists began to accept change and some integration as inevitable.[15]

By mid-November, the architects of massive resistance listened to public demands for uninterrupted education. With the federal courts and civic groups lining up against the school closings, some of the same newspapermen who launched massive resistance seemed earnest in their efforts to repeal portions of it. Even the *Richmond News Leader*'s editor could no longer commit to unyielding opposition. In an 11 November address to Richmond's Rotary Club, Kilpatrick called for a more flexible strategy against *Brown* that could keep the schools open. "I believe that the time has come for new weapons and new tactics," he explained. "I believe that the laws we now have on the books have outlived their usefulness, and I believe that new laws must be devised—speedily devised—if educational opportunities are to be preserved and social calamity is to be avoided." He told the Rotarians, "Wars are not won by such single-minded concentration on a particular pillbox." Virginians should prepare themselves to win a war, not just one battle. Rather than stick to an untenable solution, Kilpatrick advocated tuition grants for private academies and for local school districts to have the authority to shutter schools without state approval. Whites could abandon public education, and blacks would enter "empty and echoing" schoolhouses, he hoped. Kilpatrick also held out for a changed national mood and tried to restore morale. If massive resisters waited long enough, he wrote to Simmons, people outside the South "will gain so terrible an awareness of integration in their own midst that at last they will come to an understanding of the wisdom of the South's position. Virginia stands at some Corregidor, and not at Appomattox. The war has just begun. We can wage this war for years, and we will win it in the end."[16]

Kilpatrick's acceptance of the downfall of the massive resistance laws that he had helped create seemed uncharacteristic. Three years earlier, he sabotaged the Gray plan that called for tuition grants and token integration, but by late 1958, he indicated that he would tolerate them if the courts outlawed massive resistance. He was not so inflexible after all. Unlike other hard-line defenders of Jim Crow, Kilpatrick knew the limits of intransigence and interposition and could change directions to keep resistance strong and versatile. Interposition had succeeded in protesting the Court's tyranny and rousing other states into action. Kilpatrick remained proud of his interposition editorials and opposition work, but their usefulness was over.[17]

Just before announcing a less adamantine posture on resistance, Kilpatrick, Virginius Dabney, and Tennant Bryan visited Senator Harry Byrd outside Winchester to warn him about their mutiny. Friction between the newspapermen and Byrd signaled a rift in the segregationist ranks. Byrd could not accept their acquiescence. When informed of their new position, he revealed his misplaced expectations: "Virginia is the keystone to this whole fight and as long as we hold out, we can win." Undeterred, Kilpatrick, Bryan, and Dabney had sense enough to see through the political bombast, which had proven inconsequential in practice. They understood that the violation of court orders could not work indefinitely and that alternate ideas must guide their fight. Byrd, Kilpatrick believed, never knew when to quit. For all his political genius, he remained wedded to the Lost Cause and incapable of dealing realistically with the civil rights movement. The senator found it difficult to adapt to situations beyond his control and could be impatient with delicate issues. "Such reflections were alien to his nature," Kilpatrick later commented. Byrd's devotion to outright defiance of the Court surpassed the zeal of most of his stalwarts. Many Virginians began to accept the possibility of token integration, no matter its consequences. Kilpatrick also considered a small measure of desegregation and soon wrote Bill Simmons, "I think there are greater evils for the South than the admission of one Negro pupil to one white school. Mind you, I would forestall such admission as long as I could, by every device of litigation and legislation that the minds of ingenious men could conceive."[18]

Making unprecedented transitions signaled a recent trend for Kilpatrick, although change rarely moved him in progressive directions. As the fifties drew to a close, he began reassessing various facets of his public and personal life. He even reconfigured his church habits to avoid the possibility of desegregation. When Kilpatrick proposed to his Roman Catholic wife in

1942, receiving the sacrament of marriage in her church required that he become a Catholic. Over a decade later, however, racial issues challenged the conviction of his conversion. On 7 May 1954, ten days before the *Brown* decision, the Richmond Diocese of the Catholic Church announced plans to integrate its parochial schools. The pastor of St. Paul's Cathedral in Richmond, Father Thomas E. O'Connell, who instructed Kilpatrick in the Catholic faith, led the desegregation effort within the diocese.[19]

Kilpatrick's intolerance of African Americans' civil rights trumped the Mother Church's promotion of universal brotherhood and equality before a loving God. He withdrew quietly from Catholicism, and, in February 1959, during the same winter that he shifted positions on massive resistance, he, his wife, and their oldest son converted to Episcopalianism. Attending a small Episcopal church outside Richmond kept the Kilpatricks just inside the walls of Christianity. Kilpatrick insisted that his move to Protestantism stemmed from his irreconcilable theological problems with the Catholic Church concerning transubstantiation, but unspoken motives no doubt influenced his decision. Kilpatrick's longtime agnosticism, additionally, probably never allowed him to internalize Catholicism and freed him to switch churches without a crisis of conscience. He certainly lacked a convert's enthusiasm. "I attach a good deal less to the outward manifestations of religion," he mentioned to publisher Eugene Pulliam. Rumors swirled about Kilpatrick's schism. Catholics and other white Richmonders whispered that he had left because of dissatisfaction with the church's new racial policies. He preserved segregation in his own life while popular support for massive resistance floundered. The desegregation controversy shaped segregationists' private lives as profoundly as it did their public ones.[20]

At nearly the same time, in December 1958, Virginia's business and professional community announced their opposition to massive resistance. The economic development of the state obsessed businessmen, and they never endorsed interposition wholeheartedly. They thought mostly in terms of political economy, not in the framework of a racial caste system, as did diehard segregationists, and they wanted Virginia engaged in a national marketplace. Keeping schools open, even desegregated, and staffed with good teachers could draw a skilled labor force into Virginia and stimulate business growth. The Virginia Industrialization Group, comprised of nearly 100 of the commonwealth's leaders in business and the law, expressed concern with massive resistance and organized informal

meetings throughout the fall of 1958. On 19 December, at a private dinner in Richmond, the group met with Lindsay Almond and his lieutenants to discuss an end to Virginia's school closings. The governor said he
could not act until the federal court made its decision in January. The
business community, however, kept their displeasure with Almond and
the resisters to themselves to spare him ridicule and embarrassment during a crisis.[21]

Almond delivered more fiery speeches about limitless defiance to the
courts, but he conceded defeat early in the new year. On January 19, the
Virginia Supreme Court of Appeals and a three-judge federal district court
in Norfolk invalidated the school closures and ordered funding to resume
in separate cases. Kilpatrick attempted to assuage the anguish of his fellow
segregationists, noting, "Virginia's 'massive resistance' statutes have been
wiped out as if someone had taken a wet sponge to a blackboard. The slate is
clean now, and for our own part we have no particular regrets." The *Times-
Dispatch* dutifully mimicked Kilpatrick's opinion and recycled the military
metaphor from his November 1958 Rotary Club speech: "The simple fact,
disagreeable as it may be to the NAACP and its liberal cohorts," it stated,
"is that this tangible abuse of federal power has not lessened Virginia's will
to resist. We have lost the first battle, but the war has just begun." Within
a few months, a new commission headed by and named for Mosby G. Perrow Jr. revived a plan to let local school districts determine the extent of
desegregation and considered laws that would allow parents to redirect
their public school taxes into private academies. The role a hard-line approach to desegregation would play in a post-massive resistance Virginia
seemed uncertain.[22]

Rather than accept the complete loss of their power, white Virginians
began to search for new strategies to maintain some local control over the
pace of desegregation. The discontinuation of Virginia's massive resistance
laws tested the ingenuity of the state's segregationist leaders to confront
the federal government and provide an opposition platform. Only the segregationists with the fortitude to press ahead and the intelligence to change
tactics could continue the fight against racial reforms. To most southern
anti-integrationists, massive resistance meant one strategy or a single action, like Faubus's disobedience in 1957 or the theatrical stand of Governor
George Wallace in the school door at the University of Alabama in 1963.
Jack Kilpatrick, however, saw the battle against civil rights as a prolonged
war of winning public support for the white South's position, not as one defiant act. After Almond accepted court-ordered desegregation in January

1959, Kilpatrick reminded his *News Leader* audience: "There are more ways of waging a war . . . than by stubborn defense of a single fixed position. The late M. Maginot was a most admirable minister of war, but he failed in 1932 to comprehend the tanks of 1942, and in time his famous line was rendered useless."[23]

Kilpatrick sounded Burkean in his acknowledgment of massive resistance's failure, but how much to give in for segregation to survive at all still troubled him. For years to come, Kilpatrick at times seemed torn between the Burkean politics of realistic readjustment and the revanchist politics of counterrevolution. Segregationists either had to accept some changes in the racial order or cling to their ideological purism. As events tilted against Kilpatrick, the time for a different kind of fight against *Brown* had arrived. A few segregationists chose experimental ways to retaliate. Alternate strategies to interposition that redefined the terms of the white South's struggle against desegregation were already under way.

One such proposal emerged as Virginians discussed a shift from public to private education. Beginning in 1958, fifty-two-year-old Leon Sebring Dure Jr., the retired managing editor of the *Times-Dispatch*, had promoted a "freedom of choice" plan in pamphlets and numerous letters to the editor in Virginia newspapers. "Freedom of choice" involved utilizing pupil placement programs and tuition grants for private schools to block desegregation. The appeal of Dure's idea rested on its call to respect the individual's right to associate with whomever he or she wanted without being subject to government mandates or racial arguments. Though sometimes portrayed as a moderate solution in the wake of massive resistance, Dure's motives blossomed out of his desire to preserve segregation. "It was Southern violence" that moved Dure and "so many thousands of other Southerners, into the argument. Some 'way out' for a Southern rage that had brought paratroopers to Little Rock was the only original purpose" of "freedom of choice." Dure offered white Virginians an approach to limit association with blacks without explicitly forbidding or compelling interracial contact.[24]

Many state leaders welcomed Dure's freedom of choice plan. Kilpatrick, reeling from blows to segregation, praised him. "You certainly are on the right track," he wrote. The Perrow Commission worked local options for education and the phrase "freedom of choice" into its recommendations. In 1959, Virginia pushed through laws that gave students the option either to stay in their local public school system, to receive a tuition grant to attend a nonsectarian private school, or to go to a public school outside of their assigned school district. A revised program of resistance to fight federal court rulings also came forth from the Virginia General Assembly and a new public relations arm for segregation.[25]

Try, Try Again

On 7 March 1958, the state legislature authorized the creation of the Virginia Commission on Constitutional Government (CCG or VACCG). State representatives floated the idea for the commission as early as December 1955, in the heat of the interposition debate. They designated the CCG as a task force to work under the direction of the General Assembly and to report on court decisions and federal laws involving desegregation. It could advise the legislature on policy, and other states could replicate its sensibilities and strategies to foster cooperation against the national government. Two years later, in 1957, legislators introduced a bill that would form a new government body to monitor federal abuses of power and serve as a publicity agency to promote federalism and state sovereignty. In January 1958, Governor Almond asked for the creation of a commission to work with other southern states to defend the United States Constitution. By March 1958, the CCG received its title and a mandate "to develop and promulgate information concerning the dual system of government, federal and state, established under the Constitution of the United States and those of the several states." The General Assembly assigned the CCG the task of not only instructing the public about state sovereignty but also of coming up with legislation designed to protect powers reserved to the states.[26]

The CCG required an assertive director who could coordinate with the Byrd organization but withstand pressure from Southsiders and the senator. The commission's chairman, David Mays, provided the necessary management. Born in 1896, he was a natural leader among Virginia's elite and a man connected with the Byrd machine but detached from it because he owed the senator no political patronage. His independence from Harry Byrd gave him a degree of impartiality unknown to many of the state's leaders. He exercised that freedom whenever he disagreed with Byrd's ideas, as during the massive resistance campaign when Mays supported the Gray Commission. Mays, nonetheless, commanded some respect from Byrd, Almond, and Virginians in legal and business circles. As the former head of the Virginia Bar Association and a scholar of the judiciary, Mays was indispensable to obstructionists looking to thwart *Brown* with constitutional arguments rather than racial ones. Other Virginians, including white moderates, admired him as a corporate lawyer, as someone who rejected interposition and overt racism, and as a reputable academic, but a rather aloof personality made him unknown to the general populace. A professional career with a busy schedule of difficult work and studying the history of late-eighteenth-century Americans consumed Mays. He won a Pulitzer Prize in 1953 for his biography of Edmund Pendleton, Virginia's first state supreme court justice and an advocate of judicial restraint. Mays was "the ultimately reliable rock to which one anchored," recalled Kilpatrick. In their years together at the CCG, Kilpatrick and Mays became nearly inseparable but never personally close.[27]

James Kilpatrick's respect for Mays, his control of the *News Leader*, his polished writing skills, his ability to advocate a position, and his impressive political connections led to his appointment as chief of the commission's publications department. In addition to enjoying the practical benefits of working with Kilpatrick, Mays trusted him, and the two men formed a congenial relationship. They soon patched up any past differences over a lunch. To allay Mays's concerns about Kilpatrick's motives, the fiery editor promised him he would not push the school desegregation question, at least until the CCG addressed the constitutional problems arising from the Court's abuse of power. Kilpatrick and Mays also meshed well on a personal level. Both typically liked people like them: intelligent, hardworking, organized, determined, and responsible. Although they had disagreed about interposition, they had also discussed it in civil tones with mutual admiration and maintained a shared revulsion for race mixing. They were natural allies in this war.[28]

Mays's comparatively moderate views on resistance never diminished his devotion to the separation of the races. His belief in the inferiority of African Americans steeled his resolve to win. The Gray Commission's recommendations seemed like a capitulation to the integrationists, but Mays conceived them as a clever form of resistance that moved confrontation to the local level and decentralized the battle over the schools. They would have forced the NAACP to fight school boards county by county rather than all at once at the state level. Mays wanted to "deal with the colored students by attrition": they could be hazed, they could be forced to perform at unfair academic levels, or their parents could be harassed at work for enrolling their children in schools. When massive resistance began to collapse, he told a colleague, "We can lick this integration business . . . by letting in Negroes when we must, chasing them out afterwards by one method or another short of violence, and forcing them to make each incident a separate lawsuit. That will give the NAACP lawyers indigestion, assuming we haven't succeeded in running them out of the courts beforehand."[29]

Interposition prevented the Gray plan from working, but now Mays had a second chance to save segregation. Once massive resistance ran its course, Mays proposed a more disciplined and smarter fight against *Brown* through the CCG. His intellect and political pragmatism allowed him to grasp the complexity and delicacy of the segregationists' situation. Mays, like Kilpatrick, recognized indefensible situations, hated lost causes, and knew the struggle against civil rights hung on more than a single strategy. Mays did not express his opinions on the matter of civil rights with incendiary pronouncements, and he probably had more influence among his colleagues than on segregationist reactionaries.

Initially, the CCG looked incapable of warding off Virginia's radical anti-integrationists. The General Assembly intended to appoint legislators from only the Southside. In the summer of 1958, when asked to run the commission, David Mays was reluctant. He feared that a repeat of the Southsiders' racial arguments and failed policies would limit the CCG's appeal and bring further shame to Virginia. A guarantee from Governor Almond that the commission would be kept out of the school fight and under Mays's direction secured his cooperation. "I feel that we must lift it [the CCG] beyond and above the burning issue of racial matters," Almond calmed Mays.[30]

Convinced of the CCG's rationale and assured of his control, Mays agreed to head the commission. At the helm, he soon referred to it as "my CCG." The state legislature and the governor appointed fourteen individuals to the commission, and the governor served as an ex officio member. Most of them were lawyers, which made researching the history of segregation cases and states' rights easier. The CCG's publications, consequently, read like legal briefs against the federal government. The Virginians' reliance on the law to fight civil rights initiatives would differentiate them from other southern state sovereignty commissions, many of which deployed a more sordid arsenal, such as spying on and punishing activists and preaching racial animus.[31]

The commission essentially forged its ideology from desegregation battles to define and defend local white southern racial values, but Mays and Kilpatrick adopted the language of states' rights and strict constitutionalism to express their beliefs rather than focusing on school integration. Not only could the CCG formulate respectable defenses for state sovereignty based on the ideas of the American states' righters Spencer Roane, Thomas Jefferson, John Randolph, and John Calhoun, but its philosophy could serve as a launch pad for southern conservatism. Reinserting states' rights principles into the country's political vocabulary as a way to rein in the federal government preoccupied the CCG. "Our Commission is not in any sense 'at war' with the Federal government," Mays professed. "The concept of constitutional government we seek to preserve most assuredly demands a strong central government.... Our aim is simply that a balance be restored, and the States be encouraged to insist upon exercising the powers reserved to them." Mays, moreover, intended the VACCG to be a public relations bureau to increase awareness of the South's positions to diminish the region's isolation and summon outside help, which white southerners lacked during the Little Rock fiasco. Kilpatrick followed Mays's guidance.[32]

The *News Leader* editor shared Mays's desire to broaden sympathy for the South with an agenda that did not focus on race. Perhaps the CCG could even send lobbyists to Congress and secure a national hearing. "The commission's job will be to lead this sales program," Kilpatrick told his readers. In 1957, he had advised a fellow segregationist, "We can never win this thing on votes from Southern representatives alone. If we are to win . . . it must be with help from other areas of the country." Although anti-integrationists dominated the CCG, the commission avoided the race issue to recruit non-southern support. "I don't suppose I really ought to worry too much about this business of 'mongrelization,'" Kilpatrick wrote a friend in November 1958, "for it will take probably 100 years for the advocates of race-mixing to reduce the American South to the pathetic level of a Brazil or a Haiti." "But," he warned, "the corruption of constitutional process is an immediate thing, and unless this trend can be halted—or at least slowed—I will be compelled to live out the remainder of my life under a form of government abhorrent to me."[33]

The commissioners, for their part, hoped Americans would accept the wisdom of states' rights and let the South govern itself without outside interference. The CCG's plan involved reeducating the body politic at the grassroots level by distributing strict constitutionalist literature to policy makers and legislators. "This in turn leads you to a re-education of the educators," Kilpatrick told one correspondent. He hoped that an educated electorate would produce a rightward shift in national elections as voters sought presidential and congressional candidates willing to abolish the most pernicious effects of the Supreme Court's judicial activism.[34]

After assembling a list of conservative businessmen, politicians, teachers, and lawyers from across the nation, the VACCG put forth an incredible effort to change minds about the South. CCG material came in the form of pamphlets, anywhere from forty to a hundred pages, that engaged readers with a few primary documents united by a single theme. Some handouts recounted famous or recent Supreme Court decisions, and others contained reprints of well-known states' rights tracts, many of which appeared previously in Kilpatrick's interposition editorials. The commission also published a series of "For Your Reference Library" materials, including the Virginian and Kentucky Resolves, the speeches of John C. Calhoun, Thomas Jefferson's private letters on constitutional issues, and George Mason's "Virginia Declaration of Rights."[35]

To sound alarms about the Warren Court's mishandling of constitutional issues, Mays and Kilpatrick again relied on an academic approach to elevate the level of debate beyond race. In *A Question of Intent*, a transcript of Mays's 1959 testimony before the Senate Subcommittee on Constitutional Amendments, he argued that the original intent of the Fourteenth Amendment was to guarantee due process only, not equal citizenship rights for blacks or desegregated schools. Other literature on original meanings of the law distributed by the CCG included *On the Fixing of Boundary Lines* (1958), a tract defending the compact theory of government, and *The Rational Approach* (1961), written by Alfred J. Schweppe, a Seattle attorney, who condemned the Court's illegal grab for legislative power in the *Brown* case. Kilpatrick's *Did the Court Interpret or Amend?*, released in 1960, focused on the states' interpretations of the Fourteenth Amendment to prove their acceptance of racially segregated schools, and pointed out the Warren Court's misinterpretation of the amendment in the *Brown* decision. Kilpatrick believed that understanding the ratifiers' thinking on the amendment would settle the debate about segregated schools. "If the meaning and intent can be established on this basis," he explained, "the search is done. That meaning so fixed, actually becomes and is the Constitution." He also assured readers of the soundness and rationality of his racial beliefs: "This is not an argument of disgruntled Southerners" but one that all Americans could appreciate.[36]

The booklets made their way into thousands of people's homes thanks to the CCG's organization and distribution skills. The commission amassed a mailing list that included state legislators, governors, the chief justices of every state, federal judges, bar associations, the libraries of colleges and junior colleges across the nation, public libraries, law school libraries, Chambers of Commerce in each American city with a population of over 100,000, daily newspapers, college deans, economics and government teachers, editors, columnists, and periodicals with a national circulation. Mays even convinced Virginia's dental association to dispense ccg pamphlets as waiting room material to over 1,400 dentists. Ever mindful of convincing a non-southern constituency to pay attention to the South's interests, Kilpatrick and Mays reached out to congressmen and senators in Washington, D.C. "Where I could get them to do [so], I have used senators and congressmen as my 'newsboys' to distribute my pamphlets on Civil Rights, because people in Washington are far [more] likely to read them when asked by a legislator," Mays figured. By the early sixties, the ccg's distribution list grew so large that the commission ceased dispatching their booklets for free. Anyone who requested their publications picked up the tab for handling them.[37]

The Commission's literature promoting individual liberty and state sovereignty reached an immense readership. By the mid-1960s, the commission compiled a mailing list of over 30,000 organizations and private citizens presumed sympathetic to their cause. Radio and television stations across the nation received ccg documents. Kilpatrick and Mays's brochures circulated in a variety of groups: Young Republicans in Ohio, the Texas State Bar Association, Chambers of Commerce in Maryland, the Kiwanis Club of Washington, D.C., the Wyoming State Bar, and Southern Governors' Conferences. State supreme court justices, circuit court judges, and federal legislators opened boxes full of pamphlets about the legitimacy of states' rights and documents explaining the founding fathers' beliefs about the limited role of government. By December 1965, more than 1,200,000 pamphlets had been mailed to readers, and by 1969 the number mushroomed to more than two million booklets and over 16,000 books.[38]

Unsatisfied with merely a local or southern audience, and unlike many other segregationists whose influence never extended beyond their hometown or state, the ccg moved ambitiously outward. In his previous interposition drive, Kilpatrick had won national conservative support, and he again pursued that goal. The ccg's media barrage and heavy speaking schedule had an effect. In 1961, John C. Satterfield, newly selected president of the American Bar Association (aba) and longtime Mississippi segregationist, approached Mays for help. He wanted Mays to fund and hire lawyers and law professors to reshape the official policies of the Bar in regard to civil rights and constitutional issues, along the lines of limited government and judicial restraint advocated by the ccg. During his tenure as head of the aba, Satterfield relied on vaccg writings and themes in speeches. At the 1962 national aba convention, he turned his presidential address into a lecture about the encroachment of federal power upon the states.[39]

Kilpatrick's arguments about the compact theory of the Union and the strict interpretation of the Constitution reiterated the philosophy of a future U.S. presidential candidate. Barry Goldwater's 1960 classic *The Conscience of a Conservative* carried substantively the same message that Kilpatrick and the CCG peddled. The Arizona senator devoted a chapter on states' rights, which underscored Goldwater's principal objections to the expansion of federal power. Without mentioning race, he called for the elimination of socialistic federal grants-in-aid to the states for social welfare programs, which he considered blackmail.

Goldwater represented a racially heterogeneous state and never advocated overt discrimination in the book. The senator, a dues-paying member of the NAACP, campaigned for American Indian and Hispanic votes, but his racial appeal knew limits. The opening lines of his chapter on civil rights echoed the arguments of Kilpatrick: "An attempt has been made in recent years to disparage the principle of States' Rights by equating it with defense of the South's position on racial integration," he wrote. Although he did not deny connection and agreed with the "objectives" of the *Brown* decision, Goldwater rejected the notion that the federal government had the power to integrate schools. He claimed he accepted desegregation but opposed the federal intervention that achieved it. The Arizonan's awkward stance between deriding de jure racism but tolerating its de facto forms, as well as his libertarian view of the relationship between the state and the individual, would later influence his public opposition to the 1964 Civil Rights Act. Nodding wordlessly to the abuses of federal power was unacceptable," he surmised. "Any other course enthrones tyrants and dooms freedom." Kilpatrick and Mays concurred.[40]

For David Mays, the senator's endorsement of so many of the CCG's views vindicated the commission's work. "I have insisted upon from the beginning that we get our material into the hands of the leaders of the North and West who will have a much better chance of a hearing than representatives in the South," he beamed after reading Goldwater's book. Mays himself never knew the extent of uses for the CCG's pamphlets. "Unfortunately," Mays wrote, "much of what we do can't be told, because credit must go to those who use the material, not those who supply it. Our Commission will never be credited with all that it does, but that fact is unnecessary."[41]

The popularity of the propaganda from the Commission on Constitutional Government resulted from Mays and Kilpatrick's careful planning. In a painstaking effort, they worked to eliminate the taint of segregationism from the South's attachment to states' rights and focused on matters of the law that people from across the country could accept. In one CCG pamphlet, for instance, Mays reminded readers that the commission "is *not* concerned with the social aspects of racial separation in the public schools or elsewhere. Our concern with *Brown v. Board of Education* arises wholly from the impact of that decision upon long-established doctrines of constitutional law." Kilpatrick agreed because he remembered the limitations of his interposition campaign. He reminded trusted individuals that the CCG remained committed to outwitting *Brown*, albeit on a more intellectual level than massive resistance offered. Kilpatrick mentioned to one associate that the commission would not "hire anyone who is, as they say, 'soft on segregation,' but the Commission truly is not 'just another segregationist outfit.'"[42]

Combating the civil rights movement always engaged the CCG. Mays and Kilpatrick edited publications to ensure that their critics could not easily accuse them of racial insensitivity, especially when they wrote about controversial civil rights battles. In 1960, while the student sit-ins upset the racial order in nearly every southern city and led to violent reprisals by whites, the CCG tackled the problem in calm tones that explained the illegality of the protesters' actions. In the spring, the CCG produced *Race and the Restaurant: Two Opinion Pieces*. The pamphlet included the opinion of Judge Morris Ames Soper in *Williams v. Howard Johnson's Restaurant* (1960), which dealt with a restaurant owner's right to refuse service to a sit-in activist. Soper's three-judge panel sided with the proprietor on the grounds that the Fourteenth Amendment did not grant "equal protection" for citizens in private facilities. The CCG referenced *Williams* as an example of a proper judicial defense of private property rights that skirted issues of morality and race. With such evidence offered to readers, they would surely see the recklessness of the sit-ins and sympathize with the rights of the business owners. Because of his confidence in *Race and the Restaurant*, Mays stalled plans to re-release John C. Calhoun's 1831 Fort Hill Address, his well-known states' rights manifesto, to make a further case for business interests and private property based on *Williams*. Mays waited "until we can get out our folder dealing with the obvious illegality of the Negro lunch counter sit downs. This effort of the Negroes is self-defeating since they have now turned from the federal courts to extra—and illegal—actions."[43]

Always cautious about the language in their pamphlets, Mays and Kilpatrick presented civil rights initiatives as part of a stream of bad laws emanating from the Supreme Court. Other segregationists preferred sordid racial language. Mississippi state judge Thomas P. Brady's *Black Monday*

(1954), a classic among anti-integrationists, compared Negroes to chimpanzees, warned whites about the dangers of "mongrelization," and proposed the creation of a forty-ninth state for African Americans to inhabit. The CCG replaced crude racism with legal points and historical inquiry that a national audience could appreciate. To criticize the *Brown* decision, the CCG's booklets raised awareness about the Supreme Court's poor jurisprudence and the faulty evidence it used to decide desegregation cases. The commission distributed 37,000 copies of Kilpatrick's *Democracy and Despotism* and 40,000 prints of *Did the Court Interpret or Amend?* to point out the Court's attempt to legislate from the bench and, thus, its violation of the separation of powers in the Constitution. By 1966, the CCG produced *"State Action" and the 14th Amendment: A Study of Judicial Misinterpretation*, which ignored *Brown* specifically and traced the history of the Fourteenth Amendment back to its origins in June 1866. The brochure maintained that the original writers of the amendment never intended it to ban segregation, but the Supreme Court, nonetheless, started to use it as a foundation for its desegregation rulings in the mid-twentieth century with *Smith v. Allwright* (1944) and *Shelley v. Kraemer* (1948). Mays and Kilpatrick also wrote pamphlets to oppose federal grants to communities, to keep the national government out of local school programs and to warn about socialist welfare programs.[44]

To reclaim the law from the judicial activism of the Supreme Court, Kilpatrick and his accomplices maintained an inflexible stance on the meaning of constitutional law. In addition to contributing his early writings on interposition and the Tenth Amendment, Kilpatrick sponsored CCG literature that fought liberal interpretations of race-related laws. In the 1967 tome *The Reconstruction Amendments' Debates*, a 743-page investigation of the congressional debates and legislation leading up to the passage of the Thirteenth, Fourteenth, and Fifteenth Amendments, the CCG divined the framers' true intentions. The book sought an audience of judges, lawyers, politicians, and scholars—people already familiar with the legal process—to convince them of the Warren Court's misunderstanding and abuse of the Reconstruction-era laws. To increase the book's objectivity, Mays and Kilpatrick selected a nonsoutherner, Alfred Avins, to be editor because of his extensive legal knowledge and his credentials as someone sympathetic to the white South. Avins was an accomplished legal scholar, the former associate district attorney of Manhattan, staff counsel to the Senate Judiciary Committee under Strom Thurmond, and a special adviser to the CCG. He dismissed civil rights legislation as unconstitutional, wrote an article for

U.S. News & World Report that denounced the 1964 Civil Rights Act, and led a fight against provisions of the 1965 Voting Rights Act that affected New York and Louisiana. He also helped found the Washington, D.C.–based Liberty Lobby, a far right white supremacist organization.[45]

By exposing the intense debates surrounding the Thirteenth, Fourteenth, and Fifteenth Amendments, Avins questioned twentieth-century judicial interpretations of civil rights issues that ignored the history of the congressional disputes of the 1860s and 1870s. *The Reconstruction Amendments' Debates* included several exchanges from the summer of 1866 between congressmen who complained about the revolutionary nature of the Fourteenth Amendment's enforcement clause, which gave the national legislature power over the states, and representatives who denied that the amendment's equal protection clause applied to blacks as state citizens. The purpose of the book served as a warning to Americans about a radical federal government that rearranged the South after the Civil War and tried again in the 1950s and 1960s.

As part of their plan to make the CCG respectable, Mays and Kilpatrick stayed away from ultra right-wing groups. The commission disassociated itself from the John Birch Society and refused to participate in their anti-Communist witch hunts. Instead of smearing Communists and attacking public officials, the CCG promoted democracy and capitalism as self-evident alternatives to Communism. "I believe that positive teaching is necessary," Mays stated. "Prove the virtues of the American system and give communism some good kicks in the pants in passing. Nothing is done by mere negation." Even Kilpatrick, who favored many of the John Birch Society's causes and defended their freedom of speech in his editorials, confided to friends that they behaved like "a bunch of nuts."[46]

The CCG, additionally, avoided conspicuous connections to the White Citizens' Council's Virginia affiliate, the Defenders of State Sovereignty and Individual Liberties. Mays believed that a relationship with the reactionary white supremacy group that fostered the school closures in Prince Edward County would damage the CCG's reputation, and he regarded members as "a rabid crowd." The commission would not even permit the publishers of Carleton Putnam's scientific racist work *Race and Reason: A Yankee View* to use its mailing list for distribution purposes. Kilpatrick thought it a bad idea to associate with Putnam after the VACCG's toil "to stay absolutely free of the race issue. . . . Our concern is constitutional government, especially the relationship of the Federal and State governments. We want to keep it that way." The CCG's insistence on severing ties to radical organizations proved illusory. Mays and Kilpatrick knew many of the leaders in the Defenders and the Citizens' Council, including Collins Denny, the Defenders' attorney, and William Simmons. Some CCG commissioners even held a dual membership in the Defenders, including J. Segar Gravatt, one of Virginia's most outspoken massive resisters.[47]

Severing public links to demagogues and reactionaries built a reputable image for the CCG. The Virginians urged more segregationists to follow their new model of winning without recourse to racial arguments, school closures, and interposition resolutions. With massive resistance in shambles, white southerners needed to replicate the example of the Virginians and educate the public about legal options to deal with the desegregation crisis. In September 1960, David Mays accompanied Lindsay Almond to Hot Springs, Arkansas, for the annual Southern Governors' Conference. Speaking to the assemblage, Mays explained that "my Commission was not set up to deal with school litigation, but was to put on an educational program concerning basic constitutional concepts." Several governors expressed their approval of his work and resolved to spread his message at home and elsewhere. Mays eventually invited the directors of some sovereignty commissions to meet with him in Richmond to discuss the future of resistance plans. In May 1961, members of Louisiana's version of the CCG, the Rainach Committee, lunched with him at the Commonwealth Club, and within a year they decided to adopt more of Virginia's propaganda tactics and abandon efforts to disfranchise and spy on blacks. By 1964, the Alabama State Sovereignty Commission also requested the advice of the CCG and asked for its publications. The growing interest in the CCG pleased Mays, who remarked, "The word certainly gets around."[48]

Unifying segregationist politicians and state sovereignty commissions comprised merely one aspect of the CCG's work. Kilpatrick coordinated efforts to resist desegregation among members of the southern press as well. Not even newspapers could protect their communities from the social changes sweeping the region. Southern newsmen felt increasingly isolated and dislocated because of the civil rights revolution. Following his interposition campaign, Kilpatrick laid groundwork with conservative journals and thinkers to express the white South's point of view on the integration controversy.

Other segregationists had less success in winning a nonsouthern audience. When Tom Waring of Charleston, South Carolina, wrote an apology for segregation for *Harper's* magazine, its dismayed editor told him to rewrite it to remove emotional and bigoted depictions of blacks as ignorant, immoral, and debased. *Harper's* sensitivity about race relations frustrated Waring, Kilpatrick, and other segregationist journalists. Kilpatrick bristled when northern reporters gave him and like-minded southern editors negative publicity. After New York writer Jim Bishop interviewed him for a syndicated series about civil rights in 1956, Kilpatrick fumed at the story's description of him as a grim and humorless racist. Bishop scheduled Waring as his next interview, but an incensed Kilpatrick notified his friend: "He [Bishop] is a sort of cotton-mouthed son of a bitch, and the experience certainly has been an education to me. The next left wing Northern newspaper man who shows up in my office is likely to get kicked down the stairs, one step at a time. I warn you to beware of this bird if he ever shows up at your office."[49]

Annoyance turned to outrage when the restriction of segregationist views in major news periodicals combined with the northern-based media's voluntary neglect of racial problems outside the South. Kilpatrick often despaired at what he called a "paper curtain" along the Mason-Dixon Line that blocked southern accounts of the civil rights movement from reaching outside audiences. He and Waring believed that the wire services, like the Associated Press (AP), covered turmoil in southern cities but ignored racially motivated strikes and riots in the North. They wanted southern newsmen to reclaim control of race news before national newspapers and newsmagazines monopolized it and shifted public opinion against the South. As publications director of the CCG, Kilpatrick took responsibility for correcting deficiencies in the South's image in the mainstream press and encouraged segregationist colleagues to challenge the national media's bias against their homeland.[50]

Within days of the opening of Virginia's desegregated schools in March 1959, southern newsmen planned to confront nonsouthern reporting of the civil rights movement. Robert Patterson, head of the Citizens' Council in Mississippi, talked to Tom Waring about organizing the southern press to alter the country's perception of the region. Waring began to develop a campaign to deflect the nation's attention toward racial strife in the North. He sent invitations for a secret spring gathering at the Henry Grady Hotel in Atlanta to several of the South's most recalcitrant newspapermen, including Kilpatrick, Jimmy Ward of the *Jackson Daily News*, and John Temple Graves, the syndicated columnist for the *Birmingham Post-Herald*. On 6 May, nine segregationist editors convened in Atlanta and compared notes on the status of resistance in their home states. Jim Crow's future looked gloomy. The school closures proved immensely unpopular, and neither major political party in the 1960 presidential election guaranteed support for the segregationists' position. The conference also alerted Kilpatrick about the challenges that anti-integrationists faced in the public relations war, particularly in important southern cities. The press in Atlanta, Little Rock, Charlotte, Greensboro, Winston-Salem, Raleigh, and New Orleans all condoned some form of desegregation. Nashville and Memphis each had one pro- and one antisegregation daily newspaper. In Florida, Kilpatrick winced, the media prospects for segregation seemed "terrible. One seg paper."[51]

The segregationist journalists could only seek out more lecture circuits in the North to raise awareness about their point of view. They also resigned themselves to asking wire services to cover more race-related conflicts in northern cities. The editors selected Kilpatrick to find an advertising agency to correct misstatements about the South in national periodicals, but that idea went nowhere because he let the proposal settle to the bottom of his desk drawer and forgot about it.

As a regional effort, the segregationist editors' conference failed. It produced little more than feelings of frustration about desegregation and few accomplishments. Complaining to the AP about its decision not to cover the rape of a white woman by blacks in New York City amounted to the group's only endeavor. Politely asking news services to report racial violence in the North did little to win a national following for the white South. Kilpatrick returned to his work on the CCG, which had a more promising strategy to advance the South's perspective.[52]

The CCG's educational campaign reached a much broader public than the efforts of the southern editors who met in Atlanta. People across the nation demanded CCG speakers. The commission lectured to the American Bar Association, the U.S. Chamber of Commerce, universities, high schools, and on several occasions, the U.S. Senate Committee on Foreign Relations. Through the commission, Kilpatrick aspired to the role that suited him: a salesman-at-large for segregation and conservatism. Possessed of a seemingly endless supply of energy, he crisscrossed the nation. In February 1962, he flew to Arizona to, as Mays put it, "spread . . . [CCG] Gospel" and that summer met with Indiana state legislators. He also sharpened his debating skills by confronting hostile audiences in the North and West, usually on college campuses, and delighted in taking on "hapless 'liberals.'" David Mays experimented in new media to extend the VACCG's message when he produced a television program for the University of Georgia and a film for the Central Virginia Education Television Corporation that would be shown all over the country. At a June 1962 CCG meeting, Kilpatrick interpreted the group's numerous speaking engagements and television spots as a good sign: "The Commission is acquiring something of a reputation."[53]

Across America, liberals and conservatives contested the curricula of public education, and the CCG ensured that its views entered Virginia's schools. The indoctrination of Virginia's students in states' rights philosophy never bothered Kilpatrick, particularly if it replaced liberalism with conservatism. His organization's message balked at the marketplace of ideas, and he reminded one supporter: "We are not the least bit interested in academic freedom, free inquiry, or presenting both sides. We are interested in expounding what is known as the States' rights view, and that is all we are interested in." Mays envisioned the public schools as a breeding ground for conservative and states' rights thought. In January 1960, he met with members of the Virginia Department of Education to discuss a new high school course on American government and civil institutions. The CCG would also provide money for teachers to attend summer seminars to learn the material to teach the new class, and the commission's $125,000 annual budget funded teacher training and the study of economics and federalism in America. In fall 1960, all Virginia public high school seniors took a required course designed by the VACCG. It covered the history of representative government, the drafting of the Constitution, the role of local government, the separation of constitutional powers, and the benefits of free market capitalism versus socialism. For instruction in the course, Kilpatrick edited a book titled *We the States*, which contained essays and documents from the early republic that emphasized the compact theory of the Union and the protection of individual liberties from the central government. It ignored the connection between states' rights and slavery, but the Richmond editor cared little. The new text immersed students in the tenets of free enterprise and strict constitutionalism and equipped them "to combat the alien forces that will bury [them] in a Communist grave." However "great our society has changed" as a result of the radical left, Kilpatrick comforted young readers that "the principles [of the Constitution] endure."[54]

Educational initiatives did not distract the CCG from its larger mission of winning wider approval for the segregationist South's beliefs. A minor breakthrough for the CCG occurred in 1961 when it connected with northern lawmakers. A group of Pennsylvania Republicans requested a meeting with the CCG to discuss the agency's activities, specifically the campaign against federal grants-in-aid packages. Many conservatives regarded federal aid as a challenge to local control and as a form of creeping socialism.

The Pennsylvanians wanted to replicate vaccg pamphlets that explained the dangers of accepting federal money for social programs and advocated a clear boundary between state and federal powers. Their first informal talks not only proved the effectiveness of Mays and Kilpatrick's efforts to conceal their support for segregation behind more palatable constitutional issues but also showed the interests of conservatives on both sides of the Mason-Dixon Line.

In late July 1962, a contingent of thirty Pennsylvania legislators arrived in Williamsburg, Virginia, to consult with Mays and other representatives of the CCG. The envoys included prominent Pennsylvania lawmakers, such as Albert W. Johnson, the Republican minority leader in the state house of representatives, and W. Stuart Helm, chairman of the state's Republican Party. The Keystone State solons left the meeting impressed enough with the CCG's work that Helm and others formed the Dual Sovereignty Committee, a national body that wanted to revise the process of making amendments to the Constitution through state legislatures rather than the national Congress. In December 1962, Kilpatrick attended one of the committee's gatherings in Chicago to advise them about amending the Constitution. The effort fell apart the following year, but the formation of the committee hinted at the national potential for the vaccg's ideas. Even though additional plans to create a Pennsylvania version of the CCG floundered, the relationship encouraged Mays and Kilpatrick to push ahead with their efforts to win outside help. Channels of communication between conservatives from every corner of the country looked possible in ways unknown a decade beforehand.[55]

———————

Mainly, when James Jackson Kilpatrick surveyed the status of segregation in late 1958, he tried to rally the defenders of the racial caste system. "Ten years from now," he predicted to *News Leader* readers, "the South will be doing business serenely as before: Separate but equal. Sparta lost a few battles. So will the South. But 10 or 20 years is not really so long a time. This struggle on the Peloponnesus below the Potomac has barely begun." By the sixties, the desegregation of housing, public facilities, and schools continued throughout the South, but Virginia's brand of segregation transformed into a relevant component of the conservative movement. The commission's propaganda machine demonstrated some white southerners' motivation to take their case for states' rights, their respect for local communities, their strict constitutionalism, and their racial concerns to the national stage. Through the CCG, conservative Virginia blended its frustrations about *Brown*, federal authority, and the end of massive resistance into a broader attack on the role of big government and a liberal interpretation of the Constitution. The commission's pamphleteering, Kilpatrick wrote, formed part of a new, national offensive against *Brown* by accomplishing "what the repeal forces did in the early 1920's" to end Prohibition and by laboring "unceasingly to create a climate of opinion nationally in which the decision itself, if not actually reversed, will be effectively modified or controlled by Congress."[56]

In spite of the work that Kilpatrick and Mays devoted to the Virginia Commission on Constitutional Government, it stumbled in several respects. Not everyone shared their convictions or their stratagem. The CCG's gambit to recast civil rights issues as a constitutional problem came too late to prevent some segregationists from pursuing violence and obstruction, which drew the intervention of the federal government. Civil rights activists, to their credit, also thwarted the VACCG by keeping race in the headlines during the civil rights era.

Equally to blame for the commission's problems was its unwillingness to preserve official massive resistance in Virginia. Although Kilpatrick had been one of the original agents of resistance, discretion proved the better part of valor. He finished that fight on the side of segregationists who preferred a path of least confrontation with the federal courts. His teetering posture on the school closures signaled the beginning of the end of the Byrd machine as well. The rapid collapse of massive resistance in Virginia beset the Byrd organization with problems. The simultaneous emergence of black voters after the 1965 Voting Rights Act and a new wave of politicians not wedded to the Lost Cause undercut Byrd's power. In 1965, Virginians elected Mills Godwin Jr., a former resister who accepted the reality of an African American electorate. That same year, Kilpatrick tired of the CCG and wished it would go away. The commission "often seems an exercise in frustration," he admitted, and, besides, it distracted him from his newspaper writing. By the late sixties, many Virginians called for the VACCG's disbandment. Despite Mays and Kilpatrick's best efforts, it became another offshoot of the state's segregationist days and an outgrowth of its embarrassing interposition fiasco. In early 1969, the commission disbanded. The dismantling of Jim Crow, however, became an instructive preliminary to later developments in conservatism and forecast changes yet to come on the right.[57]

The Republicans would have to take the CCG agenda seriously to win the South. Race did not do the job alone. A coddling court system, crime, and activists' disrespect for authority dismayed the CCG as much as desegregation. Their last booklet, *Every Man His Own Law* (1967), associated civil rights, antiwar, and student protests with lawlessness and called for punitive governance to stabilize society. The CCG's publications, lobbying, and broadcasting built positions upon deracinated appeals, spread their ideas, and helped bring together two of the strangest bedfellows in recent southern history—southern whites and the Republican Party. By the 1960s, as many white Democrats abandoned the tenuous New Deal coalition and the right hammered more cracks in it, James Kilpatrick looked to the Republican Party "as a vehicle for conservative thought" and as a convergence point between the CCG's message and mainstream political discourse.[58]

Just as Kilpatrick plotted strategy and refused to atrophy on the political sidelines, blacks refused to cower and instead expressed indignation. While *Brown* provoked what had come to be called "massive resistance," it spurred Negroes to more vigorous radicalism. As future state senator Henry L. Marsh, an African American civil rights activist in Richmond, later maintained, massive resistance, Byrd, and Kilpatrick "strangely created a counter resistance." The goal of linking his positions to the Republicans had desensitized Kilpatrick to all the ramifications of his ideas and to the black dissidents he rankled into greater rebellion.[59]

FOUR

A Cross of Goldwater

New Year's Day 1960 fell in the middle of a winter of discontent for Richmond segregationists. The day before, columnist Lenoir Chambers stung massive resisters for the school closures with an editorial drenched in moral condemnation:

> More intelligent handling of problems of great difficulty will continue and increase only if commonsense and courage continue to direct the course of both political leadership and public opinion. The struggles for reasonable solutions are not over. The state may see setbacks of serious proportions. It is certain to encounter perplexities not easy to resolve. It may discover demagogues entranced with the thought of exploiting honest doubts and uncertainties as well as old prejudices. It needs sensible cooperation from its Negro citizenship. It needs every ounce of good will it can find from any source.
>
> But the old years of impracticality, unconstitutionalism, and futility are on the way out. If Virginia can produce more willingness to face the facts and fresh qualities of initiation and leadership in dealing with them, the year the state opened the schools can lead to a New Year of hope.[1]

Then, on 1 January, thirty-year-old Reverend Martin Luther King Jr. arrived in the city to address a rally about the school closings in the white supremacist holdout of Prince Edward County. Speaking to the commonwealth's whites, King declared that the struggle for black civil rights had only begun. "It is an unstoppable movement," he pledged. "We will wear you down by our capacity to suffer, and in the process we will win your hearts. . . . Nothing is more sublime than suffering and sacrifice for a great cause."[2]

King's words had little effect on the *News Leader*. The following day, the story of the speech and subsequent protest march through the streets made page ten of the regular news coverage. Kilpatrick's editorials ignored the presence of the preacher. The editor was more concerned about putting pressure on liberals to back off a new civil rights law and the prospect of a Republican presidential victory in the fall that would, he hoped, "take the heat of Northern radicalism off the South." Had Kilpatrick been able to acknowledge the indigenous roots of that radicalism, he might have prepared himself for the coming revolution.[3]

Behind the Paper Curtain

To many civil rights activists, the winter of 1960 felt like a resurgence. The movement shook with the promise of immediate, tangible change in the southern racial hierarchy. On the afternoon of 1 February 1960, four African American freshmen from North Carolina Agricultural and Technical State College requested service at a segregated Woolworth's lunch counter in Greensboro, North Carolina, but their hosts refused them. The next day, they returned with twenty-seven other students. By the end of the week, hundreds of students participated, and their commitment to the desegregation of public facilities in Greensboro encouraged other sit-ins as members of their generation rose in protest across the region. The black freshmen in the college class of 1960 were in junior high school during the *Brown* decision and came of age in an era of new racial possibilities. Segregation could no longer contain the young sit-in demonstrators.[4]

Civil rights activists throughout the South replicated the North Carolinians' protest, and by February 10, the demonstrations spread north into the Old Dominion. On 20 February, the first of the sit-ins that would take place in Richmond also occurred at a Woolworth's when students occupied the store's lunch counter. During the next several days, six other sit-ins and a working-class black boycott that targeted local drug stores occurred in the town. On 22 February, at Richmond's posh Thalhimers department store, a sit-in led to the arrest of student participants and triggered a boycott of the city's major department stores for months.[5]

White Virginians, like many other southerners, noted the rebirth in civil rights activity. They had rarely encountered such bold condemnations of the Virginia way of life. Observers of the Thalhimers sit-in sent word to the *News Leader* offices about the disturbance, and James Kilpatrick bounded down the stairs and then ran through the streets to witness the breach of racial etiquette. When he arrived, he saw disciplined, well-dressed black students requesting to eat alongside white customers. The young African

Americans represented a new and distressing kind of civil rights activism: impatient but composed, orderly in the midst of chaos. Worse, a bunch of unruly whites tried to break up the protest without regard for southern manners. A disgusted Kilpatrick described the scene to readers: "Here were the colored students, in coats, white shirt, ties, and one of them was reading Goethe and one was taking notes from a biology text. And here, on the sidewalk outside, was a gang of white boys come to heckle, a ragtail rabble, slack-jawed, black-jacketed, grinning fit to kill, and some of them, God save the mark, were waving the proud and honored flag of the Southern States in the last war fought by gentlemen. *Eheu!* It gives one pause." The revelation of the sit-ins slammed Kilpatrick. Despite his previous efforts to stem racial progress, the civil rights movement not only grew but also became unpredictable.[6]

Martin Luther King Jr. immediately embraced the sit-ins because of their nonviolence and respectability. In the spring of 1960, student leaders of the various sit-ins met in Raleigh, North Carolina, with King and other activists and launched a civil rights organization committed to aggressive tactics that rejected waiting for the federal government or the conscience of the white South to change race relations. The Student Non-Violent Coordinating Committee (SNCC) infiltrated segregated communities and taught blacks to lift themselves out of oppression rather than rely on outside help. A month after the creation of SNCC, a group of Nashville students used sit-ins to integrate lunch counters as well. Unlike the bus boycotts of the early and mid-1950s that occurred in just a few cities, such as Montgomery and Baton Rouge, the student sit-ins spanned the South. Nashville students and other civil rights activists fought for the right to eat at diners and enjoy access to other public facilities. The rapidity and intensity of the sit-ins drew attention from and inspired fear in segments of the white South.[7]

Kilpatrick witnessed the transformations in the black freedom struggle with a simultaneous sense of alarm and curiosity. His massive resistance program had apparently not broken the spirit of civil rights activists. The sit-ins smashed some segregationists' hopes that African Americans would accept token integration and gradual desegregation. Now, young Negro students defied the old racial hierarchy more than ever with direct confrontation, and they advanced themselves with or without the help of whites and government. "A great change has come over him [the black southerner]," Kilpatrick later commented on the new black activism. The new Negro was "no longer an Uncle Tom, or even the kind of Negro approved by

Booker T. Washington. He now talks back. He has a new self-respect, a new confidence, a new independence."[8]

In 1960, change was everywhere. Civil rights veterans like Martin Luther King worked to remain relevant to a movement pushing in experimental and unforeseen directions. As King's fame grew after the 1955–56 Montgomery bus boycott, he accepted more speaking engagements all over the country and abroad. His status as a leader of the struggle, his philosophy of nonviolence, and his ability to preach to both blacks and whites made King a menace to segregationists and a formidable opponent. Kilpatrick awaited the opportunity to confront King about the meaning of civil rights before a national audience.

The chance for a showdown between the preacher and the newsman came a few weeks after John F. Kennedy's narrow presidential victory. On 26 November 1960, Kilpatrick and King met in a New York television studio to debate the sit-ins on *The Nation's Future*, produced by the National Broadcasting Corporation (NBC). Two events, however, almost prevented that meeting. Several months earlier, in April, on the New York talk show *Open End*, Kilpatrick discussed student activism with King at a roundtable. During the program, Kilpatrick was the lone conservative voice amid a panel of liberals, who shouted him down with the help of the program's host, David Susskind. When summoned to participate in NBC's forum, Kilpatrick wrote a network producer to set the ground rules for another debate. The last time Kilpatrick appeared on television with King, he complained, "I got boobytrapped by David Susskind into the short-end of 5–1 odds. I don't propose to walk into a rigged situation again if I can avoid it." The Virginia editor refused to appear with King again unless he could meet him man-to-man without interference from a moderator.[9]

Kilpatrick was not even the original guest scheduled for the November debate. NBC wanted James H. Gray, the editor-publisher of *The Albany Herald*, the most powerful news periodical in southwest Georgia, to oppose King. Gray's chairmanship of the Georgia Democratic Party and friendship with the Kennedy family complicated that proposal. When John F. Kennedy convinced Gray not to challenge King on national television and risk injuring the candidate's efforts to win black voters, the network instead asked Kilpatrick to present the segregationist case.[10]

James Kilpatrick's intellectual talents, his familiarity with the law, and his tenacity made him a formidable debater. The broadcast, filmed before representatives from both civil rights and conservative groups, gave him a forum to put a sophisticated and rational face on segregationist beliefs.

What a sharp contrast he presented with the pious King. Kilpatrick worked to expose the reverend as a relativist with a false interpretation of the law and the founding fathers. Their televised clash primarily centered on two different understandings of Thomas Jefferson. To King, Jefferson symbolized fundamental American freedoms and natural rights bestowed by God. Kilpatrick disagreed. His Jefferson stood for the protection of individuals' rights against the federal government and for states' rights. In the debate, King proved to be more of a liability than an asset to the sit-in movement. His appeals to moral law, civil disobedience, and a mutual brotherhood of love struck Kilpatrick as self-serving and confusing. Again and again, Kilpatrick egged on King about legal and constitutional issues and respect for the property rights of store owners under siege by the student protesters. In his deep, almost gravelly voice, he demanded an explanation from King. Kilpatrick pointed out that King's choosing moral law over property rights appeared to be a matter of personal preference. King struggled for a definitive answer, thumbed through note cards, and returned to a more familiar position that adhered to the teachings of St. Augustine: "I go back to the argument, Mr. Kilpatrick, that an unjust law is no law at all."[11]

King wasted his breath on Kilpatrick. The Richmond editor, like Edmund Burke, interpreted moral law and inalienable, natural law rights as bogus premises. No human, civil, or political liberty constituted an absolute right. Rights must be rationalized to make them concrete. The right to vote should depend on a person's education about his political system. The right to own property should result from a person's payment of property taxes. Law and order broke down without proper respect for property rights. "[T]here is a pretty high degree of morality in simply abiding by the law," he scolded King. Kilpatrick concluded the program by turning the preacher's arguments against him. According to King's own logic, segregationists had the right to resist desegregation because they found *Brown* to be unjust and, therefore, not a legitimate law.[12]

Unwilling to rest on the patina of property rights, Kilpatrick inserted his personal beliefs about race relations. In examining King, Kilpatrick demonstrated his white superiority. The editor invariably refused courtesy titles for his opponent and addressed King condescendingly in the third person, not "Dr. King" or "Reverend." King did not protest the disrespect, probably to focus on the issues at hand, but perhaps also to avoid antagonizing Kilpatrick.[13]

Freed to probe many areas of King's ideas and actions, Kilpatrick jumped from his legal points to his racial beliefs. He peppered King with opinions designed to discredit the civil rights movement at large. At the onset of the debate, Kilpatrick told the television audience that the sit-ins threatened to establish a mixed-race society. "We believe," he informed viewers, "it is an affirmatively good thing to preserve the predominantly racial characteristics that have contributed to Western civilization over the past two thousand years." The declaration cut to the core of Kilpatrick's beliefs. In his opinion, King and the sit-ins endangered the natural order. Upsetting the racial hierarchy terrified Kilpatrick, and he vilified the civil rights leader as an anarchist who had no respect for the law.[14]

Kilpatrick's ability to adapt to the new medium of television and his lawyerly precision, not his racial views, won the debate. He often confused King with his references to specific cases before the courts and felt at ease addressing a hostile northern audience, which he had often encountered during speaking engagements for the CCG. At the beginning of the broadcast, Kilpatrick appeared somewhat rigid and nervous, but he finished the show with panache and humor. At one point, when King commented on the violent reprisals by whites to the sit-ins, Kilpatrick's riposte came immediately: "Well, I'm the most loving, peaceful anarchist you ever likened to meet." His dry humor elicited laughter from the crowd. Kilpatrick sat confidently behind his podium, occasionally tapping a cigarette on an ashtray between making points and bashing King.[15]

Believing that he lost the debate to the Virginia segregationist, King flew home to Atlanta. The show aired while SNCC activists met in Atlanta to decide the future of their infant organization. The students watched the program ready to applaud King's trouncing of Kilpatrick but instead sat stunned. Many of them admitted that the Nobel Prize–winning Martin Luther King appeared "no match" for Kilpatrick. It became the first of several occasions that members of SNCC doubted the effectiveness of King's leadership.[16]

King received an intellectual beating in his tangle with Kilpatrick but responded by adjusting his tactics to avoid a similar embarrassment in the future. The black minister groped for counterarguments to the constitutional points raised by Kilpatrick. He soon incorporated portions of James Madison's *The Federalist Papers* and its condemnation of tyrannical laws by an unjust majority into his language of civil disobedience. King never completely abandoned his appeals to moral law in favor of Madisonian logic, but he worked to incorporate secular, constitutional principles under the banner of heaven and moral inspection. In his later "Letter from a Birmingham Jail," King famously linked moral law to writings by the American founders. He suffered a minor defeat with Kilpatrick, but the movement itself grew larger and more popular. Kilpatrick, not King, would remain on the defensive.[17]

As the sit-ins spread, the action and then the media went with them. Protest sites popped up everywhere, most noticeably in Lower South states that seemed impervious to racial reform just a few years earlier. Kilpatrick followed the progress of the civil rights struggle anywhere it made headlines, no longer content to comment on events only in Virginia or through the CCG. If he wanted to remain a relevant avatar on racial issues, he needed to study activists and their tactics and learn to manipulate the news to tell his version of them. During the ongoing protests, he prowled for opportunities to put his own spin on the black freedom movement and found one when Mississippi tested his doctrine of interposition in an effort to prevent desegregation.

In late January 1961, James Howard Meredith, a black air force veteran and successful student at several colleges, wrote the University of Mississippi for admission. Mississippi had made little effort toward desegregation, and the state saw no reason to start with Meredith at the university. After Meredith turned to the judicial system and the NAACP for help, his case circulated through the state and federal courts until 10 September 1962, when the Supreme Court upheld his right to enroll. Many white Mississippians were furious about the ruling. Three days after the Court's verdict, the Magnolia State's wily governor, Ross R. Barnett, who had been elected in 1959 without having held any previous public office, addressed the state on television and radio: "We must either submit to the unlawful dictates of the federal government, or stand like men and tell them NEVER!" A 1960 state constitutional amendment, inspired by interposition, gave Barnett the right to close any school to prevent integration. In his speech, the governor informed citizens that he would invoke the state's powers to resist the court order and interpose himself between the federal government and the school. Under the Tenth Amendment, Barnett declared the state's sovereignty over its schools, colleges, and universities, and he cited the doctrine of interposition through a gubernatorial decree to foil the "unwarranted, illegal and arbitrary usurpation of [the state's] power" by the federal judiciary.[18]

On 17 September, the University of Mississippi's board of trustees conferred in the state capital with Barnett about the integration of the school. Barnett wanted complete resistance from the board, but several members had no intention of going to jail on contempt of court charges. Three days later, university chancellor John D. Williams, desperate to avoid conflict, stated that Meredith could enroll. Barnett, however, met Meredith on campus and prevented him from registering for his fall classes. The governor now defied the federal courts, provoked the Justice Department into enforcing the ruling, and set the stage for a deadly contest between the state and the federal governments.[19]

The story of a solitary civil rights militant facing an entire state of angry resisters captivated the American public's attention. Newsmen flooded into the small town of Oxford, located in the north central hills of the state. Overnight, the University of Mississippi became a mecca for journalists covering the civil rights beat. At least 182 reporters arrived for the standoff between the State of Mississippi and the national government. All three major television networks had crews on the scene, and the top national daily newspapers, including the *New York Times* and the *Washington Post*, sent correspondents. Mississippi's segregationist newspapers mobilized for the event as well and defended the governor's response. Although Jackson's *Clarion-Ledger* had never assigned a reporter to document the school's integration, the paper lauded Barnett as a state hero and spewed antipathy on the federal government. While most of the segregationist press stayed away from Oxford, James Jackson Kilpatrick planned to witness the climactic battle over states' rights.[20]

As the imbroglio in Mississippi heightened, Kilpatrick filed his first column on the university's crisis. In an editorial titled "Sophocles in Mississippi," he presented the story as an Attic tragedy. "From afar," he told readers, "one watches events in Mississippi unfold like so many scenes from Aeschylus or Sophocles. The antagonists are locked in a struggle from which none can withdraw; pursuing what each conceives to be right they will play out the drama to the end." He portrayed Meredith as a pawn in a tragic contest between state and federal power. Since childhood, Kilpatrick loved epics and poems. In adulthood, his fascination with classical literature, especially Greek tragedies, helped him understand the civil rights movement. "I have thought from the very beginning . . . that the whole story of the South is one long extension of Attic Tragedy," he admitted. "Where other drama brings right and wrong into conflict, Greek drama pits right against right. There are rights on both sides in our southern drama, and we are doomed by them." Using the metaphor of a Greek calamity to describe the movement fit with Kilpatrick's political beliefs and added dramatic flair to his writing. The Greeks always dealt with kings and rulers and exposed the flaws of society at its highest level. Corruption in the upper echelon of the polity always filtered down into the general population. The mistakes and abuses of America's national government affected the public with the same terrible consequences.[21]

No longer content to watch northern reporters dominate civil rights coverage, Kilpatrick flew to Mississippi on 27 September. A day later, he wrote from Oxford. Some old-fashioned, cub reporter's blood still coursed through him from his days on Richmond's various city beats. He surveyed the mood on campus and predicted violence. Kilpatrick then went to Jackson, the capital and the center of the real action, and commented on Barnett's strategy of resistance. The Richmond editor described the governor and his lieutenants as a brave band facing overwhelming odds. Barnett's deployment of interposition, however, seemed "exceedingly unlikely" to defeat the federal government, worried a realistic Kilpatrick.[22]

Kilpatrick then took an extraordinary step for a segregationist newsman and decided to capture the humanity of the person trying to desegregate the school. Before Kilpatrick arrived in Mississippi, he depicted James Meredith as a collateral figure in the game of the civil rights struggle and supported Mississippi's decision to deny him entrance on the grounds that the applicant could receive his education elsewhere. Kilpatrick, interestingly, never disputed Meredith's intelligence and said that he had the right to be admitted to a public university but not in Mississippi. Perhaps remembering his professional duties to account for all sides in a story or possibly because he recognized an exciting tale, Kilpatrick felt compelled to visit the Merediths. He drove to Kosciusko, home of the Meredith family, sat inside with the young man's mother, wife, and son, and recorded their reactions to the crisis with a degree of professionalism and dignity that few segregationist reporters possessed.[23]

During the interview, Meredith's fifty-eight-year-old mother clutched the family Bible and compared her son to Moses. "He never got to the Promised Land," she said after moments of silence. "He saw it, but he never got there. But others did. Maybe it's the same with J. H. [James Meredith]. It's in the Lord's hands now. His will be done." Kilpatrick presented Meredith's wife, June, however, as part of a new breed of assertive Negroes who formed the vanguard of the sit-ins and embodied the generation gap between young and old African Americans. Unlike Meredith's mother, his wife envisioned segregation's demise. Attending to her two-year-old son, John Howard, she taught the child the language of black resistance. "Say, I don't want to pick cotton," she instructed the boy. He chuckled and repeated, "I don't wanna pick cotton." For the Merediths, a child added incentive to fight for the rights of black Mississippians and against racial segregation. The system had to change. June Meredith showed pleasure in the response and turned to Kilpatrick: "He won't pick cotton." At best, Kilpatrick's handling of the Merediths was humane and acknowledged the family's devotion to their loved one and commitment to education. At worst, he was paternalistic and met with the Merediths to show them as simple bystanders in the larger civil rights struggle rather than agents of change. Perhaps Kilpatrick overlooked the real pawn in the battle. The editor, like many other segregationists bent on preventing integration, ignored the vulnerability of the university, an institution caught between the federal government and interposition.[24]

Meanwhile, in Jackson, the federal government turned up the heat on Barnett to comply with the Court order. September ended with constant deliberations between the governor and the Kennedy brothers as Barnett looked for ways to preserve self-respect and honor but acquiesce to the demands of the national government. He had until 2 October to follow the ruling before serving prison time. On Saturday, 29 September, thousands of students from the University of Mississippi traveled to Jackson for a night football game and waited for news from state leaders. During a halftime address, Barnett praised Mississippi's people and traditions and pledged defiance. The 40,000-plus crowd erupted into rebel yells and readied for a war. Bill Minor, the Jackson bureau chief for the New Orleans's *Times-Picayune*, observed the scene and recoiled in disbelief: "Thousands of Confederate battle flags burst forth throughout the stadium, shimmering in the night like a forest fire running before the wind."[25]

Students and resisters rushed to Barnett's home in Jackson the following day to defend him against federal officials rumored to have been sent to arrest the governor. A crowd of two thousand arrived to protect the executive mansion. The demonstration turned into a rally as people cheered for the governor and sang songs denouncing the Kennedys. Kilpatrick returned to the capital to witness them and what amounted to the state's last massive public celebration of white supremacy. While in Jackson, he discussed the events with his friend Bill Simmons. The two watched the congregation at the Governor's Mansion, which resulted from misinformation about federal marshals that Simmons had spread, and savored the moment. Kilpatrick found the Mississippians to be a noble and courteous lot. The resisters' fervor climaxed in a display of "genuinely touching love for their state," he noted. Simmons, the state's "rajah of race," according to one Mississippi segregationist, went further. "They won't give up," Simmons told Kilpatrick. "They won't ever give up. They're the finest people on earth." Inside the Citizens' Council building, the mood ranged from excitement to hostility. Edwin Walker, the militant segregationist and former army general who had reluctantly enforced the desegregation of Little Rock's Central High School, strode into the offices "flashing Messianic fire from cold, fanatic eyes," Kilpatrick recalled. At a press conference, Walker called out to the opposition to integration, "Rally to the cause of freedom in righteous indignation, violent vocal protest and bitter silence under the flag of Mississippi." White volunteers from across the South swarmed around Walker, vowing to follow him to Oxford to prevent Meredith's registration. Kilpatrick abhorred the atmosphere of violence that Simmons permitted. "War is not pretty," Simmons later told Kilpatrick, "and this was war!" A large-scale riot seemed imminent.[26]

Sunday night, a crowd of students and white people incensed about the desegregation of the school gathered in front of the Lyceum, the university's administration building. After Barnett announced that Meredith would register the next morning, the crowd turned violent and hurled bricks and explosives at the federal marshals sent to keep the peace. Throughout the night until daybreak, the mob besieged federal officials taking refuge in the Lyceum. Over two hundred military policemen from Memphis arrived to restore order that evening. Tens of thousands of federal troops also rolled onto campus. They eventually broke up the riot and made arrests. Two men lost their lives during the chaos. Around eight o'clock in the morning on 1 October, Meredith walked into the Lyceum and enrolled in his classes.[27]

Segregationist newspapers reported on the crisis from afar and let nonsouthern news periodicals cover the event. Kilpatrick traveled all the way to Mississippi to ensure that a conservative southern voice would be heard above the din of national newspaper and television coverage but then stayed in Jackson while the riot occurred. He probably sensed trouble and disassociated himself from the violence. Early Monday morning, however, Kilpatrick drove back to Oxford and arrived in time to see Edwin Walker and the last of the protesters arrested. In a unique editorial, which appeared on page one of the *News Leader*, Kilpatrick blamed the fighting on federal authorities, as did so many other southern whites. The students apparently came in peace, and the federal marshals provoked them by firing tear gas. His column also carried a resentful tone: "Long ago, this newspaper sought to warn the apostles of coerced racial integration that they were sowing the wind." During the next few weeks, his editorials placed the responsibility for the race war in Oxford on the shoulders of the Kennedys, whom he accused of abusing their power and usurping the state of Mississippi's authority. The hordes of federal troops the Kennedys unleashed, Kilpatrick charged, violated and seized private property at will and without regard for southern racial customs. In one column, Kilpatrick described a scene of Negro soldiers searching the cars of white women and children. The troops at the university, he declared, "were there to kill, to capture, to compel obedience."[28]

The *News Leader*'s regular news pages depicted the events in Oxford with similar contempt for the federal government. Pictures of armed federal troops holding back civilians in Oxford's downtown and of bayonet-wielding soldiers practicing for riot control were typical. No photographs of students assaulting federal marshals appeared in the newspaper, and white Mississippians never received any blame for their actions. Despite the outcries of the paper and Kilpatrick, the University of Mississippi had fallen to the desegregationists. The editor and the segregationist press had barely enough time to recuperate from the defeat when another stronghold of white supremacy came under attack. In Birmingham, Alabama, a local movement against Jim Crow began to take shape.[29]

Since 1956, a charismatic Baptist preacher named Fred L. Shuttlesworth led Birmingham's African American community against the city's stifling racial caste system. In early spring 1963, Shuttlesworth invited Martin Luther King and the Southern Christian Leadership Conference (SCLC) to Birmingham to desegregate public facilities. Throughout April 1963, Shuttlesworth, King, and others organized mass meetings, sit-ins, and marches to reform the city's race relations. After weeks of nonviolent protests and arrests, Birmingham exploded in violence. In the first week of May, the town's black schoolchildren poured into the streets to demonstrate against segregation, and white civic authorities responded with fire hoses and police dogs. For the rest of the month, clashes between demonstrators and law enforcement shook the city and dominated national news.[30]

From Richmond, Kilpatrick again weighed in on the civil rights struggle and covered Birmingham after weeks of silence on the situation. In April, the *News Leader* barely mentioned the Birmingham demonstrations and King's arrest for violating a court injunction against marches. The newspaper also declined to print his "Letter from Birmingham Jail." Across the hall at the *Times-Dispatch*, however, Dabney ran an editorial on King's "Letter" that ridiculed the preacher as an erratic "judge of which laws he will obey" who had "incited mobs of Negroes to turbulent street demonstrations." By May, the violence had roused the *News Leader* into action. Kilpatrick commented on Birmingham to ensure a white southern perspective because the

Birmingham News refused to report the demonstrations on its front page, pretending like the protests never occurred, and instead covered foreign affairs and national events in its headlines. The Birmingham paper gave more details on riots occurring in Syria than the ones exploding inside Birmingham's city limits. The town's white community seemed willing to ignore the movement as well, and the *News* acted as if the violence had no effect on local Negroes. One Sunday edition of the tribune pictured a black woman strolling near Kelly Ingram Park, the principal battleground for clashes between police and activists, while in the far background fire hoses blasted demonstrators. The caption read: "She appears undisturbed by disturbances in Ingram Park." As surprising as it may seem, a southern newspaper was normally the last place in the world to look for race news. *The News Leader* was exceptional. Thanks to Kilpatrick, Richmonders knew more about the crisis than Birmingham's whites, and his readers knew whom to blame.[31]

Kilpatrick attributed the Birmingham violence mostly to blacks. The editor's columns encouraged white resistance and discredited black protests. His news coverage focused on the white side of the story, particularly the police, suggested an imminent race war, and portrayed the demonstrators as threats to law and order. "It was the Negroes themselves who stoned firemen attempting to put out fires in Negro property. White persons were not involved—except as the victims of broken bottles, brickbats, and knives," he edified readers. John F. Kennedy behaved no better. Criticizing the president for federalizing the Alabama National Guard, Kilpatrick compared him to the Roman emperor Domitian, who demanded excessive tributes from imperial provinces. As he did during the University of Mississippi crisis, he accused outside agitators of disturbing the peace.[32]

The national press coverage of Birmingham troubled Kilpatrick. Nearly two hundred journalists from across America descended on the town. The May riots prompted more stories on race in the *New York Times* in two weeks than in the previous year combined. Kilpatrick sifted through every page of the Yankee newspaper to fact check for errors. The *Times*, he noted, used certain verbs and adjectives during the protests. "In Birmingham," he pouted to one correspondent, "demonstrators always were 'thrown' or 'tossed' or 'hurled' into paddy wagons; in New York, the police merely 'put' them in wagons or 'transported' them somewhere. All Southern cops are 'burly' or 'red-faced.' Northern cops are just cops." In response, Kilpatrick worked to restore the dignity of Birmingham's white community. He wrote about police commissioner Eugene "Bull" Connor, the man who authorized the use of dogs and fire hoses on demonstrators, as a hero trying to stem black violence, and he depicted the civil rights protests as an aimless rampage.[33]

The *News Leader*'s regular news pages supported Kilpatrick's interpretation of events and found ways to boil down the denial of black Birmingham's rights into a series of unruly demonstrations. Black people appeared as faceless mobs in the newspaper's photos. One picture showed only the back of a black woman sprayed by a fire hose rather than the terrified expression on her face. Several editions of the *News Leader* featured photographs of the looting and rioting taking place in Negro neighborhoods but not scenes of police violence. The newspaper depicted the police as the upholders of law and order but never mentioned the African Americans injured by their brutality. The *Times-Dispatch* also derided civil rights activists and described black student demonstrators as a "taunting crowd" that had to be "persuaded" by city police with hoses and dogs to "disperse."[34]

Richmond's black-owned and -operated newspaper offered the better source for honest and ongoing coverage of civil rights activity. Future editor Raymond H. Boone described the local black press as a "protest instrument against injustices." The *Afro-American*'s May and June accounts of the events in Birmingham were thorough and put the protests into the context of a global struggle for human rights. In contrast to the white dailies, the *Richmond Afro-American* accused Birmingham's police of "torturing defenseless citizens." The paper's front pages showed German shepherds tearing into black children and provided graphic images of protesters being dowsed with fire hoses and entering hospitals for treatment.[35]

The nation's press corps scrutinized the segregationists' violent tactics, and the nightly news showed the atrocious treatment of Birmingham's civil rights activists. Most Americans sympathized with the black protesters, and some people who had been previously indifferent to civil rights now backed it. After Birmingham, for example, *Newsweek* and *Time* magazines began praising Martin Luther King and the goals of the civil rights movement. Even John F. Kennedy, who tended to ignore domestic issues, especially civil rights, started to denounce segregation in the wake of Birmingham. In a television and radio address on 11 June 1963, Kennedy asked Congress to begin work on a comprehensive civil rights bill to desegregate public facilities. "The events in Birmingham and elsewhere," he declared, "have so increased the cries for equality that no city or state or legislative body can prudently choose to ignore them." King's August 1963 March on

Washington capitalized on Birmingham and the new political and press attention. The major television networks sent crews to the nation's capital to capture live images of the event. The *New York Times* hailed the march as "the greatest assembly for a redress of grievances that this capital has ever seen." Kilpatrick struggled to maintain his composure with the media's outpourings of support for the civil rights struggle.[36]

When Kilpatrick debated King in 1960, he wanted to make a good impression on the American public in his first major network television appearance. He had refrained from racist language, except for a brief diatribe against race-mixing, in favor of constitutional and property rights arguments. By the summer of 1963, after civil rights victories brought integrated lunch counters, classrooms at the University of Mississippi, and public facilities in Birmingham, Kilpatrick could no longer control his resentment. In June, he chimed in on the murder of Mississippi's NAACP field secretary and mourned Medgar Evers but only because his death meant more federal interference in southern affairs. "The assassination of Medgar Evers will not deter this Negro agitation for an instant; it will serve merely to give the movement new speed and fervor. The symbol lives—and the Negro-Liberal leadership can be relied upon to wring every possible advantage from it," he brooded.[37]

Following the March on Washington and King's "I Have a Dream" speech, Kilpatrick offered an intemperate commentary on the state of black life. Solicited by the *Saturday Evening Post*, he composed a screed titled "The Hell He Is Equal," in which he argued that discrimination against Negroes benefited humanity. African Americans contributed nothing to Western civilization and deserved no special treatment. Kilpatrick insisted that the

> Negro race, as a race, is in fact an inferior race. . . . Within the frame of reference of a Negroid civilization, a mud hut may be a masterpiece; a tribal council may be a marvel of social organization; a carved image may have a primitive purity all its own. Well and good. But the mud hut ought not to be equated with Monticello, nor jungle rule with Periclean Athens, nor phallic dolls with Elgin marbles. When the Negro today proclaims or demands his "equality," he is talking of equality within the terms of Western civilization. And what, pray, has he contributed to it? Putting aside conjecture, wishful thinking and a puerile jazz-worship, what has he in fact contributed to it? The blunt answer, may it please the court, is very damned little."[38]

Kilpatrick also maintained that African Americans, unlike whites, failed to add to the economic growth of the United States. Blacks' deficiencies resulted from their incompetence, laziness, and stupidity, not from restrictions placed on them by segregation. "There are respected Negro teachers, lawyers, doctors, writers. Of course, there are," he conceded. "But in general terms, where is the Negro to be found? Why, sir, he is still carrying the hod. He is still digging the ditch. He is down at the gin mill shooting craps. He is lying limp in the middle of the sidewalk, yelling he is equal. The hell he is equal." Negroes had no right to demand full citizenship if they never proved their worth or contributed to America's prosperity. Whites, on the other hand, had every reason to discriminate against them and to resent their demands for racial equality. Kilpatrick attributed the failure of African Americans to compete in America and attain the wealth and position of whites to their inability to perform like the white race.[39]

Before the *Saturday Evening Post* could publish the article in a fall 1963 issue, the racial situation took a dramatic turn. On 15 September 1963, Birmingham Ku Klux Klansmen bombed the Sixteenth Street Baptist Church in the heart of the city's black neighborhood. The blast killed four girls and nearly tore apart the town again. At the *Post*'s New York offices, editor Thomas B. Congdon Jr. canceled the release of Kilpatrick's article. He explained to Kilpatrick that publishing such a shocking article would be in "bad taste, in the extreme, and, in fact, inflammatory." Eager to reduce the emotional outcry over the terrorist act, Kilpatrick accepted the *Post*'s position. Publishing the provocative essay would stimulate support for the pending civil rights bill. "Sound legislation simply cannot be enacted in such an atmosphere," he wrote in the *News Leader*. The editor waited for a more appropriate occasion to abuse African Americans.[40]

Right Place, Wrong Time

An oasis to condemn black culture seemed nowhere in sight. Kilpatrick's thirst for the preservation of legal segregation fell on more deaf ears across the country. In Washington, national leaders reacted to the events in Birmingham and the death of John F. Kennedy with a drive for more civil rights legislation. When an assassin killed Kennedy in late November, the new president, Lyndon B. Johnson, began to promote a sweeping civil rights package that would desegregate public facilities and enforce fair hiring practices in businesses to honor his predecessor. The civil rights

movement, additionally, emerged as the sleeper domestic issue in the upcoming 1964 presidential election, and a growing consensus that welcomed
racial reforms soon dominated Congress. The rising tide of civil rights did
not augur good news for racial conservatives.

Faced with congressional legislation, sit-ins, demonstrations, and the
collapse of massive resistance, Kilpatrick had already settled on a new formula of political action to prevent more integration. "I would work for the
election of conservative Presidents," he told *Newsweek*. Outraged at the
prospect of the end of Jim Crow, a group of the most diehard segregationists, including Kilpatrick, gathered in a hotel across from Capitol Hill and
calibrated how much they could do to put a right-leaning candidate in the
White House and crush the civil rights bill.[41]

One of the ringleaders of the determined segregationists was John C.
Satterfield, the former president of the American Bar Association. In 1963,
the fifty-nine-year-old Yazoo City, Mississippi, attorney served as legal
counsel for the Mississippi State Sovereignty Commission. Over the years,
he had filled many similar positions to expose and accost outside agitators
and Communists whom he believed presented a clear and present danger
to the South. During the fifties, he belonged to the Circuit Riders, a watch-
dog group within the Methodist Church that charged church organizations,
educators, and journalists with Communist subversion.[42]

By virtue of his extensive political and legal connections, between 1955
and 1956 Satterfield served as chief of the Mississippi Bar, which launched
him into higher office. From 1961 to 1962, he used his post at the ABA as
a mouthpiece for condemning the Supreme Court's aggrandizement of
power in the federal government. As president, he coordinated with states'
righters from across the nation. In Virginia, David John Mays and Kilpatrick
agreed to supply Satterfield with counsel and ghostwriters for his speeches.
Satterfield also conspired with the director of the Federal Bureau of Investigations, J. Edgar Hoover, to remove lawyers suspected of ties with Communists from the ABA—a plan that ultimately failed.[43]

The Mississippi lawyer resisted the civil rights movement on many
fronts. He maintained a membership in the Citizens' Council and established himself as a critic of the 1954 *Brown* ruling, which he regarded as judicial tyranny. In the midst of the 1962 desegregation crisis at the University
of Mississippi, Satterfield acted as Ross Barnett's personal attorney. Satterfield later labeled Kennedy's proposed civil rights package a preliminary for
"dictatorial control" over Americans and the business community and the
usurpation of states' rights. "What purports to be an act to 'equalize' civil

rights is in fact, but 10 per cent civil rights," he chastised, "*the rest is a grasp for Federal executive power.*"[44]

In June 1963, furious at the proposed civil rights measure, Satterfield and Erle E. Johnston Jr., head of the Mississippi State Sovereignty Commission, traveled to Washington, where James O. Eastland, Mississippi's archsegregationist senator, prepared a conclave of conservative minds. The Mississippians talked with a number of people concerned about the civil rights bill. Hugh White Jr., son of the former Mississippi governor and member of the Virginia Commission on Constitutional Government, participated in the forum, as did influential northern businessmen anxious about the possibility of federal interference in their employment practices. Johnston was delighted with the conference and later reported to Governor Ross Barnett that "we in the South now have new and important allies, who never before seemed seriously concerned with states['] rights or the federal government's determination to take over private enterprise."[45]

By July 1963, more meetings had spawned a lobby to arrest the passage of the Kennedy civil rights bill: the Coordinating Committee for Fundamental American Freedoms (CCFAF). Over the following year, the CCFAF became, according to the *Washington Post*, the "best-organized and best-financed lobby" against the legislation. The men at the early gatherings formed a coterie of leaders from diverse and powerful backgrounds. Satterfield arranged one unpublicized conference attended by William B. Barton, general counsel for the U.S. Chamber of Commerce; Harvey D. Williams, assistant director of the Department of Governmental Relations of the National Association of Real Estate Boards; Henry M. Shine Jr., legislative director of the National Association of Home Builders; and Page L. Ingraham, director of research for the Council of State Government.[46]

The Coordinating Committee also landed talented writers and thinkers to discredit the civil rights legislation without resorting to the sort of racial language that might diminish the group's respectability. William Loeb, the conservative publisher of New Hampshire's largest newspaper, the *Manchester Union Leader*, chaired the CCFAF. Kilpatrick took a break from editorial proclamations about the links between "Communists and Demonstrations" within the civil rights movement to become vice chairman. Loyd Wright, another former ABA president, joined the acronymic lobby, and Satterfield, who accepted a position as secretary-treasurer, oversaw the group's finances. Finally, John James Synon, founder of the Patrick Henry Club, the Richmond-based conservative publishing house, served as full-time director. Synon, along with Satterfield, managed the day-to-day operations of the CCFAF and kept it focused on ruining Congress's civil rights plans. Attacking civil rights and liberalism was more than a job for Synon; he took pleasure in it.[47]

John J. Synon was not a behind-the-scenes kind of lobbyist but an outspoken advocate for the causes he embraced. The labels "reactionary," "zealot," and "driven" described him best. Born in 1910 in Norfolk, the heart of Virginia's Southside, Synon absorbed the culture and the segregationist sectarianism of his homeland. He attended one of Virginia's ubiquitous military high schools but then had to forego college because of inadequate funds during the Depression. After World War II, he moved to California, where he left a shadowy record directing public relations campaigns for conservative politicians, including Governor Goodwin J. Knight, and the state's Industrial Accident Commission, which he allegedly used to help friends in the insurance business undercut competitors in state contracts. During Earl Warren's governorship of California, the oil industry paid Synon to malign Warren as a Communist sympathizer. In the Golden State, Synon participated in a new generation of professional campaign managers hired to find strategies to win votes in the huge, heterogeneous state, where several candidates often ran for one office and spent millions of dollars on advertisements.[48]

In the early sixties, Synon went to Washington, D.C., to make one last, defiant stand against desegregation with the help of Kilpatrick and other Virginia leaders. Calling someone like Synon a segregationist would be kind. He distributed works of scientific racism through the Patrick Henry Press and always took the most radical stances against civil rights. "If I'm going to lose in this battle I'm determined to go down with those who think as I do," he wrote Kilpatrick before his arrival. After the courts struck down Virginia's massive resistance laws, Synon believed that segregationists should retaliate by closing all of the public schools and relying on a private school system. "[W]ipe 'em out," he grumbled to another segregationist, and just "call me Apartheid." Synon quickly solidified his reputation as a conservative political advocate and also accepted missions that promoted the segregationist South's views.[49]

George Wallace employed Synon's services to plot his 1964 run for the presidency. In January 1963, Wallace held a private summit with some of the South's leading right-wingers, including Synon. There, Synon suggested that Wallace might win the presidency if an independent elector movement consisting of a third-party bloc could capture the South, create a stalemate in the Electoral College, and force the major parties' candidates to curry favor with southerners to win. The plan never materialized, but Synon's idea helped convince Wallace to seek the presidency.[50]

Beginning in August 1963, Synon, Kilpatrick, and the other members of the CCFAF created a mailing list designed to saturate certain congressional constituencies affected by the new civil rights law with literature defending the individual right to discriminate. The Coordinating Committee compiled the names of over 230,000 professionals and businessmen and distributed nearly four million pamphlets throughout the next year. Kilpatrick also arranged with the U.S. Press Association wire service to publish a weekly editorial espousing the committee's position against the bill and released CCFAF propaganda to about 100 newspapers across the nation. Additionally, he created a directory of 14,000 editors, city editors, and editorial page directors, to whom the CCFAF sent several anonymous articles and advertisements on the proposed bill. Dean Manion, the Indiana conservative pundit, used his television and radio broadcasts, carried by 325 stations that reached over one million people, to help the CCFAF wage its ideological war against the civil rights legislation as well. Although Kilpatrick kept his involvement in the CCFAF out of the News Leader's pages, the paper's management supported the lobby's work. James Lucier, Kilpatrick's associate editor, wrote circulars for the CCFAF and excoriated civil rights leaders in conservative journals. All kinds of people lent a hand to spreading the Coordinating Committee's gospel, including the John Birch Society; "We the People"; the American Bar Association, which assisted because of Satterfield and Wright's connections; and Buckley's National Review.[51]

William Buckley looked to Kilpatrick to make the case against the civil rights legislation. In mid-1963, Kilpatrick sent the right's foremost magazine a seven-page article that outlined the National Review's opposition to the bill. Writing to the journal's publisher, Buckley admitted that he felt "a considerable debt of gratitude to the Commission for permitting us to publish free of charge and without assigning them credit, the extensive analysis of the civil rights bill by Kilpatrick eighteen months ago." In late September 1963, Kilpatrick turned the CCG pamphlet Civil Rights and Legal Wrongs into a featured article for the National Review. He argued that the right to vote was not absolute and asserted that the new bill would give the president "the powers of a despot." Kennedy's legislation jeopardized corporate America's ability to manage its own affairs, undermined property rights, and forced people to abandon freedom of choice by restricting discrimination. With the destruction of the "citizen's right to discriminate," he pled, "the whole basis of individual liberty is destroyed." Kilpatrick complained mostly about Titles II, VI, and VII of the legislation—sections that, respectively, would make discrimination in public accommodations, in federally assisted programs, and in employment illegal. Even though he never advocated discriminating on the basis of race, he also never ruled it out. Such racial statements were conversation stoppers rather than conversation starters. The point of the article was to offer, or convey the urgent need to develop, an alternative to the constitutionally reckless approach of the federal government to end segregation. It was to suggest that the substitute for that chaotic approach and the least bad choice was to strangle the invigorative powers of the central state.[52]

The impending civil rights bill was a grave matter to segregationists, and it worsened a psychological imbalance for one of Kilpatrick's principle teachers in Richmond. Liberal dominance of the federal government, egalitarianism, and the welfare state so upset John Dana Wise, the *News Leader*'s former manager, that it became his undoing. More than anything, his defense of a rapidly vanishing way of life put him in turmoil. In the late 1950s, Wise had slipped into dark premonitions about liberalism and convinced himself that the left had perverted free enterprise, individual responsibility, and America writ large. In 1957, the paper forced him to retire because of his failing mental health. Wise succumbed more and more often to bouts of depression, often spurred by his growing disdain for the expansion of federal powers. He loathed Franklin Roosevelt, derided Harry Truman, and saw Dwight Eisenhower as a false conservative. In addition, his declining mental health further isolated him. Instead of getting help, Wise descended into despair and political paranoia. "He was a man eternally besieged," Kilpatrick lamented. It seemed that "[b]arbarians of one sort or another were always battering at his gates." In retirement, Wise suffered from heart attacks and blindness. He hated weakness, infirmity, and dependence on others. Weighted down by grim prospects, Wise still oozed protocol. One early November morning in 1963, the steely taskmaster who had introduced Kilpatrick to the seminal literature of conservatism, accoutered in his hunting raiment, loaded his favorite shotgun, and blew off the top of his head. The suicide stunned Kilpatrick. "This was an unforgettable man," he eulogized, "a vital spirit, dominant, towering, his passions constantly engaged." Kilpatrick's grief over Wise was soon eclipsed by a more serious uproar over the civil rights bill.[53]

Two weeks after Wise's death, Kilpatrick submitted "Crossroads in Dixie" to Buckley and nudged conservatives to find and elect acceptable Republicans to office. If the civil rights bill's opponents could not defeat it, then Americans could vote for people who would not betray the public's welfare in the future, would block further reforms, and keep civil rights sympathizers out of office. "Daily, cold winds blow from judicial chambers; the uncertainties of reapportionment and Negro registration have men talking to themselves," Kilpatrick cautioned. He trembled, "The [voting] rolls will expand with all the wrong sort of people, and this spells trouble." The right sort of people were "honest, decent, God-fearing, anti-Kennedy, [and] conservative." In December, he followed with another article, "The South Goes Back Up for Grabs," and griped that Kennedy's recent death gave Johnson tremendous political capital to pass the civil rights legislation. He believed that the assassination might have removed some of the animus that white southerners held for Kennedy and the Democrats. Much of the white South's anger at Kennedy and liberalism, however, resurfaced as the campaign of George Wallace swung into action.[54]

Only one person on the extreme right would run in the approaching 1964 presidential election—George C. Wallace, Alabama's governor. Wallace achieved notoriety in right-wing and segregationist camps for emphasizing his anti-Washington stance and using race in his speeches to manipulate his white audiences. In his 1963 inaugural, he gained attention for his cry for "segregation today, segregation tomorrow, segregation forever." Later that year, he secured a reputation as an opportunistic, posturing politician by standing in the way of federal authorities sent to desegregate the University of Alabama. Wallace, the former boxer, preferred a good offense to dancing around issues. He forced his way into the national spotlight by politicizing white racial fears inside and outside the South and by condemning civil rights, student, and antiwar protesters, the federal government, and intellectuals.[55]

Working from the segregationist arm of the Democratic Party, Wallace entered the 1964 race as an unlikely third candidate. Few doubted that Lyndon Johnson would easily win the party's delegates at the national convention. Wallace surprised many, nonetheless, when he performed well in the Wisconsin, Maryland, and Indiana primaries with rhetoric that stirred up white anger toward civil rights reform and warned voters about invasive government oversight of businesses to ensure fair hiring practices for minorities. Kilpatrick and the CCFAF synchronized efforts with Wallace's lacerating politics and blanketed several key states, like Maryland, Wisconsin, and Indiana, with personal letters to influential citizens, such as personnel directors, lawyers, city officials, and corporate executives. During Wallace's bid to win primaries, the committee also ran expensive full-page advertisements in local newspapers "to ride his coattails" and tap into whites' hostility to civil rights by associating the threat of lost jobs with racial reform. They targeted working-class ethnic neighborhoods in immigrant papers like the *Polish Daily Zgoda*, a Chicago-based tribune that circulated in Indiana and Wisconsin, and released ads through the National Confederation of American Ethnic Groups. The conservative *Chicago Tribune* published a series of CCFAF-funded articles between mid-February and early March 1964, including one by Yale law professor Robert H. Bork, who claimed the proposed legislation misinterpreted the Fourteenth Amendment and the Commerce Clause and would coerce individuals and strip states of their powers. Harnessing that white racial prejudice and anti-government sentiment was a delicate and tricky issue.[56]

The Alabama governor often espoused the desperation of the white South and opposed the Kennedy-Johnson civil rights bill too emphatically for many northern voters. After losing the Maryland primary, he told reporters, "If it hadn't been for the nigger bloc vote, we'd have won it all." Although the Coordinating Committee refrained from the strong racial language that often bellowed from Wallace, it discreetly circulated thousands of copies of pamphlets like *The New Fanatics*, which argued that blacks could not handle the responsibility of voting and citizenship. The CCFAF's distribution efforts helped win Wallace a significant white vote against the civil rights movement in a few state primaries. Wallace recognized the committee's contribution of time and effort, referenced CCFAF material as the best analysis of the civil rights bill's effects, and sometimes pulled from their publications in his campaign hustings. Although Wallace extended some of the CCFAF's ideas, it took more than words to run their propaganda war.[57]

The Coordinating Committee would not have existed without extensive financial support. The CCFAF outspent any other organization working to block the civil rights legislation. The committee turned to anyone who shared their resentment of the impending law for monetary assistance. The state sovereignty commissions in the South initially funded the CCFAF. The Mississippi State Sovereignty Commission first financed the committee publicly with nearly $25,000 from July to November 1963. The Mississippians secretly filtered money coming from private, often out-of-state, donors. The principal contributor to the CCFAF was Wickliffe Preston Draper, a wealthy textile manufacturer and blue-blooded New Englander, who channeled funds to a variety of academic and scientific endeavors to study and promote eugenics. Draper's endowment sustained the lobbying effort against the civil rights bill. From a New York bank account he transferred nearly $125,000 in personal stocks and cash to the Mississippi State Sovereignty Commission. The commission then deposited the money in the state treasury and later withdrew it to finance the Coordinating Committee. Draper's subsidy accounted for 84 percent of the committee's money and allowed it to operate continuously for a year.[58]

With ample financial resources at their disposal, the CCFAF started a focused rhetorical campaign to win congressmen to their viewpoint. John Synon orchestrated the lobby's principal tactic of avoiding southern congressmen and representatives from liberal states, like New York and Massachusetts. The CCFAF instead targeted politicians who had large white ethnic voter bases who might resent government efforts to enforce fair hiring practices at the expense of the white working class. Synon looked for politicians who felt less compelled to back civil rights legislation because of their small African American constituencies.[59]

The lobby's impact in nonsouthern areas astonished congressmen. After reading CCFAF material, Idahoans mailed 200 letters to Senator Frank Church urging him to oppose the legislation, and the Wisconsin Chamber of Commerce came out against the bill as well. A host of midwestern and western legislators, including Gordon Allott and Peter H. Dominick of Colorado, Len B. Jordan of Idaho, Carl Hayden of Arizona, Jack Miller of Iowa, Frank Carlson of Kansas, and Clinton P. Anderson of New Mexico, also felt the pressure of CCFAF publications via angry constituent letters about the Kennedy-Johnson civil rights law. The most infamous CCFAF advertisement, designed by Synon and titled "$100 Billion Blackjack," circulated in 225 newspapers in states where senators wavered in support for the bill. The hand of a socialist waving a club, a metaphor for the federal government, and promising to withhold funding and contracts from any business that would not comply with the proposed law was a powerful visual reminder of the law's effect. The CCFAF's southern Democratic congressional allies put additional demands on fellow representatives to resist the bill, but one nonsouthern senator would decide the fate of the Civil Rights Act.[60]

To stop the bill, the Coordinating Committee had to win the support of Everett Dirksen, the Republican leader of the Senate from Illinois. Dirksen, an articulate, smooth orator, enjoyed a reputation as a moderate who liked compromise and practical solutions. Liberal Democrats knew they needed his help to sway the Republican Party to approve the bill. Segregationists also understood Dirksen's importance and wanted him as an ally in their effort to filibuster the legislation.[61]

John Synon agitated Dirksen's Chicago voter base, which consisted of unionized, ethnic Poles, Italians, Irish, and Hungarians, who feared that blacks would take their jobs through the new legislation. Synon planned to pin Dirksen between his black and white constituencies. "The question is," Synon asked, "which is his softer side? Just where is his soft underbelly?" Careful to disassociate the committee from any racial bigotry, Synon misled reporters, "We are not interested in the racial aspects of this thing at all. I have pretty much a detached view of it."[62]

Dirksen soon found himself a target of the CCFAF's lobbying pressure through the Illinois-based National Association of Manufacturers' distribution of information to corporate leaders. The CCFAF took its pleas directly to the states' business leaders and ethnic voters. The committee's broadsides called the civil rights bill worse than any New Deal measures to regulate private industries, and their advertisements in major newspapers pointed out that certain stipulations in the bill would strip businessmen of their right to operate their companies without government supervision. Courtesy of the Virginia Commission on Constitutional Government, Kilpatrick and Mays released thousands of pamphlets in Illinois to remind Dirksen of the opposition to civil rights at home. With enough public uproar, the senator might even be persuaded to weaken the legislation with amendments. "As Republican Senate leader," Mays explained, "he is the key man" to convince.[63]

The Virginians did not limit their activities to Dirksen. Kilpatrick used the VACCG and his editorials to twist public opinion against the legislation based on constitutional principles and without resorting to explicit racism. In the *News Leader*, Kilpatrick likened the bill to a new form of slavery that turned businessmen into the involuntary servants of blacks and the federal government. He also warned his readers that the proposed act would lead to a federal government composed of activist judges, despotic presidents, and emotional lawmakers. Kilpatrick warned that unless "the country rouses from its torpor, knows anger, gets involved, acts, . . . the government will be the shepherd, and men but docile sheep." The ominous cover illustration of his 1964 CCG pamphlet *Civil Rights and Federal Powers* depicted the word "Constitution" clamped by a vise, and the preface reassured readers, "This Commission is not concerned with race relations as such; this is not our function." He instead asked: "Is the bill constitutional?" The answer was no. The pamphlet became popular among conservatives, and newspapers from all over the country requested portions of it for reprinting. Harry Byrd read the entire brochure into the *Congressional Record* to filibuster the civil rights legislation, but other Virginia politicians worked to change minds in Congress as well.[64]

At the request of Howard Smith, the U.S. Representative from Virginia's Southside and chair of the House Rules Committee, John Satterfield and John Synon ventured to Washington for off-the-record meetings with congressional leaders about the bill. Opponents of the measure decided to load the legislation with several provisions that would render it unacceptable and confusing. Smith concocted the idea of inserting Title VII, a condition that barred discrimination based on sex, to reduce the civil rights law's appeal. He hoped that tying civil rights to women's rights would generate enough unrest among congressmen to make the bill a ridiculous proposition. The CCG also used Smith as an insider to distribute their materials within Congress. Other congressmen contributed to the fight against the proposed law. Six members of the House Judiciary Committee, wrote the pamphlet *Unmasking the Civil Rights Bill*, which spooked readers about the effects of helping minorities. Creating a culture of inclusion overturned centuries of restricting blacks from public life and the workplace. The new Civil Rights Act, according to the pamphlet, would destroy "the very essence of life as it has been lived in this country since the adoption of the Constitution."[65]

Many of the South's chief segregationist politicians relied on CCG pamphlets to base their opposition to the bill. Georgia's Senator Richard Russell, who led the filibuster against the Civil Rights Act, claimed that James Kilpatrick's *Civil Rights and Legal Wrongs* offered the best available criticism of the legislation and repeated the editor's arguments on the Senate floor. "[N]o member of the Reconstruction Congress, no matter how radical, would have dared to present a proposal that would have given such vast governmental control over free enterprise in this country so as to commence the process of socialism," he bellowed. In the end, the CCFAF's nationwide disruption of the passage of the civil rights bill failed. The 1964 Civil Rights Act sailed through the Senate.[66]

Dismay gripped James Jackson Kilpatrick when the civil rights bill passed. By late June 1964, the *News Leader* editor conceded defeat. "I feel as helpless as a one-legged man in an ass-kicking contest," he wrote a fellow CCG commissioner. Businesses and society could no longer prohibit blacks and minorities from the workforce and public facilities despite the deficiencies and inequalities that Kilpatrick saw in African Americans. Most of the Senate ignored the CCFAF's warnings. Only a few amendments, like a ban on federal quotas for the hiring of minorities, found their way into the final version of the act. In July, the CCFAF disbanded.[67]

Committee members returned to their respective states to carry on local fights against desegregation. When the fight over the civil rights bill ended, the presidential nomination battle intensified. The right looked determined to field a candidate with solid conservative beliefs. Many white southerners hoped for someone far to the right of Lyndon Johnson on race.[68]

Arizona Republican senator Barry Goldwater's candidacy delighted conservatives because of his western libertarianism and commitment to individual liberty. His belief that government could not fix racism pleased white southerners. The Arizonan pledged "to preserve freedom" for all individuals, not to force integration on the unwilling, and his fear of a coercive government superseded any nominal commitment to racial equality. In 1960, he had explained in *The Conscience of a Conservative* that rights only mattered if *"incorporated into the law"* already. Government should enforce the existing laws that protected individual liberty, not create new statutes. Goldwater found the *Brown* decision to be morally correct, but, he pleaded, in the course of trying to rectify race problems, "let us . . . respect the orderly processes of the law. Any other course enthrones tyrants and dooms freedom." In other words, judicial activism and the national government's expansion remained greater concerns than segregation. The senator also claimed that the Fifteenth Amendment ensured blacks' right to vote and needed no further enforcement and that the Fourteenth Amendment left the states absolute control over their schools. His doubts about the justifications of the civil rights laws and rulings could have been written by James Kilpatrick.[69]

Kilpatrick thought that Barry Goldwater could best express the sentiments of the white South and without the divisive racial language that plagued segregationist demagogues. Goldwater eschewed the racist ranting of George Wallace. The Alabama governor had served as a "vehicle" for states' rights, a political tool, but in 1964, Kilpatrick compared him to a "bull-in-the-china-shop." Kilpatrick winced at the thought of Wallace and regularly damned him as an apostate. "Just as we were beginning to make some headway in impressing rational and intelligent people with the serious shortcomings of this Bill along came George Wallace," he wrote to a correspondent a year earlier. "This vain glorious young blockhead has just about undone everything that we have spent months trying to do. . . . We need thinking men, and God sends us George Wallace! It is enough to make a man lose his religion."[70]

Technique separated Kilpatrick from Wallace just as substance differentiated Wallace from Goldwater. Wallace's constituency was disproportionately white, rural, poorly educated, and blue-collar, as well as more racially bellicose than other whites, including those who favored Goldwater in 1964. His malign, populist sophistry exploited racial fears, conflicting with Kilpatrick's tonier segregationist language and repugnance for vicious race-baiters. Kilpatrick's segregationism was conservative, not populist, presented more elegantly, and argued on the basis of civil libertarianism, free enterprise, strict constitutionalism, and natural hierarchy. Kilpatrick, furthermore, regarded Wallace as an unwelcome and worrisome distraction from the conservative movement's cause. Kilpatrick's message was not that Wallace was necessarily wrong but that he would siphon off votes from Goldwater. The Virginia editor liked some of the Alabamian's cloys against big government and civil rights, but Wallace could split the white South's conservative bloc and ruin Goldwater nationally. Republicans simultaneously had to depreciate the governor, especially if Wallace might cost Goldwater the election, and untangle conservatism from the periphery of American politics. Kilpatrick and the conservative magisterium handled the difficult task.[71]

For nine years, the *National Review*'s William F. Buckley used his journal to build a conservative revolution by publishing an assortment of attitudes from the right. By 1963 and 1964, Buckley wanted to help lead conservatives in the takeover of the Republican Party as well. The association between his magazine and Barry Goldwater had developed recently. With the publication of *The Conscience of a Conservative*, Buckley had claimed the Goldwater movement for himself and set forth much of the senator's politics, albeit from an advisory position outside the campaign staff. Even before the July GOP National Convention, he began to rally Republicans for the Arizonan. In January 1963, he asked Kilpatrick to popularize Goldwater. Perhaps Kilpatrick could persuade the white South and the nation that Goldwater's stance rested on "something more than his laissez-faire position on the Negro problem." Kilpatrick could not wait to write for Buckley again and to shift the South into the Republican column. Drafting Goldwater for the presidency offered white southerners another means to combat civil rights reform without relying on racial appeals. "Honest to God," Kilpatrick assured Buckley, in "most of the South we do get away from that tedious issue [segregation]." From the fall of 1963 until November 1964,

Kilpatrick became the presenter for the *National Review*'s positions on civil rights and the presidential campaign.[72]

In spring 1964, Buckley concocted a short-lived scheme to whip up enthusiasm for Goldwater by recruiting Dwight Eisenhower to run as vice president, and he convinced Kilpatrick to write an article in support of the idea for the *National Review*. The former president might add credibility and experienced leadership to the White House. Kilpatrick saw no constitutional restraints blocking Eisenhower from the vice presidency. Buckley told the *National Review* staff that he wanted Kilpatrick "to give form to the new vision for America," an America, he hoped, led by President Goldwater. Energizing support for Goldwater among southern voters required little effort from Kilpatrick.[73]

Many whites in Deep South states flocked to Goldwater. The Arizonan stripped the term "conservative" from its historical links to eastern big businessmen and associated it with libertarians, anti-Communists, middle-class entrepreneurs, westerners, and southerners. Goldwater also wanted to limit the reach of the federal government and seemed unwilling to oppose segregation. As the 1964 presidential campaign approached, his views made him a natural choice for Kilpatrick and southern conservatives. The senator crafted his speeches for audiences in the South to fit with their customs and beliefs, particularly in regard to states' rights and segregation. He told one group of Georgia Republicans that the "Supreme Court is not the supreme law of the land." In a 1963 address, he abandoned the subject of race and said "that the time had come for all politicians to stop appealing for votes on the grounds of race, color, or creed." Kennedy's civil rights bill also alarmed Goldwater because it threatened property rights, denied freedom of association, and encouraged the federal government to spy on private enterprises.[74]

Goldwater reached that conclusion after consultation with a trusted Arizonan. When it came time to navigate thorny civil rights matters, Goldwater turned to one of Phoenix's best constitutional experts, William H. Rehnquist, who confirmed Goldwater's doubts about the civil rights bill. Goldwater then contacted another intellectual in conservative legal circles, Robert Bork, the future solicitor general and Supreme Court nominee, for a second opinion. Bork had already stated that the issue was "not whether racial prejudice or preference is a good thing but whether individual men ought to be free to deal and associate with whom they please for whatever reasons appeal to them." Bork was also on record for his opposition to the civil rights movement. After the 1963 Birmingham demonstrations, he sided with the white citizens against the Negro "mob coercing and disturbing other individuals in the exercise of their freedom." Any criticism of the white citizenry's brutal police tactics and racial discrimination was "unsurpassed ugliness."[75]

With an eighty-five-page brief supplied by Bork and constitutional arguments at the ready, Goldwater clarified his opposition to the civil rights legislation. On 18 June 1964, he read his most important speech before the Senate during the debate of the proposed law. Goldwater fought for local antidiscrimination laws in Arizona, but the new federal law, he feared, would establish a "police force of mammoth proportions." It would also encourage workers to inform on workers and businessmen on businessmen. "These, the Federal police force and an 'informer' psychology, are the hallmarks of the police state and landmarks in the destruction of a free society," he asserted. Kilpatrick believed that Goldwater's vote against the legislation won him a place "in that small rank of statesmen—Randolph, Calhoun . . . who have had the character . . . to stand up on principle alone."[76]

Putting Goldwater in the White House dovetailed with the goals of the now moribund CCFAF and could stall implementation of the new civil rights law that became effective just days before the Republican convention. When Goldwater accepted his party's nomination on 16 July 1964, conservatives had reason to celebrate. The junior senator from Arizona roused the Republican assembly to applause with a speech about protecting American freedoms and making the nation secure against Communism. "I would remind you that extremism in the defense of liberty—is—no—vice!" he stubbornly insisted. "And let me remind you also that moderation in the pursuit of justice is no virtue!" At last, here was a national politician who understood the right's disenchantment with the liberal consensus and supported a counterattack.[77]

The morning after the nomination address, Tom Stagg Jr., a young lawyer from Shreveport, Louisiana, and an up-and-coming operative within the Republican National Committee (RNC), strolled the halls of the convention hotel unable to keep the smile off his face. In his hands, he clutched a copy of Goldwater's approval for extremism in the defense of freedom. The conservative faction of the party had finally toppled the northeastern liberal Republicans, such as Nelson Rockefeller, and moderates, like Eisenhower and Nixon, and found a home in the Grand Old Party. As Stagg waited for a RNC meeting to begin, he kept repeating the words aloud: "extremism in the defense of liberty." "I sure like that," he muttered to himself. "I sure like that." Stagg, like Kilpatrick, represented a group of white southerners who had forsaken the Democratic Party and put their hopes in the Republicans to keep government small and to prevent federal intrusions into social customs. Since 1956, the Louisiana attorney had been working on a Republican project called "Operation Dixie" to establish viable state branches of the party throughout the South and build them from the grass roots. In the 1960 presidential election, Nixon horrified Stagg with his explicit acceptance of civil rights. A repeat of that civil rights plank, Stagg believed, would "kill the Republican Party in the South." With Goldwater's candidacy, Stagg knew he had an opportunity to reshape the party's line on the civil rights movement.[78]

Kilpatrick, conversely, had reservations about Goldwater's chances. At the convention, he recognized a volatile situation when the conservative wing vied with the liberals and moderates for control. His editorial "Fratricide in San Francisco" predicted civil war among Republicans. Goldwater's nomination presented another problem. The national press would label Goldwater a fanatic for his intolerance of liberal programs, his off-the-cuff comments about using nuclear weapons against Communists, and his speech on extremism. Kilpatrick listened to the senator's acceptance address from the press gallery but felt shock instead of the exultation that Stagg experienced. A Washington reporter next to him made a "thumb-and-finger pistol and fired it through his head," Kilpatrick recalled. "Goldwater was dead in that instant. All of us knew it." The *News Leader* editor believed that the Arizonan's only chance for victory in November depended on widespread appeal within the party.[79]

A successful Goldwater run for the presidency required a civil rights package that met with general approval among Republicans but also signaled a new trajectory for the party. The growing conservative faction within the Republican Party saw an opportunity to reject the liberal state that Lyndon Johnson envisioned, including egalitarian race relations. On civil rights, Goldwaterites renounced any commitments to reform. One Texas delegate explained what the senator's victory meant: "The South took the Mason-Dixon Line and shoved it right up to Canada." Because of Tom Stagg's longtime organization of Republicans in the South, he received the appointment to head the party's civil rights committee. Predicting Goldwater's nomination, Stagg hatched plans "to moderate the language" of a new civil rights plank and win "conservative Democrats" in the South.[80]

Just before the Republican convention, Stagg asked Kilpatrick for advice about writing the forthcoming civil rights plank because he admired the editor's ideas. Kilpatrick had become a hero to young southern

Republicans, and Stagg had followed him through columns and CCG literature for years. Stagg wanted Kilpatrick to comment on a progressive civil rights memo from moderates circulating within the Republican Party that indicated their acceptance of racial reform and that they would be seeking the black vote. Stagg opposed any pro–civil rights measures but wanted to avoid "unpalatable language relative to Civil Rights" that would offend the nonsouthern delegates. He also wanted the party to abandon any notions of winning African American votes. When Stagg first approached Kilpatrick about drafting the Republican's civil rights platform, the editor responded cagily. Kilpatrick perceived the civil rights booklet passed among Republican committee chairs as a spawning ground for bad policies, but he was noncommittal about helping to revise it. He urged Stagg to "work up, in advance of the Platform Committee meeting, a brief, reasoned, moderate and responsible plank to offer as an alternative to this appalling document." Stagg persisted and begged Kilpatrick to help formulate a more suitable civil rights plank. The editor replied that he might have time to meet with Stagg to prepare a platform during the days preceding nomination night at the convention. The two men never met, but Stagg used Kilpatrick's constitutional arguments on race laws "with Yankees" at the convention in the hopes that the new Republican line on civil rights would not "turn off southerners."[81]

After Goldwater's nomination, the civil rights plank became a hotbed of controversy. A number of people debated the language of the Republican's position on race. Martin Luther King Jr. contacted party officials about the platform's wording. Liberal Republicans and Goldwaterites also pitched ideas. Some Republicans wanted a repeal of the 1964 Civil Rights Act, and others hoped for an even more progressive agenda than Johnson had promised. As a result, the plank went through a series of drafts before Goldwater's supporters won, and the Republicans offered any pro–civil rights voters an uninspiring declaration. In 1960, the GOP's progressive civil rights plank had demanded the "vigorous enforcement" of civil rights laws and "the full use of the power, resources and leadership of the federal government to eliminate discrimination." The final version of the 1964 statement pledged "full and faithful execution" of the law, but a clause added to ensure "enforcement" failed in committee. The policy instead vowed to fight "inverse discrimination" with a prohibition on racial quotas in the future and a ban on federal courts compelling children to abandon neighborhood schools to enforce integration. The plank protected voting rights, but conservatives knew that their overseeing electoral procedures could ward

Negroes away from the polls and prevent a repeat of the sort of voter fraud they suspected in Nixon's 1960 loss to Kennedy. Hints of Kilpatrick's ideas showed in the party's policies. The platform ultimately stuck close to positions Kilpatrick liked; it endorsed an unobtrusive approach by government and the individual's responsibility to end discrimination. Discrimination "is a matter of the heart, conscience, and education," the plank proclaimed.[82]

After moderate Republicans lost their civil rights platform battle, the conservative wing of the party took an apathetic stance on racial liberalism. Kilpatrick translated the party's unexciting position on race into the *National Review*'s official recommendations for Goldwater's domestic agenda. In a special July 1964 edition, he offered keynotes for a mock State of the Union address that President Goldwater would deliver. Because the precarious issue of race threatened to undermine Goldwater's run, Kilpatrick searched for unifying themes that would solidify conservative support.

Goldwater and Kilpatrick differed in their views of African Americans. "[T]he Arizonan has been as consistent as [Hubert] Humphrey" in his opposition to racial discrimination, wrote Kilpatrick in an article for the *National Review* outlining how Goldwater should win the election. Determined to bring the Goldwater campaign and the white South's defense of race relations under one umbrella, the editor geared his proposals for the senator toward the right's common goals of freeing capital from regulation and defending private property, states' rights, and individual liberty. He framed his arguments in a way that permitted his contempt for racial progress within a set of conservative values. Through emphasizing fiscal restraint and federalism, the Arizonan could counteract reckless federal spending and the new civil rights legislation. Kilpatrick encouraged Goldwater to promise to enforce the Civil Rights Act only with "moral suasion" and "State [rather than federal] regulation" and never by force and arbitration. Any infringement on privacy, furthermore, disrupted the vision of the founding fathers. "The right to own, and possess, and manage property is vital" to the freedom of Americans, wrote Kilpatrick. Instead of talking about race explicitly, he advised Goldwater to focus on his commitment to respecting state sovereignty to limit socialistic welfare and civil rights programs. Federal intervention in social problems had denied states their power and reduced them to "merely eunuchs" pitifully orbiting "a federal sun." Reinvigorating states' rights could check the infringement of the government and restore a constitutional balance that would please the nation's founders. Kilpatrick also omitted racist language from his article to diminish Goldwater's scary image. In not mentioning white supremacy,

Kilpatrick's article stayed within the limits of acceptable rhetoric about race that Goldwater and the magazine hoped to convey.[83]

Most of the *National Review*'s 60,000 readers loved Kilpatrick's pitch for the Goldwater campaign, particularly his positions on race. A survey found that 87 percent of subscribers approved of Kilpatrick and the magazine's stance on civil rights. Buckley rewarded Kilpatrick's salesmanship by elevating him to the associate editorship of the journal. Now they waited for Goldwater to implement their ideas.[84]

Kilpatrick and the *National Review* trusted that President Goldwater would not enforce certain provisions of the Civil Rights Act and expand the powers of the federal government. After all, in *Conscience of a Conservative*, Kilpatrick pointed out, Goldwater said, "My aim is not to pass laws, but to repeal them." During his campaign, the senator implemented some of Kilpatrick's suggestions. In 1960, Kilpatrick had berated LBJ as a "counterfeit confederate," a hypocrite who used civil rights to win black votes despite an older record as a segregationist. The Arizonan repeated the Richmond editor's hyperbole and questioned Johnson's sincerity about civil rights reform. Even though Goldwater eventually endorsed the 1964 Civil Rights Act, only because the president must execute the law, he said that the government could not provide a "lasting solution" to the problem of discrimination but moral suasion might work. He also avoided the subject of race when he made his case against the new civil rights law by defending private property rights and corporations against the encroachment of the federal government. Erasing race from the Republican's political language became a new priority. Goldwater often ignored topics that would harm Johnson's chances if they involved racial matters, and his campaign rhetoric knew boundaries. The urban race riots that wracked several cities during the summer and fall of 1964 received little comment from him. White voters in the South liked Goldwater because of his silence on race. He neither reminded them of his NAACP credentials nor called on them to address blacks' grievances to defer federal intervention.[85]

Goldwater distanced himself from race, but his supporters knew to conflate his racial moderation with debasing civil rights. Even though Goldwater the candidate rarely commented on the new civil rights act and racial unrest, his campaigners did. On the radio, Strom Thurmond announced, "A vote for Barry Goldwater is a vote to end judicial tyranny." John Birch Society members simply declared, "JOHNSON IS A NIGGER LOVER," on a sign in South Carolina. The RNC marshaled race with great effect in the South, where many whites blamed the despised new desegregation law on the

Democrats. Goldwaterites often saturated southern voting districts with brochures depicting African Americans negatively. The RNC also ran Goldwater commercials featuring black youths rampaging through northern streets and then asked viewers if their families and property would be safe with Johnson in the White House. Buckley predicted that civil rights protests and Negro violence would ignite "the now all but inflamed resistance of the white population at large." Critical of exciting racially reactionary passions, Goldwater trusted the conscience of the American people more than an incendiary campaign.[86]

Buckley and Kilpatrick's recruitment of Americans to Goldwater backfired. In November, Johnson handed his opponent a crushing defeat. The senator won only six states. One exit poll, reproduced in *Look* magazine, found that fewer than three million of Goldwater's nearly twenty-seven million supporters expressed enthusiasm about the candidate. Most voted for him out of party loyalty. In the North, the Arizonan faired poorly and could not stir enough white ethnic voters to divorce them from the Democrats. "White Backlash Doesn't Develop," noted the *New York Times*. Only Alabama, Mississippi, South Carolina, Louisiana, and Georgia defected from the Democrats in favor of Goldwater.[87]

Kilpatrick accepted the election results stoically. The Goldwater campaign, he later told readers in a syndicated column, "was downhill all the way, but by God, it was glorious." In spite of the loss, as the Goldwater supporters' chant went, "In our hearts we knew we were right." Although he attempted to tie the future of segregation to the outcome of a presidential contest and stumbled, Kilpatrick tried to associate national conservative values with the southern way of life and reaffirmed his belief that conservatism could persevere in America. The day after the election, he appeared to take Goldwater's defeat in stride. The right got "clobbered," he wrote in the *News Leader*, but "the conservative political philosophy has lost none of its vitality." Less than two years after the defeat, he anticipated the recrudescence of conservatism in American politics. "In a nation that is beginning to ache for a return to law and order, for a renewed respect for property rights, and for a greater measure of personal freedom," he foresaw, "the time for these ideas moves steadily toward the striking hour." In 1968, the GOP would take back the White House.[88]

Nearly a decade earlier, the conservative movement looked fragmented and rudderless as the liberal state inflicted *Brown* and other Court rulings on the nation for the protection of individual rights. The 1960s also began with a rebirth for civil rights activism, yet by 1964, conservatives mustered and controlled a major political party. The election squelched the Republican Party's fortunes in the short term but pointed the way toward new opportunities. Johnson's victory left open the possibility of conservative mobilization, and the 1964 election showed the potential for a Republican sweep of the white South. With more skill than Goldwater summoned, conservatives might finesse racial politics without perpetuating racism and intolerance to snare a national audience.

As for James J. Kilpatrick, he achieved some fame for his involvement in the Goldwater campaign,. With the senator's defeat, one chapter of Kilpatrick's life would close and another would open. His prominence on the right only increased as he started a new phase of his career as a national political commentator. By the late sixties and seventies, some saw calibration in his racial politics, and a national audience seemed more ready to hear him. His greatest victory in shaping the language of race, ironically, would come after the civil rights revolution occurred, at a time more amenable to his conservative beliefs.

In the early 1960s, Kilpatrick drew a line in the sand against the civil rights movement, asserting that the republic would be irreparably harmed if the federal government arrogated to itself the powers necessary to dismantle segregation. In 1963, Kilpatrick assessed conservatism's situation: Maybe one day, "as Americans outside the South discover for themselves some of the problems of living with massive numbers of Negroes," the right's ideas and convictions about the role of government would be more politically fashionable. "In my blue moments," he moped, "I see nothing ahead for this country but the decline that inevitably awaits those who will not learn the history of mankind." The conservative defeat in 1964 paralleled the death throes of Jim Crow and black disfranchisement but was also instructive for Kilpatrick. As the battle for men and women's minds continued, he had to stamp out tinges of racial insensitivity if he, and others on the right, hoped to gain national, not just regional, influence.[89]

FIVE

Newspeak

It's a beautiful thing, the destruction of words.
—GEORGE ORWELL, *1984* (1949)

"I find myself in a peculiar limbo just now, unwilling to identify myself with the total segregationists in their supposed hell, and twice as unwilling to identify myself with the gauzy liberals in their phony heaven," James Kilpatrick speculated about his own beliefs. By March 1961, he had left the familiarity and security of segregation for the unknown. His uncertainty came after a year of heightened civil rights activity. Brandishing old charges and clinging to segregation laws as ways to thwart Negro advancements had simply not worked. Specifically, he wrestled with the imminent downfall of Jim Crow. Wallowing in confusion but not despair, he hoped for "some sort of social and political solution that will see the Negroes treated fairly as individuals, but will stop short of surrendering our institutions to a race of people unqualified to administer them." As a result, Kilpatrick in the early 1960s admitted frustrations but also gradually yielded to desegregation. The longer he fumbled for answers, he confessed, "the more persuaded I am that we have to get rid of a few of the old stereotypes we have lived by, and that we have to begin some gradual adaptation to a genuinely new order of things." By softening his earlier bold arguments and dropping racial segregation entirely, Kilpatrick started to shift positions. What his insecurities prevented him from appreciating was that lucrative opportunities and distinguished appointments still existed for segregationists. Even notoriety carried its own celebrity.[1]

Eracism

No sure outcome surfaced amid the swirling ambiguities opened by the civil rights struggle. Kilpatrick, meanwhile, collected his thoughts and

143

prepared a defense. Despite any nagging concerns about fair treatment for blacks, he quickly tried to pull the region back to its cultural roots and re-assured southerners, in unequivocal terms, that white civilization would not only endure but prevail. In October 1962, in the aftermath of the riot at the University of Mississippi, a 220-page, dense primer called *The Southern Case for School Segregation*, featuring on the front cover two squares—one black and one white—and on the back a picture of James Jackson Kilpat-rick paused at his typewriter, found its way to bookstores. At a time when activists reinvented the region's social order at breakneck speed, Kilpatrick rejected competing dreams of the South and explained the civil rights revo-lution in a way that affirmed whites' right to rule. Claims to that authority were fraught with political import, since one who had the ability to define the South and interpret its past also held the power to outline the region's economy, culture, and politics. Kilpatrick's vision of the South's tomorrow began in the classical past.

Enamored with the ancient Greeks, Kilpatrick portrayed the segrega-tionist cause as a drama worthy of Thucydides. Like the Athenians, a people of culture, philosophy, democracy, and local self-government, the white South could win a protracted ideological war against latter-day Spartans who centralized power, restricted the rights of the individual, and broke down segregation. Kilpatrick predicted a long, drawn out battle. The "revo-lution so many Northerners jubilantly anticipated in *Brown*," he observed, "is not to be a two-day *coup d'état*, but a thirty-year Peloponnesian War."[2]

Among the many attributes of regional identity Kilpatrick called upon to defend the southern way of life were traditionalism, agrarianism, respect for private property, and resistance to change. Limited government and liv-ing with the Confederacy's defeat continued the list. While fighting over-whelming odds came naturally to many southerners, as it was their legacy, tolerating an intrusive federal government did not. Kilpatrick asserted that southerners "do not *like* authority, especially needless, lint-picking, petty authority, and a broody pessimism constantly evokes the apprehension that government, if given half a chance, will put a fast one over on the people."[3]

White southerners guarded few traits more closely than their attach-ment to segregation, or what Kilpatrick called the "consciousness of the Negro." Racial tensions permeated life in the South. He described it as "a subconscious recognition that ours are separate races, separate worlds." The importance of race concluded his discussion of southern characteris-tics. Defining southern distinctiveness, however, distracted from the book's true purpose: to displace responsibility for the region's racial problems onto the people trying to reform it. To that end, Kilpatrick worked simultaneously to redefine segregationist arguments and to question the purity of civil rights activists. Rabid segregationists like those associated with Kilpatrick, expressed a segregation of fear and often charged outside agitators, Communists, and unruly blacks with disturbing the racial order. Aside from the usual legal arguments that he employed against the judiciary's abuse of power, Kilpatrick did not single out the Supreme Court or the federal government as causes for the region's racial turmoil. He blamed African Americans for segregation and inequality.[4]

According to Kilpatrick, racial separation existed naturally because Negroes could not compete with whites. In the opening chapter, "The Evidence," Kilpatrick interjected, placed responsibility for securing black political and economic progress with African Americans. Since blacks and their allies succeeded in ending many race-based laws, let them prove their equality as a race. On that criterion, Kilpatrick argued, blacks failed. He insisted on a cultural condescension: "[I]n terms of enduring values . . . in terms of values that last, and mean something, and excite universal admiration and respect, what has man gained from the history of the Negro race? The answer, alas, is 'virtually nothing.' From the dawn of civilization to the middle of the twentieth century, the Negro race, as a race, has contributed no more than a few grains of sand to the enduring monuments of mankind." Black culture lagged behind Western civilization. To Kilpatrick, no contrary evidence existed. If African Americans deserved consideration as equals, he asked, "What library houses the works of a Nubian Thucydides? Who was the Senegalese Cicero?" To diverge from this line of reasoning would have been to acknowledge that deep social problems, not black inferiority, were responsible for Negro underperformance.[5]

Kilpatrick's summary of the "evidence" included a wide-ranging assault on the intelligence, resourcefulness, and morality of blacks. He located the crisis of the African American community squarely in their homes. The decline of the black family as a functional unit of society made African Americans a menace to the natural order. As a race, Negroes tested low on standardized tests and had high rates of illegitimate births and venereal diseases. Hundreds of years of cultural and moral unfitness left African Americans in a poor position to receive equal consideration with whites. Insisting on integration only frustrated blacks and angered whites. "Why is this so?" Kilpatrick posited. "The answer, in blunt speech, is that the Negro race . . . has not earned equality." Blaming segregationists for their plight, he snidely claimed, merely provided blacks with a "crutch, the piteous and finally pathetic defense of Negrophiles unable or unwilling to face reality. In other times and other places, sturdy, creative, and self-reliant minorities have carved out their own destiny; they have compelled acceptance on their own merit; they have demonstrated those qualities of leadership and resourcefulness and disciplined ambition that in the end cannot ever be denied. But the Negro race, as a race, has done none of this."[6]

Neither simply the desire to have the same status as whites nor the elimination of a few laws created true equality. Blacks had to demonstrate their worth and merit through self-respect and hard work. "Why are we treated as second-class citizens?" Kilpatrick asked rhetorically for blacks. "Because all too often that is what we are." The "Negro race, as a race," he asserted, "plainly is not equal to the white race." Despite Kilpatrick's claim to the contrary, the black freedom struggle, steeped in the language of Holy Scripture and the Declaration of Independence, had offered the formula for equality in modern America.[7]

Perhaps Kilpatrick needed some secondhand science to steady his arguments about blacks' supposed deficiencies. African Americans faced an uphill battle to prove their capabilities, and he had the studies of leading scientific racists to discredit them. Works by Audrey M. Shuey, Henry E. Garrett, Carleton Putnam, Frank C. J. McGurk, and Nathaniel Weyl countered the scholarship of antiracist intellectuals and anthropologists like Ashley Montague, Franz Boas, and Gunnar Myrdal who rejected fixed racial categories. Whereas Kilpatrick praised white southerners for their conservative instincts, Myrdal took them to task for their inability to recognize the rights of blacks in a nation founded on principles of liberty and equality. The Virginia editor lumped Myrdal's claims into a jumble of "specious and shabby rationalizations." Other conservatives criticized the new anthropology as well. William F. Buckley questioned Myrdal's expertise on race relations and referred to him as "Dr. Gunnar Twistmaul." David Lawrence cited numerous reports on black illegitimate birthrates as grounds for stopping integration.[8]

The Southern Case for School Segregation read clumsily on biology and anthropology as the means to prove the genetic inferiority of Negroes. As a political journalist uncomfortable with scientific debates, Kilpatrick relied more on his experiences with blacks and cultural comparisons. In the South, racial separation began "in the cradle," he observed, not in inherent, biological differences. Scientific racism, however, depended on the genetic inadequacy of the black race made observable through empirical data. Environment and culture played only minor roles in the performance of blacks and whites. Kilpatrick's incorporation of racist social science forced him into an awkward position. After using Shuey, Putnam, and others, he announced that segregationists "have regularly overestimated the factors of heredity and underestimated the factors of environment." He dismissed the debate as "largely irrelevant" because, "whether these characteristics are inherited or acquired, they *are*." Despite his vacillation on the validity of blacks' genetic inferiority, Kilpatrick privately subscribed to the teachings of scientific racism and saw animalistic qualities in African Americans. Less than a year earlier, he had told a correspondent that he carried a pistol with him when he walked his Richmond neighborhood at night to protect himself from "black ape[s]."[9]

Equivocating on racial differences measured by IQ and brain size suited a writer who admitted no scientific background. If the condition of black inferiority was inherent, he saw "nothing but disorder . . . in risking an accelerated intermingling of blood lines." If environmentally manufactured, integration put blacks, on average, in classroom settings beyond their intelligence level, and most whites would not let their children be "guinea pigs for any man's social experiment."[10]

Kilpatrick incorporated scientific racism into his argument to criticize the social science introduced by integrationists in the *Brown* case. If he could demonstrate that liberal anthropology produced a bad Court ruling, then maybe a review of that jurisprudence could create a different outcome without integration. Kilpatrick, however, made an extraneous point. The Supreme Court struck down segregation because of its harmful effects, not to prove the intellectual and moral equality of the races.[11]

None of Kilpatrick's ambiguity about intrinsic versus acquired black inferiority satisfied the segregationists' other popular writer, Carleton Putnam. Putnam, a native of New York whose airline merged with Delta Air Lines in 1953, disagreed with Kilpatrick's line of thinking "that the Constitution could save [the South]—that states' rights was its best defense." The airline executive–turned-author thought that constitutional arguments helped little and pointed instead to cognitive and biological differences between the races. Kilpatrick, who looked for a way forward rather than back to the eugenicist approach of the early twentieth century, chafed at Putnam's stress on inherent black inferiority over states' rights.[12]

Reworking segregationist arguments consumed Kilpatrick for years. With Mississippi friend Robert Patterson of the Citizens' Council, Kilpatrick planned a way to present the segregationist South's case in an effective manner that stopped short of citing eugenics but demonstrated a cultural and intellectual gulf between the races. "I think your idea of emphasizing the 'difference' instead of the 'inferiority' of the Negro race is absolutely sound," he told Patterson in 1960. Anti-integrationists needed to learn a new language to express their position. The issue was phrasing, not culture versus genetics. "Like yourself," Kilpatrick wrote his collaborator, "I believe the Negro race is inferior, and I don't see how any person who weighs the evidence objectively could come to any other conclusion. Be that as it may, the word 'inferior' is semantically bad. It goes with 'white supremacy,' which is another phrase difficult to manage in a public opinion struggle. By dwelling upon the 'difference' between the races, we can establish the case for inferiority without involving ourselves directly in a value judgment."[13] Kilpatrick meant that segregationists could let people draw conclusions about blacks after he showed them how functionally and culturally superior whites were to African Americans. Once consigned to worthlessness without recourse to genetic proof, blacks would be seen as the agents of wrongdoing through their perceived immorality, underachievement, and ignorance. If Martin Luther King Jr. wanted America to judge his children "by the content of their character," as he urged in his address at the 1963 March on Washington, Kilpatrick did too.

The segregationist writer flung the arguments of civil rights activists back in their faces. Kilpatrick put the task of creating equality and progress onto blacks and forced them to fulfill the American Dream without unfair advantages. The individual freedom to rise would determine whether Negroes could compete in an open society. If blacks lived "in terms of Western values of maturity and achievement," Kilpatrick conjectured, equality would result. In a competitive nation like America, the black race had to "develop the talents that command respect in the market place." Southerners could give the impression that they allowed blacks the freedom to advance in mainstream society while whites maintained some segregation in other aspects of their lives. "The only approach I know of is to do everything within our power, as individuals, simultaneously to preserve an essential separation of the races in certain key areas," Kilpatrick told a fellow segregationist, "and to strive in any way to see that the Negro truly is given an equal opportunity to prove himself."[14]

Since segregation restricted the freedom to compete, Kilpatrick accepted its death. Toward the end of *The Southern Case for School Segregation*, readers received a disclaimer from the author: "As a creature of the law, racial segregation in the United States is dead." Interposition, massive resistance, and segregation laws failed to halt changes in the South's racial order. "Many staunch Southerners declaring themselves unwilling to sur-render," Kilpatrick conceded, "do not realize that as a matter of law, the war is over." With segregation's demise, however, he left blacks with no excuses for their inability to gain wealth and position in society. By disguis-ing racial discrimination in the language of the free market, merit-based advancement, and cultural achievement, Kilpatrick accommodated himself to discussions of civil rights in a post-*Brown* era that would no longer tol-erate arguments based on scientific racism and genetics. Years before the 1964 and 1965 Civil Rights Acts obliterated states' rights as a check against civil rights reforms, Kilpatrick had already found a new way to oppose ra-cial progress.[15]

The Southern Case for School Segregation swapped older arguments for segregation guaranteed by race-specific laws and laced with scientific rac-ism for an attack on Negroes' character and merit. Kilpatrick dared blacks to succeed. In his new scheme, he tried to make African Americans their own worst enemy and planted an obstruction to black progress that he deemed fairer than segregation. "Jim Crow is dead, but the legal shot that felled him also put Massa in the cold, cold ground," he concluded. "The paternalism of generations is vanishing year by year, to be replaced by a healthy skepticism: The Negro says he's the white man's equal; *show me*." Kilpatrick hoped that "the separation of the races" would voluntarily last "for years to come," especially in schools, private clubs, hotels, Protestant churches, "in many fields of employment," and "in professional associa-tions." Kilpatrick came to realize that the South's best "case" to keep blacks in their place no longer required legal segregation. With Jim Crow gone, de facto segregation and occasional reminders of black cultural, intellectual, and economic inferiority would do.[16]

Mixed reviews greeted Kilpatrick's book. Many liberals regarded the work as a repetition of his earlier segregationist views and scolded him. Southern historian George Brown Tindall pointed out several inconsisten-cies, including Kilpatrick's simultaneous appeal for prolonged separation of the races and concession that segregation died. The editor's calls for white southerners to acknowledge change and give Negroes a chance to compete in society gave a few integrationists hope, however. Harry Golden, the lib-eral editor and gadfly of Charlotte, North Carolina's *Carolina Israelite* and longtime friend of Kilpatrick believed that he had extended an invitation to blacks that "exudes warmth, friendship, and affection." A reviewer for Washington's *Sunday Star* "would not want to stand up and be counted among Mr. Kilpatrick's followers in philosophy, but would be the first to congratulate him as an able spokesman for that philosophy." Though shunned by much of the mainstream press, the book received a positive reception in conservative circles. The *National Review*'s Brent Bozell saw that by offering whites an alternative to the older insistence on black genetic inferiority, Kilpatrick's ideas were a way to avoid racial strife.[17]

Kilpatrick's latest attempt to advance the segregationist cause had not originated from any personal enthusiasm for the subject. In 1961, the New York publisher Crowell-Collier had asked the Richmond editor to write an apology for Jim Crow. Crowell-Collier instructed him to present the white South's point of view as bald contempt for the civil rights movement. "The editors did not want a balanced treatment of the subject; they wanted a lawyer's brief. I was not urged to be 'fair' or impartial," Kilpatrick later told Harvard law professor Randall Kennedy. "My instructions were to do what any lawyer would do—to emphasize the evidence on one side and to rebut or ignore evidence on the other." Although the publisher promised him a large printing with distribution to college bookstores, Kilpatrick wrote more out of obligation as a prominent segregationist. "I am not at all anxious to do the book," he admitted to Henry Regnery. "Between you and me, I am so sick of this whole subject I wish I never had to write another line about it." Kilpatrick signed a contract with Crowell-Collier because they let him write freely about his racial views and because he wanted the money. He confided to Regnery that he wrote the *Sovereign States* "out of love; I'm writing this Crowell paperback largely for money. It do make a difference."[18]

The *News Leader* editor took little pleasure or pride in the book. He wrote it for a commission, and it sold too poorly to make it worthwhile. Kilpatrick also grew concerned that writing too many books on race relations would stunt his career's growth. As early as 1958, he worried about being branded a reactionary segregationist. "Sometimes you get the feeling it is like the story of the little boy who kept hollering 'Wolf, wolf!'" he wrote one man. "[My] fear has been that if I wrote too constantly about the school segregation issue, pretty soon nobody would read my editorials. They would say, 'There is Kilpatrick harping on segregation again,' and just skip it." For all his popularity among conservatives, Kilpatrick made as many enemies. William Baggs of the *Miami News* regarded him as "a grits-eating Westbrook Pegler" and "an amusing antique." In the early postwar years, conservatives and Kilpatrick had image problems. In the eyes of many Americans, they seemed out of touch, a rear guard tilting haphazardly against the modern world. Critics tarred them as colorless cranks who opposed change on principle. *Nashville Tennessean* editor John Seigenthaler summarized Kilpatrick's creed: " Nothing has happened in the past 100 years, and if it has, it shouldn't have." When interviewed by *Time* about the release of the *Southern Case for School Segregation*, Kilpatrick called the discussion of integration and race tiring. "I'm sure this book is my last effort on the subject—at least for a long while," he said. "Frankly, the subject of segregation palls." Maybe the time had come for him to find another project.[19]

Despite the *Southern Case for School Segregation*'s failure to sell and his concerns about his future, some people took James J. Kilpatrick seriously. The editor had a reputation as a sterling writer and a dedicated conservative with a rational, mostly unemotional approach to race problems. His books, articles, and editorials grabbed the interest of publishers, who wondered if he could handle a nationally syndicated column. In the 1950s and 1960s, news syndicates could pick and choose from a long list of liberal columnists, but a shortage of skilled writers on the right existed. William F. Buckley, David Lawrence, George Sokolsky, Henry Hazlitt, and Raymond Moley were the exceptions. In 1960, Barry Goldwater's column "How Do You Stand, Sir?" appeared in the *Los Angeles Times*. Maybe Kilpatrick could break into a syndicate when demand for conservative points of view ran high. His connections with Buckley, Russell Kirk, Lawrence, and Regnery made him a widely known personality in the conservative movement, but Kilpatrick still regarded himself as a provincial editor and a "fairly substantial frog in a small puddle." He might have remained obscure forever if not for his eventual success as a nationally syndicated columnist.[20]

In August 1964, Kilpatrick's column, "A Conservative View," debuted for *Newsday*, a Long Island daily newspaper that wanted a right-leaning political spokesman to balance the half dozen liberals on its roster of syndicated columnists. Harry Guggenheim, heir of mining magnate Daniel Guggenheim, owned *Newsday* and attracted big-name writers to his tabloid newspaper. Thomas Dorsey, chief of public relations for *Newsday*, flew down to Richmond for a meeting with the *News Leader* editor about a contract. Dorsey's personal touch and promise of a $5,000 one-year deal lured Kilpatrick into syndication and let him keep his editor's job. *Newsday* gave Kilpatrick a mandate "to present to a national audience the reasoned and calm point of view of a conservative white Southerner." What that meant practically was Kilpatrick should address racial problems without recourse to explicit arguments about black inferiority. His writing for the *News Leader* had catered to Tidewater dons and Southside hotheads. *Newsday* required a more sensitive style from Kilpatrick that it could market to its suburban New York audience. Dorsey knew Kilpatrick's views on race and did not want him to write columns that advocated segregation. "I was perfectly aware that I had the reputation in some quarters as an old fire-eating segregationist, one of the fathers of interposition and massive resistance and so on," Kilpatrick said. "I didn't have any idea of writing columns that would embarrass Newsday as being the rabid outpourings of a southern segregationist." Changing his stance on African Americans became a priority but unfolded through trial and error.[21]

The civil rights movement afforded Kilpatrick little time to finesse his image. After he spent a few months covering the Goldwater campaign and political news, major protests erupted in the heart of the Alabama Black Belt. In winter 1965, demonstrations and voter registration drives drew hundreds of civil rights activists to Selma, a town in Dallas County west of Montgomery. After Martin Luther King arrived, he organized a protest march from Selma to Montgomery that attracted media attention to the oppression of Alabama blacks. The first attempt to carry out King's plan ended in bloodshed when state troopers and a sheriff's posse beat marchers as they left city limits. A second effort, however, succeeded, and activists later celebrated with speeches on the steps of the state capitol. Selma gave Kilpatrick an opportunity to show some maturity as a thoughtful observer of southern race relations.

After the march, many protesters returned to Selma by automobile. Viola Liuzzo, a white housewife from Detroit, drove a carload of activists to Selma. Along the highway from Montgomery to Selma, Ku Klux Klansmen chased her car, fired shots into the driver's window, and killed Liuzzo. The murder outraged Americans, and *Newsday* expected an intelligent response from their southern opinion maker. Kilpatrick originally filed a column in which he expressed his fear that Liuzzo's slaying would prompt Congress to pass the new voting rights bill. In years past, he had responded to the deaths of civil rights figures in similar fashion. When a white supremacist killed Mississippi's NAACP leader Medgar Evers in June 1963, Kilpatrick's paranoia conjured a sinister plot since "the Negro-Liberal leadership can be relied upon to wring every possible advantage from it." Tom Dorsey stopped the publication of the feature on Liuzzo because, like Kilpatrick's commentary on Evers, it showed no compassion. Eager to please his new employer and sell his column, Kilpatrick retracted it for one that focused on the injury to white businesses caused by a boycott that King called in Montgomery.[22]

As usual, Kilpatrick's *News Leader* editorials contained the caustic commentary enjoyed by his Richmond audience. After Martin Luther King traveled to Selma to help lead the movement, Kilpatrick resorted to some old tactics and name-calling. He portrayed King as a glory-hungry, ambitious troublemaker with a self-serving interest in disturbing communities and unleashing mayhem. During the subsequent march to Montgomery, Kilpatrick described the protesters as "local followers and a gaggle of a carpetbag parson on a little hike." According to the editor, King intended to stir up "anarchy."[23]

Newsday would not print such strident comments about King, and Kilpatrick tailored his writing to reduce pejorative descriptions of civil rights leaders and their demonstrations. In many of his old *News Leader* editorials and debates, Kilpatrick addressed Martin Luther King with contempt or in the third person. A long-standing rule at the *News Leader* forbade addressing black ministers with the respectful title "Reverend." By 1965, however, Kilpatrick referred to King as "Doctor" in syndication. As the columnist exhorted to one reader, "[In] my own case, as a southern conservative, any failure on my part to use the honorary title for King would immediately be interpreted as evidence of the grossest anti-Negro prejudice."[24]

Racial integration remained a tricky subject as well. "I have hesitated to get it [integration] into my syndicated column," Kilpatrick explained. "If I write on the theme at all," he clarified, "it probably would be from a constitutional standpoint." When unable to remain silent on desegregation, he stayed away from hereditary science and stuck to arguments about blacks' character and merit. In a 1965 "A Conservative View" column, he complained that the federal government's efforts to equalize the races would "treat the Negro like a white man. God knows his race has done little enough to deserve a fate so difficult and demanding. This is to expect of the Negro . . . work; and then self-restraint; obedience to the law; respect for authority; creative imagination; right conduct."[25]

Because of the changes that Kilpatrick made to and that his publishers imposed on his writing, "A Conservative View" became a hit. By January 1965, the column had spread to over sixty newspapers. Its quick success opened more opportunities. Harry Elmlark, owner-publisher of the conservative *Washington Star*, the rival of the liberal *Washington Post* with a larger readership, and a friend of Kilpatrick since the 1950s, helped the editor acquire an even bigger name. Known as a shrewd, debonair salesman, Elmlark built his media firm through hard work and by peddling columnists. In 1962, he signed Buckley, and in 1965 he stole Kilpatrick from *Newsday* to write a biweekly column. Kilpatrick promptly agreed to a new manager despite Elmlark's reputation for leaving novice writers with fewer earnings than they expected. He liked Elmlark's tireless efforts to promote columnists and to introduce them to the Washington press corps. By March 1966, Elmlark had sold Kilpatrick's column to nearly 100 newspapers. New to writing for a national audience, Kilpatrick accepted Harry Elmlark as a "nanny" to coach the neophyte columnist. Elmlark's confidence in Kilpatrick's talent and ability to turn a profit transformed their business relationship into a friendship built on mutual trust and respect. The columnist jokingly regarded Elmlark as a surrogate parent and called him "Mother."[26]

Despite Kilpatrick's growing success as a columnist, the racial situation for white segregationists in Richmond looked bleak. In 1964 and again in 1966, local black activists organized a powerful voting bloc to challenge the white political leadership of the city. Kilpatrick backed their opposition, Richmond Forward, a group comprised of the city's managerial class and committed to a policy of annexing surrounding counties to keep Richmond's white population high and to ensure that control of the government remained in the proper hands. Throughout the election years of 1964 and 1966, Kilpatrick kept up editorial endorsement of Richmond Forward and its plans. When the African American community ran four candidates for aldermen in 1966, Kilpatrick suggested dissolving Richmond as a corporate entity and absorbing it into neighboring counties to keep whites in power. During the election, he portrayed black Richmond as divided and poorly led. In one editorial, he labeled one of the black candidates "a kind of special radical ultra-liberal lone-wolf back-handed conservative. . . . His speaking style is part bray, part babble; he is a breathless preacher of political hellfire and damnation . . . whose Pentecostal accents have left Richmonders . . . revolted for twenty years." Kilpatrick's desire to see factional infighting had blinded him to the reality of a unified Negro bloc vote. In June 1966, casting aside Kilpatrick's distressed warnings, black voters changed the composition of the city council and elected their candidates.[27]

Perhaps, in part, because of white Richmond's inability to maintain racial control, Kilpatrick considered other options for a brighter future. His rising star status as a national political commentator convinced him to retire from the *News Leader*. In 1966, he moved to Washington, and in January 1967, he relinquished control of the editorial page to become a regular D.C. insider. The departure made sense to Kilpatrick. Despite his prestige at the *News Leader*, he had disliked working at the paper more and more. Changes in the newspaper's management shortened his career at the tribune. After John Dana Wise retired, the new publisher, Alan Donnahue, tried to assert his authority but felt intimidated by Kilpatrick's power within the news offices. The two men never bonded as Wise and Kilpatrick had. By the late 1950s, Kilpatrick already contemplated possibilities outside Richmond and often contacted William F. Buckley and David Lawrence about potential positions elsewhere. Personal factors shaped his decision as well.[28]

In a clubbish city, not even Kilpatrick's elitism could win him complete acceptance. Politically and intellectually, he represented the values and the beliefs of Virginia's founding fathers, but he failed to penetrate Richmond's closely guarded high society. The exclusive Commonwealth Club, where he dined as a guest, also denied him and his wife, Marie, memberships. Despite living in Richmond for fifteen years, he never quite achieved acceptance, and with Harry Byrd's death in 1966, Kilpatrick had one fewer friend in power. "Richmond had been very good to me on the whole," he told a former associate editor, "but socially I was never there. I was still the Oklahoma boy." Kilpatrick's outsider status and ambition for more money led him away from Richmond into a new career as a national commentator on conservatism and racial controversies while the southern civil rights movement wound down.[29]

The decline of the movement coincided with the continued articulation of conservative ideas and concerns. The right tapped into political and cultural battlefields lurking within American society that pitted reform-minded and progressive individuals, who supported the Great Society, student activism, individual rights, and civil rights laws, against Americans who espoused traditional values and opposed cultural radicalism, Great Society liberalism, and racial populism and who had few national leaders to address their unease. In 1968, Richard Nixon won the presidency with the support of these "forgotten" Americans he later dubbed the "Silent Majority." The Silent Majority believed that virtually everything had gone wrong with the nation, and Nixon manipulated their frustration at having to defend values that to them seemed self-evident. He and Vice President Spiro Agnew pledged to protect society and to maintain law and order, the Silent Majority's code words for their disapproval of student activism, civil rights and antiwar demonstrations, and urban riots and violence. "I share the Nixon-Agnew philosophy," Kilpatrick proudly said.[30]

Since taking on a national column, Kilpatrick rummaged for a new voice. In the mid- to late sixties, he found the Silent Majority's. He saw them as codefenders of longtime core conservative political principles, and his columns became a beacon for their causes and concerns. With his no-nonsense tone, Kilpatrick symbolically stood beside them to face down wrongdoers. "The people," he shuddered, "are fed up with violence in their cities. They are fed up with bleeding-heart apologists for criminals who burn and steal. . . . They may not be constitutional experts, but they know something is dreadfully wrong in the country today. They want a balance restored; and they want it now." Kilpatrick drew sustenance from the Silent Majority's contempt for liberals and activists and advised readers to deal protesters a "kick . . . in the ribs" for their disregard for law and order and traditional values. He praised straight-edged, hard-working student leaders of the conservative Young Americans for Freedom as patriots opposed to the unruly truants, the "rabble of pusillanimous slobs" who embraced the counterculture and "paraded before cameras, pimpled, bearded, slack-jawed, [and] dirty. Commenting on television about Nixon's use of FBI agents to infiltrate university student groups, Kilpatrick said, "I think oppression is needed. The more oppression the better. It is high time we cut down on the bums that are blowing up the campuses."[31]

Kilpatrick could be a hero to the Silent Majority. He was like them—from areas of the country that never embraced the liberal consensus and that felt snubbed by intellectuals and D.C. elites more concerned with social justice for minorities than the needs of Middle America. "A Conservative View" cast white southerners as part of the constituency that Nixon came to champion, not as "rednecks, bigots, and racists," but as "decent, law-abiding, taxpaying Americans who are fed up with practically everything." Everything included civil rights.[32]

With racial undertones, Kilpatrick criticized civil rights campaigns that raised awareness about poverty and Lyndon Johnson's tax-funded welfare programs as rejections of "the old middle-class precepts of industry and thrift and self-reliance." Blue-collar Americans worked for a living without preferential treatment from government, while the poor and Negroes took handouts. Kilpatrick practiced naked discrimination against the poor, both black and white. Frustrated by the 1968 Poor People's March, he impugned participants as lazy, undeserving beggars. "All the visible 'poor' at Resurrection City appear remarkably well-fed. Some are downright fat," he noted. "Every man jack of them could find a job in Washington—carrying a hod, if nothing else, [but] work? Take jobs? Earn a living? Not this gang."[33]

Although contemptuous of African Americans who wanted government aid and black civil rights leaders who sought self-determination, Kilpatrick, ironically, sometimes sided with Black Power advocates. "[Stokely] Carmichael is basically right," Kilpatrick remarked. "In the end—and it will take time—the black man must make his own way," he advised. The columnist, however, usually preferred conservative blacks to Carmichael. For

Kilpatrick, Uncle Tom, Harriet Beecher Stowe's character, and Booker T. Washington were the better role models. The "serene Uncle Tom and the industrious Washington were," he believed, "superior men. They were possessed of pride in themselves, and in their race, and in their own integrity; their purpose was not to obliterate their own identity through assimilation into a predominantly white community, but to build upon that identity and to earn their own way."[34]

Praising Stowe and Washington glossed over Kilpatrick's real intention. He hoped to assuage a nervous white audience that most blacks preferred accepting the status quo to bedlam. Only immoral, irresponsible, and militant blacks would run amok and further disturb the racial system with protests and urban riots. Good blacks, however, would have little interest in seeking redress from the government, pushing for more individual rights, or blaming racism for their troubles. African American leaders should instead confront intrinsic problems within the black community. "There comes a time when the law-abiding majority of this country, imperfect as it is," Kilpatrick noted with a minimum of humility, "ought to put a hard question to large elements of the Negro community: When in the name of God are you people going to shape up?"[35]

Blacks were not alone in their need to reform their image. Kilpatrick wanted the public to see him in a new way too. Reactionary racists abounded during the heyday of the civil rights movement. Their proclamations on the inherent inferiority of blacks, however, would no longer hold up as the movement emerged victorious. Racial hatred proved difficult to expunge from the fabric of the South, but Kilpatrick had to disdain it if he wanted to remain relevant. By 1966, he had a national reputation to lose. Syndication put Kilpatrick in a bind. The very recalcitrance that fed his fire at the *News Leader* might engulf his fortunes at the *Washington Star* syndicate. Segregation haunted the polished appearance Kilpatrick hoped to convey. He needed to sound a retreat from Jim Crow and to find a surrogate for segregationism.

During the midsixties, at the height of the civil rights movement, Kilpatrick talked about seeing "through new glasses" to describe the mollification of his racial prejudice. He borrowed the expression from Mississippi's paternalistic planter William Alexander Percy, who wrote about a "barrier of glass" that separated southern whites from Negroes. As late as the 1940s, Percy viewed African Americans as unable to survive without white supervision and feared that their loss of deference for whites would ruin the South. "I discovered [*Lanterns on the Levee*] some years ago," Kilpatrick wrote to a friend, "and still return to it with the warmest sympathy and admiration. The Southern Negro never had a better friend than Percy." The columnist began to seek a measure of forgiveness without the difficulty of confronting those whom he wronged.[36]

While navigating the tangled terrain of the civil rights revolution, Kilpatrick often told other journalists that he had slowly recognized the humanity of blacks. In 1965, he informed a correspondent that he accepted the end of segregation and that many of his ideas on racial issues, like his massive resistance stand, had changed. "I would be pretty concerned about myself if they hadn't," he discussed his new attitude, "for that way lies stagnation." Kilpatrick claimed that the violent retributions against blacks shaped his newfound beliefs as well. The motley crew who greeted the sit-in activists at Thalhimers department store back in 1960 had made him more conscious of the humiliation of segregation. "Some black students came in and sat, intending to sit until they were served. They were heckled unmercifully by a bunch of white rednecks. There was this picture—the well-behaved blacks, the gaggle of loud misbehaving whites. It was bound to make an impression on anyone of moderate sensitivity," he said thirteen years after the incident. His perspective evolved even as he promoted segregation during his numerous speaking engagements. "After *Brown*, I traveled a great deal, got invited to Dartmouth, Amherst, and the West Coast and began to meet some intelligent, sophisticated blacks, including some journalists," Kilpatrick mentioned in a 1976 interview. "Thank God, I got some new attitudes."[37]

Colleagues cited Kilpatrick's exposure to the cosmopolitan Washington press pack for his avowed metamorphosis into a racial moderate. For every newspaper post he took up after his abortive attempt as a maverick reporter in junior high school, Kilpatrick adapted his opinions to fit the needs and expectations of his employers and peers. Now, he had different standards and company. It was a new world for Kilpatrick after immersion in the province of Richmond, where he had no fellow travelers but embattled segregationists. At last he could begin making an impression on the leading journalists of the country, call them friends, and fulfill his boyhood ambition of becoming a celebrated newsman. Noting the changes, a Washington friend asked in 1973,

So what's happened to Kilpo? I don't think it's been an upheaval. He's just in a new world, with a new set of issues. He's let the bitter Menckenesque part of him go. With the race issue behind him, he just sort of emerged into the daylight. Remember that he was an ambitious and striving man in the 1950s, and he was striving in a right wing crowd. And in the South, the right wingers are not the most delightful crowd you ever saw. They were just this side of John Birch and the KKK. He was a hero of that mob. Now he goes out for a drink with people like Peter Lisagor and Hugh Sidey: That's a hell of a difference.

Kilpatrick's rather graceful urbanity, his affinity for the fine arts, his risibility with colleagues, and his friendships with liberals further distanced him from his outspoken segregationist days and recast him as a canny Washington operator.[38]

After Kilpatrick's syndicated column began to take off, he felt more comfortable and self-assured in the D.C. political scene. "There was a time when my heart would go pitty-pat at meeting a United States Senator," he recalled with amusement. "My heart doesn't go pitty-pat anymore." As he settled into his surroundings, he relaxed, diminished the reactive punch in his writing, and took on a more emollient approach to civil rights issues that he assumed his comrades and audience expected and required. The sudden journey to national standing shook Kilpatrick, and he shed his segregationist dint for a Washington makeover.[39]

Gradually, Kilpatrick started to show more poise as a commentator on race, especially during crises. When a gunman assassinated Martin Luther King Jr. in April 1968, President Johnson asked the nation to mourn and unify. Kilpatrick wrote a panegyric for his fallen adversary. He wished that King had lived to cool tensions between the races. Of all the civil rights leaders, Kilpatrick believed, only King could unite the black community and negotiate with presidents. King may have been indifferent "to the Communist influences about him," jabbed Kilpatrick, but "he was the bravest man I ever knew in public life. During the terrible days that followed upon the school desegregation ruling, no white Southerner ever matched a fraction of his courage." "To watch one of his marches," he reflected, "was to sense the awesome power of strong character combined with high purpose. This is the way it must have been . . . when the early Christians braved the hate and ridicule of Rome." Only after King died could Kilpatrick pay him a compliment. He never fully reconciled with his former opponent and, along with Senator Jesse Helms of North Carolina, opposed the proposal to establish a national holiday for the preacher in the 1980s.[40]

The columnist even condemned any form of state-sanctioned segregation and encouraged efforts to end race-based laws. When the Supreme

Court handed down its 1967 *Loving v. Virginia* decision that lifted the ban on interracial marriage, Kilpatrick in the *National Review* hailed it as a "commendable advance in human freedoms. With *Loving* the last vestige of racially discriminatory law has been wiped from the statute books." Before he received absolution for his racial sins, Kilpatrick needed to exorcise one more demon.[41]

In the late 1960s, Kilpatrick, like many conservative intellectuals, backed off what was becoming a socially disgraceful point of view, renounced racism, and acknowledged the rightness and permanence of the *Brown* ruling. Because the courts and the majority of the states, and thus the will of the people, had essentially ratified *Brown* through their unwillingness to challenge the decision, he accepted it. He had to accommodate to *Brown* nearly fifteen years after the ruling or risked stigmatization as a recalcitrant, segregationist pariah. Although Kilpatrick maintained that *Brown* had been poorly reasoned, not even he could deny the failure and the consequences of *Plessy*'s "separate but equal" doctrine. The "black children were the victims" of segregation, he wrote. *Brown* also laid the groundwork for the busing programs of the late sixties and seventies, but regardless of the decision's "imperfections," Kilpatrick pronounced, it had produced "a far better America." Such a position seemed anomalous from Kilpatrick, who had lobbied hard for the eradication of every postwar civil rights bill and integration ruling. His endorsement of the ruling came with conditions that conformed to his understanding of the law.[42]

As for *Brown*, his textual reading of the decision indicated that it prohibited segregation in law but not in practice. In other words, de jure segregation was clearly unconstitutional, but reality—that parents chose to live in certain neighborhoods based on their race— fell outside the purview of the ruling. The fact that local schools ended up overwhelmingly black or white was not segregation in the legal sense. Textualists, or legalists who interpreted the law in its original context, like Kilpatrick, read *Brown* as striking down laws that allowed segregating students by race, not as directing schools to intentionally balance their racial composition through busing or court orders.

If Americans read the ruling literally, in its original intent, it did not command integration but only desegregation. Kilpatrick distinguished between desegregation and integration: the former obeyed *Brown* and the latter did not. He learned that argument from his mentor Judge John J. Parker, the first member of the federal judiciary to make such a distinction, who wrote for a three-judge panel in the 1955 South Carolina case of *Briggs v. Elliott*.

According to Parker's logic, all one had to do to comply with *Brown* was to cease legally excluding black children from school. Kilpatrick "never saw any reason to retreat from [Parker's] masterful exegesis of the subject." With the threat of integration deradicalized and restricted to desegregation, he could live with *Brown* but not its progeny of forced integration. The Court's desegregation decision produced a morally just but badly argued law that never created, thankfully to Kilpatrick, the interracial harmony that some civil rights leaders forecast. "Momentous as the decision was," he piped up, "it has produced no millennial brotherhood. Owing in part to the lunacies of racial-balance busing, racial consciousness is more than ever a factor in American life. Whatever damage may have been done to the rule of law, the blindfolded goddess who carries the scale of justice has been well served."[43]

Kilpatrick's motives for accepting *Brown* and damning state segregation laws, though, were not noble. He cultivated a more tolerant tone on race issues because it was good for business and for him. He tried to convince publishers and readers alike that the old massive resister Kilpatrick was a relic. In 1966, John Hunt, senior editor at the *Saturday Evening Post*, wanted Kilpatrick to write an essay on contemporary race relations. The magazine had scrapped Kilpatrick's 1963 article "The Hell He Is Equal" because of the church bombing in Birmingham. Three years later, Hunt suggested renaming the piece "Negroes Are Not Equal" and trying it again. After much debate, Kilpatrick decided not to publish it. Behind the public man still huddled the private, insecure Kilpatrick. Feeling his new career threatened, he explained to Hunt,

> From my own professional point of view, the problem is quite simply that I do not want—and could not possibly afford—to be publicly associated with these views, phrased with such vigor. Since the piece was written, as you may know, I have launched into the writing of a nationally syndicated column. It is going tolerably well, with about 70 papers in the fold, but my whole pitch is a reasoned and good-humored conservatism, in which I shun these racial views almost completely. My syndicate tells me that the biggest single obstacle to further sale of the column is my reputation as a[n] old-fashioned Southern racist and segregationist. If the column is to make headway, and to provide me a platform for selling dozens of ideas more important to me than the anthropological differences, if any, of the Negro race, I must continue to treat the subject, if at all, with the greatest restraint, compassion, tact, and all that.

Sometimes segregationists had other goals besides perpetuating their racial views, and those objectives often overlapped with the aims of nonracists.[44]

In his response to the editor, Kilpatrick offered a far richer passage than a black-versus-white morality play that revealed the difficulty he still had in grappling with the often unpleasant and disturbing complexities of race. With the anthropological differences, "if any," seemingly discarded, Kilpatrick could hinder black progress and deny accusations of racism. Since the beginning of his public career as a segregationist, he had always tried to find practical ways around obstacles in his path. When *Brown* violated the southern racial order, Kilpatrick dug up interposition to oppose it. After massive resistance waned, he helped build the CCG to keep the fight against desegregation alive. If editors wanted him to sacrifice his segregationist sympathies and anthropological arguments on race, he could give them the impression that he had while he continued to write against black progress. Business was business. The arresting exchange between Kilpatrick and Hunt showed that his segregationist stance could be an opportunistic one too. Where racial moderation prevailed in Kilpatrick's thinking, it manifested itself not so much in a liberalization of his racial attitudes as subordination to his business interests. In some fights, he had to contend with competing interests to negotiate his way through a controversy.

"When I wrote this piece for the Post, two and a half years ago," Kilpatrick professed to Hunt, "I was in the last throes of my Southern convictions. Since then, my views have ameliorated enormously." Such appeals came on the heels and in the midst of a gamut of segregationist activities in the 1960s. The "last throes" of his "Southern" convictions apparently subsided in the previous three years while he pushed for segregated private schools "from Southside Virginia to the MS Delta," started the year-long Coordinating Committee for Fundamental American Freedoms (CCFAF) campaign against the 1964 Civil Rights Act, and, in the *National Review*, called the 1965 Voting Rights Act a perversion of the Constitution contracted from a "virus of unreason."[45]

Perhaps Kilpatrick also never overcame his teenage fear of destitution sown by his father's abandonment during the Depression. Part of him remained the poor, scared kid from Oklahoma who worried about his next paycheck. He refused to admit failure when recognition seemed so close. Success taught Kilpatrick to suppress his belief in blacks' genetic inferiority. His principles yielded to his desire for acceptance among Washington journalists and financial security. If Hunt would not drop the article, Kilpatrick could buy his way out of bad publicity. He bargained with the *Post* editor: "In some concern, I ask where this leaves us, money-wise? It would be a helluva blow, but if necessary, I can raise the $1,500 to buy this [article] back from you, and I would rather do that than see it published. You send me back the 1963 manuscript, to be destroyed or shelved pianissimo, among my archives, and keep [a revised] copy in its place." Few segregationists could match Kilpatrick's skill in adapting to the post–civil rights world. As civil rights activists expanded their objectives in economic terms and called for equal access to schools and the workplace, the withy Kilpatrick responded in kind.[46]

Throughout the sixties, many civil rights leaders linked racial liberty to class problems and saw jobs and education as the gateways to group uplift. Activists often wanted race to play a role in hiring practices as a way to alleviate the plight of poor blacks. In 1963, Martin Luther King's "Letter from a Birmingham Jail" called for "some compensatory consideration for the handicaps" blacks "inherited from the past." His subsequent March on Washington demanded "Jobs and Freedom." The later 1968 Poor People's Campaign reinforced the connection King made between racial freedom and freedom to work.[47]

By the late sixties and early seventies, protection of African American civil rights extended into federal plans for creating equal opportunities for blacks and whites in education and employment. As African Americans made positive social gains and entered political life during and after the civil rights struggle, often for the first time since Reconstruction, liberals wanted to ensure that they continued to make progress. The victories of the movement would be hollow, however, without equal access to high-paying jobs and good schools for blacks. A society that continued to relegate minorities, particularly women and blacks, to low-paying jobs and poor schools failed in its obligation to grant full citizenship. Policies to promote access to employment and education for minority groups became collectively known as "affirmative action." Its advocates claimed that, as an example of "affirmative action," federally mandated remedial measures, recruiting minorities to diversify schools and businesses, could offset the harmful effects of past discrimination. Preferential treatment for disaffected groups and quotas to establish an adequate representation of certain minorities within public and private institutions became common tools to fashion a post–civil rights America that no longer tolerated a culture of exclusion.[48]

The remaking of America did not happen easily for everyone. Many old-guard conservatives and segregationists were hardly eager to hand their country over to the forces of racial liberalism and egalitarianism. They began to articulate a competing vision for America's future and to construct a different narrative about the meaning of equality and the rights and responsibilities of citizenship. The political coherence and success of the right in the sixties and seventies did not depend on rallying the rank and file around old phobias, like race and Communism. Instead, conservatives adopted a new language that privileged positive, rights-based claims to individual liberty and property, to choose their children's classmates, to control their schools and neighborhoods, to protect themselves from what they regarded as reckless court justices, to remain free from what they saw as dangerous encroachments by the federal government, to fix the economy with alternatives to growth economics, and to reposition themselves as defenders of fair treatment on behalf of individuals angered by the perceived deformities and arbitrariness of affirmative action programs.

Kilpatrick and his ideological confederates on the right claimed that affirmative action coerced corporations into putting less-qualified workers in positions that talented candidates deserved and pushed socialistic egalitarianism in America. Safeguarding the freedom of association let businessmen affiliate with and hire whomever they wished. The right to discriminate preserved an individual's liberty, protected property rights, fueled the free market, and "is exactly what America stands for," Kilpatrick shouted after Kennedy announced his civil rights bill. For years, the editor had made similar arguments against desegregation. In 1961, he told one supporter, "In this whole field of segregation-integration, I've come to realize that laws that prohibit are just as wrong as laws that compel. In a free society, I ought to have some right to be let alone, to pick my own companions." The government should not even proscribe religious or racial discrimination, which, according to Kilpatrick, only "voluntary process" could eliminate.[49]

Any definition of equality beyond equality of opportunity represented a socialist threat. In 1961, Kilpatrick wrote one woman that "the Republic will fall. . . . When our political leaders fall victim to the obsession that they can repeal not only the laws of man, but the laws of God, they are asking for a catastrophe. The good Lord did not create men to be equal." Other conservatives agreed. The notion of helping the dispossessed into the workplace, the *National Review*'s Frank Meyer declared, tainted Western and Christian principles of individualism and led "inexorably to barbarism and darkness." M. E. Bradford, a defender of southern conservatism, said "the 'civil rights revolution'" encouraged other Americans to expand the power of the federal government to achieve social and economic progress. Some conservatives opposed civil rights reform because it laid bare other issues they wanted to ignore, such as inequality and poverty and promised a new concept of freedom that expanded democracy to a wider segment of the population.[50]

Faced with new laws and a federal government committed to civil rights, many affirmative action opponents softened their racial attitudes to narrow the rhetorical gap between them and civil rights activists. From the late sixties through the seventies, as one historian of the modern right has shown, mainstream conservatism underwent a makeover to deny its links with racism and the obstruction of civil rights while blocking African Americans from entering schools and getting jobs. The civil rights movement took a strange turn when the right self-consciously replaced opposition to racial reforms with calls to end race-based laws. Racially conscious policies that denied hard-working whites access to the workplace and busing orders that sent children to interracial schools afforded blacks preferential treatment, conservatives argued. A new conservative assignment was to change the language of the civil rights movement, disrupt affirmative action, and block federal interference in numerous aspects of daily life.[51]

If conservatives and businessmen wanted to preserve freedom of association, they needed to curb affirmative action without resorting to race-based arguments that the government could strike. The northern neoconservative journalist Irving Kristol cautioned William F. Buckley to drop any criticism of the 1964 Civil Rights Act "in terms of racial differences." To do otherwise would be "political folly" and injure the conservative movement. A new urban and highly educated caste of conservatives wanted to scuttle any further rumblings from the right that smacked of racism. The nascent 1970s neoconservative coup, with men like Kristol holding vigil against the decay of American values and culture, provided a serious, intellectual context for prominent scholars and policy-makers to question the utility of social science in government. In domestic politics, the neoconservatives questioned the use of social science and regarded liberal tampering with the public realm as dangerous tinkering with order and authority. Neoconservatives targeted regulations, welfare, Keynesian economics, government waste, school busing, and affirmative action as roadblocks to making the federal government work properly.[52]

Kilpatrick, who also cast aspersions on the left's attempts to plan a better society using social science, closed ranks with neoconservatives by pointing out the shortcomings of the liberal state, including its inadequate defense of individual liberty. A chorus of neoconservative thinkers, such as Daniel Patrick Moynihan and Norman Podhoretz, shared his conviction that social science should not govern America. Keeping pace with the neoconservatives, who formed an armada of academics and Great Society liberals who backed the black freedom struggle, aligned older conservatives and opponents of the civil rights movement with respectable left-leaning allies. By sharing a stance with neoconservatism, Kilpatrick and Buckley were able to fashion plausible counterarguments against integration, to defuse racist language that, until then, had hindered the right in the past, and to incubate an ideology for widespread application.[53]

The credibility of former segregationists and opponents of integration depended on their ability to pass themselves off as champions of fairness. No longer could they rely on states' rights and claims about blacks' inherent inferiority to limit African Americans' advancement. A defense of the free market and individual initiative replaced the older rhetoric. Kilpatrick assisted with the new conservative counteroffensive against egalitarianism. In a 1966 article for the *National Review*, he singled out liberal economic and social policies as the culprits hampering black Americans. Welfare and civil rights reduced Negroes to dependents of the state. "If the free market were permitted to operate color-blind, and if the poor were helped simply as the poor and not as the Negro poor," Kilpatrick knew that blacks could satisfy their "needs without the blighting oppressions of . . . benefactors." Kilpatrick portrayed conservatives as the nation's true defenders of individual liberty and a color-blind tradition who halted America's slide toward despotism and egalitarianism. In 1974, he celebrated "contemporary Conservatives" as a crew of "18th Century Liberals" who resisted state-sanctioned equality and federal tyranny.[54]

James Kilpatrick concealed his contempt for racial progress behind the traditional conservative disdain for equality. The freedom to act or not to act, he insisted, rested with individuals, who could rise or fall to unequal levels. Freedom should be exercised at the expense of equality. Liberty "demands order," affirmed Kilpatrick in a 1968 "A Conservative View" column. "It demands discipline. It demands a sense of hierarchy" in which people "are inferior to their masters."[55]

For years, Kilpatrick had preached that "the international obsession with egalitarianism" blighted modern society. Real affirmative action meant letting blacks help themselves, not forcing a liberal utopia on America. Former segregationists and conservatives need not apologize for the reality of an unequal playing field. As Kilpatrick explained to one critic in 1978, "I am very wary of this business of 'making amends' for past acts of discrimination. Today's black children are owed an equal opportunity to participate in public programs, and they are owed equal access to public facilities, but I do not comprehend that today's black child is owed any 'amends' because his granddaddy was a slave. At some point the Negroes must stand on their own feet, as white persons do. Do you know who said that? Frederick Douglass, 1865." His rhetoric echoed comments Kilpatrick made about Douglass fifteen years earlier. In a 1963 essay mired in scientific racism about the bankruptcy of black culture, he referenced Douglass to prove the same point: "'What would happen to the Negroes once they were freed?' Lincoln asked [Douglass]. 'Let them take care of themselves,' Douglass replied."[56]

Kilpatrick did not hold southern segregation accountable for the creation of an inferior public education system for blacks. When Kilpatrick wrote *The Southern Case for School Segregation*, he also excused white southerners for any wrongdoing toward African Americans. "The guilt hypothesis," he nutshelled, "has been vastly overdrawn." Kilpatrick refused to believe that historical forces greater than individual accomplishment shaped educational and economic outcomes for any race. He insisted on color-blind individualism with equal opportunities for everyone. Any arbitrary leveling of the playing field or biased government intervention violated a conservative principle. The very federal bureaucrats and judges who "wronged— cruelly and maliciously wronged" the South during the civil rights movement, he argued, expanded their egalitarianism with affirmative action.[57]

Coerced equality offended Kilpatrick's sense of justice. No government assistance helped him through college or to the top of the *News Leader*. Racial quotas and affirmative action denied an individual the freedom to advance to whatever attainable height. The government's egalitarian programs took the civil rights movement to extremes in the name of correcting past discrimination. Programs that favored black job applicants and promoted black employees became one of the most politically divisive government initiatives of the 1970s. Many whites believed—and Kilpatrick encouraged them to believe—that racial quotas directly and unfairly put them at a disadvantage and imperiled their economic advancement. One of Kilpatrick's readers interpreted "remedies to correct non-existent wrongs" as tantamount to "the rape of the whites' pocketbook." An Atlanta man grumbled to Kilpatrick that the dilemma since the *Brown* decision "was not race, but the have-nots taking what the haves had produced and achieved," which threatened "us middle class people" and "liquidated" average, hardworking Americans. Affirmative action had become a personal matter for

Kilpatrick. "I know what it is to have one of my sons refused a job for which he was qualified, merely to give the job to a less qualified black," Kilpatrick commiserated with the Atlantan.[58]

Kilpatrick was, of course, hardly alone in his outlook. He succeeded in the 1970s because he tapped into grievances about affirmative action felt by the unbigoted as well as the nakedly prejudiced. While not uniformly intransigent, more Americans associated liberalism with promoting African American progress at the expense of struggling whites. White opposition emerged in a larger political context. Affirmative action's arrival came at an inopportune moment for liberals and blacks. The economic storms of the early seventies interrupted postwar prosperity. Suddenly, the liberal reform excitement of the 1960s shifted to a sense of crisis and loss of faith in the nation. Some American manufacturing jobs moved overseas, oil shortages created long gas lines, inflation rose, and consumer confidence plummeted. At a time when the nation's economy reeled, Kilpatrick blamed federal bureaucracies, government regulation, and interference in the free market for America's woes.

The U.S. Chamber of Commerce shared Kilpatrick's antipathy for government regulations. Although dedicated to the ideological traditions of fiscal restraint and the free market since its founding, the organization by the early seventies looked more liberal than right-leaning because of its tolerance for Lyndon Johnson's Great Society. By 1974, a more conservative political climate and the struggling economy encouraged a return to its original intent. The Chamber revamped itself into a lobbying powerhouse for business interests that pushed reform in bureaucracies and turned the nation's economy around. The number of subscribers to *Nation's Business*, the chamber's official journal, grew from 50,000 in 1975 to over 200,000 individuals, companies, trade and professional organizations, and local and state Chambers of Commerce by 1984 with a combined readership of two million.[59]

The rise in subscriptions correlated to the Chamber's shifted political bent and new management. Richard Lesher, the new president, thought the nation had drifted toward socialism and that capitalism was under siege from regulations. Under his direction, the Chamber put corporate politics in the hands of small businessmen and turned free enterprise into a social movement. Through mass mobilization, the Chamber rallied the business community at the grass roots and pushed tax cuts and deregulation. Lesher also proclaimed a social gospel of individual responsibility and initiative tied to a culture of traditional values.[60]

To cripple the Great Society and New Deal state, Lesher used *Nation's Business* to address the cultural divisions stirred up by the sixties. The magazine ran law and order, antifeminist, and antiunion articles. In 1974, the Chamber asked Kilpatrick to write the lead column each month to summarize the economic news from Washington and to bulk up the right's social causes. His features provided the kind of social and economic conservative commentary that the publishers wanted.[61]

The new *Nation's Business* relied on Kilpatrick to outline business's opposition to the social changes of the last decade. The counterculture's mantra of free love, he suggested in one column, coincided with college students' "left of center" standpoint on economics. Feminists, he interjected in another, attempted to redraw gender roles and threatened "the rule of law," the "truism that we live under the rule of the past," and the "Judeo-Christian ethic" of women's subordination to men. In another feature, the ordinarily agnostic Kilpatrick proselytized that traditional families and churchgoing would strengthen America during the economic recession. "Ours is not an atheistic or antireligious society" but a place where "the rituals and traditions of religious faith are part of the fabric of our national life," he commented. In other columns he ridiculed liberal government spending programs, equal employment laws, business regulations, and taxes and linked the stagnating economy of the 1970s to the egalitarianism of the 1960s. The efforts to elevate unqualified individuals, including blacks, into positions of power in jobs and at school could hamstring the American economy and block talented candidates from advancement.[62]

Kilpatrick's view of affirmative action as a swindle, a violation, and as coercion appealed both to people unwilling to admit their racial prejudice about the programs and to antiregulationist readers unswayed by bigotry but searching for corporate liberation from yet another government imposition. By attacking affirmative action as a blow against unfettered corporate capitalism, he persuaded business leaders of the risks of racial preferences and quotas to their businesses. Only through faith in unrestrained competition and the judgment of employers could minorities find better careers and opportunities. Blacks must trust in a color-blind market. Affirmative action threatened to replace time-honored hiring practices with an egalitarian "New National Nightmare," he proclaimed. The unemployed and people stuck in low-paying, dead-end jobs had only themselves to blame. Kilpatrick made similar arguments years before in *The Southern Case for School Segregation*.[63]

The columnist had revived claims about unqualified blacks that civil rights activists tried to eliminate. He constantly reminded the beneficiaries of affirmative action that they had stumbled into jobs and schools undeservingly because of their race. White job and university applicants passed over in favor of minority candidates received special mention. Kilpatrick defended the individual's right to work and enter graduate programs without interference from the courts or pressure from affirmative action advocates suits. In 1974, the Supreme Court upheld the rejection of Jewish student Marco DeFunis from the University of Washington Law School. DeFunis's lawyers argued that the school's affirmative action program welcomed unqualified blacks through a quota system but discriminated against more intelligent candidates. Kilpatrick branded the *DeFunis* ruling a "syndrome" endemic to American higher education and the ivory tower elite who touted diversity and multiculturalism. On television, he defended DeFunis as an "innocent victim of racism in reverse—that is, of discrimination against whites, in favor of blacks, Chicanos, Indians, or Filipinos." Some ethnic minorities also felt threatened by *DeFunis*. Asians were "over-represented in the sciences and professions. 'Affirmative action,' then (at least as practiced on the West Coast) ends in 'reverse discrimination' against orientals," confided Ryoji Mihara to Kilpatrick.[64]

The same year of the *DeFunis* decision, the Supreme Court heard opening arguments on affirmative action policies in the workplace. The Court guaranteed private corporations' voluntary affirmative action programs in *U.S. Steelworkers v. Weber* (1979). In a 1977 "A Conservative View" column titled "The Color of One's Skin Now the Only Measure of Merit," written during the build-up to that decision, Kilpatrick condemned the treatment of the white worker who filed suit against Kaiser Aluminum and Chemical Corporation. Kilpatrick called the company's training program that helped women and blacks at the expense of whites a racist plan that was as damaging to blue-collar whites as anything perpetrated against African Americans and a case of reverse discrimination.[65]

Supporters thronged to Kilpatrick. At least a few were as eloquent as he, and some even more so. One reader highlighted the trouble with guilt-induced, hypocritical liberal social programs: "What is happening [in affirmative action] shows not only the futility of any individual trying to deal with the injustice without first seeing his own part of it and being changed within, but the inevitability of such efforts perpetuating and increasing the evil apparently being fought." Wrong-headed, well-meaning liberals had not dealt with the problem of using prejudice to correct prejudice.

"Such insanity," the man continued, "lays the fertile ground for all kinds of exploitation such as setting up phoney [sic] minority heads to firms to responsibility."[66]

Kilpatrick remained consistent in his adherence to meritocracy and fair play even when it came to his beloved game of baseball. He agreed, for example, with an upset reader who considered the rise and domination of black athletes in professional and college sports to be a sign of America's decay: "And you may be quite right," Kilpatrick sympathized with the man, "in construing the decline of white athletes in terms of decadence of post-Augustinian Rome." He, too, longed for more "white faces on the field," but not to worry, he wrote, in "the competitive marketplace," black players must have proven their skills. He knew that baseball was a school for perseverance, not despair. The game's long season taught people something about character. In the season's trajectory, like life and politics, there were ups and downs, streaks and slumps. No one remained at the peak of his powers indefinitely, and when a player had moved past his prime, he had to find ways to make do with fewer capacities. Kilpatrick, like some aging ballplayer, adjusted, created, and compensated as he went along.[67]

Only the long season of the civil rights era could permit Kilpatrick that kind of discovery. The columnist's appeals for color-blind treatment coincided with a general shift to reevaluate the rhetoric and ideas meant to recapture what had been lost due to racial progress. In removing the debris of segregation, he returned to the old but enduring language of meritocracy. With an appeal to individual ability and achievement, he could tap many Americans' worries and validate them in ways older race talk could not. In a renewed form, he condemned the threat posed to the industrious and responsible by a privileged and untrustworthy few. Kilpatrick's columns were becoming tutorials for his increasingly suburban audience beleaguered by economic, social, and political challenges from the left. Liberalism, he notified readers, rejected middle-class values and an old-fashioned work ethic. The "[w]ell-bred citizens" of the middle class, as opposed to ill-bred minorities and the poor, were under attack. "The demonology of the Left" endangered the very lifestyle and communities of the middle class.[68]

Privileged middle-class neighborhoods came under direct assault when the federal government seemed intent on racial integration through court-ordered busing, which became a more volatile issue with the American public than either affirmative action or quotas. For nearly fifteen years after the *Brown* decision, southern states tried to fend off court directives to desegregate schools. In 1968, the federal courts imposed county- and citywide busing programs that tossed white and black children into schools together. In the North, where de facto segregated schools also existed, busing sparked intense controversy and sometimes violence as white parents resisted efforts to remove their children from neighborhood schools or refused to accept African American students and mixed-race education. For many southerners and northerners alike, busing became synonymous with affirmative action, race, and liberalism's insistence on the equality of results. It also cultivated disdain for the perceived arrogance of unelected judges. Kilpatrick warned that the courts' mandatory integration rulings would conflict with society's sense of right and wrong. Forced busing not only violated parents' freedom to control their children's schooling but also went against "a law of human nature," a built-in resistance to autocratic power over one's life.[69]

Opponents of busing programs borrowed from arguments against affirmative action. Punishing white Americans by jeopardizing children's educations to ensure racial equality and upward mobility for blacks seemed unfair and risky. Mixing students from diverse racial, socioeconomic, and academic backgrounds could have a deleterious effect on the quality of education for children. A majority of whites were not committed racists but were unlikely to support racial justice measures that interfered with their ability to control schools and neighborhoods and that veered in a direction that equated desegregation with integration. Kilpatrick knew time was on his side as more Americans questioned and resisted judicial adaptations that broke from the original *Brown* ruling. William F. Buckley also noted the "cynical-realistic" of forced integration: "Confirmed by all past experience . . . the desegregated schools will soon be resegregated anyway, so what difference does it make?"[70]

A movement against busing swept the country as parents in many communities charged the government with invading their privacy and violating their right to manage local schools. Even among its supporters, busing produced little excitement and looked like a project undertaken by a handful of liberal bureaucrats, intellectuals, and judges. Kilpatrick reached the apogee of his popularity during this immense social effort. At home among people, largely of the Silent Majority, incensed about the government's racial planning, he went on the attack against busing.[71]

Throughout the seventies, Kilpatrick wrote about busing in the majority of his syndicated columns that discussed race. He described the fight against integrated education in libertarian and coded terms that emphasized community rights, freedom of choice plans, fears of state coercion, social engineering, and racial discord. When school busing programs were first proposed in the late sixties, Kilpatrick immediately referred to them as "a kind of racism in reverse" whose only intent would be to create a "consciousness of race." On television, he excoriated busing: "If this isn't racism, the word has lost its meaning. . . . This racist manipulation of human beings—little human beings—has been a total flop. It's rekindled old animosities; it's made children more conscious than ever of race." Once again, Kilpatrick argued that he had transcended the race issue while his opponents made trouble. He sowed discord as liberals undermined the base of the Democratic Party.[72]

The busing controversy ripped apart school districts and generated enmity and militancy. Not even traditionally liberal neighborhoods avoided brawls and riots. The commitment of Boston, the former abolitionist citadel, to racial progress was soon put to the test. South Boston's Irish Catholic working class attacked black children bused to their schools. Kilpatrick took pleasure in seeing Boston, in the heart of Kennedy country, descend into a backlash against the courts and the black community. He hoped that the clashes would be a totem to other northerners about the harsh realities of race relations and point out their hypocrisy when they accused the South of racism. In a 1965 column titled "A Few Words in Defense of Mississippi," Kilpatrick had blamed northern prejudice, not southern racism, for the nation's race problems. "We will pile all our sins on the head of a scapegoat," he derided, "and drive her into a Dixie wilderness." Compared to the "jungles of Harlem and Central Park," he went on, "Jackson, Mississippi" offered an "oasis of pure tranquility." Now, in 1975, Bostonians demonstrated that they were not sanguine about racial change. One mother implored Kilpatrick to write about the fate of her children: "Someway I'll save them to be able to say when the 'agonizing [school district] reappraisal' is completed and the liberals and the judges say 'Gee, we were wrong, and those people who protested were right. Too bad, we'll have to change the laws again'; We told you so. As a nationally recognized columnist, you have a forum which is denied we who suffer. Use it. Use it to try to save someone, somewhere who hasn't been entrapped as we are in Boston."[73]

By the 1970s, many differences in the political cultures of the white South and the white North had substantially evaporated, just as Kilpatrick predicted they would during his earlier interposition gamble. "South Boston's reaction," he mocked, "tends to confirm [Bill] Simmons' Law . . . which holds that one's enthusiasm for coerced integration increases by the square of the distance by which one is removed from the actual event." The violence in Boston exposed the "Dream World of Desegregation," as Kilpatrick titled one *Nation's Business* column. He likened Yankee racial liberalism to a fairy tale. Efforts to help blacks at the expense of whites without changing hearts and minds "made racial tensions worse," he concluded. Public outrage at busing grew so intense in northern cities that the Supreme Court limited the programs beginning with the 1974 *Milliken v. Bradley* decision.[74]

According to Kilpatrick, liberals' insistence on forward mobility for unskilled minorities through special privileges discredited blacks and challenged the gains made in the civil rights struggle. He also accused the government of breeding racism. Affirmative action unleashed "scary times," he wrote to one correspondent. "The egalitarians are in command of the government . . . and many of them are fanatical. . . . They are worse racists—much worse racists—than the old Southern bigots, many of whom had an honest affection for the Negro people as individual human beings." The affirmative action "racists" gave him "the creeps." On the Columbia Broadcasting System (CBS) program *60 Minutes*, Kilpatrick called affirmative action "a return to racial discrimination" and "a nice euphemism . . . intended to slide over the ugly truth." When a San Diegan called Kilpatrick the real hypocrite for allowing the busing of white children away from blacks to segregated schools in the 1950s but opposing busing blacks to white schools in the 1970s, the columnist brooked no criticism. "I am always interested to hear from those who denounce the bad old busing of the bad old days, when children were bused to prevent integration, and simultaneously clamor for the new busing in which children are bused to compel integration," he bristled. "In either case, the children are being bused for one reason only—the color of their skin. This strikes me as a racist attitude, and for your implicit racism: Shame on you."[75]

Kilpatrick realized that he did not have to apologize or need to blame civil rights leaders directly or bash blacks as a race explicitly. African Americans were not the culprits in affirmative action. He targeted a twisted coalition of government bureaucrats, judges, and liberal intellectuals that inflicted racial equality and inclusiveness on the public and businesses from above. Government agencies, like the Equal Employment Opportunity Commission (EEOC), that supervised preferential treatment for blacks had "done more to destroy good race relations in the past ten years than the Ku Klux Klan did in a century," Kilpatrick observed. The EEOC and the Department of Health, Education, and Welfare (HEW), which oversaw welfare and uplift programs for minorities, drew his special derision. When a curious reader asked him to explain his position on the new government departments, Kilpatrick griped: "When I speak of a 'Federal bureaucrat,' I mean a son of a bitch." With the civil rights acts in place, federal bureaucracy replaced the Court as his public enemy number one.[76]

From Kilpatrick's perspective, the duplicity of federally sanctioned affirmative action made it more mephitic than the racism of the Old South. Affirmative action unfairly coupled equality to outcome and discarded equality of opportunity. It also galled whites, particularly men, that government forced blacks and women into the workplace and into education. In an effort to eliminate race as a barrier to progress, affirmative action made color-consciousness a significant factor in determining progress. Conservatives argued that markets and the workplace should remain free from any undue advantages, including racial privileges, and should operate without government restraints. Considerations of color must not influence the free market. Anyone who remained committed to racially biased policies, especially if they favored blacks, sponsored racism in reverse.[77]

Before Kilpatrick appropriated the term, "reverse racism" had several entirely different meanings. In the 1940s and 1950s, left-leaning Americans described white hate groups that targeted Jews and white liberals as reverse racists for tormenting their own race. During the 1960s, when some African Americans advocated racial self-determination, whites used the term to discredit black resentment and distrust of white people. After Kilpatrick and other conservatives referred to biased government programs for blacks as reverse racism, the expression assumed its current meaning.[78]

Kilpatrick may even have been the first conservative pitchman to call state-sanctioned policies that helped blacks "reverse racism." Reflecting on his participation in a late summer 1963 conference on the centennial of the Emancipation Proclamation where he shared the dais with civil rights personalities Roy Wilkins, James Baldwin, and James Foreman, Kilpatrick noted the innate deficiencies among African Americans that echoed arguments he made in *The Southern Case for School Segregation*. He also observed that the proposed civil rights law "petted and pampered, cuddled and coddled" blacks through "reverse racism." The prescient remark came a year before the passage of the 1964 Civil Rights Act, which unintentionally provided for later affirmative action. In 1963, few people anticipated the possibility of preferential racial policies for African Americans when they still lacked basic civil rights. Suddenly, Kilpatrick and his conservative brethren scrambled the old terminology of racism in reverse.[79]

Conservatives dreaded the results of the civil rights bill. David Lawrence reported on whites who were terrified of the "reverse discrimination" perpetrated by Kennedy's "order to advance Negro employees without re-gard to Civil Service procedures." In his 1964 campaign, Barry Goldwater spurned quotas and told crowds that the course of American society was "neither to establish a segregated society nor to establish an integrated society as such. It is to preserve a *free* society." The right's fear of undue privileges for blacks also resonated in the business community. The Na-tional Association of Manufacturers believed that Title VII of the 1964 Civil Rights Act would force employers to hire based on race and "discriminate in reverse against all other employees." By the early seventies, conservatives routinely labeled liberal racial policies as reverse racism. In 1971, Lionel Lo-kos's *The New Racism*, the first book-length study of reverse racism, received endorsements from the *National Review* and the Conservative Book Club.[80]

Indictments of reverse racism allowed conservatives like Kilpatrick to escape their ties to segregationists, to charge liberals with race-baiting, and to prevent more changes in the hierarchy of white over black. For years, liberals accused conservatives of harboring racists and foes of the civil rights revolution. Minorities may have been victims of past injustices, but conservatives convinced themselves not to feel guilty about their obstruc-tionism to the black freedom struggle. The *National Review*'s Ernest Van den Haag admitted that earlier conservatives discriminated but insisted that "current generations can bear no responsibility" for their forerunners. In the 1970s, opponents of affirmative action looked like the real trustees of the civil rights movement's appeals to eliminate racial bias and race-consciousness in society. Conservatives designed rhetoric that rejected egal-itarian programs but remained sensitive to race. A "color-blind" America that respected the civil rights struggle's quest to end racial discrimination but checked reckless egalitarianism became new tenets in the conservative movement. "As for an end to racial conflict in America," Patrick Buchanan insisted in 1976, "the first step along that road is to make the government of the United States color-blind."[81]

Kilpatrick's condemnation of racially conscious laws and liberals as the real racists was an attempt to convince skeptics that he had purged his racial prejudice. He confided to one correspondent that the "South's ex-ercise of segregated schooling was simply indefensible." As a born-again supporter of fair treatment for blacks and color blindness, he described his conversion:

> In these areas of race relations, I sometimes think I am getting to be like [the] Catholic convert who became more Catholic than the Pope.

I spent years as a Southern editor, filled with old-fashioned Southern racial prejudices, fighting to preserve segregation in our schools.
Then came the light. Today I am just as incensed as my Yankee critics
were incensed 30 years ago at what seems to me the virulent evils of a
pervasive racism throughout our society. That men and women must
be hired, promoted, educated, transported, assigned or not assigned,
solely because of the color of their skin strikes me as indefensible.

Kilpatrick's epiphany reflected no flagging of his commitment but derived from his impatience to transcend the issue of race. Such declarations
of fairness helped him to bend his racial past into an aberration. He knew
that his denunciation of segregation looked phony to many critics, however, and confessed to one reader, "That banality sounds a little hollow
coming from me."[82]
The road from massive resistance to color blindness had been a winding one. "I guess I have come a pretty far place," Kilpatrick ruminated in
1973. He talked about equal standards of treatment for the races but, as
he told journalist Morton Kondracke, "I never have believed that all men
are created equal." His uncharacteristic approval of racial fairness appalled
some former friends and allies, who thought he went too far. Bill Simmons
blanched at Kilpatrick's professed change of heart and detected a secret
agenda. When the opportunity to write a popular syndicated column presented itself, Simmons charged duplicity. Kilpatrick, critics recognized,
adjusted his attitudes to please the public. In May 1976, a cynical Simmons
confronted Kilpatrick directly. "So we have come full double circle," he
wrote disdainfully. "The Kilpatrick of Interposition now writes of race prejudice, private bias and evil." What seemed unthinkable to Simmons was
reasonable to Jack Kilpatrick. He intended his public testimony to absolve
him and conservatism of the racial animosity of which others in the nation
accused them. Difficult as it was for intractable segregationists to accept,
Kilpatrick was far from conventional and more liberal on race than they
would have liked to believe.[83]
Kilpatrick's reserve on racial malice elicited questions about his loyalty to the southern way of life and aroused wariness. Not all racial conservatives were always more comfortable with his positions. One reader
demanded that Kilpatrick acknowledge his bigoted fan mail. Tired of associating with unreconstructed racists and receiving piles of similar letters
from the radical right, Kilpatrick countered: "'[N]iggers' is a word that
happens to offend the hell out of me." Kilpatrick considered any untoward

insinuations about his racial attitudes deeply insulting and any suggestions that he was hostile toward African Americans as offensive. In animalistic terms, a Floridian described blacks in white schools as "a treefull [sic] of noisy monkeys." Something had "to be done about those bastards." Kilpatrick ruled out the reader's comparisons of blacks to animals and instead refocused him on stopping federal coercion and compelling children to love one another.[84]

Although Kilpatrick publicly renounced racism, he still believed deeply in blacks' inferiority. The columnist sometimes privately told racial conservatives that his disavowal of racism and segregation was not as sincere as they feared. After an angry segregationist accused Kilpatrick of betraying the white South, he set the "record straight." "I did not say I was sorry for my former views on racial integration," he corrected the critic. "I said, very carefully, that I was sorry I ever defended the practice of State-sanctioned segregation. There is a world of difference. Neither did I 'belatedly come to the conclusion that I was wrong about my former stand on equality of the races.' As I tried to make clear, I belatedly came to the conclusion that I was wrong about my former stand on the rightness of State-sanctioned discrimination."

He then assured the writer that he had not "fully reconciled" to integration in the public schools, either. Kilpatrick still questioned the wisdom of integrating the races in the public schools and had hijacked the *Brown* ruling's "color-blind view of the law" to serve his own purposes. *Brown* terminated the states' right to discriminate in education based on race; therefore, the federal government also could not compel egalitarian racial policies in education or jobs. If southerners could no longer govern with race-conscious laws, then neither could federal lawmakers. During the 1970s, Kilpatrick couched his distaste for integration in the respectable language of color blindness to argue against racial egalitarianism. The rhetoric Kilpatrick used to reject affirmative action—the calls for color blindness, equal treatment, racial fair play, maintaining a free market, and curtailing state regulations—was only a mask for his real concern: race.[85]

Throughout the 1960s and 1970s, Kilpatrick fought black progress on a variety of fronts. Keeping white and black schoolchildren apart, for instance, remained a priority for him. From D.C. and Virginia, he preached the gospel of private schooling. In 1963, at the request of William J. Simmons, he had begun writing on private schools for the *Citizen*, counseling rural whites about avoiding integration through tuition grant programs like those Virginia law allowed. After passage of the 1964 Civil Rights Act, private schooling became a key issue in the *Citizen*, and the Citizens' Council acted as the prime mover behind Mississippi's private academy movement. In 1964, Kilpatrick advised Simmons on the details of setting up a private education system: Never use any property or material formerly or currently used by public schools, make no mention of race in the schools' bylaws, use only private checks, and change the names of the athletic teams.[86]

Into the 1970s and 1980s, Kilpatrick's columns and articles promoted school vouchers for parents to divert tax money toward private schools and denounced the federal courts for denying tax-exempt status to schools in Mississippi and elsewhere. Government efforts in the late sixties and seventies to achieve racial balance in public schools angered many white Americans. The *National Review* provided Kilpatrick with space to elaborate on "opposition to coerced or arbitrary integration" and to defend parental control over their children's education. In a feature article, Kilpatrick documented the air-conditioned, efficient, and modern classrooms that the Citizens' Council built in Jackson, Mississippi, as a testament to the ability of private schools to compete with the best public schools. The fact that such academies remained segregated seemed "incidental" to him. He found their "return to old principles of community" impressive and pleasing.[87]

Elaborating on his theme, Kilpatrick's syndicated columns endorsed private education and school vouchers and defended them against judicial decrees. With rulings like the 1968 *Green* decision that mandated integration in public schools, he decried the federal court system for crushing "freedom-of-choice," dislodging "human beings into patterns of social behavior that are unacceptable to them," and violating "a law of human nature." When, in 1969, a U.S. Circuit Court of Appeals struck down Virginia's tuition grant laws born in the massive resistance era, Kilpatrick maintained that Virginia had broken no laws and that the state's program "transcended its origins. No racial overtones remained in the law. . . . Here was a small candle of freedom." He admitted that many of the recipients of Virginia's tuition grants were whites for all-white private academies but insisted that the program had shown signs of diversifying before the "apostles of coerced integration" snuffed it out. Rather than emphasizing race, though, Kilpatrick pled his case for school vouchers based on the right of local communities to experiment with educational models that best suited their needs and pointed out the benefits of competition for all Americans bred by the presence of private schools. After one reader of his column questioned his views on race-mixing and the importance of skin color in regard to the voucher issue, Kilpatrick shot back, "I would have them [children] taught that children ought not to be classified by the color of their skins."[88]

Seemingly unrelated stances on other major issues of the post–civil rights years supplemented and reinforced Kilpatrick's racial views and brought into doubt the sincerity of his apology for his racism. His comments on the growing abortion controversy typified the way he gave even an ostensibly nonracial issue a racial slant in a manner plainly calculated to steal the language of the left to oppose minorities. Kilpatrick defended abortion because he deemed it a right to privacy issue and because it delivered society from responsibility for unwanted children. Social engineering in this case served a racial and an economic purpose he could endorse. If abortion was illegal, he noted, poor women and blacks on welfare would "dump their progeny on the taxpayers for life." Lumping together abortion and race to argue for welfare cuts was certainly not necessary or convincing for all readers; one need only be callous about the poor or stingy to accept Kilpatrick's argument.[89]

Although Kilpatrick was not associated with the increasingly influential and vocal religious right, he did advocate traditional values, and he volunteered to be a culture warrior to defend Western civilization. Many of Kilpatrick's views were not out of place with the ascendant cultural conservatism of the 1970s and 1980s. He was neither conventionally pious nor one to emphasize a providential order of Creation, but he did affirm a hierarchy in human affairs and was deeply concerned with the upkeep of the nation and the character and natural endowments of its people. Only certain persons possessed the right knowledge and habits to run America and prevent the roots of society from withering. Based on that premise, many newcomers to the country did not meet his patriotic standards. Noting the increase in non-European immigrants to the country since the 1965 Immigration Act, he feared a "tidal wave" of "racial and ethnic groups with little understanding of Western values." Included in Kilpatrick's condemnation of non-Western immigrant groups were attacks on the developing world, especially southern Africa, where he saw potential for disorder in the absence of white rule.[90]

Throughout the 1970s and 1980s, Kilpatrick's foreign policy views mimicked positions he took in *The Southern Case for School Segregation*. He insisted that whites in America and abroad should maintain the right to rule societies because of their cultural and economic superiority. With little regard for democratic development, Kilpatrick wrote of his support for white minority regimes and apartheid in Rhodesia and South Africa and backed efforts to resist independence and human rights movements. "The white regimes are no more undemocratic than many of the black ruled countries nearby," he wrote in 1973, "and their more aggressive industrial development will eventually produce better living for blacks there than they would have if they ruled themselves from the outset." According to Kilpatrick, whites built the only civilized societies in Africa and thus deserved to control the governments and natural resources. When the Portuguese rule of Angola ended in 1975, Kilpatrick could think of nothing good to say. He observed an old adage that "he never feared for the black man at the hands of his oppressors half as much as at the hands of his liberators. . . . The Portuguese have exchanged a bad dictatorship for a worse one." Whether he commented on decolonization, welfare, immigration, or affirmative action, Kilpatrick tried to rout advancement for minorities, people of color, and the poor on nearly every matter and continent. Though his positions often served as a ruse for his discomfort with changes to traditional racial patterns, something more complex and subtle than a facsimile of segregation had evolved in Kilpatrick's thinking.[91]

Kilpatrick had provided conservatism some of the argot of segregationism minus the overt racism in the wake of civil rights victories. His linguistic ingenuity and sophisticated arguments put Kilpatrick into the thick of a conservative movement that sought to recapture America and discredit civil rights gains rather than to recover segregation. Taken in this wider context, his appeal for color blindness appeared more rhetorical, less than altruistic and certainly not race neutral. Yet, because of his cleverness, he had gone from artifact to archetype in the battle against racial egalitarianism. One measure of Kilpatrick's adjustment to the post–civil rights world came with his redefinition of racism, but even it triggered controversy and coincided with a reexamination of the white South's identity in the 1970s.

The Briar Patch

In *I'll Take My Stand*, a 1930 volume written in objection to industrialism and modernity, Robert Penn Warren's essay, "The Briar Patch," defended segregation and the agrarian South as the best way of life for blacks. On farms, away from cities, factories, and the North, Negroes would live decently and prevent racial tension in the region. "The Briar Patch" was a more than suitable title for Warren's chapter because it excused southern white responsibility for racial problems and imagined the rural, Jim Crow South as a place of safety. Warren's idea of the South—free of racial woes and with a social structure reminiscent of antebellum days—was conservative and instructive. In Warren's South, people were bound to the land and no one disturbed the racial status quo. On the form and substance of the South, he pictured an unmolested, georgic society that could be reincarnated under duress and that stirred generations of southerners, including Kilpatrick and those close to him. A member of Kilpatrick's newspaper family, Louis Decimus Rubin, would carry on southern agrarianism into the mid-twentieth century and along with it a chance for the preservation of a distinctive South. Rubin, thoroughly southern in background, presented a coherent and careful defense of agrarianism as the heart of southern identity. In Kilpatrick's thinking, agrarianism would accomplish more. It would again cloak resistance to integration in a palatable form for a national audience.[92]

Born in 1923 in Charleston, South Carolina, Louis Rubin grew up with Lost Cause mythology and around old Confederate veterans, and, in 1932, he witnessed one of their reunion parades in Richmond. After finishing college at the University of Richmond, Rubin earned a doctorate in English at Johns Hopkins University in 1954. There, he contemplated writing a dissertation on Confederate general James Longstreet under the supervision of C. Vann Woodward, the dean of southern history. Rubin's fascination with nearly all things southern also introduced him to the Southern, or Nashville, Agrarians, the twelve white southerners based at Vanderbilt University who critiqued modern, urban, capitalist society in their manifesto *I'll Take My Stand*.[93]

Rubin was teaching American Studies at the University of Pennsylvania when white southern resistance to the *Brown* decision began. Colleagues at Penn, however, harbored no affection for the South or southern literature. Alone in the North when desegregation threatened the South, Rubin longed to return to Virginia. Though Rubin espoused no special commitment to segregation, he took the associate editor job at the *News Leader* from 1956 to 1957. Caught up in the frenzy of the paper's massive resistance stance, Rubin momentarily embraced segregation. "As the chorus of criticism grew in the southern press, for a brief period I was even able to rationalize myself into an intellectual concurrence in the traditional Southern position on race," Rubin later reflected. "It was totally an abstraction: I had no contacts with black people whatever."[94]

By fall 1956, Rubin started to question the wisdom of Kilpatrick and massive resistance. Increasingly, he felt at odds with the editor and "on the wrong side of the segregation business," he disclosed to Robert Penn

Warren, who had since recanted his support of segregation. When the *News Leader* admonished the southern liberal historian C. Vann Woodward for welcoming the end of segregation, Rubin took umbrage. "I made a much better Diehard Confederate when away from the scene of the crime," he later mentioned to Allen Tate, another of the original Agrarians. Rubin's rejection of massive resistance made him the third associate editor to break ranks with Kilpatrick.[95]

Kilpatrick and Rubin stayed friendly despite the disagreement. Rubin esteemed Kilpatrick's writing abilities and remained grateful to him for the opportunity to write in the city and region they both loved. The two men, additionally, subscribed to a set of cultural values that held the South aloft from modernity and change. For Rubin, the South's sense of community in-sulated it from larger forces of "spiritual and moral dislocation" in America. In 1957, Rubin recruited Kilpatrick to co-edit an anthology on the South similar to the Vanderbilt Agrarians' *I'll Take My Stand*. Titled *The Lasting South: Fourteen Southerners Look at Their Home*, the book opened with the assertion that the South's identity was "worth preserving." Rubin's intro-ductory essay, "An Image of the South," revealed a picture of the region he would develop into a grander design based on Agrarian ideals.[96]

Rubin's preoccupation with the Agrarians began in the 1950s just be-fore he worked for Kilpatrick. From 1954 to 1956, Rubin served as execu-tive secretary of the American Studies Association and, in 1956, organized the Southern Agrarians' reunion at Vanderbilt. Rather than seeking a prag-matic application of agrarianism, however, Rubin absorbed their views as testimony to pure, southern culture, or as a "symbol, a metaphor even, for a much larger cultural position," he told Allen Tate. Putting aside the im-practicality of the Vanderbilt Agrarians' economic positions in an industri-alized America, Rubin accepted the mythic aspects of their vision. For him, the Agrarians championed the best elements of the South. His apolitical reading of the Southern Agrarians ignored their racial bigotry and instead focused on only their good qualities in the form of a spiritual protest. They had, he reflected, dared to imagine

[a] society that very likely never existed, but one that should have ex-isted, in which men could live as individuals and not as automatons, aware of their finiteness and their dependence on God and nature, imbued with a sense of the deep inscrutability of nature, dedicated to the enhancement of the moral life in its aesthetic and spiritual di-mensions. In contrast to the hurried, nervous pace of life in modern

cities, the agrarian South was the image of a society in which human beings could live serenely and harmoniously. Not dominated by lust for money and power, they could be free of the tension and harassment of the modern industrial community.

The serene South dreamed of by the Agrarians and given new life by Rubin offered a touchstone "in which all was fixed and ordered, and everyone knew everyone else, and who he was, and who and what his family was."[97]

When Kilpatrick worked on Rubin's omnibus, he knew little about the history of the Agrarians and had mostly peripheral connections to them. After the publication of *The Sovereign States*, Kilpatrick had garnered praise from Richard Weaver, the intellectual most responsible for carrying the Agrarians' vision of rootedness and traditionalism into the postwar years. In Weaver's opinion, the whole Enlightenment project had undermined the God-centered universe and left modern man in a relativistic, materialistic daze. Kilpatrick also came to know Donald Davidson, another charter member of the Nashville Agrarians, who had enjoyed the editor's interposition crusade. Davidson, a professor of English at Vanderbilt University and a leader in Nashville's Citizens' Council, shared Kilpatrick and Weaver's insistence on the preservation of a transcendent order and their opposition to civil rights for blacks.[98]

Rubin and Kilpatrick may have diverged on the segregation issue, but they retained a cultural affinity, a mutual attachment to an ideal southern community, and an agreed sense of place. Rubin's "Image of the South" essay outlined a unique way of life grounded in southerners' attachment to family, history, and regional identity. While the earlier Agrarians had shunned factories, however, Rubin accepted the realities of industrial America. Rubin's "'lasting South,'" wrote Paul Murphy in his intellectual history of the Agrarians, "was an identity, not an economy." Rubin also jettisoned Kilpatrick, Davidson, and Weaver's white supremacy in favor of looking at how best to preserve values and accept blacks in a desegregating South.[99]

The Lasting South opened with questions about the retention of a southern identity in an industrialized, postsegregation world. Kilpatrick finished the book with a political essay that skirted the segregation issue and fused the South's values with the conservative movement. The "'race issue' alone," asserted Kilpatrick, could not define the South's conservatism. Like their Jeffersonian and Agrarian predecessors, mid-twentieth-century white southerners shared a "love of place" and a "sense of community." The South's culture "remains basically agrarian in its politics, its economy, its outlook," Kilpatrick wrote, "[and preserves a] tradition of man's dependence on the soil and his independence by reason of this." Southerners' manners, customs, and devotion to God differentiated them from other Americans, but their states' rights attachment to local government made them fundamentally American. The "Southern States," he insisted, "were [not] alone in demanding a plain explication of the State-Federal relationship."[100]

Addressing the postwar federal government's growth, Kilpatrick linked the South's reservations about state-centered consolidation to the conservative movement's fear of a "bulldozer society" that "will dominate men's lives and control their destinies." The perceived threat of an "omniscient state" based in Washington transcended "the immediate issue of school segregation in the Southern States" as well. Conservatism also could not rely on a smear campaign against liberals to win. Conservatives' "efforts to label opposition as 'Socialists' or 'statists' seem not to have taken hold," he wrote. The South must serve as a bastion of traditionalism while the forces of conservatism weathered "the storm." If the South could slow the ruination of the Republic, then "Southern conservatism one day will be counted not as bigotry but a blessing." Agrarianism, properly interpreted in the tradition of southern antistatism, according to Kilpatrick, was really a politics.[101]

In 1957, as the civil rights movement intensified, Kilpatrick and Rubin's remarks presented a heroic view of southern culture and politics that would become, in the 1970s, part of a major revitalization of the contemporary American South. Political and economic changes well under way in the late sixties and seventies not only brought the South's viability as a distinct region into question but also redefined the southern community. As resistance to civil rights collapsed, Kilpatrick and other southerners explored their identity and what role race would play in white consciousness.

The new realities were unmistakable and grounded in cultural, political, and economic changes. Since the Second World War, the number of factories in the South had tripled, and the region's agrarian identity had greatly diminished as a result. By 1980, more than fourteen million southerners had left farms and the land. Black southerners led the exodus as waves of them migrated north and west throughout the twentieth century. The African Americans who stayed behind became a major force in southern politics. The Civil Rights Act of 1964 and the Voting Rights Act of 1965 ushered in a new generation of black voters. African Americans in even the most racially obsessed southern states registered to vote. In Mississippi, the number of blacks registered to vote skyrocketed from 6.7 percent, before the Voting Rights Act, to 67 percent, by the early seventies.[102]

White southern politicians took note of African Americans' surging political power. In the 1970s and 1980s, moderate-to-progressive southern governors viewed black voting and the end of segregation with optimism. William Waller and later William Winter in Mississippi, Dale Bumpers in Arkansas, John West in South Carolina, Edwin Edwards in Louisiana, and Reuben Askew in Florida accepted the new racial reality and worked for change in their states. In 1971, Jimmy Carter, a former peanut farmer, won the governorship of Georgia and then, in 1976, the presidency.[103]

In the nation's eyes, Carter's election symbolized southern change. During the 1970s, while not all Americans forgave the South for the ferocity of its resistance to civil rights, they rediscovered the place and seemed captivated by the region. During the bicentennial, *Saturday Review* portrayed the South as "the New America." The region reunited with the nation not just as a prodigal son but as an exemplar of racial reconciliation and redemptive values at a time when troubled Americans searched for ways to cope with the country's burdens. In its September 1976 special edition focusing on Jimmy Carter and the presidential contest, *Time* magazine celebrated "The South Today." The Lost Cause mythology that Louis Rubin gushed about and the states' rights rhetoric that James Kilpatrick spouted had been "drowned out by a new beat—the frank clang of cash registers, of buildings going up, of dirt roads being paved . . . of expectations that no longer seem visionary or Utopian," announced *Time*. The burst of activity and the atmosphere of change had not diminished the region's distinctiveness. The South represented "the last American arena with a special, nurtured identity, its own sometimes unfashionable regard for the soil, for family ties, for the authority of God and country." Popular music, television, and films propagated regional chauvinism too. Tanya Tucker and Lynyrd Skynyrd tunes, *The Dukes of Hazzard* and *The Waltons*, and a slew of Burt Reynolds movies helped solidify the new, positive image.[104]

Aware of the efforts to rehabilitate the South, the nation's top conservative political columnist chimed in, and he came equipped for the portents of change. In some ways, the newest New South reflected James Kilpatrick's prevailing experiences. Key influences in his early life prepared him for progress, modernity, and growth, not for inertia. His timber-dealing father helped cut down southern forests. The Bryan family in Richmond built their newspaper empire on investments in railroads and mining. Kilpatrick made cities—Oklahoma City, Richmond, and Washington—not the country-side, his homes. But now, in the 1970s, defenders of the South described their community in terms of the land and rural traditions, and, perhaps strangely, Kilpatrick did too. Because Kilpatrick was no country boy, his contributions to preserving the South's rural image during the seventies were all the more remarkable and atypical. For him and some other conservatives, the agrarian South seemed the model of community and a stable political order.[105]

Along with Richard Weaver and M. E. Bradford, a *National Review* contributor and student of Donald Davidson at Vanderbilt, Kilpatrick reclaimed agrarianism as a political ideology. Agrarianism was part of a genealogy of southern conservatism Kilpatrick knew well from his time in Virginia. Reaching back to the antistatist country gentlemen John Taylor, Thomas Jefferson, and John Randolph of Roanoke, who envisioned a nation of independent freeholding farmers, Kilpatrick did not draw a new battle line for southern conservatism; he deepened the trench. Like his antebellum predecessors of the Old Dominion, Kilpatrick imagined an organic society infused with republican antifederalism. During the last days of the civil rights era, the fight was to be joined not only against the federal government but also against an America turned away from community, patriarchy, and order. The political genius of antebellum southern theorists of states' rights and an organic society took on new meaning as Kilpatrick translated their wisdom into a politics of identity and a narrow ethic of old-fashioned social thinking. Symbolism soon became Kilpatrick's preferred means of describing a nomothetic society based on habits and wisdom drawn through the generations.[106]

To rewrite an old script for a changing South, Kilpatrick changed venues. In 1969, he and his wife built a farmhouse/work studio named White Walnut Hill on thirty-seven acres of land at the headwaters of the Rappahannock River in the foothills of Virginia's Blue Ridge Mountains. Two flags flew over their home: the Stars and Stripes and an old Revolutionary War flag featuring a black snake and the inscription "Don't Tread on Me." His weekend getaway near the Rappahannock County community of Woodville, eighty-five miles southwest of Washington, developed into a haven for dropouts, artists, farmers, and writers. The western part of the county was piedmont and the eastern half was in the Virginia hunt country. Residents lived with few amenities and no supermarkets, fast food chains, or stoplights. General stores served as community gathering sites. Although bordered on three sides by the Baltimore-D.C. metro area, Rappahannock lagged behind. No highways or railroads disrupted the pastoral fields, orchards, and million-dollar estates. The county was not on the way to anywhere. Secluded from Beltway politics, Kilpatrick lived like a gentleman-planter and observed Nature's rhythms.[107]

While Kilpatrick held on to the remnants of an agrarian society, something else was lost. The Watergate scandal, most recently, had furthered his distaste for urban living and the Washington political beat. "You have to rethink all these things now," marveled Kilpatrick. "I've been writing for years that Nixon is an astute politician. But is he? The paranoia. The secrecy. The abuse of power! . . . You begin to wonder if the things you've supported all these years aren't rotten all the way down." Kilpatrick took Watergate personally, and he desperately wanted normality. His conservative instincts and apprehension about progress drew him into peregrinations for steadfast truths and purity. He looked first to the ambiance of the new Kilpatrick homestead: "[A]t night when all the lights are out in the country, you can feel that just a few feet away from the house there is another world moving. The animals . . . the fields . . . the stars. That world doesn't change." Even before the woeful abyss of Watergate, pressure on Kilpatrick's world, with its southern locus, had increased. Toward the end of the civil rights era, he and other white southerners tried again to limit their political and cultural vulnerability.[108]

After Kilpatrick abandoned Nixon to a likely impeachment, his columns focused more on ideas that he had developed since 1966. From the vantage point of his Rappahannock manor, he moved into a personal, reminiscent mode of writing that dealt with his domestic world and its natural surroundings. Living like a squire, Kilpatrick described a slow-paced, unadulterated South where each man knew his position, respected his neighbors, and lived in harmony with nature and society. In an effort to forget about the unrest of the sixties and escape the discord of the seventies, Kilpatrick reconstructed a hamlet—Scrabble, Virginia—that reflected his roots. "Hardscrabble" better described the byline for the new column since it reflected Kilpatrick's beginnings on the plains of Oklahoma and implied age-old ethics of hard work and self-improvement. Scrabble was a last frontier for Kilpatrick, and he turned to this legendary place as an oppositional model against an anomic America averse to self-sacrifice and building solid communities.

Kilpatrick filed the "Scrabble" articles, hundreds of them, every couple weeks or months in his "A Conservative View" and *Nation's Business* columns, and they contained short stories about his home and family, the animals on his property, the county's residents, and the seasons of the land. Until about 1937, Scrabble had been a real place with its own post office. It had even appeared on some old Civil War maps of the area. Kilpatrick liked to make old things live again, and he datelined the columns "Scrabble." Confused readers often addressed letters to him using the village name rather than Woodville and received replies from the postal service that no such town existed.[109]

Though not an incorporated city or town or a fictional Camelot or Yoknapatawpha, "Scrabble most certainly *is*," Kilpatrick assured readers. Rappahannock County had few physical markers, but that was fine by its inhabitants: no liquor store, no golf course, no pool hall, and no bookstore. Kilpatrick summed up the county's infrastructure: "[R]udimentary" law enforcement, "minimal" public health services, weak public schools, dirt roads, no hospital, no chain fast food, and only a volunteer fire department. The only school in the ruins of Scrabble itself was an abandoned building, empty since desegregation. As Kilpatrick put it, Rappahannock was a road-block to the "Holy Name of Progress." "The action was someplace else," Kilpatrick wrote with relish. "That's the story of Rappahannock."[110]

Such a relaxed pace of living seemed unfitting for a city boy who liked concert halls and the rooms of swirling political discussion. But, for Kilpatrick, there was "a certain freedom in captivity, a certain peacefulness in being prisoner" in the mountains. There, he found a community where one need only "look after the elementary necessities of existence." In the hills of Rappahannock and at the heart of Scrabble, there "is no end, and no beginning either." "Rappahannockers are great ones for continuity," Kilpatrick wrote with admiration. "Families remain; place names echo long-gone generations; the mountains never change." The county's denizens lived unburdened by the present. They fished, made hay, moonshined, raised cattle, grew fruit, and regarded industry as sacrilegious. In the late fall they slaughtered hogs, in the summers they held tent revivals, and on weekends they auctioned livestock.[111]

Scrabble offered Kilpatrick more than continuity, it gave him another way, albeit obliquely, to fix political and racial problems. For over twenty years, from *Brown* to affirmative action, race had disrupted the tranquility of the South and had obsessed Kilpatrick. In one early Scrabble column, he cursed the 1960s and called for a retreat to a simpler time:

Perhaps this was the story of the past decade: mixed good and ill, trees fallen, roads blocked and opened and blocked again, rough winds keening from a ragged sky. This was the violent decade; color it angry red—shots in the night, Watts burning, glass breaking, and sirens forever winding tight spirals through the skull. It was a decade of crime, brutality, bloodshed, blurred by tears for young men dead. The violence was more than physical. This was the decade in which civility was lost. The wind rips at our Rappahannock earth built by centuries: manners, courtesy, tolerance, respect for authority—the Sixties saw these hurled in massive drifts across our roads.

Many readers shared Kilpatrick's fears and longing for familiarity. One man discovered in Scrabble a quality "that strengthens one's beliefs, and reaffirms what one feels about the things that are really basic, true and abiding in what often seems to be a world completely without any but the wrong direction."[112]

Within his rejection of the sixties, Kilpatrick provided a corrective to the era's depravity, reaffirmed his beliefs, and plugged core southern values. With Scrabble, Kilpatrick revisited an older political model in which prescriptive community values ruled. Any American, not just the southerner, disaffected by the strife of the previous decades could find sanctuary in Scrabble, a place where people still cherished privacy and property rights, learned to settle disputes in county and state courts without outside interference, and relied on inner strength. Local customs and self-rule allowed the people to solve problems effectively in accord with community needs. "[A]ll of us dwell, in city or suburb or town or country, in our own Rappahannock Counties," Kilpatrick remarked. "It is not necessary to look to Congress, or to the high court, or to the White House," to find the will of the people. The federal government was only noticeable by its absence in Scrabble. He believed that most Americans, no matter what their background, had always veered toward individualism and local politics and remained leery, if not distrustful, of centralized authority. By putting greater faith in individuals and communities than in national institutions, Scrabble's residents, and those they symbolized, lived free from federal rule. This kind of conservatism was a philosophy universally applicable but also inextricably linked to what Kilpatrick considered "southern."[113]

Just as Kilpatrick wrote about the South's guardianship of the land against disruptions to its aesthetic orthodoxy, Scrabble provided a synergy of natural order and racial hierarchy. Sheltered from modern America and the federal government, Scrabble represented a fabled South, a romanticized version of the Jim Crow past, that saluted a white ideal by ignoring divisive racial issues. Kilpatrick described Scrabble as "a loose, unbounded nineteenth century community where white man, bound slave, and free Negro once scrabbled side by side in the same shale for a living." Retreating to an antebellum concept of society, as the Agrarians had, meant returning to a period of slaveholders who believed only white property owners could rule society. White freedom and discrimination against minorities in the early constitutional republic, the era dearest to Kilpatrick, had forged important bonds between whites. The republicanism of the late eighteenth and early nineteenth centuries had depended on a natural order of things, including the political exclusion of blacks, to unify whites. Using Scrabble to reinstate cohesion would glue contemporary America at a time of rapid social upheaval and divisions.[114]

In a late-twentieth-century America scarred by continuous unrest, Kilpatrick felt a "certain shock" and had reestablished a stable southland that still respected manners and order. "Values are slipping away," he fretted. "If I can write on the earth . . . something good and solid," it would benefit the public and be of "therapeutic value" for him. Through Scrabble, Kilpatrick could think "upon changing times and eternal verities." In seclusion, he could ponder the issues of the day and refresh his spirit. Although the South changed around him, he created a refuge that survived the civil rights movement and the Warren Court. "Laws change," he noted, "but hills and hearts and humans stay the same." Scrabble was both a physical and a metaphysical setting. Kilpatrick's paeans to the peaceful, pristine, rolling hills of Virginia served as a break from his Washington-beat writing as well as its "state of mind."[115]

An eclectic array of sources buttressed Kilpatrick's reconstruction of a political tradition of tapered rights, limited government, and patriarchal authority. His interest in bandaging all three together into an organic whole was more academic than practical. Kilpatrick recognized the need to give the abstract Scrabble some intellectual grounding in the hopes of reversing the South's and the nation's trajectory. Russell Kirk, the best-known conservative traditionalist in America, obliged Kilpatrick. Kirk pushed for continued "resistance to the idea of a planned society, through restoration of an order which will make the planned society unnecessary and impracticable." He also pointed out society's perpetual struggle with the "problem of spiritual and moral regeneration" and advocated "the restoration of the ethical system and the religious sanction upon which any life worth living is founded." Kilpatrick had little use for religious-based traditionalism but drew on the postwar revival of interest in Edmund Burke fostered by

Kirk. The individual's political self depended upon social connections and a sense of rootedness. "[T]o cultivate a love for one's own land, as . . . Burke reflected year's ago," Kilpatrick noted, "is to forge the first link in the chain that leads from a love of one's own community to a love of country, and thence to a love of all mankind."[116]

Burke and Kilpatrick's assertion of an individual's identity fixed in an organic community meshed well with the views of an unlikely ally. In 1978, former Democratic senator Eugene J. McCarthy, the anti-Vietnam presidential campaigner, moved into an eighteenth-century stone farmhouse in Rappahannock County and became Kilpatrick's neighbor. On many nights, the two men from opposite ends of the political spectrum talked poetry, philosophy, art, literature, and religion over bourbon. Agrarianism also drew the men together. McCarthy grew up on a farm in Minnesota during the Depression. Influenced by the Catholic rural life movement, whose adherents envisioned the land as a source of freedom and stability and as a base of community, he eventually joined the Minnesota Farm Labor Party, an amalgamation of socialists, agrarians, and utopians. McCarthy's Catholic education at a Benedictine university pitted him against the modern, secular world. Modernity threatened community, isolated people, and damaged the family. One biographer described McCarthy as a "conservative lamenting the passing of tradition" rather than "a liberal confidant in the march of progress." A belief in order, hierarchy, and tradition put McCarthy in line with a European-derived conservatism stretching back to thinkers like John Henry Cardinal Newman and Edmund Burke. Russell Kirk's *Conservative Mind*, which drew Kilpatrick to the conservative intellectual movement, plotted the same path. McCarthy, like Kilpatrick, also admired Burke for the value he placed on traditions and cultural institutions.[117]

In the wake of the epochal civil rights movement, the South had to somehow avoid too much change. As Kilpatrick assessed behavioral changes in whites caused by the movement, he submitted mythic Scrabble and agrarianism as a way out of the cultural morass. If southern behavior could be so dramatically altered in what had seemed a morally evil society, perhaps the region's redemption still could be achieved through agrarianism. Yet the morality projected in Kilpatrick's contemporary South was not the same as that preached by the 1930s Nashville Agrarians. They believed in the South as the last noncapitalist hope against a wave of materialism that had engulfed Europe and the northern United States.

Kilpatrick's background gave him a perspective on the South's economics and demography at variance with the Agrarians. As a son of the New

South, Kilpatrick found that extolling the beauty and wonder of a rural past seemed easier than offering correctives for the burdens of capitalism and southern history. His idea of the South ignored the evils of the invisible hand. Kilpatrick spent his youth in boomtown Oklahoma City and Upper South Virginia; he had not grown up in the Black Belt or experienced first-hand the depredation of sharecropping and textile mills. Squaring free-market capitalism with agrarianism had never occurred to the Depression-era Agrarians.[118]

Something unholy to the Vanderbilt Agrarians had seeped into Scrabble's soul, but Kilpatrick worked to fuse his South with theirs. He retained, for example, the Southern Agrarians' vision of a diversity of local economies and cultures. Fifty years after the publication of *I'll Take My Stand*, in a photographic essay on Scrabble titled *The American South: Four Seasons of the Land*, Kilpatrick argued, "There is no such thing as *the* Southerner." The experience of an East Tennessean could be quite distinct from that of a Charlestonian or a Texan. In *The American South: Towns and Cities* (1982), a companion volume, Kilpatrick paid homage to the original Agrarians' assertion that there existed a "definable South, that retains certain distinctive elements," but unlike them, he added that "we cherish our cities." A cohesive southland, he contended, had survived into the late twentieth century amid air-conditioned skyscrapers and shiny cities.[119]

In his Scrabble books and articles, Kilpatrick blamed the decline of a patriarchal, organic social order on the increasing power of the state and liberal individualism, not on cities or capitalism. Misery loved company, or corporations, more precisely, at this time. As the blame game worsened during the 1970s, Kilpatrick, and Americans in general, often refused to indict industry for industry's failures. Government and unions served as the more conspicuous culprits. For the most part, Kilpatrick, as did many others, equivocated on the role of the market in the social order. According to his version of agrarianism, scrolled in the partisan pages of *Nation's Business*, traditional culture depended on premodern values but not on a premodern economy. The free market and corporate capitalism were compatible with agrarianism, and he spent little to no time considering the negative relation between culture and economics. Kilpatrick seemed to believe that without the deforming presence of the activist state, liberal social planning, and cultural radicals, traditional culture would assume the shape it always had.

The Nashville Agrarians never would have made that claim. They criticized industrial capitalism and confronted the modern cult of progress with a call to slow down, to return to a simpler, more leisurely way of life, one, they believed, that history and tradition supported. Kilpatrick echoed their call for a return to an earlier way of life and their sense of nostalgia but not their economics. The Agrarians helped him to point out the hollowness of liberalism's planned society and big government, but he mutated their agrarianism into a capitalist-friendly version of republican political philosophy. Stripped of its radicalism and anticapitalism, Kilpatrick's agrarianism served the free market, celebrated rugged individualism, and promoted his social view of the South.[120]

Out of the experience of civil rights, Kilpatrick reawakened Scrabble as a new southern Eden in an updated briar patch. Ignoring the deleterious problems of the past, he urged the South to embrace a different heritage, symbolized not by racism and segregation but by reverence for local government, regional identity, and the land. Kilpatrick approved all three as aspects of a cultural revitalization emerging out of the fear that the South would not survive the civil rights era as a distinct entity.

Regional writers, though, kept alive the idea of the South as a potentially redemptive community. Channeling the Agrarians' spirit in the absence of Jim Crow, Kilpatrick affirmed southern worth within the 1970s rejuvenation of southern culture. Massive resistance had failed to unify the South, but Kilpatrick argued for a return to tradition as the South faced postindustrial, post–civil rights America. He understood that, forged in a fear of the federal government and liberalism and blended with provincialism, despite modernity and the detritus of segregation, the South had lessons to teach Americans on the necessity of preserving community and order.

As the nation contemplated the South and the ripple effects of civil rights, Kilpatrick had again transformed himself. During the same years that he emerged as an opponent of "reverse racism," his facility for self reinvention knew few boundaries. Kilpatrick was the king of such conceits. With his welcoming of agrarianism, he not only worked to shed his unsavory reputation without abandoning more of his racial philosophy but also adopted a new identity as a gentleman-farmer belonging to another minority group, the agrarian-southerner.

Consistent with his other post–Jim Crow makeovers, Kilpatrick's neoagrarianism helped him to escape the confines of his ordeal over integration and the legacies of the South's past. With Scrabble, similarly, he was able to ignore painful questions about race and to disregard blacks' suffering from poverty and degradation. Kilpatrick's positive portrayal of the South had a special appeal to whites who worried about the post–civil rights South's embrace of blacks into political life. On the surface, Kilpatrick had abandoned racial politics, but he had also repaired the white southern belief in organic hierarchy. Scrabble had simply stifled race and presented what sort of community Kilpatrick envisioned to make it agreeable to more Americans.

By the late 1960s and 1970s, the problem of race in the white mind had not yet resulted in a triumph for egalitarianism. Conflicts between democratic ideals and everyday realities pervaded race relations throughout the nation, not just in the South or in Scrabble. Clashes over busing and affirmative action were only the most recent, visible fights over race and equal access in America's neighborhoods and schools. Scrabble, however, provided a cheery celebration of the country through the South and instilled regional pride for a place that had earned negative publicity. Kilpatrick erected Scrabble, a place of stability, order, and strength, as a tribute to everything positive about the South. His platitudes probably satisfied many white readers, but they also pointed out what remained implicit and left undone.

Through Scrabble, Kilpatrick's nostalgia exposed some Americans' abiding inability or unwillingness to confront the difficulties and gritty history of race in the South. Scrabble censored the energy and power of the civil rights era because Kilpatrick refused to acknowledge the countless frustrations and humiliations in the lives of blacks. Instead of using the Virginia village to address centuries of racial tragedies, Kilpatrick retracted from reconciliation. For Kilpatrick, the South's segregated past and the southern way of life had no relation to the inequality, discrimination, and prejudice African Americans continued to suffer.

In important ways, Kilpatrick's Scrabble was at odds with the harmonious, biracial South that liberals and moderates hoped to establish. Questioning that optimism coincided with and intensified a general loss of faith in public institutions and government solutions that balkanized the nation. By the time Ronald Reagan appeared on the scene to bind the nation's wounds, a fear of change prevailed, and many Americans clung to a conservative antistatism, hence their susceptibility to a vocabulary that excused the opponents of racial reform of any wrongdoing and evoked a mythological time when government was not big and people did for themselves. In Kilpatrick's final act, he tapped into the newest form of media to spin this nostalgic tale of individualism, small-town values, and limited government before the federal government intervened in racial matters and created social upheaval and, at the same time, to rewrite his own legacy regarding race. Scrabble and racial Newspeak presaged a novel form of conservatism that produced not only an alternate history and language but one that Americans could grasp easily and without guilt.

Silas Rogers and
James J. Kilpatrick,
1953. Courtesy
of Richmond
Newspapers, Inc.

Editorial cartoon
by Art Wood, from
the *Richmond
News Leader*,
30 November
1955. Courtesy
of Richmond
Newspapers, Inc.

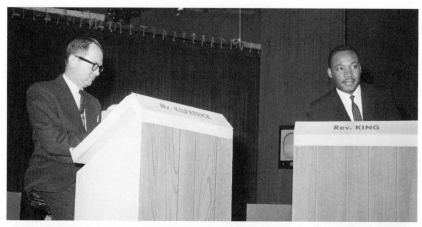

(top) James J. Kilpatrick and Martin Luther King Jr. debate
on *The Nation's Future*, 1960. Courtesy of Associated Press.

(bottom) Senator Harry Byrd (left) and James J. Kilpatrick after a hike
outside Winchester, Virginia, 1960. Papers of James J. Kilpatrick, 1925–1966,
Accession #6626-c, University of Virginia Library, Charlottesville, Va.

(top) James J. Kilpatrick on the job at the *Richmond News Leader*, 1962. Courtesy of Richmond Newspapers, Inc.

(bottom) James J. Kilpatrick and Richard Nixon talking at the White House, 1974. Courtesy of Richmond Newspapers, Inc.

James J. Kilpatrick at home in Rappahannock County, 1976.
Courtesy of Richmond Newspapers, Inc.

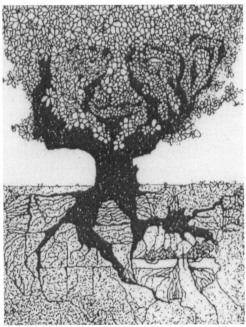

A cartoon that accompanied an article by Philip Hilts in the *Washington Post*, 23 September 1973. The illustrations capture Kilpatrick's growth from southern roots to the national scene. Courtesy of Philip Hilts and the *Washington Post*.

SIX

The Revolution Will Not Be Televised

On a Thursday afternoon in September 1973, James J. Kilpatrick stood behind a podium waiting for television studio cameras to start rolling. A flamboyant African American technician walked into the set. Glancing at the young man's pink and purple, high-heeled, platform shoes, Kilpatrick exclaimed, "Wow!" "Do you wear those out on the street?" he asked with a coy little chortle. "Only out to the car and back," laughed the technician as he studied Kilpatrick's footwear. Then, he reprimanded Kilpatrick, "You still wearing wingtips? You ought to be ashamed!" The columnist's sartorial dress for televised appearances was immaculate, down to his brown wingtip shoes. "Well, I have an image to preserve you know," Kilpatrick joked. "I used to wear cowboy boots." The flash of a red light on the camera cued Kilpatrick to speak. "At the risk of sounding like an old fogey," he began, "let me sound like an old fogey." Kilpatrick rattled through a list of topics, including home rule for the District of Columbia, the Constitution, and wildlife preservation. When the red light flickered off, he returned to his dressing room, sat in front of his makeup mirror, and assessed his performance.[1]

To report a position, Kilpatrick tried to get into his subject's mind. "You have to see these things through their eyes just the way they would see them," he explained to a *Washington Post* correspondent. In the fall of 1973, Kilpatrick struggled to understand the players in the Watergate scandal. Few journalists in the Washington press corps had greater access to the Nixon White House than Kilpatrick. He and Nixon met in 1948 at the Alger Hiss hearings, and, by 1961, Nixon "had a particularly high regard for the vigor and accuracy of the *News Leader* editorials."[2]

The columnist had come far and fast since his days in Richmond. His praise and defense of Nixon and the Silent Majority earned Kilpatrick dinner invitations and exclusive interviews at the White House, and he occasionally attended Sunday prayers with the president. Sometimes Nixon even consulted with Kilpatrick, whom he and others considered a respected bellwether for the health of American conservatism. When news of the

Watergate scandal broke, Kilpatrick imagined his response if he were president: "I would have picked up the phone and said, 'Get McCord up here! I want Liddy's ass in my office right now!' I would call him every kind of pluperfect son of a bitch . . . ! It would have been over in 24 hours. Lyndon Johnson would have done that." Despite his confidence and proximity to power, it took Kilpatrick a minute to calm.[3]

Kilpatrick's career had brought him close to the elite, whether they were Virginia kingpins, *National Review* insiders, or Washington journalists, and he won the respect of influential Republican politicians. Nixon's aides took Kilpatrick seriously, and the White House regarded him as a loyalist, but the Watergate scandal steadily wore down Kilpatrick's support. "Watergate! The very word rings like the drowned bells of a sunken cathedral," he moaned in one syndicated column. At first, Kilpatrick concocted fantasies to save Nixon, including one in which the Cubans had framed the president. Gradually, the Nixon administration's deceptions proved too great to ignore. After White House tapes exposed the "smoking gun" of Nixon's coverup of the break-in and obstruction of justice, Kilpatrick was unable to clear the president's name. Saddled with grief, he nearly sobbed: "I am close to tears. My President is a liar. I wish he were a crook instead," he groaned.[4]

Nixon's misdeeds did not preclude Kilpatrick's evolving expression of conservatism, however. While the hubbub at the White House preoccupied the nation, he had again been refining the presentation of his message. Thanks, in part, to Kilpatrick's television appearances and syndicated columns, the seventies generated a political glow in which conservatism would bask for years despite the failures of Nixon and that other herald of divisions between real and fake Americans, George Wallace. The politics of pageantry was conservatism's inheritance, not Watergate or Wallace's politics of rage. The movement entered a fresh phase and presented a new face in the mainstream media. Entering the 1970s, the adept Kilpatrick spun conservatism into ideological performance art. The conservative movement, not the civil rights revolution or Kilpatrick's dark past with race, would be televised. Through commentators like Kilpatrick, partisan politics became more ideological and alluring than ever before. Kilpatrick's role in expanding conservatism's reach enhanced his stature and led to greater involvement in various activities.[5]

The Politics of Celebrity

During the late sixties and seventies, Kilpatrick became a highly sought after conservative analyst in the national media. His political message resonated powerfully among Americans. In 1970, over 170 newspapers carried his syndicated column. By 1980, his commentary on public and political affairs appeared from coast to coast in 538 dailies with a collective circulation of more than twenty million. Kilpatrick's writing skills and political connections had paid impressive dividends. The former Goldwater supporters and throngs of Nixon's Silent Majority who read his columns made him an annual income in excess of $150,000 and one of the most popular syndicated political writers of the decade.[6]

Kilpatrick's columns made him more than money. They also showcased his brilliance—losing. He had learned to be a good loser by sidestepping and upending the application of civil rights goals. Kilpatrick could not stop the civil rights movement, but his defiant campaigns and media savvy reoriented race issues and forged a national conservative constituency against the laws, court rulings, and ideas that he disliked. He became fluent in the language of the right and its adherence to private property rights, hostility toward central government, faith in disciplinary authority to defend order, adherence to free market capitalism, and indifference to racial advancement for blacks. The rank and file of the conservative base was his core audience, and Kilpatrick was truly an institution in his own right. "He seems to have a constituency, and I think they're legion and they're loyal," Peter Lisagor of the *Chicago Daily News* noted. "It's almost as if he's a congressman from some huge district." *Washington Post* correspondent Philip Hilts called Kilpatrick the "representative of Right 'n Proud-of-it Country" and "the king of the country conservative spokesmen."[7]

Writing his political column gave Kilpatrick enormous cachet with all kinds of conservatives and a sense of personal satisfaction. "It's a fun field," he remarked. Kilpatrick had "never been happier." As an editorialist, he mastered the art of advocacy: communicating ideas, defending them, and convincing others of their soundness. Syndicated columns also forced him to stay sharp and pay attention to his audience to remain a success or risk losing them. "I'm a free enterpriser," he continued. If he wrote "a good column, my papers will keep me. But I'm keenly aware that I'm going to lose those papers if I don't. . . . So I have to stay aware; there's not much security in this business."[8]

Kilpatrick pursued an exhausting schedule after he entered the D.C. press scene. In one day, he sped through three radio tapings, two television shows, and three TV commentaries. He also wrote three weekly syndicated columns. Combined with his lectures, the several magazine articles he wrote a year, and his books, Kilpatrick amassed an impressive body of work. Fame, however, came from his television appearances. As the Republican Party gained strength, more networks wanted conservative talking heads on their political talk shows, but there were only a few available on which to model. Kilpatrick became a journalist-celebrity in an era that saw the rise of George F. Will, Robert Novak, Pat Buchanan, Fred Barnes, and Stan Evans. He and other political commentators gained national recognition by virtue of their wit and through the overwhelming number of newspapers owned by Republicans, and the high-priced lecture series sponsored by business groups that liked conservatives.

In the late 1960s, Kilpatrick's reputation as a writer and right-leaning polemicist earned him television slots on political talk shows like *Meet the Press* and *Inside Washington*. In 1969, Washington television producers had hired him as one of four regulars on Martin Agronsky's political roundtable, *Agronsky & Company*. *Agronsky*, one of the first television news programs in D.C., became required viewing for politicians and political insiders. Notable journalists like Kilpatrick, George Will, Carl Rowan, Peter Lisagor, and Hugh Sidey were regular guests. Presidents Richard Nixon, Jimmy Carter, and Ronald Reagan watched it routinely. For a dozen years, *Agronsky* was the most popular Washington talk show on the air.[9]

The producers of current-affairs programs encouraged provocative commentary and wanted confrontation over rather than discussion of issues. On *Agronsky*, the producers pitted Kilpatrick against four moderates/liberals. They even ran local television ads that previewed Kilpatrick's contentious comments. "Some liberals insist he is ten miles to the right of Ivan the Terrible," said one. "But to those of us who love him, he's only a little to the south of John C. Calhoun." In 1970, Don Hewitt, the producer and creator of CBS's *60 Minutes* paired him with *Washington Post* new left journalist Nicholas Von Hoffman in three-minute "Point/Counterpoint" debates that first aired in September 1971. "We weren't screamers," recalled Von Hoffman, but they did practice a "form of political wrestling." As the segment's right half, Kilpatrick adopted the same adversarial style and offered the same controversial opinions that he had as an editor. His criticism of welfare programs sometimes drew accusations from Von Hoffman that he was a racist who advocated policies that intentionally harmed blacks.[10]

The commentators' weekly sparring ended without reconciliation, anticipating the one-sided pundit shows and ranting personalities that would dominate cable television news in the future. Bill Press, former co-host of the Cable News Network's *Crossfire*, which aired from 1982 to 2005, credited "Point/Counterpoint" as his show's inspiration. "They established the format, and we all followed in their footsteps," said Press. Even Hollywood mimicked the right-versus-left television spot. In 1976, CBS producer Norman Lear developed *All's Fair* (1976–77) as a sitcom spinoff of "Point/Counterpoint." The show, set in Washington, featured actor Richard Crenna, who played the conservative columnist modeled on Kilpatrick, and Bernadette Peters, his younger, liberal wife. To portray the conservative view correctly, Lear invited Nixon speechwriter, Ben Stein, to help write the show's dialogue. *All's Fair* was as short-lived, however, as Von Hoffman's tenure as Kilpatrick's liberal antithesis.[11]

When CBS fired the contrarian Von Hoffman for defaming Richard Nixon in 1974, *Life* journalist and *Newsweek* columnist Shana Alexander, a blue-blooded liberal whose father wrote the great Democratic anthem "Happy Days Are Here Again," replaced him and turned the segment into a battle of the sexes. Kilpatrick bantered with her over the Equal Rights Amendment, government-funded health care, and a host of other matters. Once, when she pushed for expanded Social Security benefits, he snapped back, "When your heart bleeds, it bleeds in buckets. . . . You're full of mushy sentimentality and mushy economics too."[12]

Although Kilpatrick had earned a fearsome reputation, he had a softer side. The little group at CBS saw Kilpatrick in both his varieties, both the curmudgeonly and the congenial. Off camera, he was affable, even impish, with colleagues and not proprietary with his professional talents. He and Alexander choreographed their skirmishes and read from teleprompters, and Kilpatrick taught her to make their fights more dramatic. On one occasion, he suggested that they debate "the plight of 700 million women and children dying of famine. My idea, naturally, is to let 'em starve. Does your heart bleed? Would you do good? We have to get into role reversal." He perfected playing the conservative villain against his liberal cohorts, and he thrived on the scrupulous discipline required of him to squeeze an argument into a ninety-second segment. His ability to make concise and powerful points came from years of editorial and syndicated writing. Alexander observed that the performance came naturally to Kilpatrick: "Jack didn't have to do any research as he had made up his mind on all the issues thirty years ago."[13]

"Point/Counterpoint" was unlike other outlets for the right because conservatives were not talking only to each other anymore. The segment featured both liberal and conservative slants while providing the right a platform to repay attacks on liberals after years of having few conservative voices in mainstream publications and politics. Such programming gave conservatives the chance to "stick it to the liberals," remarked Richard Viguerie, who, through his direct-mail campaigns, became a revolutionary leader in disseminating conservative ideas. The power of television to mold opinions cannot be underestimated. In the 1970s, Kilpatrick fine-tuned the image of conservatism through his skillful blend of narrative and emotion on TV spots. People expected more personal relationships with those bringing them the news and commentary. The press had exposed the Watergate scandal, after all, and seemed like some of the last good guys in an America adrift in political failure at its uppermost levels. Viewers wanted "a much more personalized journalism than tradition has permitted," Kilpatrick understood. With a keen interest in how he appeared on television, he sensed instinctively what few other political tacticians did, that conservatism needed new techniques to proliferate itself. An emotive TV persona could sell ideas better than plain facts could. Kilpatrick's gift was in creating a mood around issues and turning his conservatism into theater.[14]

Kilpatrick, now in his fifties, emerged as the conservative spokesman extraordinaire of the 1970s. On and off the television screen, he was confident and articulate. His skill in imbuing even the dullest political issues with significance made him nationally famous. Today, most Americans expect political commentary to be delivered with personality and flair, but in the seventies, Kilpatrick's anthropomorphic punditry was groundbreaking. He played the role easily, and other political journalists registered fascination about Kilpatrick's self-importance wherever he went. Covering the 1972 Democratic primaries in New Hampshire for *Rolling Stone* magazine, Hunter S. Thompson recoiled when Kilpatrick, "the famous crypto-nazi newspaper columnist," strolled into the same bar one night. Kilpatrick made no attempt to sit with peers, and, Thompson scoffed, "he made sure everybody in the room knew exactly who he was." As is true of most innovative artists, Kilpatrick tended to go over the top, but such braggadocio helped spearhead a stylish conservatism into political hoopla.[15]

By the 1970s, therefore, Kilpatrick was both a television curiosity and a tough spokesman. He was genteel and colorful. He was at home among bustling Washingtonians and provincial Virginians. Oklahoma City, New Orleans, and Richmond had all contributed to his upbringing and outlook. Kilpatrick had become unusually equipped for the enormous task of addressing broad swaths of Americans. On television, Kilpatrick settled on one identity to speak his mind. Adopting the rich speech of the Virginia tobacco aristocracy, he presented himself as a country gentleman with simple southern roots. Assuming the same mien of a homespun patrician that he developed through his Scrabble columns, the cosmopolitan Kilpatrick ordained himself the avuncular voice of the common man. Anyone who saw past his TV charade learned a little more about the man. Kilpatrick was someone who wanted respect and to influence his audience.

All politics is local, so the saying goes, or, in other words, people's immediate reality informs their political philosophy. Kilpatrick reversed the old maxim. On television, politics shaped reality. Many saw Kilpatrick as more than a conservative with *a* view. His supporters typically evaluated his politics as prognostications and judged him exactly right in expressing their beliefs. "If only more of us could make ourselves heard, or have the opportunity to be read, with the same cooperation from the newspapers and television, that you are given," trumpeted one woman, "just maybe the vast silent majority, would not be taking the back seat, and permitting this 'vocal minority' to remove all our rights and good freedoms." A Milwaukeean reacted similarly after seeing Kilpatrick on *60 Minutes*. "Sometimes I get the feeling that ESP is really alive," she marveled.[16]

The popularity of "Point/Counterpoint" and the increasing presence of conservatives on television demonstrated that the right resonated with audiences in the 1970s. Kilpatrick was a recognizable figure on television throughout the decade. By 1980, *60 Minutes* had climbed to number one in the television ratings with over 100 million viewers. Thanks in part to point men like George Will and James Kilpatrick, conservatism was more accessible than ever. Their work went far beyond the right's days as a literary, intellectual movement, and they rallied conservatives.[17]

The appeal of Kilpatrick's approach to conservatism lay in his uncomplicated, vivacious way of expressing himself and his departure from earlier, less effective means of framing the conservative challenge. In 1955, during the infancy of conservative political discourse, how representative the *National Review* was of the nation's conservatism remained unclear. As important as Buckley's role was in steering the movement's heading, his magazine received criticism for its esoteric tone. Ironically, because of his masterful use of language, Buckley's proclaimed conservatism of inclusion did not appeal to all readers. One woman urged that he "*not* make it [the *National Review*] too erudite for the average reader." Another advised, "Please ask your writers to use plain simple language, and not to hide their meaning under sarcastic double-talk." Since then, highbrow, intellectual conservatism for the most part has been displaced by the televised, emotive form pioneered by Kilpatrick and the still greater communicator, Ronald

Reagan. Conservative politicians often relied on wordsmiths for assistance in making sense of their positions for the public. Barry Goldwater readily conceded his inability to articulate his conservatism, which he demonstrated routinely on and off the stump. "I don't devote an overabundance of time to my thoughts," the senator reflected late in life, because "I've been through the situation so often, so long, the answers just sort of pop out." In 1978, Goldwater complimented Kilpatrick on his columns and television programs. "I think conservatism is becoming a decent term again," he wrote, "thanks to you."[18]

Kilpatrick was conscious of his contributions and bombast on television: a splendid peacock in the service of showbiz. "On television," he confessed, "if you're going to make any impact at all you have to say things emphatically. There's just not time for qualifiers, nuances, and flourishes." Kilpatrick sacrificed the polish of his syndicated writing for the cut and parry of heated debate. Neither his age nor his small frame diminished his screen presence. Most of his power was in his candid blue eyes. When he frowned, he glared with an intensity that meant that if pushed, he would deliver on his gaze's implied threat, burst through the camera, and run right over the television audience. For added effect, he sometimes puffed out his chest, put his head in his hands, or removed his glasses to scowl at an opponent from under the heavy eyebrows he inherited from his father. Kilpatrick took his showmanship seriously and even carried his own cosmetic kit to prepare himself if the studio's makeup staff was too busy. He had learned the cadence of sound-bite commentary on political talk shows and sparred with curt, antiquated words like "bosh" and "balderdash" when he disliked an opponent's position. A viewer who had seen him debate on *Agronsky* advised Kilpatrick to seek therapy and anger management counseling. "If looks could kill, (thank goodness they can't)," he teased, "there would be no more Carl Rowan." The cranky conservative had so many and so much to slate in the errant 1970s.[19]

To Kilpatrick, everything seemed wrong with America and the world. On one show, Kilpatrick might mutter about antiwar protesters, the counterculture, urban crime rates, judicial activism, or government deficits. On another segment, he might defend abortion because it prevented women from dumping their children on the taxpayers, or he might point out the dangers of affirmative action. Squaring off against Shana Alexander in January 1977, he testified to the merits of an individual's right to discriminate: "I had supposed that freedom of association is everyone's right in a free society. The right to discriminate in one's choice of golf partners and drinking companions is precious. The right not to believe in wall-to-wall brotherhood is a fine right. . . . So it's discrimination. It's also freedom."[20]

Kilpatrick walked a fine line between freedom and discrimination. Critics often detected a dose of racism, albeit obliquely expressed, in his opposition to busing, in his genial indifference to the problems of poor people, and in his attacks on affirmative action. When, in November 1977, he and Alexander disputed a program that rewarded minority-owned firms with federal contracts, Kilpatrick asked: "How would you like to ride in an elevator constructed by an Eskimo, Chicano, or Black?" The quip offended more than a few viewers. "Kilpatrick has given credibility to the deleterious elements of his devotees," complained one man. Kilpatrick had ignored contributions by minority businesses to urban economies, bailouts for major corporations by the government, and the paucity of federal subsidization for minority-owned private companies. A New Yorker demanded that CBS tell Kilpatrick to "apologize publicly to all people concerned for such an insensitive, bigoted, and ignorant statement." As criticisms picked up, Kilpatrick contacted the president of CBS to explain, not excuse, himself. Originally, he said, he had intended only to target blacks given contracts because of the color of their skin but had "recast the question" to include other minorities as well. He promised to apologize but continued to defend his line of inquiry.[21]

Though affirmative action and busing comprised most of Kilpatrick and Alexander's commentaries on race, the television audience understood many other policies discussed on the show as a conspiracy either against blacks and their interests, if he spoke, or against white southerners and American values, if she did. On 3 August 1975, the evening's debate centered on New York City's financial crisis and the collapse of its mini–welfare state. Alexander blamed "George Wallace's Alabama" for causing the out-migration of blacks and swelling welfare rolls in northern cities. Kilpatrick countered that "welfare mamas" and "welfare cheats," namely Puerto Ricans and blacks, were the reason for the city's spending woes. A South Carolinian took issue with Alexander and other "blind, unrealistic, misguided 'do-gooders'" who were "as dangerous and frightening as the chiefs of the Soviet Politburo and friends." Another frustrated viewer targeted Kilpatrick: "What in the Lord's name does he want New York City to do? Send the blacks to Africa, the Puerto Ricans to Puerto Rico, the welfare recipients to Welfare Island?" Despite chastisement, Kilpatrick refused to compromise his opinions and renewed his assaults each week.[22]

For nine years, audiences tuned in to CBS on Sunday nights after the National Football League gridiron for political football with Kilpatrick. In 1978, Kilpatrick became a part of popular culture when Dan Aykroyd spoofed his exchanges with Alexander, portrayed by Jane Curtin, in pugilistic spectacles that deviated from their well-versed arguments on the *60 Minutes* program. Aykroyd's version of Kilpatrick on NBC's *Saturday Night Live* was a blowhard whose response to Curtin's Alexander, "Jane, you ignorant slut!" became a catchphrase. The misogynist punch line not only punctuated the act but also demonstrated the shifting importance of issues in the 1970s with the ascension of feminism and the waning of the civil rights movement. Even *Saturday Night Live* had deconditioned Kilpatrick's racial politics in favor of sexist jibes, but the parody belied more contentious matters.[23]

For all Kilpatrick's successes and popularity, a dilemma would not go away: how could he reconcile the public persona he had created with his past. In his syndicated column, Kilpatrick betrayed a discomfort about himself as an artist. His reaction to poet Ezra Pound's death in 1972 indicated that no matter the changes in Kilpatrick's status, he felt tested by a heritage of bigotry. In his obituary for Pound, Kilpatrick's perception of his life seemed sensitive, and he described him as a

> great poet, but by establishment standards, a bad man. He admired Fascists; he hated Jews. The question he leaves behind—the question I find so hard to answer—is whether the world of letters should officially honor a great poet who is also a bad man. Can the artist be judged apart from the artist's life? Writing last month in *World* magazine, critic Irving Howe said, no: He finds pervasive anti-Semitism beyond forgetting and forgiving. I have no answer. Should we see poetry as poetry, acting as acting, singing as singing, or do we properly look beyond that work of art? I think Pound, the poet, should have been honored in his lifetime, his badness kept out of the balance. But it is a question on which reasonably minded men will disagree, and I do not press the point.[24]

Unpacking the relationship between Kilpatrick's art and beliefs is part of determining his political relevance. By the end of the 1970s as he looked toward retirement, Kilpatrick had emerged as a polemicist-fixture on the right. An artifact of massive resistance but no longer the odd man out thanks to his television exposure and the popularity of his columns, he had transmogrified into a mainstream conservative. Kilpatrick's Sinaitic search for acceptance in the elite ranks of journalism was at an end. What had started years earlier as an adventure without a sure destination as a cub reporter in Richmond had become an influential career in Washington. Kilpatrick's racial prejudice, regardless of his attempts to dissociate it from his accomplishments late in life, would remain the paramount peril to a positive legacy for him.

Nature's Rhythms

The man who helped popularize both interposition and TV conservatism gradually learned to live in an America without segregation and continued to write. In 1981, Kilpatrick started a new column on English usage called "The Writer's Art" and returned to his first love. Pontificating on grammar reinforced his conservatism and the desire to preserve some order and convention despite the changes around him. At least grammar would never depreciate without his permission. Syntax and the structure of language, he argued, should remain unaltered, ubiquitous, and obeyed. Cadence, he often advised readers, counted in good writing and imposed rhythm on sentences. With his "Writer's Art" columns, he could act as gatekeeper to the English language. Although he approved of some innovation with words and usage, he insisted that writers use standard grammar, because it showed that a writer had put some thought into the formation of ideas and that one had observed the norms of society. Like Kilpatrick's Scrabble columns, "The Writer's Art" afforded him a position from which to right wrongs.[25]

Refereeing language, in fact, was a "matter of metaphysical import to Jack," one admirer noted. In a published collection of his writing recommendations and rules, *The Writer's Art* (1984), Kilpatrick even titled the second chapter "Faith, Hope, and Clarity" as a play on the Christian virtues. Kilpatrick warned writers to stay away from complicated language in favor of simplicity. Using a word meant to impress readers with one's vocabulary was "like knowing a sin." He went on, "Sitting at their typewriters, all writers know the experience. The word is seductive. It slithers along, wet-lipped, scented with exotic perfume; it gazes at the writer with a come-hither glance. 'Take me,' says this gorgeous creature. 'I dare you.' Thus are we led into temptation."[26]

Focusing on the art of writing coincided with Kilpatrick's move into semi-retirement, first in Charleston, South Carolina, and later in Washington's

Georgetown district. His advancing age required that he reduce his speaking engagements and public appearances, but he still wrote weekly columns on the Court and writing. Failing health forced him to retire from covering the Supreme Court in 2008, and from his beloved writing column in January 2009. Even though he was away from the limelight, the events of his years as a diehard segregationist still came up in Kilpatrick's conversations and columns.[27]

Kilpatrick spent much of his career trying to ditch his ugly past. Privately and publicly, he portrayed himself as an erstwhile segregationist. Immediately after the passage of the 1964 Civil Rights Act, he insisted that he accepted the demise of state-sanctioned segregation. With some apprehension, he told one disgruntled Alabamian, "We will discover that one does not necessarily contract contagious diseases by eating in a restaurant that also serves Negroes, or suffer some other calamity by taking a room in a hotel that also books Negroes. It will take us time to discover some of these things, but in the end it will be better than catfish. I just won't be coerced, that's all." On his sixtieth birthday, sixteen years after he made that remark, he wrote, "If I were cataloguing the good things that have happened in my lifetime," the end of state-sponsored segregation ranked first.[28]

In the seventies and eighties, Kilpatrick framed the legacy of the civil rights movement as a quest for racial harmony. Rather than promote the black freedom struggle's expanded goals of social equality, including affirmative action, he accentuated the impracticality of interracial brotherhood, which busing and quotas shattered. Kilpatrick evaluated the success of the movement based on individuals' acceptance of racial egalitarianism and commitment to reform. The realization of a racial utopia looked doubtful. Desegregation knew limitations. Laws changed, but hearts and minds did slowly or not at all. On racial issues, Americans, he suspected, preferred patient evolution to constitutional revolution. "The difficulty, perhaps, is that in some areas of human relationships neither the carrot nor the stick is very effective," he wrote. "Government can go so far, but no farther. The American people are a reasonably docile lot, ordinarily obedient to governmental coercion, but at some point they get their backs up."[29]

Americans tolerated only so much racial progress before they applied the brakes and resisted integration. The *Brown* decision and desegregation created space for better race relations, but not panaceas. The future of racial liberalism seemed uncertain, and Kilpatrick forecast continual obstacles for *Brown*. On the twentieth anniversary of the ruling, he told *60 Minutes* viewers that *Brown* "broke the dams of racial discrimination. In the resulting flood, a lot of wrongs were washed away, but I wonder if some rights haven't been destroyed as well." In a 1975 syndicated column, he feared that the Supreme Court would eventually have to force the hiring of blacks "just because they are black. This is the kind of equality that George Orwell once described—an equality in which some are more equal than others. . . . Soon after the turn of the century, in 2004, the Civil Rights Commission of that day doubtless will release a report entitled 'Fifty Years After Brown.' Will that report look with pride upon universal brotherhood and totally integrated schools? It's not a proposition on which to bet your bottom dollar." For all the energy that the integrationists expended to desegregate society, Kilpatrick, from the vantage point of 1989, viewed their cause as a "sad pursuit. A vast deal of the taxpayer's money has been squandered. The children, both black and white, probably are more race conscious than they were before *Brown*. Many school districts have effectively resegregated. The whole miserable business has been an exercise in folly." The revolution that some liberal policymakers had expected fell short of their goals.[30]

Kilpatrick's many crusades against racial progress tainted comments that he made about the impact of civil rights. He never completely eliminated his association with segregation. His past, he accepted, "will follow me to the grave." Whenever pressed about his role in interposition, Kilpatrick maintained that he had acted appropriately and had done the best he could given the context of the times: someone had to defend the constitutional order and dampen racial hostility. "I remember one rabid redneck, a real minuteman type, who stormed into my [*Richmond News Leader*] office angry as hell," he proudly recalled. "But as soon as I got him talking about the 14th Amendment and ratification, he calmed down like a kitten. He really got interested in the issues, and he started writing long pieces on the Constitution and ratification. . . . Those strong and violent passions were channeled off." Kilpatrick believed his actions sidelined the possibility of a race war and had simply been misguided. "I can't apologize for that [interposition] campaign. It is a part of my record, and not altogether a credit. We never really thought we could stop integration, we wanted to delay it. I think that was a reasonable thing to do," Kilpatrick said on another occasion. He rarely confessed to mistakes.[31]

When cornered about his drive for massive resistance, Kilpatrick went on the defensive and refused to accept responsibility for fomenting a crisis. "Very few of us, I suspect, would like to have our passions and profundities at age 28 thrust in our faces at 50," he reminded a *Time* reporter. He was actually thirty-five when he began writing the interposition editorials, and he claimed that his attack on *Brown* lacked emotion and twinge. Satisfied with his innocence, Kilpatrick excused Harry Byrd and the other fathers of massive resistance too. "Harry Byrd was no racist. God knows he wasn't," he pled to one interviewer. Kilpatrick rejected the charge that the resisters' motives and actions had been governed only by race, arguing, "It's cruelly unkind to refer to them as racists." It was states' rights and strict constitutionalism that had inspired segregationists.[32]

For years, the *News Leader* also dodged its participation in interposition and massive resistance. After Kilpatrick, Ross Mackenzie, a younger and more reactionary version of his predecessor, had assumed the editorship and continued the fight against racial reform. In May 1973, when the U.S. Supreme Court rejected a federal district judge's order to consolidate Richmond's predominantly black public schools with heavily white-populated schools in nearby counties, the *News Leader* had celebrated. "We won! With today's decision from the Supreme Court, let us have no more attempts to impose abstraction on reality," Mackenzie proclaimed in a manner reminiscent of Kilpatrick. "We all have endured enough." Civil rights supporters had to wait two more decades for something resembling an apology from the paper's management about its obstruction of the movement and *Brown*. In 1992, *Times-Dispatch* publisher Tennant Bryan, for his part, expressed sorrow that states' rights could not prevail against the courts. Not until 2003 did the *Times-Dispatch* take responsibility for its actions and promotion of an "unjust policy" and "a horrible thing." The tribune asked Richmonders to accept its "profound regret." History may have been different had the white Richmond papers and their editors led the community toward moderation, but they chose the path of defiance.[33]

In 2009, the *Times-Dispatch* released a rare front-page editorial that again expressed regret for its endorsement of the "dreadful doctrine" of massive resistance. The paper's impact on the state's race relations affected many others, and a few were especially mindful of its harm. Former governor L. Douglas Wilder, who was elected in 1989 as the nation's first black governor, found the editorial inadequate. He appreciated the newspaper's admission of wrongdoing, but the editorial failed to acknowledge the injury it had caused. State senator Henry L. Marsh III of Richmond noted the editorial did not mention civil rights lawyers Oliver W. Hill Sr. and Samuel W. Tucker, who stood up to segregation. Marsh also cited the paper's failure to account for the numerous victims denied an equal education by massive resistance. "Many remember. We understand. Words have consequences," the editorial concluded.[34]

Though the pangs of massive resistance remained, James Kilpatrick ducked grappling with his role in the preservation of segregation. Kilpatrick had many opportunities to demonstrate remorse for his part in white resistance to civil rights, but he never recognized the role his ideas played at places like Little Rock and the University of Mississippi. To have acknowledged that his work may have led others to violence or prolonged the racial conflict of the era might have ruined his new status as a national authority on conservatism or been too agonizing. A simpler and smoother route for him to accept came through the verdict of his fans and popularity that his history did not injure his career. Seldom one to go spelunking in men's souls, he rarely revealed any serious misgivings about his segregationist days.

As the first histories of the movement appeared in the 1980s, the demand for an account from Kilpatrick mounted. To distance himself from segregation, he provided scant information. It seemed obvious why Kilpatrick said little. He sided against the civil rights struggle and proselytized with positions that later Americans widely repudiated. When one historian asked for Kilpatrick to comment on how he had come to grips with the anathema of desegregation, he fell back on a bad memory. "I find it astounding that someone as keenly interested in history as your writings reveal you to be would accept the notion that the past is past, and is best forgotten," complained the inquisitive scholar. The columnist equivocated without contrition or anything complex. Kilpatrick countered, "You should make a distinction between events and their consequences. The events of 1954–1960 are indeed over and done with—the bills passed, the speeches made, the editorials written, the persons elected to office. The stream of history goes on. Thirty years ago I made a very small contribution to that stream. You ask me for a time-consuming exercise in retrospection; you want me to tell you how I came to terms with the end of racial segregation. Such an exercise would be a painful and profitless expenditure of my time."[35]

Llewellyn Smith, associate producer for the Public Broadcasting Service's *Eyes on the Prize* documentary series on the civil rights movement also wrote Kilpatrick to see if he would provide insights about the segregationist defense. Kilpatrick declined and said he could not remember: "My memory of events thirty years ago has greatly faded, and it would be a wholly profitless undertaking for me to do the research necessary to freshen my recollection." On his history with race, he usually remained mum and preferred to live an unexamined life. Besides, by the mid-1980s, Kilpatrick felt too secure in his views to worry about serious challenges to his reputation.

One reader urged him to "take it easy on the anti-affirmative action columns. . . . To argue at this point that affirmative action is reverse discrimination cannot help your image." Kilpatrick, however, was content with his position and the courts': "I am getting too old, and have been in the news business too long, to worry much about my 'image.' Little by little the courts are coming around to the point of view I have expressed so many times . . . that ours is a color-blind Constitution."[36]

Kilpatrick did not, nonetheless, remain unaffected by the racial changes around him. His willingness to remove overt racism from his arguments in itself was an admission of a new racial order. He adapted and sometimes even offered regrets for his views. It formed part of the strange process that many white southerners underwent after the movement years. They slowly accepted certain alterations and actively opposed other transformations. If the tempo of change was unhurried and whites limited their contact with blacks, Kilpatrick and others like him could live with the movement's results, including limited integration. In 1985, a reader from Indiana noted that Kilpatrick did not share his belief that "the entire thrust of our racial efforts must be towards setting up social institutions which will make it difficult or impossible for the races to crossbreed." Kilpatrick replied, "I long ago abandoned my advocacy of state-sanctioned segregation, and while I still regard interracial marriage as regrettable—especially for the children of such unions—three decades have quieted my fears. Miscegenation remains an infinitesimal factor in our culture. For the social and genetic reasons you mention, I hope that it always will remain an aberrant condition, to be tolerated in the name of a free society but not to be encouraged."[37]

In his published remarks about mixed-race education, Kilpatrick revealed few of his old fears. Despite having stirred up the prolonged and often bitter public debate about interracial schooling, his later writings occasionally had positive messages. In a 1977 book, he talked about his granddaughter's excitement as she started kindergarten and made all kinds of new discoveries and friends, even black children. The columnist's acceptance of change, however conditionally, was more than many segregationists offered. The fact that Kilpatrick no longer referred to the inherent inferiority of African Americans or raised concerns about interracial sex in his syndicated columns and books signaled that he, and America, had passed a critical point in race relations. The nation had become more diverse and inclusive, and Kilpatrick knew it.

Though his tone softened, his argument for a color-blind society was an unwavering, double-edged sword cutting against restorative measures to help minorities as often as it supported equal opportunities for the races. One of Kilpatrick's 1993 columns lacked any incendiary pronouncements about racial differences, but it denounced a pervasive political culture that welcomed diversity. Despairing of the new racial climate, he worried that "all the posturing gestures of 'diversity' and 'multiculturalism' and 'affirmative action' are making bad matters worse. Our country ideally should be colorblind. We have become color obsessed." While his position on affirmative action remained constant, the aging columnist tried to amend his notoriety for racism and resistance.[38]

As long as Kilpatrick controlled the conversation about racial issues, he could discuss and repudiate racism. He changed his tune on civil rights as the times warranted. In an article in the *Raleigh News and Observer* in 1988, for example, he said: "I ardently supported [the Voting Rights Act of 1965] because I knew, as only a white Southerner can know, what chicanery my people had employed to prevent blacks from voting." At the time of the bill's proposal, however, he wrote in the *National Review* that the proposed act "strikes with the brute and clumsy force of a wrecking ball at the very foundations of American federalism." In a 2002 article, after Mississippi senator Trent Lott complimented Strom Thurmond at a birthday party, a seemingly contrite Kilpatrick wrote about his own racial prejudice. He called Lott's tribute to Thurmond "a stupid thing to say, profoundly wrong, deeply offensive." Lott, unfortunately, said the United States would have avoided "all these problems" if then-segregationist Thurmond had been elected in 1948. He had "fecklessly attempted to defend the indefensible." Whereas the Mississippian never discarded his racist beliefs, Kilpatrick "outgrew those roots." Kilpatrick's family, he attested, broke from segregation. He mentioned a granddaughter who married a Moroccan Muslim and another who wed a Mexican. Kilpatrick characterized his change of heart regarding race as a rocky pilgrimage ending with an epiphany, a turning point in his sense of right and wrong. Yet it would take more than a revelation to wipe out the problems of his past, and his account rang hollow. On some events, he dissembled the historical record. In the same article, he claimed that he had sympathized with the sit-in protesters of 1960, that he had "severed the last vestige of Southern segregation" by 1970, and that his grandfather had put down a nineteenth-century black "insurrection" in New Orleans. His disparagement of the sit-in movement, his promotion of segregated, private schools, and his grandfather's participation in a white supremacist paramilitary coup against municipal authorities contradicted his memory.[39]

While Kilpatrick mothballed certain aspects of his heritage, he also made important contributions to the conservative movement. Once he became involved in the mainstream media, his role rapidly expanded. Transferring his talents from print to television was easy, popular, and impressive. "In the dark ages of conservatism—before direct mail, before Rush [Limbaugh], before the Fox News Channel, and way before the Internet," remarked Richard Viguerie, the creator of direct mail for conservative political causes, "there was Kilpatrick with his columns and national television appearances. He gave encouragement to millions of conservatives as he expressed their beliefs."[40]

Kilpatrick had turned his outsider status to his advantage in a changing political landscape. The political and racial philosophy that he concealed behind his push for color blindness captured the spirit of American freedom from constraint and free enterprise and updated it for a new generation searching for individualism and community reinvention in the midst of social upheaval. He helped make southern conservatism conspicuous by thrusting it into the mainstream press. He also resurrected states' rights as a strategy of resistance to the national government but in a way that pared back its parallel with racism. Kilpatrick honed his defense of segregation by framing it as an ideological clash between national control and individual freedom with a conviction about human nature that did not require southerners to export their racial politics. By linking whites' reservations about integration and constitutional arguments to opposition against the 1964 Civil Rights Act, affirmative action, busing, and judicial activism, he helped extend unstated, but powerful, vestiges of massive resistance and invigorated the conservative movement. Kilpatrick understood that associating his ideas with national conservative values was the best way to rid himself of his image as a marginalized segregationist. White southerners, he also recognized early on, could be powerful allies for conservatives in their attempts to undermine the liberal national political culture and the countermovements for equality and democracy and return authority to home rule.[41]

Important conservative movement figureheads also paid attention to the kinds of arguments Kilpatrick put forth. After the 1970s, conservatives did not encode demagogic fury into their oppositional rhetoric. They embraced a calmer, race-neutral mantle. Kilpatrick crafted his message far more carefully than some ranting Klansman or ax-wielding governor. His and others' identification of "colorblindness" with conservatism and "reverse racism" with liberalism showed up in the most prominent of conservative intellectual and legal circles. Reinterpreting the language of the civil rights movement for conservatives' ends had become ordinary for the right.

Color-blind rhetoric and efforts to reverse the effects of *Brown* eventually appeared in the Supreme Court, where the desegregation issue originated. Justice Antonin Scalia detested affirmative action because "restorative justice" for blacks hampered whites. In 2007, the judiciary reversed a Hawaii circuit court decision that had allowed a school for native Hawaiians to limit enrollment of non-natives. In a column about the case, Kilpatrick had expressed his hope that the Court would open the school to white students to teach the Hawaiians something about a color-blind reading of the law. "Sometimes nothing fits so comfortably as a shoe upon another foot," he chided liberals.[42]

The Supreme Court never took cues directly from Kilpatrick, but its rulings on racial matters were symbolic of the kind of government positions he advocated. In the same year as its Hawaiian school ruling, the Court also denied local school districts in Louisville and Seattle the right to use race-conscious strategies to keep schools integrated in *Parents Involved v. Seattle*. Writing the opinion, Chief Justice John G. Roberts noted the disputes about whether racial diversity in schools benefits students. The Court, Roberts asserted, need not resolve the issue, however. In both Louisville and Seattle, the districts' plans called for racial balance for its own sake. Mandating racial programs to achieve certain levels of diversity, he cited, would run counter to the judiciary's insistence that "at the heart of the Constitution's guarantee of equal protection lies the simple command that the Government must treat citizens as individuals, not as simply components of a racial, religious, sexual or national class." The dissent by Justice Stephen Breyer respected the right of democratically elected school boards to achieve integrated education.[43]

The disagreement touched on more than the choice between returning to *Brown*'s emphasis on desegregation or the racial mixing that integrationists desired. The two cases raised questions about the real purpose of Kilpatrick's conservatism. Covering the Court for his online syndicated column, Kilpatrick anticipated the bench's decision, which would halt the cities' forced racial balancing plans. "Far beyond Seattle and Louisville," he calculated, "the whole country will be listening" to the Court's verdict. Ironically, rather than defend the local communities' right to control their schools without the federal government's intervention, Kilpatrick encouraged the Court to interfere and end the voluntary busing program. He folded on his states' rights and Burkean principles. In the 1950s, Kilpatrick churned against robust judicial circumscription of democracy, but in 2007 he applauded the Court's hostility toward local government and social experimentation because the majority's opinion stated that "the way to stop discrimination on the basis of race is to stop discriminating on the basis of race." Kilpatrick reprimanded the four dissenting justices who claimed the ruling undermined *Brown* for their inability to see the validity of a color-blind version of the law. He ridiculed the "misguided cohort" for believing "that our nation's residual racism will be cured by a little more racism." As long as the Court ordered action that he agreed with, the mandate did not constitute government intrusion.[44]

The emblematic significance of *Seattle* and *Louisville* was substantial. Conservatives could now shape the courts on racial matters. The columnist's ideas had paved the way for conservative jurisprudence on race and education, but over fifty-two years after *Brown*, he could breathe only a partial sigh of relief. His hope that the federal government would establish a color-blind standard became entangled with a troubling incongruity for a conservative. According to Kilpatrick's logic, America and the Court did well to expand the purview of the federal government to end Jim Crow and racial discrimination. Otherwise, his admonitions were nothing more than a deception to perpetuate racial inequality.

For one reason or another, most Americans shared Kilpatrick's point of view: they wanted the courts to release them from imposed racial balancing programs. other Americans accepted the *Brown* opinion's nondiscrimination principle and the idea that people should not be treated a certain way based on their race. Desegregation fit with America's new postwar morals that rejected scientific racism and racial demagoguery. Integration, however, did not. Many Americans instead chose freedom of association, defended the right to live in neighborhoods with similar-looking and -working people, and rejected integration.[45]

By the beginning of the twenty-first century, Kilpatrick no longer bided his time or worried whether his racial views were in line with mainstream opinion. Perhaps widespread conservative principles were nearer the nation's true path all along. There was no mistaking the harmony between conservatism and Kilpatrick's predictions as events unfolded. Many public schools had effectually resegregated or debated voucher programs. Communities across the country contested the offspring of the *Brown* ruling. "Judicial activism" and "affirmative action" had become dirty words among conservatives. The right embraced states' rights rhetoric. The Republican Party dominated the South and large sections of the nation.

Kilpatrick did not look like such a failure. A popular army of protest continued to mobilize. Scores of conservatives identified with his positions and resisted not only excessive, mandated alterations in race relations but also the seemingly monolithic liberal consensus. Government's laws cannot change people's hearts, Kilpatrick had warned. Change flowed in a natural rhythm and depended on the community's readiness for it. His father had taught him that lesson years ago, and Kilpatrick had followed that steady course ever after.

Kilpatrick's 1955 defiance of the Court and inability to see the value of racial integration to American culture had launched him onto the national stage. His racial politics, however, contributed to a progression of conservative thought that required no racial backlash to congeal. Kilpatrick was no atavistic barbarian. His curious and sometimes perplexing blend of color-blind fairness and opposition to racial progress allowed him to talk and write in ways that expressed the hopes of people groping for stability in race relations but who tended to ignore social justice issues. Kilpatrick channeled the inchoate concerns of Americans who already shared his unease about racial liberalism and the reach of the federal government. The conservatism he preached gave form to a preexisting, and not always coherent, set of political ideas based on the protection of the status quo and the defense of values close to home.[46]

Kilpatrick's post-1955 career and personality has sometimes baffled observers because he violated expectations of what a segregationist ought to be. While Kilpatrick the columnist and commentator succeeded in spite of his past and segregation's downfall, he remained true to many beliefs that he acquired as a young man. His public grappling with civil rights reinforced his sense of obedience to community norms and individual responsibility and achievement. The same self-reliance and sense of order that enabled him to survive the Depression in Oklahoma and the challenges of the civil rights era also directed his later endeavors.

States' rights, strict constitutionalism, and segregation defined a career that began with an uncomplicated goal. Kilpatrick's journey from the plains of Oklahoma to the press rooms of the nation's capital started with a boyhood passion for writing and working for newspapers. In subsequent years, Kilpatrick's legacy as the editor-architect of interposition and nemesis of the civil rights movement threatened his career as a writer, journalist, and commentator. His public respectability and personal prejudice were at odds. He chose to preserve his political ideology and aspects of his racial positions despite fluctuating situations and the requirements of his audiences and employers. Though caught in the middle of twin impulses to succeed as a columnist and to preserve a semblance of the old racial caste system, he was not ineffectual. He molded and sold his racial views that transcended regional boundaries while achieving professional distinction. Did other segregationists match Kilpatrick's nimbleness in keeping resistance resilient while overhauling their self-images after the civil rights era?

The hell he had an equal.

NOTES

Abbreviations Used in the Notes

CCGP   Virginia Commission on Constitutional Government Papers,
Library of Virginia, Richmond, Va.

DMP   David J. Mays Papers, Virginia Historical Society, Richmond, Va.

JJK   James J. Kilpatrick

JJKP   James J. Kilpatrick Papers, University of Virginia,
Special Collections, Charlottesville, Va.

MD   David J. Mays Diary, David Mays Papers,
Virginia Historical Society, Richmond, Va.

NYT   *New York Times*

RNL   *Richmond News Leader*

RTD   *Richmond Times-Dispatch*

TRWP   Thomas R. Waring Jr. Papers, South Carolina Historical Society,
Charleston, S.C.

UVA   University of Virginia, Special Collections, Charlottesville, Va.

WFBP   William F. Buckley Jr. Papers, Yale University Library, Manuscripts
and Archives, New Haven, Conn.

WP   *Washington Post*

Introduction

1. Kilpatrick, "My Journey from Racism" (quotations).

2. Nash, *Conservative Intellectual Movement*, 200 (quotation on 202). For more on the American conservative movement, see Hodgson, *World Turned Right Side Up*; Lichtman, *White Protestant Nation*; Philips-Fein, *Invisible Hands*; and Farber, *Rise and Fall*.

3. Scholarly understanding of white segregationists began in the aftermath of the civil rights movement. See Bartley, *Rise of Massive Resistance*, and McMillen, *Citizens' Council*. For other notable recent histories of segregationists, see Marsh, *God's Long Summer*; Roche, *Restructured Resistance*; Eagles, "Toward New Histories"; and Chappell, *Stone of Hope*, 170–71.

4. For literature on the conservative elite, see Perlstein, *Before the Storm*; Perlstein, *Nixonland*; Goldberg, *Barry Goldwater*; Dallek, *Right Moment*; Reinhard, *Republican Right Since 1945*; Brennan, *Turning Right in the Sixties*; Phillips, *Emerging Republican Majority*; Blumenthal, *Rise of the Counter-Establishment*; Judis, *William F. Buckley, Jr.* Nancy MacLean's recent work credits the men atop

the *National Review* and prominent politicians and intellectuals with much of the right-wing's prominence. See MacLean, *Freedom Is Not Enough*. For two important studies of grassroots conservatism in the 1960s, see Farber and Roche, *Conservative Sixties*, and McGirr, *Suburban Warriors*.

5. The latest scholarship to postulate the South as America writ small and as lacking in regional distinctiveness includes Lassiter and Crespino, *Myth of Southern Exceptionalism*, 5–7; Nickerson and Dochuk, *Sunbelt Rising*. Egerton, *Americanization of Dixie*; Lassiter, *Silent Majority*; and Crespino, *In Search of Another Country*. Scholarship that does not deny an exceptional South is sometimes discarded as the "backlash thesis." See Lassiter and Crespino, *Myth of Southern Exceptionalism*, 7, 9, 11. For more on the overlap of southern and American political culture, see Carter, *Politics of Rage*. In his milestone biography of former Alabama governor George Wallace, Carter notes the popularity of racial politics in the North as the "southernization" of American politics. Following Wallace through the 1960s and 1970s, Carter documents how his coded crypto-racism helped him gain politically. Wallace's denunciations of liberal intellectuals, integration, immorality, and sixties' radicalism polarized issues that successive waves of conservatives manipulated. For excellent refutations of the backlash school, see Sugrue, *Origins of the Urban Crisis*; Durr, *Behind the Backlash*; Hirsch, *Making the Second Ghetto*; Dochuk, *From Bible Belt to Sunbelt*; Gregory, *Southern Diaspora*; and Link, *Righteous Warrior*. For a defense of the South's identity within national change, see John Shelton Reed, *Enduring South*.

6. On 16 August 2010, James J. Kilpatrick died of congestive heart failure at age eighty-nine in Washington, D.C. See Bernstein, "James J. Kilpatrick, 89, Dies." This study builds on Glenn Feldman's case for the South's regional and political continuity. See Feldman, review of *The Myth of Southern Exceptionalism*, 783–86.

7. For an interpretation of postwar conservatism in the South that understands taxes, property rights, law and order, and other suburban issues as "color-blind," see Lassiter, *Silent Majority*. For a study that interprets suburban conservative politics as separate from race, see McGirr, *Suburban Warriors*. For more on the complex relationships informing post–civil rights conservatism, see MacLean, *Freedom Is Not Enough*, and Kruse, *White Flight*. Lassiter and Kruse express an emerging standard among histories of the civil rights–era South for understanding white behavior. They argue for a rising willingness of the middle class and elite to moderate their racial bigotry with bourgeois, color-blind arguments. This class-based narrative insists that the working class stuck to racist beliefs while their economic betters ditched reactionary politics. The elite position—personified in Kilpatrick—did not always or necessarily overcome racism by countermanding economic, political, and cultural interests, however.

8. Myrdal, *American Dilemma*.

9. Foner, *Who Owns History* (Jordan quoted on 10). For more on Kilpatrick's legacy, see Epps, "Littlest Rebel," and Hirsch, *Talking Heads*. Kilpatrick himself

tried to have the last word about his reputation in 2002. See JJK, "My Journey from Racism."

10. Myrdal, *American Dilemma*.

Chapter One

1. Gibson, *Oklahoma*, 3–5; Elazar, "Political Culture on the Plains," 262; Scales and Goble, *Oklahoma Politics*, 6; Peirce, *Great Plains States of America*, 247; McReynolds, Marriott, and Faulconer, *Oklahoma*, 161; Goble, *Progressive Oklahoma*, 9–12, 145. For more on "Okie culture," see Gregory, *American Exodus*.

2. Bureau of the Census, *Tenth Census, 1880*; JJK to John Finnegan, February 12, 1957, in JJKP (quotation); Hilts, "Saga of James J. Kilpatrick"; Corley, "James Jackson Kilpatrick," 1–2.

3. Bureau of the Census, *Seventh Census, 1850*; Bureau of the Census, *Eighth Census, 1860*; Bureau of the Census, *Tenth Census, 1880*; Bureau of the Census, *Twelfth Census, 1900*; JJK to Elizabeth Moore, 5 February 1964, and JJK to W. B. Gilmer, 28 March 1956, in JJKP; JJK, *Southern Case for School Segregation*, 22; Booth, *Records of Louisiana Confederate Soldiers*.

4. JJK, "My Journey from Racism"; Federal Writers' Project, *New Orleans City Guide*, 33; Ryan, *Civic Wars*, 260–81; Nystrom, *New Orleans After the Civil War*.

5. JJK to Mr. and Mrs. Ira Erickson, 13 October 1964; and JJK to Moore, 4 February 1964, in JJKP; Hilts, "Saga of James J. Kilpatrick."

6. Gibson, *Oklahoma*, 165; Federal Writers' Project, *Oklahoma*, 45; Bake and Kilpatrick, *American South*, xviii; interview with Sean Kilpatrick.

7. Bureau of the Census, *Twelfth Census, 1900*; Bureau of the Census, *Fifteenth Census, 1930*; JJK, "A Conservative View," 16 November 1978, in JJKP.

8. Hilts, "Saga of James J. Kilpatrick."

9. JJK, "A Conservative View," 16 November 1978, in JJKP; "James Jackson Kilpatrick," 162; Grauer, *Wits and Sages*, 181 (quotations). Kilpatrick thought the magazine was *Child's Life*, but he was unsure. See JJK, *Fine Print*, x.

10. JJK to Mary Jeanne Hansen, 9 September 1963, in JJKP (quotation); JJK, "Our Poet Laureate."

11. JJK, *Writer's Art*, 18–19.

12. JJK to Sidney Morton, 11 June 1962, and JJK to Edgar Shannon, 25 March 1965, in JJKP.

13. Grauer, *Wits and Sages*, 181 (first quotation); Hilts, "Saga of James J. Kilpatrick" (second quotation); JJK to Jane Gubelin, 25 August 1994, in JJKP.

14. Federal Writers' Project, *Oklahoma*, 170–71; Bake and Kilpatrick, *American South: Four Seasons of the Land,* xvii (quotation).

15. Gibson, *Oklahoma*, 270; JJK to Lloyd Unsell, 7 and 8 December 1959, in JJKP.

16. Bake and Kilpatrick, *American South: Four Seasons of the Land*, 67 (quotation).

17. "Southern Living Magazine" folder, in JJKP; Bake and Kilpatrick, *American South: Four Seasons of the Land*, xviii–xx, 103; JJK, *Foxes' Union*; JJK to Harry F. Byrd Sr., 23 April 1963, in Harry Byrd Sr. Papers, UVA.

18. Bake and Kilpatrick, *American South: Four Seasons of the Land*, xvii–xviii (first and second quotations); interview with James J. Kilpatrick. See also JJK, CBS "Sixty Minutes" Transcript for "Point-Counterpoint," 7 September 1975, in JJKP.

19. Key, *Southern Politics*, 277 (first quotation). Key gave the Republican Party in the South only one chapter out of thirty-one, suggestively titled "A Note on the Republican Party." JJK, *Foxes' Union*, 166 (second quotation); Farber, *Sloan Rules*, (third quotation on 95); Scales and Goble, *Oklahoma Politics*, 111.

20. Bryant, *Alfalfa Bill Murray*, vii–viii, 255; Dabney, "Spokesman for the Privileged Class," in "James Jackson Kilpatrick" folder, WFBP.

21. JJK to James Boehling, 12 February 1959, and JJK to B. J. McIver, 30 December 1965, in JJKP; interview with James J. Kilpatrick; Novak, *Joy of Sports*, 19, 21, 27.

22. JJK to Charles Hayes, 11 March 1965, and JJK to Ralph Hunting, 3 December 1956, in JJKP (quotation).

23. Novak, *Joy of Sports*, 58, 59, 63; Burke, *Baseball in Oklahoma City*; JJK, *Foxes' Union*, 67.

24. JJK, *Foxes' Union*, 69; JJK, "Grand Old Game," 17–18; Bake and Kilpatrick, *American South: Four Seasons of the Land*, 65 (quotation).

25. Franklin, *Mirror to America*, 15–16; JJK, *Southern Case for School Segregation*, 23–24 (quotation); JJK, "My Journey from Racism," C3.

26. JJK to Walter J. Suthon Jr., 25 February 1957, in JJKP; Viles, *University of Missouri*, 423 (quotation); Stephens, *History of the University of Missouri*, 607; Olson and Olson, *University of Missouri*, 47–49; Williams, *Twenty Years of Education*, 413–14.

27. JJK, *Fine Print*, 1 (quotation).

28. Interview with James J. Kilpatrick; "Intercollegiate Press Association—1951" folder, JJK to Donald Cole, 22 October 1956, and JJK to E. B. Parks, 24 October 1957, "Roscoe Ellard" folder, in JJKP (quotation); Viles, *University of Missouri*, 423.

29. Egan, *Worst Hard Time*, 2–10, 281; Grauer, *Wits and Sages*, 181.

30. Grauer, *Wits and Sages*, 181; JJK to Jane Kilpatrick, 31 October 1956 (quotation), and JJK to James J. Kilpatrick Sr., 11 June 1957, in JJKP; Gregory, *American Exodus*, xvi–xvii; *California Death Index, 1940–1997 Record*.

31. JJK, *Fine Print*, x (quotation); Dabney, "Spokesman for the Privileged Class," in "James Jackson Kilpatrick" folder, WFBP. Alma Kilpatrick later took a secretarial job at Tinker Air Force Base in Oklahoma City. See interview with Sean Kilpatrick.

32. JJK to Anthony Britti, 10 March 1982, in JJKP (quotation).

33. Hilts, "Saga of James J. Kilpatrick"; Grauer, *Wits and Sages*, 181; Riley, *Biographical Dictionary*, 157; *Missouri Student*, 21 September 1938; JJK, *Fine Print*, 27; JJK to John Thornell, 24 September 1964, in JJKP.

34. Corley, "James Jackson Kilpatrick," 4; Bake and Kilpatrick, *American South: Four Seasons of the Land*, 19; Roberts and Klibanoff, *Race Beat*, 113 (first quotation); JJK, "Smell of Printer's Ink Lingers On" (second quotation).

35. Bake and Kilpatrick, *American South: Towns and Cities*, 19–20 (quotations); Hilts, "Saga of James J. Kilpatrick"; Roberts and Klibanoff, *Race Beat*, 113.

36. Dabney, *Richmond*, 9–10, 14–15, 20; Wilkinson, *Harry Byrd*, 177; Rouse, *We Happy WASPs*, 94–95; Sartain and Dennis, "Richmond, Virginia," 209; Tyler-McGraw, *At the Falls*, 270–71; Federal Writer's Project, *Virginia*, 285.

37. Douglas Southall Freeman, "Spirit of Virginia," in Federal Writers' Project, *Virginia*, 3–4 (quotation); Rouse, *We Happy WASPs*, 94–95; Peirce, *Border South States*, 37.

38. Heinemann, *Harry Byrd of Virginia*, 80; Key, *Southern Politics*, 26 (first quotation), 32; Lassiter and Lewis, *Moderates' Dilemma*, 176 (second quotation). One of the few voices of black dissent in Richmond was the editor of the *Richmond Planet*, John Mitchell Jr., who wrote against racial injustice into the 1920s. For more on Virginia's African Americans and opposition to Jim Crow in the years between World War I and 1954, see Smith, *Managing White Supremacy*; Tyler-McGraw, *At the Falls*, 276; Rouse, *We Happy WASPs*, 41–42; Sartain and Dennis, "Richmond, Virginia," 209; Franklin, *Mirror to America*, 30; Goldfield, *Cotton Fields*, 152, 158, 165, 169; and Silver and Moeser, *Separate City*, 26, 28, 42.

39. Bass and DeVries, *Transformation of Southern Politics*, 346; Hershman, "Massive Resistance Meets Its Match," 104–5; Sweeney, *Race, Reason, and Massive Resistance*.

40. Key, *Southern Politics*, 19–20 (quotation on 19).

41. Ibid., 20–26.

42. Wilkinson, *Harry Byrd*, 37–38; Lassiter and Lewis, *Moderates' Dilemma*, 14; Bureau of the Census, *Eighteenth Census, 1960*, 349; JJK, "A Conservative View," 14/15 October 1967, in JJKP.

43. Joseph Bryan also amassed power in Richmond by investing in railroads and mining. See Johnson, *Douglas Southall Freeman*, 86, 109–10; and Rouse, *We Happy WASPs*, 111–12.

44. Dunford, *"Richmond Times-Dispatch,"* 9–11; Johnson, *Douglas Southall Freeman*, 10 and 275; Rouse, *We Happy WASPs*, 59; Dabney, *Across the Years*, 148–49.

45. Harris, "Virginia's Voice of Conservatism Says 'Nevermore'"; Mason, "Newspaper Days," 347; Johnson, *Douglas Southall Freeman*, 136–37 (quotation). With the absence of a twenty-four-hour news cycle and with network television nightly news in its infancy, Kilpatrick's editorials in an afternoon newspaper were more amplified.

46. Johnson, *Douglas Southall Freeman*, 38–39, 80–84, 106.

47. Ibid., 72; Hamilton, "Time Was 'Irreplaceable' and Never Wasted," *RNL*, 30 May 1992 (second quotation); Bake and Kilpatrick, *American South: Towns and Cities*, 21–23 (first and third quotations on 21).

48. JJK, "Smell of Printer's Ink Lingers On"; Hilts, "Saga of James J. Kilpatrick." During the war, Kilpatrick served as brigade leader of a firehouse in neighboring Henrico County. Obsessed with financial security, Kilpatrick took on extra jobs and wrote for magazines and other newspapers. When the U.S. Patent Office opened in Richmond during the war, he submitted a 1,000-word piece each week on the new patents for the *New York Times*. See JJK, *Fine Print*, 152.

49. JJK, "Another 'Unfortunate Event'"; JJK to Judge Edgar S. Vaught, 12 August 1957, and JJK to Milton Honemann, 25 March 1975 (quotation), in "Intercollegiate Press Association" folder, JJKP; interview with James J. Kilpatrick. In 1930, the NAACP blocked Judge Parker's nomination to the U.S. Supreme Court because of his segregationist views. See Goings, *"NAACP Comes of Age."*

50. JJK, "Another 'Unfortunate Event'" (quotation); JJK, "My Journey from Racism," C3.

51. JJK to Judy Wubnig, 10 July 1985, in "Kilpatrick, J. J. (Personal)" folder, "Richmond Afternoons Columns—1947" folder, JJKP; JJK, *Writer's Art*, 118; JJK, *RNL*, 6 January 1950 (quotation), 16 June 1947; Hilts, "Saga of James J. Kilpatrick"; interview with Roger Mudd. For examples of his court beat writing, see JJK, *RNL*, 26 June and 8 July 1947. Harold L. Ickes was Franklin D. Roosevelt's secretary of the interior, and Jonathan Daniels was the moderate editor of the *Raleigh News and Observer*. Kilpatrick followed Tuck to the 1952 Democratic National Convention in Chicago, where the two men discussed political issues over dinner.

52. "George Wallace" folder, in JJKP; JJK, *RNL*, 5 September 1949 (quotation).

53. In 1788, Gibbon finished his history of the Roman Empire's final days. See Gibbon, *History of the Decline and Fall*; JJK to Judy Wubnig, 7 July 1985, and JJK to Joseph Bryan, 23 July 1964, in JJKP; JJK, *RNL*, 6 January 1950; JJK, "South Will Be Vindicated," 128; Bake and Kilpatrick, *American South: Towns and Cities*, 29; Corley, "James Jackson Kilpatrick," 5–6.

54. "James Jackson Kilpatrick"; Hilts, "Saga of James J. Kilpatrick" (quotations); JJK to Metropolitan Life Insurance Company, 8 February 1957, and JJK to James J. Kilpatrick Sr., 11 June 1957, in JJKP; "James Jackson Kilpatrick" folder, WFBP.

55. "James Jackson Kilpatrick"; Hilts, "Saga of James J. Kilpatrick"; Roberts and Klibanoff, *Race Beat*, 113–14; interview with Richard Whalen.

56. "Press" (first quotation); Roberts and Klibanoff, *Race Beat*, 113 (second quotation); Corley, "James Jackson Kilpatrick," 6; Bake and Kilpatrick, *American South: Towns and Cities*, 23 (third quotation); Dunford, *"Richmond Times-Dispatch,"* 318–19; JJK, "The 17 Happy Years of a Fire-Breathing Editor," *RNL*, 30 May 1992; "Man Who Took Richmond," 55; Johnson, *Douglas Southall Freeman*, 327 (fourth quotation).

57. "James Jackson Kilpatrick," 162; Bake and Kilpatrick, *American South: Towns and Cities*, 24; JJK to George Modlin, 7 July 1953, in "Kilpatrick, J. J. (Personal)" folder, JJKP (quotation). In the early 1950s, the *News Leader* reached

96,000 households. The *Times-Dispatch*, next door, reached 120,000. See Thomas, "Television News."

58. McElway, "Steering a Conservative Course," *RTD*, 15 October 2000.

59. Lohmann, "A 20th Century Newspaper Ends Its Run," *RNL*, 30 May 1992 (quotation); Egerton, *Speak Now against the Day*, 256.

60. Bake and Kilpatrick, *American South: Towns and Cities*, 21; Dunford, *"Richmond Times-Dispatch,"* 322–23 (first and second quotations on 319); Roberts and Klibanoff, *Race Beat*, 31, 114, 417 n. 16; Dabney, *Across the Years*, 232 (third quotation). "Tarheels" referred to Ashmore's upbringing in North Carolina.

61. Hilts, "Saga of James J. Kilpatrick" (quotations); Roberts and Klibanoff, *Race Beat*, 114; Corley, "James Jackson Kilpatrick," 6; JJK, "A Conservative View," 8 June 1971, in JJKP; "James Jackson Kilpatrick," 163; interview with James J. Kilpatrick. Kilpatrick referred to his early years as a liberal at the paper as his "salad days." As a young professional journalist, he believed he had a responsibility to present both sides of a story. See JJK to John J. Wicker Jr., 7 November 1957, in JJKP; and interview with Louis Rubin. Kilpatrick even struck many as prickly partly because he was always a bit brisk with people. He also intimidated his colleagues with his political ties to the Byrd regime, his tough reporting style, and his bureaucratic connections at the paper.

62. JJK to Perry Millikin, 23 September 1954 (quotation), and JJK to Rexmond Cochrane, 25 April 1955, in JJKP.

63. Nash, *Conservative Intellectual Movement*, 164–66, 191–92; Kirk, *Conservative Mind*, 52, 142–43, 154–60; JJK to John Temple Graves, 30 August 1957 (first quotation), "Prince Edward Academy Dedication of J.J.K. Library" folder; and JJK, "A Conservative View," 28 April 1970, in JJKP; Burke, *Reflections on the Revolution in France*. In an interview with the author, Kilpatrick said, "If I had a single conservative influence, it was John Dana Wise" (interview with James J. Kilpatrick).

64. JJK, *RNL*, 4 November 1963 (first and second quotations); JJK, "New National Nightmare," 12 (third quotation); Dunford, *"Richmond Times-Dispatch,"* 322–23; Bake and Kilpatrick, *American South: Towns and Cities*, 21. Kilpatrick remained a compulsive reader throughout his life. He maintained memberships in several book clubs that issued monthly readings, and he was particularly fond of the classics of Western literature. His 1953 reading list, for example, included Fyodor Dostoyevsky's *Brothers Karamazov*, Ralph Waldo Emerson's *Essays*, Virgil, Robert Louis Stevenson's *Gulliver's Travels*, Mary Shelley's *Frankenstein*, Sir Arthur Conan Doyle's Sherlock Holmes stories, and Charles Dickens's *Bleak House*. He loved to read Mark Twain, poetry, and sometimes the Bible as well. He also subscribed to the *Congressional Record* to stay current with events in Washington, D.C., the major national newspapers, conservative journals like *National Review*, and liberal periodicals like the *New Republic*. See "Account Journal 1951–53" folder, in JJKP.

65. D'Evelyn, "Columnist Kilpatrick on Language," LexisNexis; Corley, "James Jackson Kilpatrick," 8–9; JJK to Owen J. Roberts, May 1953 (first

quotation), and JJK, "A Conservative View," 18/19 November 1978 (second quotation), in JJKP.

66. For Kilpatrick's self-identification as a Whig, see JJK to Rexmond Cochrane, 25 April 1955 (quotation), and JJK to Mary Demas, 23 December 1964, in JJKP. The Whigs were the early-nineteenth-century critics of Andrew Jackson. They regarded his powerful presidency as a tyranny and feared his popularity among a large uneducated electorate. Whigs also tended to favor business interests and market capitalism. In late-eighteenth-century and early-nineteenth-century Britain, Whigs opposed crown rule and fought for increased parliamentary power. Kilpatrick later named himself the recording secretary of the True Whig Party. Edmund Burke was a Whig. See "South of John C. Calhoun."

67. Cobb, *Away Down South*, 109–11.

68. Hobson, *Serpent in Eden*, 6–7; JJK, "Rotary Club of Columbia, Missouri" speech, in JJKP (first quotation); JJK, *Writer's Art*, 52 (second quotation). Kilpatrick's identification with Mencken affected his writing even before he became editor and won him some criticism. Roscoe Ellard, Kilpatrick's former mentor, warned him: "You are genuinely bright and you have a real flair for style. But your emotional attachment for H. L. Mencken is, I think, giving your writing a New Yorkerish flavor that is not the most adroit approach for Richmond, Virginia" (Ellard to JJK, 28 November 1950, in JJKP).

69. Freeman, *RNL*, 14 September 1948; JJK, *RNL*, 29 March 1950 and 5 March 1951 (quotation).

70. JJK, *Writer's Art*, 52; JJK, "The 17 Happy Years of a Fire-Breathing Editor," *RNL*, 30 May 1992, 72; Hilts, "Saga of James J. Kilpatrick"; Dunford, *"Richmond Times-Dispatch,"* 319; JJK, "Rotary Club of Columbia Missouri" speech (first quotation), and JJK to Cochrane, 25 April 1955, "Roscoe Ellard" folder (second quotation), in JJKP. Kilpatrick took every aspect of his job seriously, including personally answering almost all of his reader mail. It was common for him to reply to as many as eighty-four letters in one day. See Roberts and Klibanoff, *Race Beat*, 113.

71. JJK to Millikin, 23 September 1954, in JJKP; Roberts and Klibanoff, *Race Beat*, 113; JJK, *RNL*, 1 July 1949 (first quotation), 8 July 1949 (second quotation), 7 September 1951 (third quotation), 15 November 1951 (fourth quotation).

72. "Pi Delta Epsilon" speech folder (first quotation), JJK to Willis Robertson, 14 July 1953 (second quotation), "Rotary Club of Missouri" speech (third quotation), in JJKP.

73. Roberts and Klibanoff, *Race Beat*, 114; Rouse, *We Happy WASPs*, 43; Egerton, *Speak Now against the Day*, 135, 137–38; Kneebone, *Southern Liberal Journalists*, 211–13; Sosna, *In Search of the Silent South*, 123–37 (first quotation on 137); John Dana Wise to Virginius Dabney, 6 January 1943, Virginius Dabney Papers, UVA; Dabney, *Across the Years*, 166 (second quotation).

74. JJK, *RNL*, 11 August 1949.

75. JJK, *RNL*, 23 January (first quotation), 30 January (second quotation), 7 December 1951 (third quotation).

76. JJK, *RNL*, 4 June 1953.

77. John Dana Wise to JJK, 10 April 1950, in JJKP (quotation).

78. JJK, *RNL*, 13 March 1951.

79. *Silas Rogers v. Commonwealth of Virginia*; "The Case of Silas Rogers," 50; JJK, *RNL*, 29 December 1950, 18 January and 8 March 1951; Dunford, *"Richmond Times-Dispatch,"* 318; Hilts, "Saga of James J. Kilpatrick"; JJK to John S. Battle, 9 May 1952, in JJKP (quotation). After only ten years in Richmond, Kilpatrick was familiar enough with the governors to call Battle by his first name.

80. JJK, *RNL*, 29 December 1950 (first quotation); Carter, *Scottsboro*; "The Case of Silas Rogers," 51 (second quotation); Roberts and Klibanoff, *Race Beat*, 63.

81. "The Case of Silas Rogers," 50–51; JJK to V. M. Newton, 6 July 1956, in JJKP (quotation).

82. Roberts and Klibanoff, *Race Beat*, 115; John Cook Wylie to JJK, 19 August 1953, in JJKP; Epps, "Littlest Rebel," 22.

Chapter Two

1. Kluger, *Simple Justice*, 749; Mayer, "With Much Deliberation."

2. Wall, *Farmville Herald*, 21 May 1954.

3. Kluger, *Simple Justice*, 713–14; Heinemann, *Harry Byrd of Virginia*, 326–27 (first quotation); Muse, *Virginia's Massive Resistance*, 5 (second quotation); Thorndike, "'Sometimes Sordid Level,'" 53; Dabney to John Dana Wise, 21 May 1954, and Dabney to Tennant Bryan, 23 September 1954, Virginius Dabney Papers, UVA; Dabney, *RTD*, 18 May 1954; Chodorov, "Solution of Our Public School Problem." Dabney instead wrote an essay for the *Saturday Evening Post* on John Marshall to remind southerners that the Supreme Court's edicts were the law of the land. See Dabney, "He Made the Court Supreme," 36, 121–22, 124.

4. JJK, *RNL*, 2 October 1953 (first quotation), 18 May 1954 (second quotation); Kilpatrick speech at the University of Richmond, in JJKP (third quotation); Thorndike, "'Sometimes Sordid Level,'" 54.

5. JJK to Harry Byrd Sr., 20 May 1954, in JJKP (first quotation); JJK, *RNL*, 18 May 1954 (second quotation).

6. Richard Tuggle to JJK, *RNL*, 20 May 1954; June Purcell Guild to JJK, *RNL*, 4 June 1954 (first quotation); JJK to Jean Guyton, 30 October 1956, in JJKP (second quotation). See also Guild, *Black Laws of Virginia*.

7. JJK to Harry Byrd Jr., 20 May 1954, in JJKP (quotation). For a temperate response to *Brown*, see JJK, *RNL*, 28 May 1954.

8. "May 1954" folder, Thomas B. Stanley Gubernatorial Papers, Library of Virginia, Richmond; Heinemann, *Harry Byrd of Virginia*, 326–33 (first quotation); Ely, *Crisis of Conservative Virginia*, 12; Heinemann, "Thomas B. Stanley," 340 (second quotation); Muse, *Virginia's Massive Resistance*, 6–8 (third quotation).

9. JJK to William M. Tuck, 21 June 1954 (first quotation), and JJK to Barrye Wall, 14 June 1954, in JJKP (second and third quotations).

10. JJK, *RNL*, 30 August and 25 September 1954 (quotation); Thorndike, "'Sometimes Sordid Level,'" 54–55.

11. JJK, *RNL*, 27 November (first quotation) and 25 September 1954; JJK to Lindsay Almond, 5 November 1954, in JJKP (second quotation).

12. Lewis, "Virginia's Northern Strategy," 118; entries dated 11 (quotation), 19, and 25 January 1955, in MD; Latimer, "Rise and Fall of Massive Resistance." Mays was also William Tuck's business partner and a formidable lobbyist who represented the Virginia Highway Association (trucking industry), the Virginia Bankers Association, and the Virginia Meatpackers Association in the General Assembly. See Sweeney, *Race, Reason, and Massive Resistance*, 18.

13. Entries dated 19 November 1954 (quotation), 6 and 10 January 1955, in MD.

14. Entries dated 12, 16, 23, and 24 June 1955, in MD.

15. Roberts and Klibanoff, *Race Beat*, 72.

16. JJK, *RNL*, 1 June 1955.

17. Miles, *Odyssey of the American Right*, 274; Thorndike, "'Sometimes Sordid Level,'" 55–56.

18. Thorndike, "'Sometimes Sordid Level,'" 56; JJK, *RNL*, 14 November 1955 (quotation).

19. Heinemann, *Harry Byrd of Virginia*, 332–33; Gates, *Making of Massive Resistance*, chap. 6; Ely, *Crisis of Conservative Virginia*, 37–39; Bartley, *Rise of Massive Resistance*, 110–11; Muse, *Virginia's Massive Resistance*, 115–19; Thorndike, "'Sometimes Sordid Level,'" 56.

20. JJK to Tom Waring, 7 November 1955, in TRWP.

21. "Sigma Delta Chi" folder, in JJKP. Olds and Kilpatrick were not the first segregationists to advocate interposition as a means of resisting civil rights reform. In Georgia in 1951, U.S. senator Herman Talmadge called for interposition to stymie civil rights laws proposed in Congress. See Epps, "Littlest Rebel," 22.

22. JJK to Bill Workman, 24 April 1957, and Collins Denny to JJK, 24 December 1958, in JJKP; McKelway, "Pressing for Resistance," *RTD*, 16 May 2004.

23. JJK to James O. Eastland, 22 December 1955, in JJKP; JJK, *RNL*, 21 November 1955; Thorndike, "'Sometimes Sordid Level,'" 56.

24. JJK, *RNL*, 21 November 1955. "Fundamental principles" was Calhoun's phrase in his Fort Hill address for the defense of states' rights as the basis for the American system of government.

25. JJK, *RNL*, 22 November 1955.

26. "The Case for States' Rights" speech, in JJKP (quotation); JJK, *RNL*, 21 November 1955; Thorndike, "'Sometimes Sordid Level,'" 57.

27. JJK, *Southern Case for School Segregation*, 8 (first quotation); "Jim Bishop" folder, in JJKP; JJK, *RNL*, 25 January 1956 (second quotation); interview with James J. Kilpatrick.

28. Roberts and Klibanoff, *Race Beat*, 116–17; *Southern School News* 1 (1956), 10 (quotation).

29. Rolfe, "Columnist Mellowed"; JJK, *RNL*, 28 November (first and second quotations), 25 November 1955 (third and fourth quotations). See also JJK, *RNL*, 24 and 26 November 1955.

30. JJK, "Repeal the 22nd Amendment," *WP*, 8 January 1991; *Brown v. Board* 347 U.S. 483 (1954) (first quotation); Gibbon, *History of the Decline and Fall*, 518 (second quotation); JJK, *RNL*, 25 January 1957 (third quotation); "Open End" debate, JJK to Jameson G. Campaigne, 20 January 1956, in JJKP (fourth quotation).

31. Twardy, "James Jackson Kilpatrick," 225; JJK, *RNL*, 23 November 1955 (first quotation); JJK to Harry Byrd Sr., 3 December 1955 (second quotation), and JJK to Charles Glasgow, 23 March 1956, in JJKP.

32. Hilts, "Saga of James J. Kilpatrick"; Thorndike, "'Sometimes Sordid Level,'" 58; JJK, *RNL*, 22 November 1955 (quotation).

33. JJK, *RNL*, 22 November 1955 (first quotation); Epps, "Littlest Rebel," 32; JJK to W. R. Baker Sr., 28 December 1956, JJK to James Clendinen, 6 February 1956 (second quotation), and JJK to William Flax, undated (February 1961?) (third quotation), in JJKP.

34. See Wills, *Necessary Evil*.

35. Hilts, "Saga of James J. Kilpatrick"; Bartley, *New South*, 188–89; JJK University of Richmond speech, in "Speeches, University of Richmond on Integration" folder, in JJKP; Anthony Lewis, "South Is Talking of 'Interposition,'" *NYT*, 22 January 1956.

36. JJK, *RNL*, 23 November 1955 (first quotation); JJK to Paul D. Hastings, 28 December 1955, in JJKP (second quotation); Thorndike, "'Sometimes Sordid Level,'" 52.

37. JJK to Felix Morley, 16 January 1956 (first quotation), and JJK to Joe Lee Frank, 2 January 1956 (second quotation), in JJKP; JJK, *RNL*, 28 November and 30 December 1955 (third quotation); Thorndike, "'Sometimes Sordid Level,'" 52; Parkinson, "First from the Right," 6. Kilpatrick referred to the Hartford Convention in New England, Wisconsin's objection to the 1850 Fugitive Slave Act, and Iowa's post–Civil War objections to state charters for railroads. That a majority of northerners had the same ideas about states' rights—and maybe even about racial issues—as southerners but were reluctant to confess it had been a mantra of southern politicians at least since Strom Thurmond ventured to New York to recruit support for his Dixiecrat campaign in 1948. George Wallace's presidential bids in the 1960s would follow suit.

38. Parkinson, "First from the Right," 2–3.

39. Hilts, "Saga of James J. Kilpatrick."

40. Thorndike, "'Sometimes Sordid Level,'" 62; Roberts and Klibanoff, *Race Beat*, 118; FitzGerald Bemiss to Prescott Bush, 21 December 1955, in JJKP.

41. Waring, *Charleston News & Courier*, 24 November 1955 (first quotation); *Jackson Daily News*, 24 January 1956 (second quotation); Bartley, *Rise of Massive Resistance*, 130. Pulliam, one of the powerful forces behind Barry Goldwater's campaigns, owned the *Arizona Republic*, the *Phoenix Gazette*, and the *Indianapolis Star*. Kilpatrick often cited the *Star* as proof of his appeal with Midwesterners and nonsoutherners. See JJK, *RNL*, 10 January 1956, and Goldberg, *Barry Goldwater*, 93–94.

42. Harry Byrd Sr. to JJK, 3 December 1955, in JJKP (first quotation); Jeffries, *Justice Lewis F. Powell, Jr.*, 149 (second quotation); "General Assembly 1955–1957" folder, in James H. Latimer Papers, Library of Virginia, Richmond.

43. JJK to Harry Byrd Sr., 28 December 1955 (first quotation), and JJK to Tom Waring, 9 December 1955 (second quotation), in JJKP. Several historians have argued that Kilpatrick's interposition editorials hardened Virginia's position on desegregation and removed the chance for compliance with *Brown*. See Heinemann, *Harry Byrd of Virginia*, 332–33; Ely, *Crisis of Conservative Virginia*; and Muse, *Virginia's Massive Resistance*, 20–21.

44. JJK to Waring, 9 December 1955, in TRWP (first quotation); "Kilpatrick, J.J. (Personal)" folder, in JJKP; Thorndike, "'Sometimes Sordid Level,'" 59; Haley quoted in *Dallas Morning News*, 12 April 1956; Bartley, *Rise of Massive Resistance*, 126–27 (second quotation).

45. JJK to James Clendinen, 6 February 1956 (first quotation), and JJK to Harry Byrd Sr., 30 January 1956 (second and third quotations), in JJKP.

46. Thorndike, "'Sometimes Sordid Level,'" 59, 63.

47. JJK, *RNL*, 10 January 1956 (quotation); Heinemann, "Thomas B. Stanley," 338–45.

48. Entries dated 25 November 1955, 13 January (quotation), and 6 February 1956, in MD.

49. Jeffries, *Justice Lewis F. Powell, Jr.*, 137, 146 (quotation on 148); "Biographical—Historical Memoranda—re Byrds of Virginia" and "Biographical—Historical Memoranda—The 'Massive Resistance' Movement in Virginia" folders, in Lewis F. Powell Jr. Papers, Washington and Lee University School of Law, Lexington, Va.

50. Bartley, *Rise of Massive Resistance*, 134–35.

51. JJK, *RNL*, 10 January (first quotation) and 23 (second quotation) 1956; Gates, *Making of Massive Resistance* (Whitehead quoted on 114).

52. Coleman quoted in the *Baltimore Evening Sun*, 31 January 1956; entry dated 24 January 1956, in MD; George Lewis, *White South*, 42. Marvin Griffin would later urge Arkansas governor Orval Faubus to oppose desegregation during Little Rock's Central High School crisis based on interposition. See Epps, "Littlest Rebel," 24.

53. Collins Denny to JJK, 24 December 1958, in JJKP (first quotation). Denny was a Southside lawyer and charter member of the Citizens' Council's Virginia affiliate, the Defenders of State Sovereignty and Individual Liberties. He consulted with Kilpatrick throughout the interposition campaign. See Thorndike, "'Sometimes Sordid Level,'" 62; Gates, *Making of Massive Resistance*, 110; and Muse, *Virginia's Massive Resistance*, 21 (second quotation).

54. Bartley, *New South*, 194–95; Williams quoted in *Birmingham News*, 26 January 1956.

55. *Race Relations Law Reporter* 1 (April 1956): 447 (quotation); Bartley, *Rise of Massive Resistance*, 132.

56. Bartley, *Rise of Massive Resistance*, 110–11 (quotation), 113; Bartley, *New South*, 197–98; Roberts and Klibanoff, *Race Beat*, 118; Goldfield, *Black, White, and Southern*, 80.

57. Epps, "Littlest Rebel," 25; Latimer, "Rise and Fall of Massive Resistance," A1 (quotation).

58. JJK speech to North Carolina editorial writers, May 1958, in JJKP.

59. Nitschke, "Virginius Dabney of Virginia," 245; Rubin, *Honorable Estate*, 175; McKelway, "Pressing for Resistance," *RTD*, 16 May 2004.

60. Folsom quoted in *Southern School News*, 5 January 1956, 5 (first quotation); Chambers, *Virginia-Pilot*, 1 December 1955 (second quotation); Roberts and Klibanoff, *Race Beat*, 117–18; Muse, *Virginia's Massive Resistance*, 96; Morris, *Courting of Marcus Dupree*, 88–89 (third quotation). Prominent federal judge John Minor Wisdom of the Fifth Circuit Court of Appeals called interposition "a fantasia." See interview with Wisdom, 31 October 1985, disc 1, program 2, "Fighting Back," *Eyes on the Prize* (1986; DVD edition, 2006).

61. *Interposition: Editorials and Editorial Page Presentations*, 12 (first quotation); JJK to Marian Gattermann, 27 March 1957, in JJKP (second quotation). Joseph Thorndike has also argued that Kilpatrick shifted toward winning an outside audience in late 1956. See Thorndike, "'Sometimes Sordid Level,'" 63.

62. Thorndike, "'Sometimes Sordid Level,'" 64; JJK to Marian Gattermann, 6 June 1957 (first quotation), and JJK to Jay Bell, 5 November 1956 (second quotation), in JJKP.

63. JJK to Anthony Harrigan, 27 March 1956 (quotation), JJK to Henry Regnery, 29 February 1956, and JJK to Meredith Butterton, 13 June 1974, in JJKP.

64. JJK, *Sovereign States*, xi (quotation). The Hartford Convention (1814–15) was organized in Hartford, Connecticut, by New Englanders angered about the 1812 War with Britain. Some New Englanders threatened secession to protest the war and the injury it did to international trade, especially with the British.

65. Buckley, *God and Man at Yale*; Kirk, *Conservative Mind*; JJK, "Not to Be Solved on a Slide Rule."

66. Henry Regnery to JJK, 19 May 1955 and 17 April 1972 (quotation), in Henry Regnery Papers, Hoover Institution Archives, Palo Alto, Calif.; Regnery, "Emerging Conservatism," 237–38.

67. JJK, *Sovereign States* manuscript, undated (1956?), in JJKP. See also boxes 66 and 67, 6626-b, in JJKP.

68. JJK, *Sovereign States*, 283.

69. Schlesinger, *New Viewpoints in American History*, 239, 243; General Assembly of Virginia, *Doctrine of Interposition*.

70. JJK to Robert B. Patterson, 7 November 1960 (first quotation), and JJK to Frank Chodorov, 6 March 1956 (second quotation), in JJKP.

71. JJK, *Sovereign States*, 256 (first quotation); JJK to Fitzhugh L. Brown, 19 June 1957, in JJKP (second and third quotations). Kilpatrick referred to three U.S. Supreme Court decisions on school desegregation at the university level: *State of Missouri ex rel. Gaines v. Canada* 305 U.S. 337 (1938); *Sweatt v. Painter* 339 U.S. 629 (1950); and *McLaurin v. Oklahoma State Regents for Higher Education* 339 U.S. 637 (1950).

72. Parkinson, "First from the Right," 9–10; Jefferson, *Notes on the State of Virginia*, 139 (quotation). A Citizens' Council publication advised parents

against race-mixing because Jefferson also opposed it. See *Citizens' Council* 2 (1957): 1.

73. JJK to John Briggs, 21 June 1957, "Book Reviews" folder, in JJKP (quotation). See also Bickel and Wellington, "Legislative Purpose and the Judicial Process."

74. Murphy, review of *The Sovereign States*, 1505–6.

75. JJK to Clendinen, 6 February 1956, in JJKP (quotation); Murphy, review of *The Sovereign States*, 1507–9.

76. Murphy, *Congress and the Court*, 85–91.

77. Kirk, "Prescription, Authority, and Ordered Freedom," 35 (first quotation); Weaver, *Southern Tradition at Bay*, 167–68 (second quotation); Kendall, *Conservative Affirmation*, 16–17 (third quotation); MacLean, *Freedom Is Not Enough*, 46–49. Kirk devoted an entire issue of *Modern Age* to denouncing civil rights reform. See Kirk, "Norms, Conventions, and the South." Less than three months after publishing Kilpatrick's defense of segregation, Kirk offered Kilpatrick the editorship of the magazine. Kilpatrick declined because of work constraints at the *News Leader*. See Russell Kirk to JJK, 29 January 1959, in JJKP.

78. Thorndike, "'Sometimes Sordid Level,'" 67; Nash, *Conservative Intellectual Movement*, 187, 211–12. Nash devoted considerable attention to conservative ideas in the postwar period but mostly ignored conservative intellectuals' views on race and civil rights. See Morley, *Freedom and Federalism*. Morley also supported Kilpatrick's ideas on states' rights in major news periodicals. See, for example, Morley, *Wall Street Journal* (18 February 1956).

79. Perlstein, *Before the Storm*, 70–75; Judis, "Remnant," 28 (quotation).

80. Judis, *William F. Buckley, Jr.*, 35–51; Henry Regnery to Buckley, 27 December 1956, in WFBP; Nash, *Conservative Intellectual Movement*, 187. Brent Bozell, Buckley's brother-in-law and *National Review* editor, opposed segregation. See Nash, *Conservative Intellectual Movement*, 200.

81. Gottfried, *Conservative Movement*, 19; MacLean, *Freedom Is Not Enough*, 47–48; *National Review*, March 1956 (first quotation); Buckley, "Why the South Must Prevail," 149 (second quotation); Burner and West, *Column Right*, 50–51; Harrigan, "The South *Is* Different," 225–27 (third quotation).

82. Nash, *Conservative Intellectual Movement*, 153, 187; JJK, "Down to the Firehouse"; MacLean, *Freedom Is Not Enough*, 46 (quotation). Buckley also allowed Kilpatrick the opportunity to denounce the 1957 integration of Little Rock's Central High School. Kilpatrick wrote that race-mixing would destabilize the community. See JJK, "Right and Power in Arkansas." Kilpatrick and Buckley remained lifelong friends. In 1984, Kilpatrick said Buckley was "the closest male friend I have." See Hutchinson, "Dateline Scrabble."

83. Lentz, *Symbols*, 16–19; Lawrence, *New York Herald Tribune*, 2 February and 17 May 1956; Shelly, "David Lawrence and Ralph McGill," 4, 75, 78; JJK, "The South Will Be Vindicated," 126–29.

84. Lora and Longton, *Conservative Press*, 416; Richard M. Weaver to JJK, 23 September 1957, Clarence Manion to JJK, 9 December 1955 (third quotation), and Strom Thurmond to JJK, 5 September 1957, in JJKP; Davidson quoted in

Maxwell, "Heritage of Inferiority," 310 (second quotation). For examples of Kilpatrick's writing for *Human Events*, see JJK, "'Right to Interpose,'" "Sovereign States," and "School Integration."

85. Wolters, *Race and Education* (Wilkins quoted on 102); Thurgood Marshall, Columbia Oral History Project, quoted in the *WP*, 24 January 1993; Garrow, *Bearing the Cross* (King quoted on 284).

86. Roberts and Klibanoff, *Race Beat*, 118–19.

87. For evidence of Kilpatrick's direct links to the Little Rock crisis, see Muse, *Virginia's Massive Resistance*, 70; Freyer, *Little Rock Crisis*, 68–82; Talbot Field Jr. to JJK, 27 April 1959, in JJKP; and Epps, "Littlest Rebel," 26. Faubus certainly relied on Kilpatrick to justify opposing the desegregation order. See Reed, *Faubus*, 354.

88. Thorndike, "'Sometimes Sordid Level,'" 70; Newby, *South*, 485.

Chapter Three

1. JJK to William J. Simmons, 17 July 1957, in JJKP.

2. JJK to William J. Simmons, 24 July 1957 (first quotation), and JJK to Don Shoemaker, 12 August 1957 (second quotation), in JJKP; Roberts and Klibanoff, *Race Beat*, 147–48.

3. JJK to Nell Battle Lewis, 19 June 1956 (first quotation), and JJK to Francis Sedgwick, 2 October 1957 (second quotation), in JJKP. Kilpatrick's associate editor, Richard Whalen, observed a fellow reporter, Robert W. Harper, cry in the newsroom. See interview with Richard Whalen.

4. Roberts and Klibanoff, *Race Beat*, 179–81; JJK to Marvin Mobley, 9 September 1957, in JJKP (first quotation); Chappell, *Stone of Hope*, 160 (second quotation).

5. JJK, *RNL*, 6 September 1957 (first quotation), 21 September 1957 (second quotation); JJK, "Right and Power in Arkansas," 275 (third quotation).

6. JJK, *RNL*, 26 September 1957 (first quotation), 9 October 1957 (second quotation).

7. Wilkinson, *Harry Byrd*, 240; Klarman, *From Jim Crow to Civil Rights*, 417–18; Ely, *Crisis of Conservative Virginia*, 70 (quotation).

8. Webb, *Fight against Fear*, 73; JJK, *RNL*, 7 July 1958 (quotation).

9. Friedman, "One Episode," 175, 178–81; Bloch, *States' Rights*.

10. Friedman, "One Episode," 177; Webb, *Fight against Fear*, 73 (quotation).

11. JJK to Carl Andrews, 4 September 1959, "Prince Edward Academy Dedication of J.J.K. Library" folder, and JJK to Kate O'Brien, 12 August 1959, in JJKP.

12. Lassiter and Lewis, "Massive Resistance Revisited," 12; Muse, *Virginia's Massive Resistance*, 96; Roberts and Klibanoff, *Race Beat*, 208.

13. Roberts and Klibanoff, *Race Beat*, 210 (quotation). Richard Whalen, Kilpatrick's associate editor at the time, believed the school closings were "antithetical" to Thomas Jefferson's vision of public education and wrote against massive resistance for a period in the *News Leader* while Kilpatrick was out of town. See interview with Richard Whalen.

14. Sweeney, *Race, Reason, and Massive Resistance*, 235 (quotations).

15. JJK speech at the University of Richmond, undated (first quotation), and JJK to M. H. Sass, 12 November 1958 (second quotation), in JJKP; Thorndike, "'Sometimes Sordid Level,'" 68; Bartley, *New South*, 197 (third quotation). Pickett's Charge refers to the failed Confederate attack on the third day of Gettysburg.

16. Bartley, *New South*, 246; Epps, "Littlest Rebel," 26; "Tactics in the School War" speech at the Richmond Rotary Club, 11 November 1958, in JJKP (quotations); Lewis, "Emergency Mothers," 92. Winning a war rather than a battle was the same advice John Dana Wise gave Kilpatrick about segregation a few years before. The Japanese drove American troops from the Philippines in the battle for Corregidor.

17. Thorndike, "'Sometimes Sordid Level,'" 69.

18. Lechner, "Massive Resistance," 637 (first quotation); JJK, "A Conservative View," undated (second quotation), and JJK to William J. Simmons, 23 July 1959 (third quotation), in JJKP; Roberts and Klibanoff, *Race Beat*, 210–11.

19. JJK to James Boehling, 12 February 1959, in JJKP.

20. Fogarty, *Commonwealth Catholicism*, 512; interview with Gerald Fogarty; JJK to Boehling, 13 February 1959, and JJK to Eugene Pulliam, 13 February 1959 (quotation), in JJKP. Kilpatrick attended a small Episcopal church in neighboring Goochland County. As a member of the vestry, he immediately opposed funding the National Council of Churches, an ecumenical, integrationist organization. "Our pastor, a political innocent, is very much in favor of this outfit," he wrote a friend. "I hope to educate him a little over the next few years." See JJK to Elizabeth Osth, 12 April 1960, in JJKP. Toward the end of his life, Kilpatrick described his religious beliefs like any good eighteenth-century Deist would. He wrote an Anglican clergyman that his faith went no further than "the first sentence of the Creed" and that everything else was just "reciting words, not affirming belief." See JJK to Rev. Charles A. Cesaretti, 13 May 1992, in JJKP.

21. Hershman, "Massive Resistance Meets Its Match," 105; Jeffries, *Justice Lewis F. Powell, Jr.*, 151–53; Lewis, "Emergency Mothers," 93.

22. JJK, *RNL*, 20 January 1959 (first quotation); *RTD*, 20 January 1959 (second quotation).

23. *RTD*, 20 January 1959. The Maginot Line was the French defensive network built between the world wars designed to prevent another German invasion.

24. Dure first outlined his "freedom of choice" proposal in a January 1958 *Times-Dispatch* article. See *RTD*, 20 January 1958 and 10 November 1993; Hershman, "Massive Resistance Meets Its Match," 127–30. Hershman regards Dure and the Perrow Commission as setting a moderate tone for post–massive resistance Virginia.

25. JJK to Leon Dure, 24 February 1959, in Leon Dure Papers, UVA (quotation); JJK to Henry Regnery, 20 January 1960, in JJKP.

26. JJK to Tom Waring, 9 December 1955, in TRWP; "Report to Governor, December, Yearly," in CCGP; Entries dated 8 and 25 June 1958 in MD; Lewis,

White South, 148–49; Lewis, "Virginia's Northern Strategy," 115–16; JJK, *RNL*, 26 January 1966; VaCCG pamphlet, General Collection JK 2439 M45, in DMP.

27. Latimer, "Rise and Fall of Massive Resistance," *RTD*, 22 September 1996, A1; JJK, *RNL*, 18 February 1971 (quotation).

28. Entries for 2 July 1958 and 8 December 1964, in MD.

29. Latimer, "Rise and Fall of Massive Resistance"; entry for 15 September 1958, in MD (quotations).

30. Entry for 27 June 1958, in MD. Kilpatrick's wish to elevate the level of debate above the race issue percolated through Virginia's leadership ranks all the way to the governor.

31. For examples of "my CCG," see entries for 17 July 1961 and 31 May 1962, in MD; Lewis, "Virginia's Northern Strategy," 122. As many as eleven lawyers served simultaneously on the CCG. In 1965, Governor Albertis Harrison appointed author John Dos Passos to the CCG to lend more credibility to the group. Dos Passos served on the commission until its final days. See Albertis Harrison to John Dos Passos, 26 January 1965, in John Dos Passos Papers, UVA.

32. VaCCG pamphlet, General Collection JK 2439 M45, in DMP.

33. JJK, *RNL*, 21 February 1958 (first quotation); JJK to Robert T. Stevens Jr., 12 April 1957 (second quotation), and JJK to Charles Packard, 26 November 1958 (third quotation), in JJKP.

34. JJK to Dan Walter, 7 August 1961 (first quotation), and JJK to Edward Lane, 7 January 1960, in JJKP; JJK, *RNL*, 21 February 1958.

35. Bartley, *Rise of Massive Resistance*, 183.

36. CCG, *We the States*, 314; CCG, *On the Fixing of Boundary Lines*; CCG, *Rational Approach*; O'Neill, *Originalism*, 76; Lewis, "Virginia's Northern Strategy," 142; CCG, *Did the Court "Interpret" or "Amend"?*, 4 (quotation). Alfred J. Schweppe was a legal scholar and attorney. His career included numerous appointments to the American Bar Association and as dean of the University of Washington Law School. The VaCCG chose him, a nonsoutherner, to emphasize the CCG's national appeal.

37. Lewis, *White South*, 196; entries for 2 October 1961 and 19 February 1964, in MD (second quotation); John Synon to JJK, 17 March 1961, in JJKP.

38. Latimer, "Constitutional Commission Prepares for New Legal Fight," *RTD*, 21 March 1965, B7; "David J. Mays speeches" folder, "James J. Kilpatrick" folder, "Publicity" folder, in CCGP; Lewis, *White South*, 151. In 1963 alone, CCG publications inundated 1,807 college departments, 887 college libraries, 955 college newspapers, 546 high schools, and 1,618 newspapers. The commission's publications arrived on the desks of traditional allies, like the Citizens' Council, which put the reading material on their recommended literature list for members. See Lewis, "Virginia's Northern Strategy," 122.

39. JJK to Louis Hollis, 20 March 1961, in JJKP; entries for 13 May 1961 and 5 April and 6 August 1962, in MD.

40. Goldwater, *Conscience of a Conservative*, 25–31, 32 (first quotation), 38 (second quotation); Perlstein, *Before the Storm*, 64.

41. Entries for 25 September 1960 (first quotation) and 19 March 1964 (second quotation), in MD.

42. VaCCG pamphlet, General Collection JK 2439 M45, in DMP (first quotation); JJK to William Ball, 10 June 1959, in JJKP (second quotation).

43. CCG, *Race and the Restaurant*; *Williams v. Howard Johnson's Restaurant*; entry for 8 April 1960, in MD (quotation); Lewis, "Virginia's Northern Strategy," 120.

44. Brady, *Black Monday*; CCG, *Democracy and Despotism*; CCG, *Did the Court "Interpret" or "Amend"?*; CCG, *"State Action,"* 15–17; *Shelley v. Kraemer*; *Smith v. Allwright*; Lewis, "Virginia's Northern Strategy," 120–21. See also CCG, *Federal Grants-in-Aid*.

45. CCG, *Reconstruction Amendments' Debates*; "Avins" folder, in CCGP; Robert H. Williams, "Legal Scholar Alfred Avins Dies at Age 64," *WP*, 11 June 1999; O'Neill, *Originalism*, 85; Avins, "Maybe It's Time to Look at the Antislavery Amendment," 82–84; Mintz, *Liberty Lobby*;.

46. Lewis, *White South*, 149, 150 (first quotation); JJK to George Richardson, 14 September 1965, in JJKP (second quotation); JJK, "A Conservative View," 1 October 1964, in JJKP. The *News Leader* office was supportive of the John Birch Society despite Kilpatrick's public reservations. Kilpatrick subscribed to their magazine, *American Opinion*, and James Lucier, his associate editor in the early to mid-1960s, wrote frequently for them. Lucier did not belong to the John Birch Society but published fourteen articles for them between 1963 and 1966. See Link, *Righteous Warrior*, 204–5.

47. Entry for 26 June 1964, in MD (first quotation); Putnam, *Race and Reason*; JJK to Fred Davis, July 1962(?), in JJKP (second quotation); Lewis, *White South*, 149.

48. Entries for 28 September 1960 (first quotation) and 10 and 15 May and 13 September 1961 (second quotation), in MD; Lewis, "Virginia's Northern Strategy," 123, 126.

49. JJK to Tom Waring, 27 March 1956, in JJKP; Roberts and Klibanoff, *Race Beat*, 212.

50. Roberts and Klibanoff, *Race Beat*, 212–14.

51. Ibid., 215–21; Waring to James Gray, 12 May 1959, in TRWP (quotation).

52. Roberts and Klibanoff, *Race Beat*, 215–21.

53. Entries for 28 February (first quotation) and 7 May 1962 (second quotation), 7 and 9 August 1963, and 29 April 1965, in MD; "CCG Minutes, Meetings, 1960–1963," 21 June 1962, in JJKP (third quotation); Lewis, "Virginia's Northern Strategy," 126.

54. JJK to William Ball, 8 January 1959, in JJKP (first quotation); entry for 21 January 1960, in MD; VaCCG pamphlet, General Collection JK 2439 M45, in DMP; JJK, *RNL*, 7 July and 3 October 1960 (second quotation); CCG, *We the States*, viii (third quotation).

55. *Report of the Virginia Commission on Constitutional Government*, 4 January 1962, 10–11; entry for 24 July 1962, in MD; "The Virginia Commission on Constitutional Government and the Pennsylvania Republican Forum: Minutes

of Meeting Held at the Williamsburg Inn, Williamsburg, Virginia, July 23 and 24, 1962," in JJKP; Lewis, "Virginia's Northern Strategy," III, 130–39. Lewis probably argues too strongly for cooperation between the Pennsylvanians and Virginians, which disintegrated quickly after their meeting.

56. JJK, *RNL*, 31 December 1958; JJK to Edward C. Lane, 7 January 1960, in JJKP (quotation).

57. Entries for 14 February and 1 March 1968, in MD; Bass and DeVries, *Transformation of Southern Politics*, 348–54; JJK to Addison Hagan, 5 April 1965, in JJKP (quotation). In early 1968, the General Assembly passed bills authorizing the CCG to disperse the following winter.

58. CCG, *Every Man His Own Law*; Lewis, "Virginia's Northern Strategy," 146; JJK to Richard McCullough, 11 June 1965, in JJKP. For the CCG's political platform calling for tax reduction and reform, see CCG, *We the States*, xxx–xxxi. During the 1950s and 1960s, conservative Americans became increasingly distressed about the Warren Court's protection of subversives, unions, minorities, and criminals. A string of judicial decisions, like the 1957 Red Monday rulings and the *Miranda* case, reinforced their fears. See *Yates v. United States* 354 U.S. 298 (1957); and *Ernesto Arturo Miranda v. State of Arizona* 384 U.S. 436 (1966).

59. Henry L. Marsh III, Voices of Freedom Collection, Virginia Commonwealth University Libraries Digital History Collection (quotation).

Chapter Four

1. Lenoir Chambers, "The Year Virginia Opened the Schools," *Virginian-Pilot*, 31 December 1959.

2. *WP*, 2 January 1960, A9.

3. *RNL*, 2 January 1960; JJK, *RNL*, 8 January 1960 (quotation).

4. Bartley, *New South*, 298; Roberts and Klibanoff, *Race Beat*, 294.

5. Randolph and Tate, *Rights for a Season*, 33.

6. JJK, *RNL*, 22 February 1960. The sit-ins and later integration crisis at the University of Mississippi consumed Kilpatrick's attention like few other civil rights events in the early 1960s. In 1961, for example, Kilpatrick traveled to the Soviet Union during the spring Freedom Rides. The *News Leader*, however, still provided scathing editorials against the integration of the bus lines. Ten days after white supremacists attacked the Freedom Riders in Anniston, Alabama, the *News Leader* ran an editorial that called the activists "militant Negroes" bent on a "maliciously destructive trip." See *RNL*, 25 May 1961.

7. Carson, *In Struggle*, 22–23.

8. JJK, *Southern Case for School Segregation*, 99 (quotations).

9. Branch, *Parting the Waters*, 554; Carson, *Papers of Martin Luther King, Jr.*, 459, 556, 638; JJK to Robert Allison, 7 November 1960, in JJKP (quotation); "Virginian to Debate Rev. King on TV," *Atlanta Constitution*, 2 November 1960.

10. Branch, *Parting the Waters*, 554; Carson, *Papers of Martin Luther King, Jr.*, 459, 556, 638.

11. Carson, *Papers of Martin Luther King, Jr.*, 40. Carson's edited collection contains the entire broadcast transcript of the NBC debate. Less than a month after the debate, Kilpatrick took issue with NBC's documentary *White Paper* on the Nashville sit-ins. He accused the network of pairing "the most articulate Negro and integrationist whites they could find" against "a few dull-witted whites as typical Southerners." "We call it dirty pool," he remarked, "unfair, untruthful, and . . . irresponsible." The smart, polished Kilpatrick pitted against King challenged television audiences' stereotypes about segregationists. See "Speaking from the South," 49.

12. JJK to Andrew Blunt, 22 November 1963, in JJKP; Allen, "Martin Luther King's Civil Disobedience," 94; Carson, *Papers of Martin Luther King, Jr.*, 560 (quotation).

13. Carson, *Papers of Martin Luther King, Jr.*

14. Branch, *Parting the Waters*, 380–81 (quotation). Presenting King as a disturber of the peace was commonplace among conservatives in the 1960s. One of King's first biographers, Lionel Lokos, a popular writer for the right, believed that King's legacy was lawlessness. See Lokos, *House Divided*.

15. Carson, *Papers of Martin Luther King, Jr.*, 560 (quotation).

16. Branch, *Parting the Waters*, 380–81; Garrow, *Bearing the Cross*, 150 (quotation).

17. Hamilton, Madison, and Jay, *Federalist Papers*. The essays comprising the *Federalist Papers* started to appear in 1787. Allen, "Martin Luther King's Civil Disobedience," 95–96. For another example of King's linking the founders to morality, see Martin Luther King Jr., "Love, Law, and Civil Disobedience," *New South*, 12 December 1961, 3–11.

18. Sansing, *University of Mississippi*, 280–87, 289–90 (first quotation); Roberts and Klibanoff, *Race Beat*, 270, 274; Eagles, *Price of Defiance*, chap. 11, 282, 283 (second quotation).

19. Sansing, *University of Mississippi*, 291–94; Branch, *Parting the Waters*, 648–49.

20. Sansing, *University of Mississippi*, 279; Roberts and Klibanoff, *Race Beat*, chap. 17.

21. JJK, *RNL*, 26 September 1962 (first quotation); JJK to Robert Needles, 7 November 1963, in JJKP (second quotation).

22. JJK, *RNL*, 29 September and 1 October (quotation) 1962.

23. JJK, *RNL*, 29 September 1962; Roberts and Klibanoff, *Race Beat*, 284; interview with Hank Klibanoff.

24. Roberts and Klibanoff, *Race Beat*, 284; JJK, *RNL*, 1 October 1962 (quotations). Had Kilpatrick bothered to research the Meredith family's history, he would have found a long-standing commitment to education as the pathway to black advancement. See Eagles, *Price of Defiance*, 205–8. The *Louisville (Ky.) Courier-Journal* called the university the "pawn" in the 23 September 1962 edition.

25. Sansing, *University of Mississippi*, 298–99; Roberts and Klibanoff, *Race Beat*, 289 (quotation).

26. Roberts and Klibanoff, *Race Beat*, 289; JJK, *RNL*, 1 October 1962 (first, third, and fourth quotations); Eagles, *Price of Defiance*, 322 (second quotation); Walker quoted in the *Jackson (Miss.) Clarion-Ledger*, 30 September 1962 (fifth quotation); Simmons to JJK, 4 August 1964, in JJKP (sixth quotation).

27. Sansing, *University of Mississippi*, 303; Branch, *Parting the Waters*, 668–69; Roberts and Klibanoff, *Race Beat*, 297.

28. JJK, *RNL*, 1 (first quotation), 3, 5 (second quotation) October 1962.

29. *RNL*, 1, 2, 3, 16 October 1962.

30. Eskew, *But for Birmingham*, 121, 216, 272. See also Manis, *Fire You Can't Put Out*.

31. JJK to Mary Louise Meeks, 20 May 1963, in JJKP; Thomas, "Television News"; Dabney, *RTD*, 5 June 1963 (quotation); JJK, *RNL*, 4, 6, and 8 May 1963.

32. JJK, *RNL*, 21 and 22 May 1963 (quotations).

33. Perlstein, *Before the Storm*, 203–4; JJK to Joe Nadler, 31 December 1965, in JJKP (quotation); JJK, *RNL*, 4, 6, and 8 May 1963.

34. Raymond H. Boone, Voices of Freedom Collection, Virginia Commonwealth University Libraries Digital History Collection (first quotation); Thomas, "Television News"; JJK, *RNL*, 8, 10, and 13 May 1963; *RTD*, 5 May 1963 (second quotation).

35. Thomas, "Television News" (quotation); *Richmond Afro-American*, 11 and 18 May 1963.

36. Garrow, *Protest at Selma*, 166–69; Bartley, *New South*, 338 (first quotation); Roberts and Klibanoff, *Race Beat*, 323, 346–47 (second quotation). For more on King's evolving image in the media, see Lentz, *Symbols*.

37. JJK, *RNL*, 13 June 1963.

38. JJK, "The Hell He Is Equal."

39. Roberts and Klibanoff, *Race Beat*, 350; JJK, "The Hell He Is Equal" (quotations); MacLean, *Freedom Is Not Enough*, 63.

40. Thomas B. Congdon Jr. to JJK, 16 September 1963 (first quotation), and JJK to Congdon, 19 September 1963, in JJKP; Roberts and Klibanoff, *Race Beat*, 350–51; JJK, *RNL*, 19 September 1963 (second quotation).

41. "Speaking from the South," 49 (quotation).

42. *Group Research Report* 2 (12 August 1963): 57; Crespino, *In Search of Another Country*, 60–61. *Group Research Report* was the left's response to Joseph McCarthy's investigations of Communist influences in government. The United Auto Workers funded its publication and reported the activities of the extreme right.

43. Entry for 11 April 1961, in MD; Anthony Lewis, "Bar Chief Assails High Court Views," *NYT*, 7 August 1962; Jack Anderson and Les Whitten, "Clash of Lawyers," *WP*, 24 October 1977.

44. Katagiri, *Mississippi State Sovereignty Commission*, 123.

45. JJK to Mrs. Harold Hundley, 20 February 1964, in JJKP; Crespino, *In Search of Another Country*, 92–93; Katagiri, *Mississippi State Sovereignty Commission*, 122 (quotation).

46. Katagiri, *Mississippi State Sovereignty Commission*, 122 (quotation). For a brief history of the CCFAF, see Brown, "Role of Elite Leadership."

47. Katagari, *Mississippi State Sovereignty Commission*, 123–24; "L-1961" folder, in JJKP; JJK, *RNL*, 15 July 1963. In April 1963, Synon traveled to Mississippi to meet with William J. Simmons and others about "thickening some plots" to stop the civil rights legislation and plan joint resistance in the Magnolia State, Virginia, and elsewhere. See Simmons to JJK, 30 April 1963, in JJKP. Bill Loeb was a colorful addition to the CCFAF. The newspaperman wore a pearl-handled revolver and reported that he infiltrated the state's Communist Party. He also made sure that New Hampshire backed Senator Barry Goldwater in the 1964 presidential primary. His front-page editorials dubbed liberal candidate Nelson Rockefeller a "spoiled, rich glamour boy." Republican presidential aspirants desperately courted Loeb to win the Granite State's primary. See *Manchester Union Leader*, 1 July 1963, i; Veblen, *"Manchester Union Leader"*; Perlstein, *Before the Storm*, 268.

48. Carter, "New Dixie Colonel"; Carter, *Politics of Rage*, 201; Worden, "Tales of the Kingmakers."

49. Synon to JJK, 10 July 1959, in JJKP (first quotation); JJK to Tom Waring, 31 August 1961, in TRWP (second quotation). Sometimes Synon's ideas struck even Kilpatrick as too extreme. When Synon wanted to abolish the public schools in Virginia, Kilpatrick told him, "That is a negative response. The constitutional fight is not thus won, or even fought out; the issue is merely mooted." See JJK to Synon, 3 August 1959, in JJKP.

50. Carter, *Politics of Rage*, 201–2.

51. Mississippi State Sovereignty Commission Final Report to CCFAF, Inc., 15 June 1964, SCRID#6-70-0-1-16-1-1 and #6-70-0-1-17-1-1: Mississippi State Sovereignty Commission Records, 1994–2006, <http://mdah.state.ms.us>; Blackmon, "Silent Partner"; Danzig, "Rightists, Racists, and Separatists," 30; Crespino, *In Search of Another Country*, 95–97. Lucier wrote articles critical of Martin Luther King for *American Opinion*, the John Birch Society magazine, and *Human Events*. He later worked for Jesse Helms as his chief legislative assistant in the Senate. See *Group Research Report* 3 (31 January 1964): 7; and Link, *Righteous Warrior*, 204.

52. Buckley to William A. Rusher, 2 February 1965, in WFBP (first quotation); JJK, "Civil Rights and Legal Wrongs," 231–34 (second quotation on 236, third quotation on 234); MacLean, *Freedom Is Not Enough*, 69; CCG, "Civil Rights and Legal Wrongs." Buckley agreed to advertise the CCG's booklet *We the States* as a special reward for their assistance. *National Review* normally forbade advertisements by lobbyists.

53. "Correspondence W" folder (undated), in JJKP (first and second quotations); interview with James J. Kilpatrick; Bake and Kilpatrick, *American South: Towns and Cities*, 21; Dunford, *"Richmond Times-Dispatch,"* 322–23; JJK, *RNL*, 4 November 1963 (third quotation); K. V. Hoffman, *RTD*, 4 November 1963.

54. JJK, "Crossroads in Dixie," 435 (quotations); JJK, "South Goes Back Up for Grabs."

55. Carter, *Politics of Rage*, 12, 157 (quotation). Carter noted that Wallace "thrust himself forward as the authentic defender of the 'common man.'" See Carter, *Politics of Rage*, 313–14.

56. Mississippi State Sovereignty Commission Final Report to CCFAF, Inc., 15 June 1964, SCRID#6-70-0-1-16-1-1 and #6-70-0-1-17-1-1, Mississippi State Sovereignty Commission Records, <http://mdah.state.ms.us>; Crespino, *In Search of Another Country*, 95; "Civil Rights Act–Title VII" folder, in CCGP.

57. Carter, *Politics of Rage*, 206–10; Wallace quoted in the *NYT*, 21 May 1964; Tucker, *Funding of Scientific Racism*, 124; Massey, *New Fanatics*. The National Putnam Letters Committee, the leading publishing house of books on scientific racism, released Massey's book with the help of the CCFAF.

58. Tucker, *Funding of Scientific Racism*, 122; Katagiri, *Mississippi State Sovereignty Commission*, 124–25.

59. Mississippi State Sovereignty Commission Final Report to CCFAF, Inc., SCRID#6-70-0-1-7-1-1; 13-1-1; 14-1-1, Mississippi State Sovereignty Commission Records, <http://mdah.state.ms.us>; Tucker, *Funding of Scientific Racism*, 1, 2, 6–8, 70–71, 124; Blackmon, "Silent Partner."

60. "Spring 1964: Bloom and Boom," 17; JJK to Thaddeus Crump, 14 April 1964, in JJKP; Carter, "New Dixie Colonel"; Perlstein, *Before the Storm*, 307.

61. Mann, *Walls of Jericho*, 238, 395, 409.

62. Carter, "New Dixie Colonel."

63. Entry for 2 April 1964, in MD.

64. JJK, *RNL*, 11 May and 26 June (first quotation) 1964; CCG, *Civil Rights and Federal Powers*, preface (second quotation); Lewis, "Virginia's Northern Strategy," 142. Kilpatrick repeated such ideas about the constitutional effects of the bill in other editorials. See, for example, JJK, *RNL*, 4 and 7 February, 13 April, and 9 June 1964.

65. "Civil Rights Legislation" folder, in CCGP; Mississippi State Sovereignty Commission, "A Brief 'Resume' of Activities of the CCFAF," SCRID#6-70-0-1-18-11 and #6-70-0-374-1-1, Mississippi State Sovereignty Commission Records, <http://mdah.state.ms.us>; Coordinating Committee on Fundamental American Freedoms, *Unmasking the Civil Rights Bill*, 56 (quotation).

66. Entry for 3 December 1963, in MD; Whalen and Whalen, *Longest Debate* (Russell quoted on 142). The pamphlet repeated arguments that Kilpatrick made for Buckley in fall 1963.

67. JJK to J. Segar Gravatt, 23 June 1964, in JJKP (quotation); Crespino, *In Search of Another Country*, 99–100.

68. John C. Satterfield returned to Mississippi and, over the next decade, fought for the Citizens' Councils' private school system. He became lead defense lawyer in *Holmes v. Alexander* (1969), where the Supreme Court ruled an immediate end to racially based school segregation in the South. Seriously ill and near death, Satterfield told the Methodist bishop of Mississippi that he had been on the wrong side of the segregation battle. In 1981, he committed suicide. John James Synon retired to Richmond, where he managed the Patrick Henry Press and published books about the genetic and intellectual inferiority

of blacks for the next eight years and wrote articles for the *Citizen*. He moved into the fringes of the right-wing community and eventually died of cancer in 1972. His friends draped his coffin with a Confederate flag. See Simmons, "In Memoriam"; Tucker, *Funding of Scientific Racism*, 110; and Crespino, *In Search of Another Country*, 271.

69. Perlstein, *Before the Storm*, 89 (first quotation); Goldwater, *Conscience of a Conservative*, 33–37 (second and third quotations); Goldberg, *Barry Goldwater*, 89; Mayer, *Running on Race*, 45.

70. JJK, *RNL*, 19 June 1964 (first quotation); JJK to Lance Phillips, 2 July 1964, and JJK to S. L. Gentry, 27 September 1963 (second), in JJKP;. Wallace's greatest sin may have been politicizing race, but the libertarian Goldwater's was devaluing the positive role of big government and institutions on behalf of the public good. Historians have noted the damaging effects of Goldwater's positions, even his "color-blind" ones, on black civil rights. See Chen, *Fifth Freedom*, 21–22.

71. Kilpatrick believed Wallace's performance in the primaries was courageous, but afterward, he needed to leave the political scene to prevent divisions in the southern electorate. Kilpatrick and Wallace shared the states' rights philosophy and an antipathy toward the civil rights bill, but the editor saw the governor's campaign as pointless. For more on Wallace voters, see Carlson, *George C. Wallace*, 53, 89, 94–98, 120, 168, 238, 245, 261.

72. Buckley to JJK, 21 January 1963, WFBP (first quotation); JJK to Buckley, 23 January 1963, in JJKP (second quotation); Goldberg, *Barry Goldwater*, 183. The *National Review* even reprinted material from the Virginia Commission on Constitutional Government and advertised the agency in its pages, which violated Buckley's long-standing policy of not promoting political groups that employed friends of the magazine. Buckley made the exception because he was indebted to Kilpatrick. The *News Leader* editor had already begun work on a comprehensive analysis of Goldwater's domestic agenda that the *National Review* would use in the upcoming election.

73. JJK, "The Ike Plan Cometh"; JJK, *RNL*, 13 May 1964; Buckley to William A. Rusher, 16 February 1965, in WFBP (quotation).

74. Mayer, *Running on Race*, 46 (first quotation); Perlstein, *Before the Storm*, 363–64 (second quotation); Roche, "Cowboy Conservatism," 84.

75. Perlstein, *Before the Storm*, 363; Margolis, *Last Innocent Year*, 239; Bork, "Civil Rights—A Challenge" (quotations).

76. Perlstein, *Before the Storm*, 363; Goldwater quoted in *Congressional Record—Senate*, 18 June 1964, no. 14318 (first quotation); JJK, *RNL*, 22 June 1964 (second quotation).

77. Perlstein, *Before the Storm*, 391.

78. Novak, *Agony of the G.O.P.*, 1–2 (quotation); Perlstein, *Before the Storm*, 86–87.

79. JJK, *RNL*, 13 June 1964; JJK, "A Conservative View," 24/25 February 1968, in JJKP (quotation). "A Conservative View" was Kilpatrick's nationally

syndicated column. Kilpatrick was skeptical about Goldwater's chances from the beginning of the campaign. See JJK, *RNL*, 16 July and 5 November 1964.

80. Perlstein, *Before the Storm*, 384 (first quotation); interview with Tom Stagg (second quotation).

81. Stagg to JJK, 17 June 1964 (first quotation), JJK to Stagg, 19 June 1964 (second quotation), Stagg to JJK, 22 June 1964, and JJK to Stagg, 25 June 1964, in JJKP; interview with James J. Kilpatrick; interview with Tom Stagg (third quotation).

82. Goldberg, *Barry Goldwater*, 203 (first quotation); Bjerre-Poulsen, *Right Face*, 254; Mayer, "LBJ Fights the White Backlash"; *Proceedings of the Twenty-Eighth Republican National Convention*, 275–76 (second and third quotations).

83. JJK, "Domestic Affairs," 588 (first, second, and third quotations), 587 (fourth quotation); JJK, "National Review July 14, 1964" folder, in JJKP. Some recent scholarship argues that segregationists and business conservatives, including Goldwater, who defended the right to discriminate in employment based on property rights and the free market, had a compatible race-based, color-blind ideology. See MacLean, *Freedom Is Not Enough*, and Chen, *Fifth Freedom*. Goldwater's beliefs must be understood within the broader context of racial politics in the sixties. In general, Goldwater contributed to political strategies and policies that had a long-standing, negative impact on race relations and African Americans. Goldwater, however, was not the same kind of political creature as George Wallace and the gaggle of southern demagogues who preached segregation and was less guided by race.

84. Buckley to *National Review* staff, 9 June 1964, "Inter-Office Memo" folder, "Inter-Office Memos—Jan.–June 1965" folder, in WFBP. Kilpatrick's name appeared on the masthead from October 1964, when he was made associate editor. By the late 1960s, Kilpatrick was the magazine's primary contributor for assessing the Supreme Court and southern, and often national, politics. See JJK to Buckley, 8 February 1969, in WFBP.

85. JJK, "Domestic Affairs," 589 (first quotation); Goldberg, *Barry Goldwater*, 146 (second quotation); Bjerre-Poulsen, *Right Turn*, 132; Goldwater quoted in *NYT*, 28 October 1964 (third quotation); JJK, "Lyndon Johnson"; Mayer, *Running on Race*, 54. Goldwater reiterated points made by other conservatives like Kilpatrick. Kilpatrick revived the attacks on LBJ's shaky commitment to civil rights in editorials as well. See JJK, *RNL*, 13 August 1964.

86. Goldberg, *Barry Goldwater*, 208 (first quotation); Perlstein, *Before the Storm*, 486–87, 465 (second quotation); Buckley, "Black Madness," 263 (third quotation). Rus Walton of the RNC and F. Clifton White of Citizens for Goldwater-Miller were the principal exploiters of whites' racial fears during the Goldwater campaign.

87. Perlstein, *Before the Storm*, 513; *NYT*, 5 November 1964.

88. JJK, "A Conservative View," 18 October 1979, in JJKP (first quotation); JJK, *RNL*, 4 November 1964 (second quotation); JJK, "New Right" (third quotation); Twardy, "James Jackson Kilpatrick," 229. As the Reagan revolution

approached, Kilpatrick could wax poetic about the Goldwater campaign. Whereas Kilpatrick sensed a conservative resurgence, Richard Hofstadter, the best-known scholar of the right in the 1960s, predicted that the Cow Palace convention "may come to be seen as the high tide of the radical right." See Hixson, *Search for the American Right Wing* (Hofstadter quoted on 112).

89. JJK to Alex McKeigney, 31 May 1963, in JJKP (quotation). Dan Carter's work suggests the opposite in conservatism's rising prominence and finds racism everywhere in the national Republican Party. See Carter, *From George Wallace to Newt Gingrich*. Though race was central to Kilpatrick's conservatism, a monolithic, racially deterministic view of American conservatism would be narrow and insulting to many on the right.

Chapter Five

1. JJK to Raymond Wheeler, 21 March 1961 (first quotation), and JJK to Mr. and Mrs. James Mitchell, 27 March 1961 (second quotation), in JJKP.

2. JJK, *Southern Case for School Segregation*, 37 (quotation).

3. Ibid., 29 (quotation).

4. Ibid., 27 (first quotation), 42 (second quotation).

5. Ibid., 49–50.

6. Ibid., 96 (first quotation), 97 (second quotation). Newby, *Challenge to the Court*, 170–73. Other sophisticated segregationists, like Jesse Helms, one of Kilpatrick's good friends, also pointed out the problems in the black community to discredit the civil rights movement. See Link, *Righteous Warrior*, 75–76; and JJK to Allen Taylor, 12 August 1963, in JJKP.

7. JJK, *Southern Case for School Segregation*, 97 (first quotation), 26 (second quotation).

8. Myrdal, *American Dilemma*; JJK, *Southern Case for School Segregation*, 68 (first quotation); Southern, *Gunnar Myrdal*, 181 (quotation); Pate, "Pregnancies Grow in Washington Schools." Scientific racism had mostly disappeared by the 1930s but rebounded in the fifties and sixties thanks to an assortment of writers angry about integration. See Newby, *Jim Crow's Defense*, 195–96. Henry Garrett was a professor at the University of Virginia's School of Education and former chair of Columbia University's psychology department. Kilpatrick often relied on his ideas for *News Leader* editorials as well.

9. JJK, *Southern Case for School Segregation*, 23 (first quotation), 71 (second and third quotations); Newby, *Challenge to the Court*, 147, 171; JJK to Tom Sloan, 17 and 21 March 1961, in JJKP (fourth quotation).

10. JJK, *Southern Case for School Segregation*, 70–73.

11. Tucker, *Funding of Scientific Racism*, 111; Epps, "Littlest Rebel," 34.

12. Putnam, *Race and Reason*, 20.

13. JJK to Robert Patterson, 7 November 1960, in JJKP. Kilpatrick liked eugenics arguments. He subscribed to *Mankind Quarterly* and even tried to use the CCG to encourage the journal's distribution in the Virginia school system. See JJK to Donald Swan, 10 November 1960, in JJKP.

14. JJK, *Southern Case for School Segregation*, 101 (first quotation), 97 (second quotation); JJK to Florence Schiele, 28 June 1963, in JJKP (third quotation). Kilpatrick believed that talented and exceptional blacks should be allowed to enter white schools but warned that this would deny weaker black students the intellectual stimulation of superior ones. He considered deserving black students ones who had entered with whites' permission whereas undeserving blacks were ones who challenged the system. See JJK, *Southern Case for School Segregation*, 90.

15. JJK, *Southern Case for School Segregation*, 183–84.

16. Ibid., 184–85, 191 (first quotation), 192 (second quotation).

17. Tindall, "The Unfinished Emancipation," *The Progressive* 26, no. 12 (December 1962); and Golden, "The Interesting James Jackson Kilpatrick," *Carolina Israelite* (first quotation), both in JJKP; Mary Lou Werner, "The Segregation Issue From the Losing Side," *Sunday Star*, 4 November 1962 (second quotation); Bozell, "To Mend the Tragic Flaw."

18. JJK to Kennedy, 14 July 1986, in JJKP (first quotation); JJK to Regnery, 19 October 1961 (second and third quotations), 31 January 1962 (fourth quotation), in folder 2, Henry Regnery Papers, Hoover Institution Archives, Palo Alto, Calf.

19. JJK to Donald Hagler, 1 June 1964, JJK to Tom Bradbury, 7 June 1963, and JJK to Virgil Gil, 2 February 1958 (first quotation), in JJKP; "Petulant Plea," 57 (second, third, and fourth quotations). Westbrook Pegler was a well-known anti–New Deal conservative columnist who wrote for the Hearst syndicate. Crowell-Collier published Kilpatrick's book in October of 1962 in the wake of the Ole Miss riot. The timing of its release made it unpopular. The publishing house also did not publicize the book or contact Kilpatrick for almost a year after its publication. Kilpatrick waited a year to receive a royalty check. See JJK to Donald Hagler, 1 June 1964, in JJKP.

20. Perlstein, *Before the Storm*, 6; Hilts, "Saga of James J. Kilpatrick" (quotation); "James Jackson Kilpatrick," 162.

21. "James Jackson Kilpatrick," 162; JJK to Ben Moreel, 20 January 1965, in JJKP (first quotation); Mason, "Newspaper Days," 347; Keeler, *Newsday*, 351–53 (second quotation on 353). After Guggenheim and Dorsey recruited widely known writers, *Newsday*'s popularity soared. By 1967, its circulation reached 450,000.

22. JJK, *RNL*, 13 June 1963 (quotation); JJK, unpublished and published "A Conservative View" articles, 1 April 1965; JJK to A. M. Bachman, 25 October 1965, in JJKP.

23. JJK, *RNL*, 10 February and 10 March (quotation) 1965. The *News Leader*'s descriptions also ignored the harsh realities of white resistance to civil rights. The day Alabama state troopers drove back marchers with cattle prods and clubs in March 1965, the paper covered the event with one picture of police calmly approaching the protesters. The photograph's caption explained that protesters left the scene as state policemen "broke up" the demonstration. Activists who sustained severe injuries during the attack had to be "put on the ground" by local law enforcement. See *RNL*, 8 March 1965.

24. JJK to G. S. Manelty, 11 June 1965, in JJKP (quotation). In the early 1950s, incoming *News Leader* reporters were handed stylebooks that informed writers never to call black ministers "The Reverend," a title reserved for whites, but just "Reverend." See Mudd, *Place to Be*, 7.

25. JJK, "A Conservative View," 19 August 1965, in JJKP.

26. Hilts, "Saga of James J. Kilpatrick"; Lowry, "On the Right @ 40"; Kerr, "James J. Kilpatrick"; JJK to John Fischer, 11 March 1966, "Harry Elmlark Correspondence" folder, in JJKP. *Newsday* promised Kilpatrick a one-year contract, which was their customary offer for new columnists. Elmlark, however, gave Kilpatrick a five-year deal with an office in Washington, D.C., which put him close to political action. *Newsday* could not match Elmlark's offer. See Keeler, *"Newsday,"* 353.

27. Dickinson, "Myth and Manipulation," 39–42, 75–78, 100–101; JJK, *RNL*, 30 May and 15 June (quotation) 1966.

28. Hilts, "Saga of James J. Kilpatrick." The *News Leader* replaced Kilpatrick with Grover Hall, the segregationist editor of the *Montgomery Advertiser*. See Hall, *RNL*, 2 January 1967; Roberts and Klibanoff, *Race Beat*, 74, 123; JJK to Tom Waring, 30 January 1958, TRWP; JJK to Buckley, 30 January 1958, WFBP; and interview with James J. Kilpatrick. In the late fifties, Kilpatrick also interviewed for editor of Phoenix's *Arizona Republic*, owned by conservative newspaper mogul Eugene C. Pulliam. See interview with Richard Whalen.

29. Rubin, *Honorable Estate*, 186. Richard Whalen also noted Kilpatrick's problematic outsider status in Richmond. White Richmonders referred to anyone born outside the Old Dominion as being "away." See interview with Richard Whalen.

30. "South of John C. Calhoun" (quotation); Perlstein, *Nixonland*, 277–78.

31. JJK, "A Conservative View," 4/5 May 1968 (first quotation), 4/5 September 1965 (second quotation), 17 May 1966 (third quotation), in JJKP; "South of John C. Calhoun" (fourth quotation).

32. JJK, "A Conservative View," 17 September 1968, in JJKP (quotation); Lassiter, *Silent Majority*, 5. During the late sixties and seventies, Kilpatrick worked with the *National Review* to discredit George Wallace as a reactionary populist and help the South transition into the Republican Party. See Buckley to JJK, 5 February 1969, and JJK to Buckley, 8 February 1969, WFBP; JJK, "What Makes Wallace Run?"

33. JJK, "A Conservative View," 19/20 February 1966 (first quotation), in JJKP; Kilpatrick quoted in "Talkathon of Comment" (second quotation).

34. JJK, "A Conservative View," 16 August 1966 (first and second quotations), 16 February 1965 (third quotation), in JJKP.

35. JJK, "A Conservative View," 22 August 1967, in JJKP.

36. JJK, "South Sees Through New Glasses" (first quotation); Percy, *Lanterns on the Levee*, 273–75, 299, 312 (second quotation); JJK to Delia Brock, 26 February 1965, in JJKP (third quotation).

37. Hilts, "Saga of James J. Kilpatrick"; JJK to Herman Barbour, 22 February 1965, in JJKP (first quotation); Kondracke, "James J. Kilpatrick" (second quotation); Rolfe, "Columnist Mellowed," G3 (third quotation).

38. Hilts, "Saga of James J. Kilpatrick" (quotation); interview with Roger Mudd. Journalist Hugh Sidey covered the White House for *Time* magazine for decades. Peter Lisagor, syndicated columnist and Washington bureau chief of the *Chicago Daily News*, appeared with Kilpatrick on many network political talk shows. Kilpatrick maintained his relationship with journalist Harry Golden, befriended Senator Eugene McCarthy during the 1968 election and later wrote a political satire with him, and, late in life, married liberal political columnist Marianne Means after his wife Marie died in 1996. See Kilpatrick and McCarthy, *Political Bestiary*.

39. Kilpatrick and McCarthy, *Political Bestiary* .

40. JJK, "A Conservative View," 9 April 1968, "Race" folder, in JJKP. In 1980, Kilpatrick referred to King as "the father of civil disobedience" and as a leader who "promoted the doctrine of selective obedience to the law." He also argued that honoring King with a national holiday would disrupt the flow of the business week. See JJK, "A Conservative View," 8 January 1980, in JJKP. Kilpatrick and Helms had been friends and regularly corresponded since around 1963. During the 1960s, they were pioneering cohorts in a media-savvy southern conservatism. Helms was vice president of and spokesman for WRAL-TV in Raleigh-Durham. See JJK to Allen Taylor, 12 August 1963, in JJKP; and Link, *Righteous Warrior*, 261–69.

41. JJK, "Term's End," 805; *Loving v. Virginia* 388 U.S. 1 (1967). For more on the *Loving* case, see Wallenstein, *Tell the Court I Love My Wife*, chap. 15.

42. Kondracke, "James J. Kilpatrick" (first quotation); JJK, "A Conservative View," 21/22 June 1969 and 11/12 May 1974 (second quotation), in JJKP.

43. *Briggs et al. v. Elliott et al.*; JJK, "A Conservative View," 1 August 1974, and JJK to Milton Honemann, 25 March 1975 (first quotation), in JJKP; *Charlotte Observer*, 13 May 1979 (second quotation). He added: "After 25 years, *Brown* still fits the description some scholars gave it at the time: Good justice, bad law." Parker's opinion, known as the "Briggs Dictum," held sway in the courts until the mid-1960s. "The Constitution," wrote Parker, "does not require integration. . . . It merely forbids the use of governmental power to enforce segregation." See Patterson, *"Brown v. Board of Education,"* 143, 145.

44. John Hunt to JJK, 25 January 1966, and JJK to Hunt, 31 January 1966 (quotation), in JJKP.

45. JJK to Hunt, 31 January 1966, in JJKP (first quotation); JJK, *RNL*, 27 August 1963 (second quotation); JJK, "Must We Repeal the Constitution?" (third quotation); JJK, "Voting Rights Postscript."

46. JJK to Hunt, 31 January 1966, in JJKP (quotation).

47. King, *Why We Can't Wait*, 134.

48. MacLean, *Freedom Is Not Enough*, chap. 2; Skrentny, *Minority Rights Revolution*, chap. 4; Anderson, *Pursuit of Fairness*, chap. 2.

49. JJK, *RNL*, 29 July 1963 (first and third quotations); JJK to Thomas Smith, 1961, in JJKP (second quotation).

50. Kilpatrick to Mrs. Hagan, 29 June 1961, in JJKP (first quotation); Meyer, "Equality Ad Absurdum" (second quotation); Bradford, "Fire Bell in the Night," 11 (third quotation); MacLean, *Freedom Is Not Enough*, 234.

51. See MacLean, *Freedom Is Not Enough*, chaps. 2 and 7. Matthew Lassiter argues that the southern wing of the Silent Majority refused to accept affirmative action because it threatened their middle-class prosperity and insisted on color-blind individualism and equality of opportunity as ways to stop it. See Lassiter, *Silent Majority*, 2, 4–5, 169. Other critiques of color-blind conservatism include Brown et al., *Whitewashing Race*; Kousser, *Colorblind Injustice*; Steinberg, *Turning Back*; Hall, "Long Civil Rights Movement."

52. Irving Kristol to Buckley, 23 November 1964, in WFBP (quotation); MacLean, *Freedom Is Not Enough*, 64; MacLean, "Scary Origins."

53. MacLean, *Freedom Is Not Enough*, 198, 230. See also Murray Friedman, *Neoconservative Revolution*, and Dorrien, *Neoconservative Mind*.

54. MacLean, *Freedom Is Not Enough*, 230, 259–60; JJK, "Our Man at the Golliwog Lounge," 257, 258 (first quotation); JJK to Mary Demas, 23 December 1964, and JJK to F. Evans Farwell, 20 February 1974 (second quotation), in JJKP.

55. JJK, "A Conservative View," 2 May 1968, in JJKP.

56. JJK, "Notes for Informal Talk to Association of Senate Press Secretaries," 30 January 1969 (first quotation), and JJK to Isham Parker, 9 January 1978 (second quotation), in JJKP; JJK, "View from a Southern Exposure," 128 (third quotation); MacLean, *Freedom Is Not Enough*, 234.

57. JJK, *Southern Case for School Segregation*, 21.

58. William M. Horner to JJK, 4 July 1975 (first quotation), and JJK to Bob Cherry, 11 June 1979 (second quotation), in JJKP; MacLean, *Freedom Is Not Enough*, 233. For more on affirmative action violating white rights, see JJK, CBS "Sixty Minutes" Transcript from "Point-Counterpoint," 27 November 1977, in JJKP. No government assistance aided Kilpatrick's ascent within the *News Leader* unless one considers the military draft, which exempted him from service but also removed his competition at the paper.

59. Lora and Longton, *Conservative Press*, 72.

60. Phillips-Fein, *Invisible Hands*, 200–203.

61. Ibid., 205–6; Lora and Longton, *Conservative Press*, 72.

62. Lora and Longton, *Conservative Press*, 72; JJK, "Why Students Are Hostile," 11–12 (first quotation); JJK, "Case against ERA," 9–10 (second quotation); JJK, "Rulings That Penalize Private Schools," 19–20 (third quotation); JJK, "Flow of Power," 17–18; JJK, "Turning America Around." Thanks to Kilpatrick's columns, *Nation's Business* became a popular publication again. Felix Morley, a colleague of Kilpatrick's at the *National Review*, wrote the features for the magazine prior to Kilpatrick..

63. JJK, "New National Nightmare"; MacLean, *Freedom Is Not Enough*, 50.

64. JJK, "DeFunis Syndrome"; JJK, CBS "Sixty Minutes" Transcript for "Point-Counterpoint," 28 April 1974 (first quotation); Ryoji Mihara to JJK, 25

October 1974, in JJKP (second quotation); MacLean, *Freedom Is Not Enough*, chap. 7.

65. JJK, "The Color of One's Skin Now the Only Measure of Merit," "A Conservative View," December 1977, in JJKP; *Kaiser Aluminum and Chemical Corporation and United States Steelworkers, AFL-CIO v. Brian F. Weber* 443 U.S. 193 (1979). MacLean, *Freedom Is Not Enough*, 219, 233–34.

66. Richard McWilliams to JJK, 3 January 1978, in JJKP (quotation).

67. JJK to Joseph Armbrust, 27 June 1977, in JJKP.

68. JJK, "A Conservative View," 19/20 February 1966, in JJKP (quotation); MacLean, *Freedom Is Not Enough*, 257. Matthew Lassiter believes that southern moderates in the suburbs embraced color-blind rhetoric and freedom-of-choice plans in schools as a way to replace the racial caste system and create racial harmony in a newly prosperous region. See Lassiter, *Silent Majority*, 40–43. His account somewhat downplays racism and accepts bourgeois southern claims to racial moderation. Kevin Kruse argues that white moderates used racially neutral language, like the phrases "protecting private property" and "neighborhood schools," to express discomfort with rapid changes in the South. See Kruse, *White Flight*, chap. 9.

69. JJK, "A Conservative View," 4 June 1968, in JJKP.

70. Buckley, *National Review* 22 (22 September 1970): 986–88 (quotation).

71. Mayer, *Running on Race*, 115–16. See also Wilkinson, *From "Brown" to "Bakke,"* chaps. 7 and 8.

72. JJK to Norman Terhune, 28 March 1966 (first quotation), and JJK, CBS "Sixty Minutes" Transcript for "Point-Counterpoint," 18 January 1976 (second quotation), in JJKP.

73. JJK, "A Conservative View," 8 January 1965, in JJKP (first quotation); Crespino, "Mississippi as Metaphor," 108; Nancy H. Hannan to JJK, 15 April 1975 (second quotation), in JJKP. Kilpatrick's apology for Mississippi drew immediate criticism from readers outraged about the recent murders. See JJK to John Palm, 15 January 1965.

74. JJK, "A Conservative View," 21/22 September 1974 (first quotation), 14 September 1976 (second quotation), in JJKP; *Milliken v. Bradley*, 418 U.S. 717 (1974). Kilpatrick reveled in pointing out northern hypocrisies. In 1965, he wrote a "defense of Mississippi." Although he admitted that a "terrible sickness" of racial violence existed in Mississippi, his real concern was not white racists. "We pile all our sins on the head of the scapegoat, and drive her into a Dixie wilderness," Kilpatrick wrote. The "blunt truth" was that in contrast to the "jungles of Harlem and Central Park, Jackson [Mississippi] is an oasis of pure tranquility." See Crespino, *In Search of Another Country* (Kilpatrick quoted on 107). In a 1966 column, after a summer of urban riots in the North, Kilpatrick sarcastically asked: "Is it conceivable that those Northern spokesmen who have spent ten years in denouncing the Southern sickness [of racism] were infected with the same virus all along?" ("A Conservative View," 16 August 1966, in JJKP).

75. JJK to Marie Cooper, 17 August 1977 (first quotation); JJK, CBS "Sixty Minutes" Transcript from "Point-Counterpoint," 2 October 1977 (second quotation);

Michael W. Freund to JJK, 20 March 1975; and JJK to Freund, 2 April 1975 (third quotation), in JJKP.

76. JJK to Brent Hall, 19 March 1979 (first quotation), and JJK to Daniel Elazar, 18 January 1966 (second quotation), in JJKP.

77. MacLean, *Freedom Is Not Enough*.

78. *National Review* 23 (19 November 1971): 1265. *Oxford English Dictionary*, *WP*, *Merriam-Webster's Dictionary*, and *NYT* archives indicate that the term "reverse racism" was not in common usage until the end of the 1960s.

79. JJK, "View from a Southern Exposure," 107, 110–11 (quotation); MacLean, *Freedom Is Not Enough*, 63.

80. David Lawrence, *St. Louis Post Dispatch*, 12 June 1963 (first quotation); Goldberg, *Barry Goldwater*, 230 (second quotation); National Association of Manufacturers quoted in MacLean, *Freedom Is Not Enough*, 67; Loko, *New Racism*. Arlington House was the self-declared publishing house of the Silent Majority and flagship press for the conservative movement.

81. Van den Haag, "Reverse Discrimination" (first quotation); Buchanan, *Conservative Votes*, 52, 69, 71, 172 (second quotation). Buchanan started out as an editorialist for the right-wing *St. Louis Globe Democrat*, where he smeared civil rights leaders with information leaked by J. Edgar Hoover. See Buchanan, *Right from the Beginning*, 320–22; MacLean, *Freedom Is Not Enough*, 235. For more on conservatives who advocate color blindness and argue that affirmative action causes current race problems, see Murray, *Losing Ground*; Sowell, *Civil Rights*; Thernstrom and Thernstrom, *America in Black and White*; and Sleeper, *Liberal Racism*.

82. JJK to Erle Cato, 14 July 1977 (first quotation), JJK to Ralph May, 21 July 1978 (second quotation), and JJK to Waights Henry, 10 September 1981 (third quotation), in JJKP.

83. Kondracke, "James J. Kilpatrick" (first quotation); Rolfe, "Columnist Mellowed" (second quotation); William J. Simmons to JJK, 5 May 1976, in JJKP (third quotation); Roberts and Klibanoff, *Race Beat*, 405–6, 461. Simmons honestly believed that Kilpatrick sold out the segregationist cause. See interview with William J. Simmons.

84. JJK to Dan Cubbin, 7 September 1978 (first quotation), Philip Weilding to JJK, 18 March 1975 (second quotation), and JJK to Weilding, 25 March 1975, in JJKP.

85. JJK to Reginald Jones, 18 October 1977 (first quotation), and JJK to Kennedy, 14 July 1986 (second quotation), in JJKP; MacLean, *Freedom Is Not Enough*, 257.

86. Crespino, *In Search of Another Country*, 243–44; JJK to William J. Simmons, 14 September 1964, in JJKP. Erle Johnston Jr., acting director of the Mississippi Sovereignty Commission, a states' rights and segregationist government agency, also contacted Kilpatrick for advice about setting up private high schools in Mississippi. See Johnston to JJK, 17 March 1964, in JJKP.

87. JJK, "Back to Segregation," 614–15, 626 (quotations). For more examples of columns in which Kilpatrick expressed his support for private schools, see

JJK, "A Conservative View," 20 January and 28 March 1970, in JJKP; and JJK, "Rulings That Penalize Private Schools," 19–20.

88. JJK, "A Conservative View," 4 June and 14 November 1968 (first quotation), in JJKP; *Green v. County School Board of New Kent County*, 391 U.S. 430 (1968); JJK, "One Small Candle of Freedom," *Evening Independent*, 20 February 1969 (second quotation); JJK, "A Conservative View," 26 February 1974 (third quotation); JJK, "Tuition Voucher Idea Merits Consideration," *Eugene Register-Appeal*, 24 December 1970. Kilpatrick continued his defense of school vouchers, private schools, and tuition grant programs into the early 1990s. See JJK, "States Now Hold Key to Tuition Vouchers," *Ocala Star-Banner*, 6 December 1992.

89. JJK, "A Conservative View," 2/3 July 1977, in JJKP.

90. JJK, "A Conservative View," 24 January 1978, in JJKP (quotation). Kilpatrick had made a foray into the 1960s culture wars when he characterized the fight against pornography and obscenity as a "war" between "the Philistines and the literati." See JJK, *Smut Peddlers*, 288.

91. Kondracke, "James J. Kilpatrick" (first quotation); JJK, CBS "Sixty Minutes" Transcript for "Point-Counterpoint," 20 July 1975, in JJKP (second quotation). Since the 1960s, Kilpatrick understood the interconnectedness of black liberation in America and Africa. In syndication and *News Leader* editorials, he supported white European governments' grip on power in Africa. Along with William F. Buckley and other conservatives, he defended and funded white separatists and their mercenaries in the Belgian Congo's mineral-rich region of Katanga. See JJK, *RNL*, 1 July 1 1964; and boxes 29–34, 6626-b, in JJKP.

92. Twelve Southerners, *I'll Take My Stand*, 246–64.

93. Murphy, *Rebuke of History*, 220.

94. Ibid. (Rubin quoted on 223).

95. Ibid., 223 (quotations); Woodward, *Strange Career of Jim Crow*. The two other editors who opposed massive resistance were Jack Hamilton and Guy Friddell. Friddell took a job as editor of the *Norfolk Virginian-Pilot* writing anti-Byrd editorials. After Hamilton defected, Kilpatrick and Bryan hired only confirmed conservatives as associate editors, including Garry Wills, James Lucier, Grover Hall, Dick Whalen, and Ross Mackenzie. See Rubin, *Honorable Estate*, 180.

96. Murphy, *Rebuke of History*, 222 (first quotation); Rubin and Kilpatrick, *Lasting South*, ix (second quotation); JJK to Clendinen, 22 February 1956, in JJKP.

97. Murphy, *Rebuke of History* 221 (first quotation); Rubin, *Faraway Country*, 159 (second quotation), 5 (third quotation).

98. Weaver, *Ideas Have Consequences*, 3–6, 16; Scotchie, *Barbarians in the Saddle*; JJK to Davidson, 1959, in JJKP. For Weaver's praise of Kilpatrick's massive resistance stand, see Weaver, *Ideas Have Consequences*, chap. 2.

99. Murphy, *Rebuke of History*, 224; Rubin and Kilpatrick, *Lasting South*, 10–12.

100. Rubin and Kilpatrick, *Lasting South*, 188 (first and second quotations), 193 (third quotation), 199 (fourth quotation).

101. Ibid., 204 (first and second quotations), 189 (third quotation), 205 (fourth quotation).

102. Murphy, *Rebuke of History*, 212; Black and Black, *Vital South*, 214.

103. Murphy, *Rebuke of History*, 212; Wilson, "Myth of the Biracial South," 9–10.

104. Murphy, "South as the New America"; "Spirit of the South" (first and second quotations); Schulman, *Seventies*, 102, 114–15, 117; Cobb, *Selling of the South*, 185–86.

105. In the 1970s, a number of authors located the South's sense of community in its agrarian past. See, for example, Reed, *Enduring South*; Foxfire Students, *Foxfire 40th Anniversary Book*; Murphy, *Rebuke of History*, 264, 266–67; Berry, *Unsettling of America*; and Rosengarten, *All God's Dangers*.

106. Murphy, *Rebuke of History*, 251–53; Wilson, *Defender of Southern Conservatism*.

107. JJK to Darton Greist, 2 August 1977, in JJKP; JJK, *Foxes' Union*, 5; "South of John C. Calhoun"; Hardcastle, "Refuge for Urbanites"; Tazewell, "Washington Outside the Beltway."

108. Hilts, "Retreat of James J. Kilpatrick" (first quotation); JJK, "A Conservative View," 5 June 1969, in JJKP (second quotation).

109. Havard, "Journalist as Interpreter of the South," 18–19; JJK, "A Conservative View," 5 November 1970, in JJKP; JJK, *Fine Print*, 33; Smith, *Myth, Media, and the Southern Mind*, 70–71.

110. JJK, *Foxes' Union*, 46 (first quotation), 72–73 (second quotation), 77 (third quotation); Hutchinson, "Dateline Scrabble." Yoknapatawpha is the fictional Mississippi county William Faulkner wrote about in many of his novels.

111. JJK, *Foxes' Union*, 82 (first quotation), 136 (second quotation), 48 (third, fourth, and fifth quotations), 50.

112. JJK, "A Conservative View," 1 January 1970 (first quotation), and Kevin M. O'Connell to JJK, 9 January 1978 (second quotation), in JJKP.

113. JJK, "Beauty of America," 10 (quotations); Farber, "Democratic Subjects," 319–32.

114. JJK, "Beauty of America," 9 (quotation).

115. Endres, "James J. Kilpatrick" (first quotation), JJK, "A Conservative View," 20 June 1968 (second quotation), and JJK to W. C. Nesmith, 17 June 1975 (third quotation), in JJKP; Roberts and Klibanoff, *Race Beat*, 117.

116. Kirk, *Conservative Mind*, 414 (first and second quotations); JJK, *Foxes' Union*, 17 (third quotation).

117. Sandbrook, *Eugene McCarthy*, 26 (quotation), 27, 276; Rising, *Clean for Gene*, 5. Kilpatrick and McCarthy also meshed because neither man paid much deference to Washington and both regarded themselves as political outsiders. See JJK, "Impolitic Politician."

118. Conkin, *Southern Agrarians*; King, *Southern Renaissance*.

119. Bake and Kilpatrick, *American South: Four Seasons of the Land*, xxix (first quotation); Bake and Kilpatrick, *American South: Towns and Cities*, 4 (second quotation), 12 (third quotation).

120. Murphy, *Rebuke of History*, 254.

Chapter Six

1. Hilts, "Saga of James J. Kilpatrick."

2. Ibid. (first quotation); Richard M. Nixon to JJK, 7 September 1961, in JJKP (second quotation).

3. Hilts, "Saga of James J. Kilpatrick" (quotation); "South of John C. Calhoun." James McCord and G. Gordon Liddy were the principal directors of Nixon's Committee to Re-Elect the President, the organization responsible for the break-in.

4. JJK, "A Conservative View," 19/20 May 1973 (first quotation), 5 August 1974 (second quotation), in JJKP; Hilts, "Saga of James J. Kilpatrick."

5. I owe these observations about the changing nature of American conservatism in the 1970s and beyond to Jeff Roche.

6. Hilts, "Saga of James J. Kilpatrick."

7. JJK, *Fine Print*, 67; Hilts, "Saga of James J. Kilpatrick" (quotations).

8. "James Jackson Kilpatrick," 164.

9. Hilts, "Saga of James J. Kilpatrick"; Hirsch, *Talking Heads*, 4–5; Frohnan, Beer, and Nelson, *American Conservatism*, 470–71; O'Reilly, *Nixon's Piano*, 363–64, 370; Richard Pearson, "Political Talk Show Pioneer Agronsky Dies," *WP*, 27 July 1999, 6; interview with George F. Will; Kurtz, *Hot Air*, 154–55. In terms of the number of viewers, only Robert MacNeil's *Washington Week in Review* rivaled *Agronsky*. Ronald Reagan would sometimes call George Will or Kilpatrick after watching the program to discuss the show.

10. "South of John C. Calhoun" (first quotation); Hirsch, *Talking Heads*, 26, 162–63; Fay, *Eminent Rhetoric*, 104; Hagey, "James Kilpatrick" (second quotation). In retrospect, Kilpatrick's outbursts seem mild when compared to those of Rush Limbaugh, Bill O'Reilly, and Glenn Beck, but he blazed a trail for them, back in the days when the Federal Communications Commission's Fairness Doctrine still required a counterpoint. Kilpatrick certainly was not the first angry conservative commentator on the air, however. Before the 1970s, Fulton Lewis Jr. had made a successful career as radio's "voice with a snarl." Clarence Manion and John T. Flynn also had radio programs, albeit with limited audiences. See Nimmo and Newsome, *Political Commentators*, 95, 171–79.

11. Hagey, "James Kilpatrick" (quotation); Stein, *View from Sunset Boulevard*. Actor Michael Keaton made his debut on television in *All's Fair* as the character Lanny Wolf.

12. JJK, CBS "Sixty Minutes" Transcript for "Point-Counterpoint," 9 March 1975, in JJKP.

13. JJK to Shana Alexander, 16 December 1974, in JJKP (first quotation); Alexander, *Happy Days*, 301, 336 (second quotation). Kilpatrick was just as antagonistic of women's rights and the ERA in his syndicated columns. On the women's rights amendment, he wrote, "Gadzooks! Zounds! Horsefeathers! What in the world came over the House? This constitutional time bomb is the

contrivance of a gang of professional harpies." See "South of John C. Calhoun." Kilpatrick enjoyed an advantage on TV against less effective opponents. Von Hoffman often took loopy positions, and Alexander's upbringing in Manhattan's high society left her unfit for rough banter with Kilpatrick. Alexander, in fact, regarded her time on *60 Minutes* as an unwelcome distraction from her writing. "Before I ever heard about '60 Minutes,' I had been a writer, a columnist for Life magazine. . . . I care about my writing. I'm not a quack-quack TV journalist," she later remarked. Quoted in McLellan, "Shana Alexander."

14. Viguerie, *America's Right Turn*, 218; unknown author, *Daily Oklahoman*, no date, in JJKP (second quotation).

15. Thompson, *Fear and Loathing*, 70 (quotation).

16. Mrs. H. W. Suddick to JJK, 12 July 1978 (first quotation), and Ellen Bourget to JJK, undated (second quotation), in JJKP.

17. "Shana Alexander" folder, in JJKP; Murray, *Encyclopedia of Television News*, 237; Blum, *Tick . . . Tick . . . Tick*, 124.

18. McPherson, *Conservative Resurgence*, 140 (first quotation); Goldberg, *Barry Goldwater*, 177–78 (second quotation); Barry Goldwater to JJK, 23 June 1978, in JJKP (third quotation). Prominent newspaper editors, like Kilpatrick, served as mediums for public and political leaders. Kilpatrick's personal papers are an extraordinary source for both elite and grassroots conservative thought. Late in life, Kilpatrick encouraged conservatives to use words and phrases easily understood by the majority of the public. He criticized elite conservative leaders and intellectuals who failed to communicate broadly to diverse audiences. See Kilpatrick's exchange with Buckley on *Firing Line*: "Language and Journalism," 2 and 9 February 1997, Catalog ID T: 60616, The Paley Center for Media, New York, N.Y.

19. Hilts, "Saga of James J. Kilpatrick"; Hirsch, *Talking Heads*, 155, 163–64 (first quotation); Kondracke, "James J. Kilpatrick"; Edward H. Haessler to JJK, 9 April 1981, in JJKP (second quotation).

20. JJK, "A Conservative View," 2/3 July 1977; January 1977 episode, "Sixty Minutes," Transcripts 1977–1979, (quotation), in JJKP.

21. Guin N. Jones to John Backe, 1 December 1977 (first and third quotations), Earl R. Graves to Don Hewitt, 30 November 1977 (second quotation), and JJK to Richard Slant, 14 December 1977 (fourth quotation), in JJKP.

22. Carol Wesley to JJK, 1975 (first quotation); Ava Torre-Bueno to "60 Minutes," 3 August 1975 (second quotation); Tom Fly to JJK, 1975 (third quotation); and Richard A. Denew to "60 Minutes," 1975 (fourth quotation), in JJKP.

23. It is interesting to note *SNL*'s preference for a sexual attack over a racial one. By the late 1970s, the American mainstream had accepted the basic tenets of the civil rights movement, including a rejection of racism, but the on-going women's movement was still fair game for ridicule and condescension. When Curtin replied to Aykroyd, she often retorted, "Dan, you pompous ass."

24. JJK, "A Conservative View," 11/12 November 1972, in JJKP. In 1957 and 1958, Kilpatrick published several columns advocating Pound's release from St. Elizabeth's mental hospital outside Washington, D.C. The two men met only

once and were never close friends. Kilpatrick respected Pound as an artist but did not understand his anti-Semitism, love of fascism, or poetry. See Stock, *Life of Ezra Pound*, 227, 230, 243.

25. JJK, "Why Do We Study Grammar?" David Foster Wallace has pointed out that arguments about writing have actually been a platform for authority and politics. According to Wallace, the politics of the English language matter more than effective written communication in American society. See Wallace, *Consider the Lobster*, 66–127.

26. Babbin, "James Jackson Kilpatrick, RIP" (first quotation); JJK, *Writer's Art*, 29 (second quotation), 35–36 (third and fourth quotations).

27. McDermott, "A Wordsmith Hangs up His Quill"; JJK to Ashbel Green, 17 May 1965, in JJKP. His final "A Conservative View" column appeared in 1992. Elmlark eventually steered Kilpatrick to the Universal Press Syndicate, which absorbed the *Washington Star* syndicate in 1979. See Kerr, "James J. Kilpatrick."

28. JJK to Ray Jenkins, undated, in JJKP (first quotation); JJK, "On Reaching Threescore Years," 13 (second quotation).

29. JJK, "A Conservative View," 18 March 1975, in JJKP.

30. JJK, CBS "Sixty Minutes" Transcript for "Point-Counterpoint," 19 May 1974 (first quotation), JJK, "A Conservative View," 18 March 1975 (second quotation), and JJK to Gene Boyett, 28 March 1989 (third quotation), in JJKP.

31. JJK to David Lindsay, 24 February 1976, in JJKP (first quotation); Hilts, "Saga of James J. Kilpatrick" (second quotation); Michael Issikoff, "Virginia Tradition: Richmond Editor Keeps Passions Stretched Tight," *WP*, 19 September 1982, A1 (third quotation).

32. "South of John C. Calhoun" (first quotation); interview with Richard Whalen; Hutchinson, "Dateline Scrabble" (second and third quotations).

33. McKelway, "Pressing for Resistance," *RTD*, 16 May 2004 (first and second quotations); *RTD*, 5 February 2003 (third quotation); Lassiter, *Silent Majority*, 287–88. U.S. District Judge Robert H. Merhige Jr. took a leading role in Richmond's busing program. Kilpatrick wrote guest columns for his old paper during its antibusing crusade. He condemned Mehrige's ruling and accused him of "doctrinaire racism." See *RNL*, 11 and 15 January 1972.

34. O'Dell, "Va. Paper Expresses Regret."

35. Laurence Shore to JJK, 12 September 1985 (first quotation), and JJK to Shore, 30 September 1985 (second quotation), in JJKP.

36. JJK to Llewellyn Smith, 3 October 1985 (first quotation), Walter M. High to JJK, 4 March 1986 (second quotation), and JJK to High, 17 March 1986 (third quotation), in JJKP. When I interviewed Kilpatrick, he did not refer to race or *Brown* until I asked about them. See interview with James Kilpatrick. Late in life, he also claimed no knowledge of the CCFAF's existence and activities. See Crespino, *In Search of Another Country*, 303 n. 47.

37. Maurice Fleming to JJK, 22 July 1985 (first quotation), and JJK to Fleming, 29 July 1985 (second quotation), in JJKP. Angered by the response, Fleming wrote him back and asked if Kilpatrick would accept incest in small doses as well. See Fleming to JJK, 23 August 1985, in JJKP.

38. JJK, *Foxes' Union*, 173; JJK, "Columnist's (Kind of) Farewell" (quotation). Kilpatrick's appeals for color blindness were consistent. His motto was "Make whole the identifiable victims of racial discrimination, and stop there." He recognized that racism existed but did advocate measures to advance blacks. See JJK to Kennedy, 14 July 1986, in JJKP.

39. JJK, "Judicial Redistricting Carries Voting Rights Act Too Far," *Raleigh News and Observer*, 7 December 1988 (first quotation); JJK, "Must We Repeal the Constitution to Give the Negro the Vote?," 319 (second quotation); JJK, "My Journey from Racism" (third, fourth, fifth, and sixth quotations); Epps, "Littlest Rebel." Kilpatrick expressed profound regrets about his opposition to *Brown* and civil rights in an interview with me as well.

40. "Richard Viguerie on the Death of James J. Kilpatrick."

41. Twardy, "James Jackson Kilpatrick," 222, 229–30; interview with Jeffrey Hart. Even in old age, Kilpatrick still clung to states' rights as one of the few viable checks against a reckless federal government. Although the political philosophy of state sovereignty looked dead at the start of the twenty-first century, he recollected the heyday of states' rights in the nineteenth century as a "brief shining moment to recall" and an American "Camelot." See JJK, "Back to the Sovereign States!" For another conservative southerner who fought integration without abrasive racism, see Collins, *Whither the Solid South?* Years after white southerners and other conservatives appealed for the defense of states' rights as a way to prevent changes to the racial order, their arguments showed up in the mainstream press. Thomas Woods Jr.'s *Politically Incorrect Guide to American History*, a *New York Times* bestseller released by the Right's oldest and most venerable publisher, Regnery, has a Confederate officer on its cover and puts a positive spin on states' rights. The book includes a subchapter called "Why Nullification Isn't as Crazy as It Sounds," mentions that the southern states had the right to secede, and denounces the Fourteenth Amendment as unconstitutional. See 83–92 (quotation on 40). See also MacLean, "Neo-Confederacy vs. the New Deal."

42. Scalia, "Disease as Cure" (first quotation); JJK, "Hula at the High Court" (second quotation). For more on Scalia's insistence on color-blind justice to eliminate the effects of the nation's racist past, see Yarbrough, *Rehnquist Court and the Constitution*, 265.

43. *Meredith v. Jefferson County Board of Education* 551 S. Ct. (2007); *Parents Involved v. Seattle*, 127 S. Ct. 2738 (2007), 2755–56 (quotation), 2821; Wolters, *Race and Education*, 296–97.

44. *Parents Involved v. Seattle*, 127 S. Ct. 2738 (2007); JJK, "Segregation" (first quotation); MacLean, "Scary Origins" (second quotation); JJK, "Advancing to the Rear."

45. Wolters, *Race and Education*, 304–5. The political left must accept partial responsibility for the failures and limitations of integration in the forms of busing and affirmative action. Just as there were many different kinds of opposition to integration on the right, there were also some weak spots in the liberal application of it as an official policy.

46. Twardy, "James Jackson Kilpatrick," 229–30.

BIBLIOGRAPHY

Manuscript Collections

CHARLESTON, SOUTH CAROLINA
South Carolina Historical Society
Thomas R. Waring Jr. Papers

CHARLOTTESVILLE, VIRGINIA
University of Virginia, Special Collections
Harry F. Byrd Sr. Papers
Harry F. Byrd Jr. Papers
Everett R. Combs Papers
Virginius Dabney Papers
Colgate W. Darden Papers
Defenders of State Sovereignty and Individual Liberties Files
John Dos Passos Papers
Leon Dure Papers
Douglas Southall Freeman Papers
James J. Kilpatrick Papers
Fred O. Seibel Cartoons
Howard W. Smith Papers
G. Fred Switzer Papers

JACKSON, MISSISSIPPI
Mississippi Department of Archives and History, Digital Collections
Mississippi State Sovereignty Commission Records

LEXINGTON, VIRGINIA
Washington and Lee University School of Law
Lewis F. Powell Jr. Papers

NEW HAVEN, CONNECTICUT
Yale University Library, Manuscripts and Archives
William F. Buckley Jr. Papers

NEW YORK, NEW YORK
The Paley Center for Media

OXFORD, MISSISSIPPI
University of Mississippi, J. D. Williams Library, Department of Archives
and Special Collections
Citizens' Council Collection

James O. Eastland Collection
John C. Satterfield/American Bar Association Collection

PALO ALTO, CALIFORNIA
Hoover Institution Archives
  Henry Regnery Papers

RICHMOND, VIRGINIA
Library of Virginia
  J. Lindsay Almond Jr. Gubernatorial Papers
  James H. Latimer Papers
  Richmond Times-Dispatch/New Leader Microfiche
  Thomas B. Stanley Gubernatorial Papers
  Virginia Commission on Constitutional Government Papers
Edward H. Peeples Papers (private collection)
Richmond Times-Dispatch Archives
  James J. Kilpatrick Files
Virginia Commonwealth University Libraries Digital Collections
  Voices of Freedom Collection
Virginia Historical Society
  J. Lindsay Almond Jr. Papers
  Samuel M. Bemiss Papers
  David Tennant Bryan—Vertical File
  John Stewart Bryan Papers
  Marie Pietri Kilpatrick—Vertical File
  David J. Mays Papers
  James R. Sydnor Papers

Microfilm

Facts on Film.
Papers of the National Association for the Advancement of Colored People.
  Edited by August Meier. Frederick, Md.: University Publications of
  America, 1982.

Government Documents

Baker v. Carr. Supreme Court of the United States. 369 U.S. 186; 82 S. Ct. 691;
  7 L. Ed. 2d 663; 1962 U.S. LEXIS 1567.
Briggs et al. v. Elliott et al. U.S. District Court. 132 F. Supp. 776 (1955).
Brown v. Board of Education of Topeka. Supreme Court of the United States.
  347 U.S. 483; 74 S. Ct. 686; 98 L. Ed. 873; 1954 U.S. LEXIS 2094.
California Death Index, 1940–1997 Record. Sacramento, Calif., 1999.
Ernesto Arturo Miranda v. State of Arizona. Supreme Court of the United
  States. 384 U.S. 436; 86 S. Ct. 1602; 16 L. Ed. 2d. 694; 1966 U.S. LEXIS 2817;
  10 A.L.R. 3d 974.

Garcia v. San Antonio Metropolitan Transit Authority. Supreme Court of the
United States. 469 U.S. 552 (1985); 105 S. Ct. 1005; 83 L. Ed. 2d 1016; 85 U.S.
LEXIS 48.

General Assembly of Virginia. *Doctrine of Interposition: Its History and
Application*. Senate Joint Resolution No. 3. Virginia Senate. Richmond, Va.,
1956.

Green v. County School Board of New Kent County. Supreme Court of the
United States. 391 U.S. 430 (1968); 88 S. Ct. 1689, 20 L. Ed. 2d 716.

Griswold v. Connecticut. Supreme Court of the United States. 381 U.S. 479; 85
S. Ct. 1678; 14 L. Ed. 2d 510; 1965 U.S. LEXIS 2282.

"Interposition: The Barrier Against Tyranny." *Congressional Record*. 84th
Cong., 2d sess., vol. 102 (January 25, 1956). Washington, D.C.: GPO, 1956.

Louisiana Birth Records Index, 1790–1899. New Orleans, La., 1901.

Loving v. Virginia. Supreme Court of the United States. 388 U.S. 1; 87 S. Ct.
1817; 18 L. Ed. 2d 1010; 1967 U.S. LEXIS 1082.

McLaurin v. Oklahoma State Regents for Higher Education. Supreme Court
of the United States. 339 U.S. 637; 70 S. Ct. 851; 94 L. Ed. 1149; 1950 U.S.
LEXIS 1810.

Milliken v. Bradley. Supreme Court of the United States. 418 U.S. 717; 94 S. Ct.
3112; 41 L. Ed. 2d 1069; 1974 U.S. LEXIS 94.

Murray v. Curlett. Supreme Court of the United States. 374 U.S. 203; 83 S. Ct.
1560; 10 L. Ed. 2d 844; 1963 U.S. LEXIS 2611.

National League of Cities v. Usery. Supreme Court of the United States. 426
U.S. 833 (1976).

*Parents Involved in Community Schools v. Seattle School District No. 1, et al.;
Meredith v. Jefferson County Board of Education*. Supreme Court of the
United States. 551 U.S. —; 127 S. Ct. 2738; 75 U.S.L.W. 4577; 20 Fla. L.
Weekly Fed. S 490.

Plessy v. Ferguson. No. 210. Supreme Court of the United States. 163 U.S. 537;
16 S. Ct. 1138; 41 L. Ed. 256; 1896 U.S. LEXIS 3390.

Roe v. Wade. Supreme Court of the United States. 410 U.S. 113; 93 S. Ct. 705; 35
L. Ed. 2d 147; 1973 U.S. LEXIS 159.

Senate Joint Resolution, No. 3. Commonwealth of Virginia General Assembly.
Richmond, Va., February 1, 1956.

Shelley v. Kraemer. No. 334. Supreme Court of the United States. 334 U.S. 1; 68
S. Ct. 836; 92 L. Ed. 1161; 3 A.L.R. 2d 441.

Silas Rogers v. Commonwealth of Virginia. 183 Va. 190 (1944).

Smith v. Allwright. No. 321. Supreme Court of the United States. 321 U.S. 649
(1944).

"The Southern Manifesto." *Congressional Record*. 84th Cong., 2nd sess., vol.
102 (March 12, 1956). Washington, D.C.: GPO, 1956.

State of Missouri ex rel. Gaines v. Canada. Supreme Court of the United States.
305 U.S. 337; 59 S. Ct. 232; 83 L. Ed. 208; 1938 U.S. LEXIS 440.

Swann v. Charlotte-Mecklenburg Board of Education. Supreme Court of the
United States. 402 U.S. 1; 1971.

Sweatt v. Painter. Supreme Court of the United States. 339 U.S. 629; 70 S. Ct. 848; 94 L. Ed. 1114; 1950 U.S. LEXIS 1809.

U.S. Bureau of the Census. *Seventh Census of the United States, 1850*. Washington, D.C., 1853.

———. *The Eighth Census: Population of the United States in 1860*. Washington, D.C., 1864.

———. *Ninth Census, 1870*. Vol. 1, *The Statistics of the Population of the United States*. Washington, D.C., 1872.

———. *Tenth Census, 1880*. Vol. 1, Population. Washington, D.C., 1883.

———. *Twelfth Census of the United States, 1900*. Vol. 1, Population. Washington, D.C., 1902.

———. *Fourteenth Census of the United States, 1920*. Vol. 3, Population. Washington, D.C., 1922.

———. *Fifteenth Census of the United States, 1930*. Vol. 3, Population. Washington, D.C., 1932.

———. *Seventeenth Census of the United States: Statistical Abstract of the United States: 1955*. Washington, D.C., 1957.

———. *Eighteenth Census of the United States: Statistical Abstract of the United States: 1960*. Washington, D.C., 1962.

———. *Eighteenth Census of the United States*, Vol. 1, *Characteristics of the Population: Virginia*. Washington, D.C., 1963.

Virginia Commission on Constitutional Government. *Civil Rights and Federal Powers*. Richmond, Va.: William Byrd Press, 1964.

———. *Civil Rights and Legal Wrongs*. Richmond, Va.: William Byrd Press, 1963.

———. *Democracy and Despotism: An Excerpt from Part II of Democracy in America, by Alexis de Tocqueville*. New York: Alfred A. Knopf, 1963.

———. *Did the Court "Interpret" or "Amend"? The Meaning of the Fourteenth Amendment, in Terms of a State's Power to Operate Racially Separate Public Schools, as Defined by the Courts*. Richmond, Va., May 1960.

———. *Every Man His Own Law; A Commentary by the Virginia Commission on Constitutional Government Concerning the Unparalleled Lawlessness in the Streets of the Nation Today*. Richmond, Va., 1967.

———. *Federal Grants-in-Aid: Report of the CCG: A Comprehensive Analysis of Federal Grants-in-Aid to All the States, with a Detailed Analysis of Programs in Effect in Each City and County of Virginia*. Richmond, Va., 1961.

———. *On the Fixing of Boundary Lines*. Richmond, Va.: William Byrd Press, 1958.

———. *Race and the Restaurant: Two Opinion Pieces*. Richmond, Va.: William Byrd Press, 1960.

———. *The Rational Approach*. Richmond, Va.: William Byrd Press, 1961.

———. *The Reconstruction Amendments' Debates: The Legislative History and Contemporary Debates in Congress on the 13th, 14th, and 15th Amendments*. Edited by Alfred Avins. Richmond, Va., 1967.

————. *The Reconstruction Amendments' Debates: The Legislative History and Contemporary Debates in Congress on the 13th, 14th, and 15th Amendments, Supplement.* Edited by Alfred Avins. Richmond, Va., 1967.

————. *The Right Not to Listen.* Richmond, Va.: William Byrd Press, 1964.

————. *Sockdolager!: A Tale of Davey Crockett, in Which the Old Tennessee Bear Hunter Meets up with the Constitution of the United States.* Richmond, Va.: William Byrd Press, 1958.

————. *"State Action" and the Fourteenth Amendment.* Richmond, Va.: William Byrd Press, 1966.

————. *The Supreme Court of the United States: A Review of the 1964 Term.* Richmond, Va.: William Byrd Press, 1965.

————. *Voting Rights and Legal Wrongs.* Richmond, Va.: William Byrd Press, 1965.

————. *We the States: An Anthology of Historic Documents and Commentaries thereon, Expanding the State and Federal Relationship.* Richmond, Va.: William Byrd Press, 1964.

————. *When Virginia Joined the Union: A Backward Look at the Powerful Prophecy of Men Who Foresaw in 1788 the Trend of Events in 1963.* Richmond, Va., 1963.

Virginia State Board of Education. *Superintendent of Public Instruction: Annual Report, 1954–1955.* Vol. 38 (October 1955).

Williams v. Howard Johnson's Restaurant. U.S. Fourth Circuit Court of Appeals. No. 342 F.2d 727 (1960).

Yates v. United States. Supreme Court of the United States. 354 U.S. 298; 77 S. Ct. 1064; 1 L. Ed. 2d 1356; 1957 U.S. LEXIS 1957.

Periodicals

Charlottesville Daily Progress

Congressional Record

Evening Star

Farmville Herald

Group Research Report

Human Events

Manchester Union Leader

Missouri Alumnus

Missouri Student

National Review

Nation's Business

New York Herald Tribune

New York Times

Race Relations Law Reporter

Richmond Afro-American

Richmond News Leader

Richmond Times-Dispatch

Southern School News

St. Louis Post Dispatch

St. Petersburg Times (Florida)

Virginian-Pilot

Washington Post

Online Databases

LexisNexis *Academic*

Interviews and Correspondence

Buckley, William F., Jr. Correspondence, March 2007.
Byrd, Harry F., Jr. Telephone interview, November 2006.
Fogarty, Gerald, S.J. Interview, October 2006.
Hart, Jeffrey. Telephone interview, June 2007.
Kilpatrick, James J. Interview, April 2007.
Kilpatrick, Sean. Telephone interview, August 2011.
Klibanoff, Hank. Telephone interview, August 2006.
Mudd, Roger. Telephone interview, May 2007.
Peeples, Edward H. Interview, November 2006.
Regnery, Alfred S. Telephone interview, May 2007.
Rubin, Louis. Telephone interview, June 2007.
Simmons, William J. Interview, July 2007.
Stagg, Tom. Telephone interview, November 2011.
Whalen, Richard. Telephone interview, July 2007.
Will, George F. Telephone interview, May 2007.

Articles and Pamphlets

Abbott, Carl. "The Norfolk Business Community." In *Southern Businessmen and Desegregation*, edited by Elizabeth Jacoway and David R. Colburn, 98–119. Baton Rouge: Louisiana State University Press, 1982.
Alexander, Holmes. "Richmond Editor in Bold Stand." *Nashville Banner* (15 April 1957).
Allen, Barbara. "Martin Luther King's Civil Disobedience and the American Covenant Tradition." *Publius: The Journal of Federalism* 30 (Fall 2000): 71–113.
Anderson, Jack, and Les Whitten. "Clash of Lawyers' Groups in 1950s." *Washington Post* (24 October 1977), B11.
Avins, Alfred. "Maybe It's Time to Look at the Antislavery Amendment." *U.S. News & World Report* 50 (11 May 1964): 82–84.
Babbin, Jed. "James J. Kilpatrick, RIP." Article online. Available from http://spectator.org/archives/2010/08/17/james-jackson-kilpatrick-rip. Accessed 17 August 2010.
Badger, Tony. "Southerners Who Refused to Sign the Southern Manifesto." *Historical Journal* 42 (June 1999): 517–34.
Bagdikian, Ben H. "The Newsmagazines: I - *U.S. News and World Report*." *New Republic* 140 (2 February 1959): 11–16.
Baker, Robert. "Rights for Sale." *Washington Post* (19 April 1964), E1.

Bell, Daniel. "The Dispossessed." In *The Radical Right*, edited by Daniel Bell. Garden City, N.Y.: Doubleday, 1963.

Bernstein, Adam. "James J. Kilpatrick, 89, Dies; Conservative Columnist Formerly on '60 Minutes.'" *Washington Post* (17 August 2010).

Bickel, Alexander M., and Harry H. Wellington. "Legislative Purpose and the Judicial Process: The Lincoln Mills Case." *Harvard Law Review* 71 (November 1957): 1–39.

Black, Isabella. "Race and Unreason: Anti-Negro Opinion in Professional and Scientific Literature Since 1954." *Phylon* 26, no. 1 (1965): 65–79.

Blackmon, Douglas A. "Silent Partner: How the South's Fight to Uphold Segregation Was Funded Up North." *Wall Street Journal* (11 June 1999).

Bork, Robert H. "Civil Rights—A Challenge." *New Republic* 149 (31 August 1963): 22–23.

Boyd, Tim. "The 1966 Election in Georgia and the Ambiguity of the White Backlash." *Journal of Southern History* 75 (May 2009): 305–40.

Bozell, L. Brent. "To Mend the Tragic Flaw." *National Review* 10 (12 March 1963): 199–200.

Bradford, M. E. "A Fire Bell in the Night: The Southern Conservative View." *Modern Age* 17 (Winter 1973): 9–15.

Brest, Paul. "The Misconceived Quest for Original Understanding." In *Interpreting the Constitution: The Debate over Original Intent*, edited by Jack N. Rakove. Boston: Northeastern University Press, 1990.

Brinkley, Alan. "The Problem of American Conservatism." *American Historical Review* 99 (April 1994): 409–29.

Brown, Sarah H. "The Role of Elite Leadership in the Southern Defense of Segregation, 1954–1964." *Journal of Southern History* 77 (November 2011): 827–64.

Buckley, William F. "Black Madness." *National Review* 16 (7 April 1964): 263.
———. "A Clarification." *National Review* 4 (7 September 1957): 199.
———. "Why the South Must Prevail." *National Review* 4 (24 August 1957): 148–49.

Burchard, Hank. "John J. Synon, Fought for Conservative Causes." *Washington Post* (8 April 1972), B10.

Byrnes, James F. "The Supreme Court Must Be Curbed." *U.S. News and World Report* 42 (18 May 1956): 50–58.

Carter, Dan T. "Reflections of a Reconstructed White Southerner." In *Historians and Race: Autobiography and the Writing of History*, edited by Paul A. Cimbala and Robert F. Himmelberg, 33–50. Bloomington: University of Indiana Press, 1996.

Carter, Luther J. "A New Dixie Colonel." *Washington Post* (12 April 1964): E3.

"The Case of Silas Rogers." *Time* 61 (5 January 1953): 50–51.

Chappell, David L. "Did Racists Create the Suburban Nation?" *Reviews in American History* 35 (March 2007): 89–97.
———. "The Divided Mind of Southern Segregationists." *Georgia Historical Quarterly* 72 (Spring 1998): 45–72.

————. "What's Racism Got to Do with It? Orval Faubus, George Wallace, and the New Right." *Arkansas Historical Quarterly* 57, no. 4 (Winter 1998): 453–71.

Chemerinsky, Erwin. "Reconceptualizing Federalism." *New York Law School Law Review* 50 (3, 2005–2006): 729–55.

Chodorov, Frank. "A Solution of Our Public School Problem (brought up to date)." *Human Events* 11 (19 May 1954).

————. "Virginia Shows a Way." *Human Events* 13 (21 January 1956).

Coordinating Committee on Fundamental American Freedoms. *Unmasking the Civil Rights Bill*. Washington, D.C.: Coordinating Committee on Fundamental American Freedoms, Inc., 1964.

"Coping with the New Reality." *Time* 107 (14 June 1976): 70–72.

Court, John. "Integration in Historical Perspective." *Modern Age* 2 (Fall 1958): 365.

Crespino, Joseph. "Mississippi as Metaphor: Civil Rights, the South, and the Nation in the Historical Imagination." In *The Myth of Southern Exceptionalism*. Edited by Joseph Crespino and Matthew D. Lassiter, 99–120. New York: Oxford University Press, 2010.

Dabney, Virginius. "He Made the Court Supreme." *Saturday Evening Post* 228 (24 September 1955): 36, 121–22, 124.

Dailey, Jane. "Sex, Segregation, and the Sacred after *Brown*." *Journal of American History* 91 (June 2004): 119–44.

Danzig, David. "Rightists, Racists, and Separatists: A White Bloc in the Making?" *Commentary* 38 (August 1964): 28–32.

DeWar, Helen. "Home Guard Urged for Riots." *Washington Post* (29 October 1967): A1.

Eagles, Charles W. "Toward New Histories of the Civil Rights Era." *Journal of Southern History* 66 (November 2000): 815–48.

Eisenberg, Ralph. "Virginia: The Emergence of Two Party Politics." In *The Changing Politics of the South*. Edited by William Havard. Baton Rouge: Louisiana State University Press, 1972.

Elazar, Daniel J. "Political Culture on the Plains." *Western Historical Quarterly* 11 (July 1980): 261–83.

Epps, Garrett. "James J. Kilpatrick and the Soft-Focus of Historical Memory." Article online. Available from http://www.theatlantic.com/nationa/archive/2010/08/james-j-kilpatrick-and-the-soft. Accessed August 18, 2010.

————. "The Littlest Rebel: James J. Kilpatrick and the Second Civil War." *Constitutional Commentary* 10 (Winter 1993): 19–36.

Evans, Rowland, and Robert Novak. "Concession to the South." *Washington Post* (19 July 1964).

Farber, David. "Democratic Subjects in the American Sixties: National Politics, Cultural Authenticity, and Community Interest." *Mid-America: An Historical Review* 81 (Fall 1999): 319–32.

Feldman, Glenn. Review of *The Myth of Southern Exceptionalism*, edited by
   Matthew D. Lassiter and Joseph Crespino. *Journal of Southern History* 77
   (August 2011): 783–86.
Ferguson, Andrew. "The Happy Curmudgeon: James J. Kilpatrick, 1920–
   2010." *Weekly Standard* 15 (30 August 2010).
"Fifteen Years of Publishing: Henry Regnery Company." *Human Events* 20 (23
   February 1963): 151.
"Folksy Bar Leader: John Creighton Satterfield." *New York Times* (31 August
   1960): 14.
Franklin, Ben A. "Mississippi Funds Fight Rights Bill." *New York Times* (4
   November 1963): 16.
Friedman, Barry. "The Birth of an Academic Obsession: The History of the
   Countermajoritarian Difficulty, Part Five." *Yale Law Journal* 112 (16 October
   2002): 155–259.
Friedman, Murray. "One Episode in Southern Jewry's Response to
   Desegregation: An Historical Memoir." *American Jewish Archives* 33
   (November 1981): 170–83.
Goldstein, Richard. "James J. Kilpatrick, Conservative Voice in Print and on
   TV, Dies at 89." *New York Times* (16 August 2010).
Goodgame, Dan, and Karen Tumulty. "Lott: Tripped up by History" (16
   December 2002). Article online. Available from http://archives.cnn.
   com/2002/ALLPOLITICS/12/16/timep.lott.tm/. Accessed 8 February 2011.
Hagey, Keach. "James Kilpatrick Set Stage for Political TV Talk." Article
   online. Available from www.politico.com. Accessed 16 August 2010.
Hall, Jacquelyn Dowd. "The Long Civil Rights Movement and the Political
   Uses of the Past." *Journal of American History* 91 (March 2005): 1233–63.
Hamlin, Christopher, and John T. McGreevy, "The Greening of America,
   Catholic Style, 1930–1950." *Environmental History* 11 (July 2006): 464–99.
Hardcastle, James R. "A Refuge for Urbanites in Back Country Virginia." *New
   York Times* (26 September 1999).
Harrigan, Anthony. "The South *Is* Different." *National Review* 5 (8 March
   1958): 225–27.
Harris, John F. "Virginia's Voice of Conservatism Says 'Nevermore.'"
   Washington Post (30 May 1992).
Hart, Jeffrey. "The American Dissent: A Decade of Modern Conservatism."
   National Review 17 (30 November 1965): A1–A48.
Havard, William C. "The Journalist as Interpreter of the South." *Virginia
   Quarterly Review* 59 (Winter 1983): 15–21.
"The Heart of Darkness." *Time* 68 (22 December 1961): 16–21.
Heinemann, Ronald L. "Thomas B. Stanley: Reluctant Resister." In *The
   Governors of Virginia: 1860–1978*, edited by Edward Younger and James
   Tice Moore, 333–47. Charlottesville: University Press of Virginia, 1982.
Hershman, James H., Jr. "Massive Resistance Meets Its Match: The
   Emergence of a Pro-Public School Majority." In *The Moderates' Dilemma:*

Massive Resistance to School Desegregation in Virginia, edited by Matthew D. Lassiter and Andrew B. Lewis, 104–33. Charlottesville: University Press of Virginia, 1998.

Hilts, Philip J. "The Retreat of James J. Kilpatrick." *Washington Post* (2 December 1973).

———. "The Saga of James J. Kilpatrick." *Washington Post* (23 September 1973).

Hoffelt, Mary. "Leaning Right, but Looking Both Ways." *Seattle Post-Intelligencer* (12 November 1974).

Holton, Linwood. "A Former Governor's Reflections on Massive Resistance in Virginia." *Washington and Lee Law Review* 49 (Winter 1992): 15–21.

Hutchinson, Daphne. "Dateline Scrabble: Believe It or Not, Columnist James J. Kilpatrick Wasn't Always a Conservative." *Rappahannock News* (19 July 1984).

"If Rights Bill Passes—How to Hire, Fire, Promote." *U.S. News & World Report* 56 (February 24, 1964): 113–15.

Interposition: Editorials and Editorial Page Presentations, "The Richmond News Leader," 1955–1956. Richmond, Va.: 1956.

"Interposition vs. Judicial Power: A Study of Ultimate Authority in Constitutional Questions." *Race Relations Law Reporter* 1 (April 1956): 465–99.

Jackson, John P., Jr. "In Ways Unacademical: The Reception of Carleton S. Coon's *The Origin of Race*." *Journal of the History of Biology* 34 (June 2001): 247–85.

Jacoway, Elizabeth. "Jim Johnson of Arkansas: Segregationist Prototype." In *The Role of Ideas in the Civil Rights South*. Edited by Ted Ownby, 137–56. Jackson: University Press of Mississippi, 2002.

"James Jackson Kilpatrick." *Quill* (25 October 1975): 162–14.

Judis, John B. "The Remnant: William F. Buckley, counter-revolutionary." *New Republic* (26 March 2008): 28.

Kerr, Kathie. "James J. Kilpatrick: The Journalist Who Made 'Curmudgeons' Chic." Universal Press Syndicate News Releases (2005). Article online. Available from http://www.amuniversal.com/ups/newsrelease. Accessed 19 January 2007.

Kilpatrick, James J. "Abortion, Equal Rights, and Robert's Rules of Order." *National Review* 29 (23 December 1977): 1481–85.

———. "Advancing to the Rear" (11 July 2007). Article online. Available from http://www.uxpress.com/coveringthecourts/. Accessed 31 July 2007.

———. "The Age of 'No.'" *Nation's Business* 60 (September 1972): 38–40, 42.

———. "The Anatomy of Liberalism." *National Review* 7 (10 October 1959): 396–97.

———. "Another 'Unfortunate Event'" (6 June 2007). Article online. Available from http://www.uxpress.com/coveringthecourts/. Accessed 12 June 2007.

———. "Are They Carpetbaggers, or Grave Diggers?" *Sunday Star* (1 March 1970).

———. "Back to Segregation, By Order of the Courts." *National Review* 22 (16 June 1970): 611–26.

———. "Back to the Sovereign States!" (11 April 2007). Article online. Available from http://www.uexpress.com/coveringthecourts/. Accessed 13 April 2007.

———. "The Beauty of America." *Nation's Business* 63 (September 1975): 9–10.

———. "But It Won't Stay Buried." *National Review* 5 (8 March 1958): 235–36.

———. "The Byrd Machine Will Survive: Exploding a Myth about the Virginia Senator." *Human Events* 16 (23 September 1959).

———. "The Case against ERA." *Nation's Business* 63 (January 1975): 9–10.

———. "Civil Rights and Legal Wrongs." *National Review* 15 (24 September 1963): 231–36.

———. "Civil Rights and Wrongs." *Nation's Business* 69 (March 1981): 17.

———. "Columnist's (Kind of) Farewell." *Register-Guard [Eugene, Oreg.]* (3 January 1993): B2.

———. "The Confidence Tree." *Nation's Business* 62 (January 1974): 9–10.

———. "A Conservative Prophecy: Peace Below, Tumult Above." *Harper's* 230 (April 1965): 160–64.

———. "Crossroads in Dixie." *National Review* 15 (19 November 1963): 433–35.

———. "The DeFunis Syndrome." *Nation's Business* 62 (June 1974): 13–14.

———. "Domestic Affairs." *National Review* 16 (14 July 1964): 586–89.

———. "Doomsday for Public Education?" *Nation's Business* 68 (February 1980): 13–14.

———. "The Doors Hang Awry: Reflections upon the House of Our Forefathers." Richmond, Va.: Virginia Bankers Association, 1963.

———. "Down to the Firehouse." *National Review* 6 (20 December 1958): 397–98.

———. "The Flow of Power." *Nation's Business* 62 (May 1974): 17–18.

———. "The Good Old Time of Conservatism." *Nation's Business* 66 (December 1978): 13–15.

———. "The Grand Old Game." *Nation's Business* 63 (June 1975): 17–18.

———. "Guiding Principles for America's Third Century." *Nation's Business* 64 (July 1976): 24–28.

———. "The High Court—Where Now?" *National Review* 23 (19 November 1971): 1287–91.

———. "A Hula at the High Court" (18 April 2007). Article online. Available from http://www.uexpress.com/coveringthecourts/. Accessed 21 April 2007.

———. "The Ike Plan Cometh." *National Review* 16 (16 June 1964): 483–86.

———. "An Impolitic Politician." *National Review* 20 (9 April 1968).

———. "Jesse Helms: The Admirable 'No' Man." *Seattle Times* (18 October 1990).

———. "The Little Touch" (7 September 2008). Article online. Available from http://www.uexpress.com/coveringthecourts/. Accessed 12 September 2008.

———. "Lyndon Johnson: Counterfeit Confederate." *Human Events* 17 (25 August 1960).

———. "Mr. Byrd of Virginia: At 70, He Continues His Great Career." *Human Events* 14 (10 August 1957).

———. "Must We Repeal the Constitution to Give the Negro the Vote?" *National Review* 17 (20 April 1965): 319–22.

———. "My Journey from Racism." *Atlanta Constitution-Journal* (22 December 2002): C3–C4.

———. "The New National Nightmare." *Nation's Business* 63 (August 1975): 11–12.

———. "The New Right: What Does It Seek?" *Saturday Review* 49 (8 October 1966): 29–31, 124–25.

———. "Not to Be Solved on a Slide Rule: A Southerner Looks at the Problem of Integrated Schools." *Human Events* 12 (14 May 1955).

———. "On Reaching Threescore Years." *Nation's Business* 68 (December 1980): 13.

———. "Our Man at the Golliwog Lounge." *National Review* 18 (22 March 1966): 257–58.

———. "Our Poet Laureate—What's His Name?" (26 August 2007). Article online. Available from http://www.uexpress.com/coveringthecourts/. Accessed 31 August 2007.

———. "The Oxford Incident: Its Past, Its Present, and Its Future." *Human Events* 29 (27 October 1962): 815–18.

———. "The Reagan Presidency: A Pattern of Significant Change." *Nation's Business* 71 (January 1983): 32–36.

———. "Right and Power in Arkansas." *National Review* 4 (28 September 1957): 273–75.

———. "'The Right to Interpose': An Old and Honored Doctrine Gives the People of the Several States a Chance to Regain Effective Control of Their Constitution." *Human Events* 12 (24 December 1955).

———. "Rulings That Penalize Private Schools." *Nation's Business* 64 (September 1976): 19–20.

———. "The Rural South and Private Schools." *Citizen* (September 1963): 13–14.

———. "School Integration—Four Years After: The South vs. the High Court's 1954 Ruling." *Human Events* 15 (12 May 1958).

———. "Segregation: How Much Longer Lord?" (14 June 2006). Article online. Available from http://www.uexpress.com/coveringthecourts/. Accessed 20 June 2006.

———. "The Smell of Printer's Ink Lingers On" (21 March 1991). Article online. Available from Lexis-Nexus. Accessed 3 January 2008.

———. "The South Goes Back Up for Grabs." *National Review* 15 (17 December 1963): 523–25, 527.

———. "The South Sees Through New Glasses." *National Review* 10 (11 March 1961): 141.

———. "The South's 'Granitic Opposition.'" *National Review* 6 (21 September 1957): 259.

———. "The South Will Be Vindicated: Long-Range Analysis of the Battle Over State Powers." *U.S. News & World Report* 43 (25 October 1957): 126–29.

———. "The Sovereign States—How Americans Can End Federal Usurpation." *Human Events* 13 (3 November 1956).

———. "States' Rights Make a Comeback." *Nation's Business* 64 (October 1976): 12 and 14.

———. "Term's End." *National Review* 19 (25 July 1967): 789–805.

———. "This Much at Least: The Court." *National Review* 25 (28 September 1973): 1047–52.

———. "A Time for Unfrocking." *Citizen* (November 1962): 17–18.

———. "Tuition Grants and Trojan Horses." *Nation's Business* 66 (October 1978): 17–18.

———. "Turning America Around." *Nation's Business* 72 (May 1984).

———. "The Uses of Adversity." *Nation's Business* 62 (February 1974): 11–12.

———. "A Very Different Constitution." *National Review* 21 (12 August 1969): 794–800.

———. "View from a Southern Exposure." In *100 Years of Emancipation*. Edited by Robert Goldwin. Chicago: Rand McNally & Company, 1963.

———. "Voting Rights Postscript." *National Review* 17 (4 May 1965): 351–52.

———. "The Way to Reduce Crime." *Nation's Business* 63 (April 1975): 7–8.

———. "What Makes Wallace Run?" *National Review* 19 (18 April 1967): 400–409.

———. "What a Southern Conservative Thinks." *Saturday Review* (25 April 1964): 15–18.

———. "When Virginia Joined the Union." *The Commonwealth: The Magazine of Virginia* 30, no. 11 (November 1963): 21–25, 60.

———. "Why Do We Study Grammar?" (23 March 2008). Article online. Available from http://www.uexpress/coveringthecourts/. Accessed 21 November 2008.

———. "Why Students Are Hostile to Free Enterprise." *Nation's Business* 63 (July 1975): 11–12.

King, Richard H. "The Struggle against Equality: Conservative Intellectuals in the Civil Rights Era, 1954–1975." In *The Role of Ideas in the Civil Rights South*. Edited by Ted Ownby, 137–56. Jackson: University Press of Mississippi, 2002.

Kirk, Russell. "Norms, Conventions, and the South." *Modern Age* 2 (Fall 1958): 338–45.

———. "Prescription, Authority, and Ordered Freedom." In *What Is Conservatism?*. Edited by Frank S. Meyer. New York: Holt, Rinehart, and Winston, 1964.

Klarman, Michael J. "How *Brown* Changed Race Relations: The Backlash Thesis." *Journal of American History* 8 (June 1994): 81–118.

Kondracke, Morton. "James J. Kilpatrick." *Washingtonian* (October 1973). James J. Kilpatrick Papers, Special Collections, University of Virginia.

Lassiter, Matthew D., and Andrew B. Lewis. "Massive Resistance Revisited: Virginia's White Moderates and the Byrd Organization." In *The Moderates' Dilemma: Massive Resistance to School Desegregation in Virginia*. Edited by Matthew D. Lassiter and Andrew B. Lewis, 1–21. Charlottesville: University Press of Virginia, 1998.

Latimer, James. "The Rise and Fall of Massive Resistance." *Richmond Times-Dispatch* (22 September 1996): A1.

Lawrence, David. "Undoing a Fraud." *U.S. News & World Report* 49 (12 August 1963): 83–84.

Lechner, Ira M. "Massive Resistance: Virginia's Great Leap Backward." *Virginia Quarterly Review* 74 (Autumn 1998): 631–40.

Lewis, Andrew B. "Emergency Mothers: Basement Schools and the Preservation of Public Education in Charlottesville." In *The Moderates' Dilemma: Massive Resistance to School Desegregation in Virginia*. Edited by Matthew D. Lassiter and Andrew B. Lewis, 72–103. Charlottesville: University of Virginia Press, 1998.

Lewis, Anthony. "Bar Chief Assails High Court Views." *New York Times* (7 August 1962): 7.

———. "Virginia, N.A.A.C.P. Collide in Court." *New York Times* (25 March 1959): 21.

Lewis, George. "Virginia's Northern Strategy: Southern Segregationists and the Route to National Conservatism." *Journal of Southern History* 62 (February 2006): 111–46.

Lowry, Rick. "On the Right @ 40." *National Review* 54 (6 May 2002). Article online. Available from www.nationalreview.com. Accessed 22 January 2007.

MacLean, Nancy. "Neo-Confederacy vs. the New Deal: The Regional Utopia of the Modern American Right." In *The Myth of Southern Exceptionalism*. Edited by Matthew D. Lassiter and Joseph Crespino. New York: Oxford University Press, 2010.

———. "The Scary Origins of Chief Justice Roberts's Decision Opposing the Use of Race to Promote Integration" (6 August 2007). Article online. Available from http://hnn.us/articles. Accessed 10 March 2008.

———. "Southern Dominance in Borrowed Language: The Regional Origins of American Neo-Liberalism." In *New Landscapes of Inequality:*

Neoliberalism and the Erosion of Democracy in America. Edited by Jane Collins, Micaela di Leonardo, and Brett Williams. Sante Fe, N.M.: School of American Research Press, 2008.

"The Man in the Middle." *Time* 63 (24 May 1954): 44, 46.

"Man Who Took Richmond." *Time* 58 (16 July 1951): 55.

Mason, Robert. "Newspaper Days." *Virginia Quarterly Review* 78 (Spring 2002): 342–47.

Mayer, Jeremy. "LBJ Fights the White Backlash: The Racial Politics of the 1964 Presidential Campaign." *Prologue* 33 (Spring 2001). Article online. Available from www.archives.gov. Accessed 3 November 2007.

Mayer, Michael S. "With Much Deliberation and Some Speed: Eisenhower and the *Brown* Decision." *Journal of Southern History* 52 (1986): 43–76.

McDermott, Alan. "A Wordsmith Hangs up His Quill" (1 February 2009). Article online. Available from http://www.uexpress.com/coveringthecourts/. Accessed 13 February 2009.

McLellan, Dennis. "Shana Alexander, Famed for "Point-Counterpoint,' Dies." *Los Angeles Times* (26 June 2005).

Meyer, Frank S. "Conservatism." In *Left, Right, and Center: Essays on Liberalism and Conservatism in the United States*. Edited by Robert A. Goldwin. Chicago: Rand, McNally, 1966.

———. "Equality Ad Absurdum." *National Review* 18 (15 November 1966): 1168.

Moore, Leonard. "Good Old-Fashioned New Social History and the Twentieth-Century American Right." *Reviews in American History* 24 (1996): 555–73.

Murphy, Reg. "The South as the New America." *Saturday Review* (4 September 1976): 8–11.

Murphy, Walter. Review of *The Sovereign States*, by James J. Kilpatrick. *Yale Law Journal* 67 (1958): 1505–10.

Murrell, Amy E. "The 'Impossible' Prince Edward Case: The Endurance of Resistance in a Southside County, 1959–64." In *The Moderates' Dilemma: Massive Resistance to School Desegregation in Virginia*. Edited by Matthew D. Lassiter and Andrew B. Lewis, 134–67. Charlottesville: University Press of Virginia, 1998.

Nelson, Robert Colby. "Vigorous Foe of Civil-Rights Bill." *Christian Science Monitor* (27 March 1964): 3.

O'Dell, Larry. "Va. Paper Expresses Regret for Backing Segregation." Yahoo!News (16 July 2009). Article online. Available from http://news.yahoo/s/ap/us_school_desegregation. Accessed 27 July 2009.

Parkinson, Robert G. "First from the Right: Massive Resistance and the Image of Thomas Jefferson in the 1950s." *Virginia Magazine of History & Biography* 112, no. 1 (2004): 2–35.

Pate, John R. "Pregnancies Grow in Washington Schools." *U.S. News & World Report* 43 (12 July 1957): 66–69.

Pearson, Drew. "Lobby Inspires Anti-Rights Mail." *Washington Post* (4 April 1964): B7.

Peeples, Edward H. "Richmond Journal: Thirty Years in Black & White." *Race Traitor: Treason to Whiteness Is Loyalty to Humanity* 3 (Spring 1994): 35–46.

"Petulant Plea." *Time* 80 (26 October 1962): 56–57.

"The Press: Merger in Richmond." *Time* 47 (22 April 1940).

Purcell, Edward A., Jr. "Evolving Understandings of American Federalism: Some Shifting Parameters." *New York Law School Law Review* 50 (3, 2005–2006): 635–98.

Raskin, Jamin B. "Affirmative Action and Racial Reaction." *ZMagazine* (May 1995). Article online. Available from http://www.zmag.org. Accessed 1 February 2007.

Regnery, Henry. "Emerging Conservatism: Kilpatrick, Morley, and Burnham." *Modern Age* 22 (Summer 1978): 237–46.

"Richard Viguerie on the Death of James J. Kilpatrick" (16 August 2010). Article online. Available from http://www.christiannewswire.com. Accessed 10 September 2010.

Roberts, Dick. "Patrice Lumumba and Revolution in the Congo." *Militant* 65 (23 July 2001).

Roche, Jeff. "Cowboy Conservatism." In *The Conservative Sixties*. Edited by David Farber and Jeff Roche, 79–92. New York: Peter Lang, 2003.

———. "Political Conservatism in the Sixties: Silent Majority or White Backlash?" In *The Columbia Guide to America in the 1960s*. Edited by David Farber and Beth Bailey. New York: Columbia University Press, 2001.

———. "Roche on Kruse and Lassiter." H-1960s Discussion Log (31 May 2007). Article online. Available from http://h-net.msu.edu. Accessed 17 June 2007.

Rolfe, Shelley. "Columnist Mellowed, Moved Toward Center." *Richmond Times-Dispatch* (3 October 1976): G1–G3.

Sartain, James A., and Dennis M. Rutledge. "Richmond, Virginia: Massive Resistance Without Violence." In *Community Politics and Educational Change*. Edited by Charles V. Willie and Susan L. Greenblatt. New York: Longman, 1981.

"Satterfield, Ex-ABA Chief, Dies at 76." *Jackson Clarion-Ledger* (7 May 1981): 10B.

Scalia, Antonin. "The Disease as Cure: 'In Order to Get Beyond Racism, We Must First Take Account of Race.'" *Washington University Law Quarterly* 147 (1979): 152–153.

Setegn, Lea. "Ann Merriman, Retired T-D Editor, Dies." *Richmond Times-Dispatch* (27 August 2005).

Shermer, Elizabeth Tandy. "Origins of the Conservative Ascendancy: Barry Goldwater's Early Senate Career and the De-legitimization of Organized Labor." *Journal of American History* 95 (December 2008): 678–709.

Simmons, William J. "In Memoriam: John J. Synon." *Citizen* (May 1972).

Singal, Daniel Joseph. "Beyond Consensus: Richard Hofstadter and American Historiography." *American Historical Review* 89, no. 4 (October 1984): 976–1004.

Sokolsky, George C. "What Sort of Integrationist Is Editor Harry Ashmore?" *Citizen* (August 1958).

Somers, Dale A. "Black and White in New Orleans: A Study in Urban Race Relations, 1865–1900." *Journal of Southern History* 40 (February 1974): 19–42.

"South of John C. Calhoun." *Time* 96 (30 November 1970): 46.

"Speaking from the South." *Newsweek* 57 (2 January 1961): 49.

"The Spirit of the South." *Time* 102 (26 September 1976): 30–31.

"Spokesman for Conservatism." *Time* 90 (10 July 1964).

"Spring 1964: Bloom and Boom." *Newsweek* 63 (30 March 1964): 15–21.

Stewart, Douglas K., and Ted C. Smith. "Celebrity Structure of the Far Right." *Western Political Quarterly* 17 (June 1964): 349–55.

Stevens, William K. "Nearly $500,000 in Va. Money Talks Conservatism." *Virginian-Pilot* (4 February 1966): 29.

Synon, John J. "Knowland at the Crossroads: The Cause of His Primary Defeat—And How to Reverse It." *Human Events* 15 (16 June 1958): 1–4.

———. "A Southern President? The South May Very Well Rise Again." *Human Events* 15 (11 August 1958): 1–4.

"Talkathon of Comment." *Time* 94 (26 July 1968).

Tazewell, William L. "A Washington Outside the Beltway." *New York Times* (27 December 1987).

Thomas, Robert, Jr. "Carleton Putnam Dies at 96; Led Delta and Wrote on Race." *New York Times* (16 March 1998).

Thomas, William G., III. "Television News and the Civil Rights Struggle: The Views in Virginia and Mississippi." *Southern Spaces* (3 November 2004). Article online. Available from http://www.southernspaces.org. Accessed 15 October 2006.

Thorndike, Joseph J. "'The Sometimes Sordid Level of Race and Segregation': James J. Kilpatrick and the Virginia Campaign against *Brown*." In *The Moderates' Dilemma*. Edited by Matthew D. Lassiter and Andrew B. Lewis, 51–71. Charlottesville: University Press of Virginia, 1998.

Thurber, Timothy N. "Goldwaterism Triumphant? Race and the Republican Party, 1965–1968." *Journal of the Historical Society* 7 (September 2007): 349–84.

Tillett, Paul. "The National Conventions." In *The National Election of 1964*. Edited by Milton C. Cummings Jr. Washington, D.C.: Brookings Institution, 1966.

Twardy, Edward S. "James Jackson Kilpatrick: Southern Conservative." In *American Conservative Opinion Leaders*. Edited by Mark J. Rozell and James F. Pontuso. Boulder, Colo.: Westview Press, 1990.

Van den Haag, Ernest. "Reverse Discrimination: A Brief against It." *National Review* 24 (29 April 1977): 492–95.

Voegeli, William. "Civil Rights and the Conservative Movement." *Claremont Review of Books* (Summer 2008).

Walker, Anders. "Legislating Virtue: How Segregationists Disguised Racial Discrimination as Moral Reform Following *Brown v. Board of Education*." *Duke Law Journal* 47 (November 1997): 399–424.

Waring, Thomas R. "The Southern Case *Against Desegregation*." *Harper's Magazine* 212 (January 1956): 39–45.

Whalen, Richard. "Rural Virginia: A Microcosm." *National Review* 5 (8 March 1958): 229–31.

Whittaker, Charles E. "Can 'Integration' Be Forced By Federal Law?" *U.S. News & World Report* 56 (23 March 1964): 99–101.

Williams, Robert H. "Legal Scholar Alfred Avins Dies at Age 64." *Washington Post* (11 June 1999): B06.

Williams, Roger. "A Regional Report: Newspapers of the South." *Columbia Journalism Review* (Summer 1967): 26–35.

Wilson, Charles Reagan. "The Myth of the Biracial South." In *The Southern State of Mind*. Edited by Jan Nordby Gretlund, 3–22. Columbia: University of South Carolina Press, 1999.

Woo, Elaine. "James J. Kilpatrick Dies at 89; Newspaper Columnist and Arbiter of Language." *Los Angeles Times* (17 August 2010).

Worden, William L. "Tales of the Kingmakers." *Saturday Evening Post* 231 (23 May 1959): 28–29, 65–70.

Wren, Mark. "Editor Says North-South Fight Should Get Out of Racial 'Mud.'" *Charleston News and Courier* (16 March 1956).

Wyatt, Edward. "D. Tennant Bryan, 92, Chief of Newspaper and TV Empire." *New York Times* (12 December 1998): A19.

Yuill, Kevin L. "The 1966 White House Conference on Civil Rights." *Historical Journal* 41, no. 1 (1998): 259–82.

Books

Alexander, Holmes. *Never Lose a War: Memoirs and Observations of a National Columnist*. Greenwich, Conn.: Devin-Adair, 1984.

Alexander, Shana. *Happy Days: My Mother, My Father, My Sister & Me*. New York: Doubleday, 1995.

Allitt, Patrick. *Catholic Intellectuals and Conservative Politics in America, 1950–1985*. Ithaca, N.Y.: Cornell University Press, 1993.

Alterman, Eric. *Sound and Fury: The Making of the Punditocracy*. Ithaca, N.Y.: Cornell University Press, 1999.

Anderson, Terry H. *The Pursuit of Fairness: A History of Affirmative Action*. New York: Oxford University Press, 2004.

Ashmore, Harry S. *Civil Rights and Wrongs: A Memoir of Race and Politics*. New York: Pantheon Books, 1994.

Atkinson, Frank. *The Dynamic Dominion: Realignment and the Rise of Virginia's Republican Party Since 1945*. Fairfax, Va.: George Mason University Press, 1992.

Baird, W. David, and Danney Goble. *The Story of Oklahoma*. Norman: University of Oklahoma Press, 1994.

Bake, William A., and James J. Kilpatrick. *The American South: Four Seasons of the Land*. Birmingham, Ala.: Oxmoor House, 1980.

———. *The American South: Towns and Cities*. Birmingham, Ala.: Oxmoor House, 1982.

Baker, Keith Michael. *Inventing the French Revolution: Essays on French Political Culture in the Eighteenth Century*. Cambridge: Cambridge University Press, 1990.

Bartley, Numan V. *The Creation of Modern Georgia*. Athens: University of Georgia Press, 1983.

———. *The New South, 1945–1980: The Story of the South's Modernization*. Baton Rouge: Louisiana State University Press, 1995.

———. *The Rise of Massive Resistance: Race and Politics in the South during the 1950's*. Baton Rouge: Louisiana State University Press, 1969.

Bass, Jack, and Walter DeVries. *The Transformation of Southern Politics: Social Change and Political Consequence Since 1945*. New York: Basic Books, 1976.

Beagle, Ben, and Ozzie Osbourne. *J. Lindsay Almond: Virginia's Reluctant Rebel*. Roanoke, Va.: Full Court Press, 1984.

Bears, Sara B., John T. Kneebone, J. Jefferson Looney, Brent Tarter, and Sandra Gioia Treadway, eds. *Dictionary of Virginia Biography*. Vol. 2. Richmond: Library of Virginia, 2001.

Belknap, Michael. *Federal Law and Southern Order: Racial Violence and Constitutional Conflict in the Post-"Brown" South*. Athens: University of Georgia Press, 1987.

Berger, Raoul. *Government by Judiciary: The Transformation of the Fourteenth Amendment*. Cambridge, Mass.: Harvard University Press, 1977.

———. *Federalism: The Founders' Design*. Norman: University of Oklahoma Press, 1987.

———. *The Fourteenth Amendment and the Bill of Rights*. Norman: University of Oklahoma Press, 1989.

Berman, William C. *America's Right Turn: From Nixon to Clinton*. Baltimore: Johns Hopkins University Press, 1994.

Berry, Wendell. *The Unsettling of America: Culture and Agriculture*. San Francisco: Sierra Club Books, 1977.

Bissett, Jim. *Agrarian Socialism in America: Marx, Jefferson, and Jesus in the Oklahoma Countryside, 1904–1920*. Norman: University of Oklahoma Press, 1999.

Bjerre-Poulsen, Niels. *Right Face: Organizing the American Conservative Movement, 1945–65*. University of Copenhagen: Museum Tusculanum Press, 2002.

Black, Earl, and Merle Black. *The Vital South: How Presidents Are Elected*. Cambridge, Mass.: Harvard University Press, 1993.

Bloch, Charles J. *States' Rights: The Law of the Land*. Atlanta: Harrison, 1958.

Blum, David. *Tick . . . Tick . . . Tick: The Long Life and Turbulent Times of "60 Minutes."* New York: Harper Collins, 2004.

Blumenthal, Sidney. *The Rise of the Counter-Establishment: From Conservative Ideology to Political Power.* New York: Times Books, 1986.

Booth, Andrew B., ed. *Records of Louisiana Confederate Soldiers and Confederate Commands.* Vol. 2. New Orleans, 1920.

Bork, Robert H. *The Tempting of America.* New York: Free Press, 1997.

Boyle, Sarah Patton. *The Desegregated Heart: A Virginian's Stand in Time of Transition.* New York: William Morrow and Company, 1962.

Bozell, L. Brent. *The Warren Revolution: Reflections on the Consensus Society.* New Rochelle, N.Y.: Arlington House, 1966.

Brady, Thomas P. *Black Monday.* Winona, Miss.: Association of Citizens' Councils, 1954.

Branch, Taylor. *Parting the Waters: America in the King Years: 1954–1963.* New York: Simon and Schuster, 1988.

Brennan, Mary C. *Turning Right in the Sixties: The Conservative Capture of the GOP.* Chapel Hill: University of North Carolina Press, 1995.

Brock, David. *The Republican Noise Machine: Right-Wing Media and How It Corrupts Democracy.* New York: Crown Publishers, 2004.

Brooks, David. *On Paradise Drive: How We Live Now (And Always Have) in the Future Tense.* New York: Simon and Schuster, 2004.

Brown, Michael K., Martin Carnoy, Elliott Currie, Troy Duster, and David B. Oppenheimer. *Whitewashing Race: The Myth of a Color-Blind Society.* Berkeley: University of California Press, 2003.

Brundage, W. Fitzhugh. *Lynching in the New South: Georgia and Virginia, 1880–1930.* Urbana: University of Illinois Press, 1993.

Bryan, John Stewart. *Joseph Bryan: His Times, His Family, His Friends.* Richmond, Va.: 1935 (privately printed).

Bryant, Keith L., Jr. *Alfalfa Bill Murray.* Norman: University of Oklahoma Press, 1968.

Buchanan, Patrick J. *Conservative Votes, Liberal Victories: Why the Right Has Failed.* New York: Quadrangle/New York Times, 1975.

———. *Right from the Beginning.* Boston: Little, Brown, 1988.

Buckley, William F., Jr. *God and Man at Yale: The Superstitions of "Academic Freedom."* Chicago: Henry Regnery, 1951.

Buni, Andrew. *The Negro in Virginia Politics, 1902–1965.* Charlottesville: University Press of Virginia, 1967.

Burke, Bob. *Baseball in Oklahoma City.* Mount Pleasant, S.C.: Arcadia, 2003.

Burke, Edmund. *Reflections on the Revolution in France.* 1790. New York: Prometheus Books, 1987.

Burner, David, and Thomas R. West. *Column Right: Conservative Journalists in the Service of Nationalism.* New York: New York University Press, 1988.

Butler, Ian, Lesley Scanlan, Margaret Robinson, Gillian Douglas, and Mervyn Murch. *Divorcing Children: Children's Experiences of Their Parents' Divorce.* New York: Jessica Kingsley, 2003.

Cappon, Lester. *Virginia Newspapers, 1821–1935: A Bibliography with Historical Introduction and Notes*. New York: D. Appleton-Century, 1936.

Carlson, Jody. *George C. Wallace and the Politics of Powerlessness*. New Brunswick, N.J.: Transaction, 1981.

Carpenter, Jesse T. *The South as a Conscious Minority: 1789–1861*. Gloucester, Mass.: Peter Smith, 1963 (second printing).

Carr, Virginia Spencer. *Dos Passos: A Life*. Garden City, N.Y.: Doubleday, 1984.

Carson, Clayborne. *In Struggle: SNCC and the Black Awakening of the 1960s*. Cambridge, Mass.: Harvard University Press, 1981.

———. ed. *The Papers of Martin Luther King, Jr*. Vol. 5. Berkeley: University of California Press, 2005.

Carter, Dan T. *From George Wallace to Newt Gingrich: Race in the Conservative Counterrevolution, 1963–1994*. Baton Rouge: Louisiana State University Press, 1996.

———. *The Politics of Rage: George Wallace, the Origins of the New Conservatism, and the Transformation of American Politics*. Baton Rouge: Louisiana State University Press, 1995.

———. *Scottsboro: A Tragedy of the American South*. Baton Rouge: Louisiana State University Press, 1969.

Chambers, Lenoir, and Joseph E. Shank. *Salt Water and Printer's Ink: Norfolk and Its Newspapers, 1865–1965*. Chapel Hill: University of North Carolina Press, 1967.

Chafe, William H. *Civilities and Civil Rights: Greensboro, North Carolina, and the Black Struggle for Freedom*. New York: Oxford University Press, 1980.

Chappell, David L. *A Stone of Hope: Prophetic Religion and the Death of Jim Crow*. Chapel Hill: University of North Carolina Press, 2004.

Chen, Anthony S. *The Fifth Freedom: Jobs, Politics, and Civil Rights in the United States, 1941–1972*. Princeton, N.J.: Princeton University Press, 2009.

Cobb, James C. *Away Down South: A History of Southern Identity*. New York: Oxford University Press, 2005.

———. *The Selling of the South: The Southern Crusade for Industrial Development, 1936–1990*. Baton Rouge: Louisiana State University Press, 1982.

Cohen, Warren I. *The Chinese Connection: Roger S. Greene, Thomas W. Lamont, George Sokolsky, and American–East Asian Relations*. New York: Columbia University Press, 1978.

Collins, Charles Wallace. *Whither the Solid South? A Study in Politics and Race Relations*. New Orleans: Pelican, 1947.

Conkin, Paul K. *The Southern Agrarians*. Knoxville: University of Tennessee Press, 1988.

Coontz, Stephanie. *The Way We Never Were: American Families and the Nostalgia Trap*. New York: Basic Books, 1992.

Cottrol, Robert J., Raymond T. Diamond, and Leland B. Ware. *"Brown v. Board of Education": Caste, Culture, and the Constitution*. Lawrence: University Press of Kansas, 2003.

Crespino, Joseph. *In Search of Another Country: Mississippi and the Conservative Counterrevolution*. Princeton, N.J.: Princeton University Press, 2007.

Critchlow, Donald T., and Nancy MacLean. *Debating the American Conservative Movement: 1945 to the Present*. New York: Rowman & Littlefield, 2009.

Dabney, Virginius. *Across the Years: Memories of a Virginian*. Garden City, N.Y.: Doubleday, 1978.

———. *Richmond: The Story of a City*. Rev. ed. Charlottesville: University Press of Virginia, 1990.

———. *Virginia: The New Dominion*. Garden City, N.Y.: Doubleday, 1971.

Dailey, Jane. *Before Jim Crow: The Politics of Race in Postemancipation Virginia*. Chapel Hill: University of North Carolina Press, 2000.

Dallek, Matthew. *The Right Moment: Ronald Reagan's First Victory and the Decisive Turning Point in American Politics*. New York: Free Press, 2000.

Davies, David R., ed. *The Press and Race: Mississippi Journalists Confront the Movement*. Jackson: University Press of Mississippi, 2001.

Debo, Angie. *Prairie City: The Story of an American Community*. New York: Alfred A. Knopf, 1944.

Diggins, John P. *Up from Communism: Conservative Odysseys in American Intellectual History*. New York: Harper & Row, 1975.

Dochuk, Darren. *From Bible Belt to Sunbelt: Plain-Folk Religion, Grassroots Politics, and the Rise of Evangelical Conservatism*. New York: W. W. Norton, 2010.

Dorr, Gregory Michael. *Segregation's Science: Eugenics and Society in Virginia*. Charlottesville: University of Virginia Press, 2008.

Dorrien, Gary J. *The Neoconservative Mind: Politics, Culture, and the War of Ideology*. Philadelphia: Temple University Press, 1993.

Dudziak, Mary L. *Cold War Civil Rights: Race and the Image of American Democracy*. Princeton, N.J.: Princeton University Press, 2000.

Duke, Maurice, and Daniel P. Jordan. *A Richmond Reader, 1733–1983*. Chapel Hill: University of North Carolina Press, 1983.

Dunford, Earle. *"Richmond Times-Dispatch": The Story of a Newspaper*. Richmond, Va.: Cadmus, 1995.

Durr, Kenneth D. *Behind the Backlash: White Working-Class Politics in Baltimore, 1940–1980*. Chapel Hill: University of North Carolina Press, 2003.

Dworkin, Ronald. *A Matter of Principle*. Cambridge, Mass.: Harvard University Press, 1985.

Eagles, Charles W. *The Price of Defiance: James Meredith and the Integration of Ole Miss*. Chapel Hill: University of North Carolina Press, 2009.

Edsall, Thomas B., and Mary D. Edsall. *Chain Reaction: The Impact of Race, Rights, and Taxes on American Politics*. New York: W. W. Norton, 1991.

Egan, Timothy. *The Worst Hard Time: The Untold Story of Those Who Survived the Great American Dust Bowl*. Boston: Houghton Mifflin, 2006.

Egerton, John. *The Americanization of Dixie: The Southernization of America*. New York: Harper's Magazine Press, 1974.

———. *Speak Now against the Day: The Generation Before the Civil Rights Movement in the South*. New York: Alfred A. Knopf, 1994.

Elazar, Daniel J. *Cities of the Prairie: The Metropolitan Frontier and American Politics*. New York: Basic Books, 1970.

Ely, James W., Jr. *The Crisis of Conservative Virginia: The Byrd Organization and the Politics of Massive Resistance*. Knoxville: University of Tennessee Press, 1976.

Epstein, Benjamin R., and Arnold Forster. *The Radical Right: Report on the John Birch Society and Its Allies*. New York: Random House, 1966.

Eskew, Glenn T. *But for Birmingham: The Local and National Movements in the Civil Rights Struggle*. Chapel Hill: University of North Carolina Press, 1997.

Fairclough, Adam. *Race and Democracy: The Civil Rights Struggle in Louisiana, 1915–1972*. Athens: University of Georgia Press, 1995.

Farber, David. *The Age of Great Dreams: America in the 1960s*. New York: Hill and Wang, 1994.

———. *The Conservative Sixties*. Edited by David Farber and Jeff Roche. New York: Peter Lang, 2003.

———. *The Rise and Fall of Modern American Conservatism: A Short History*. Princeton, N.J.: Princeton University Press, 2010.

———. *Sloan Rules: Alfred P. Sloan and the Triumph of General Motors*. Chicago: University of Chicago Press, 2002.

Farrar, Ronald T. *A Creed for My Profession: Walter Williams, Journalist to the World*. Columbia: University of Missouri Press, 1998.

Fay, Elizabeth A. *Eminent Rhetoric: Language, Gender, and Cultural Tropes*. Westport, Conn.: Bergin & Garvey, 1994.

Federal Writers' Project. *New Orleans City Guide*. Boston: Houghton Mifflin, 1938.

———. *Oklahoma: A Guide to the Sooner State*. Norman: University of Oklahoma Press, 1941.

———. *Virginia: A Guide to the Old Dominion*. New York: Oxford University Press, 1940.

———. *The WPA Guide to 1930s Missouri*. 2nd ed. Lawrence: University Press of Kansas, 1986.

Fisher, Paul L., and Ralph L. Lowenstein, eds. *Race and the News Media*. New York: Frederick A. Praeger, 1967.

Fogarty, Gerald P. *Commonwealth Catholicism: A History of the Catholic Church in Virginia*. South Bend: University of Notre Dame Press, 2001.

Foxfire Students, *Foxfire 40th Anniversary Book*. New York: Anchor Books, 2006.

Franklin, Jimmie Lewis. *Journey Toward Hope: A History of Blacks in Oklahoma*. Norman: University of Oklahoma Press, 1982.

Franklin, John Hope. *Mirror to America: The Autobiography of John Hope Franklin*. New York: Farrar, Straus, and Giroux, 2005.

Frederickson, George M. *The Black Image in the White Mind: The Debate on Afro-American Character and Destiny, 1817–1914*. New York: Harper & Row, 1971.

Freyer, Tony. *The Little Rock Crisis: A Constitutional Interpretation*. Westport, Conn.: Greenwood Press, 1984.

Friedman, Murray. *The Neoconservative Revolution: Jewish Intellectuals and the Shaping of Public Policy*. Cambridge: Cambridge University Press, 2005.

Frohnan, Bruce, Jeremy Beer, and Jeffrey O. Nelson, eds. *American Conservatism: An Encyclopedia*. Wilmington, Del.: Isi Books, 2006.

Gallagher, Gary W. *Lee and His Army in Confederate History*. Chapel Hill: University of North Carolina Press, 2001.

Garrow, David J. *Bearing the Cross: Martin Luther King, Jr., and the Southern Christian Leadership Conference*. New York: William Morrow, 1986.

———. *Protest at Selma: Martin Luther King, Jr., and the Voting Rights Act of 1965*. New Haven, Conn.: Yale University Press, 1978.

Gaston, Paul M. *The New South Creed: A Study in Southern Mythmaking*. New York: Alfred A. Knopf, 1970.

Gates, Robbins L. *The Making of Massive Resistance: Virginia's Politics of Public School Desegregation, 1954–1956*. Chapel Hill: University of North Carolina Press, 1962.

Genovese, Eugene D. *The Southern Tradition: The Achievement and Limitations of an American Conservatism*. Cambridge, Mass.: Harvard University Press, 1994.

Gibbon, Edward. *The History of the Decline and Fall of the Roman Empire*. New York: Penguin Books, 1995.

Gibson, Arrell Morgan. *Oklahoma: A History of Five Centuries*. 2nd ed. Norman: University of Oklahoma Press, 1981.

Gillon, Steven M. *"That's Not What We Meant to Do": Reform and Its Unintended Consequences in Twentieth-Century America*. New York: W. W. Norton, 2000.

Gitlin, Todd. *The Whole World Is Watching: Mass Media in the Making and Unmaking of the New Left*. Berkeley: University of California Press, 1980.

Glasscock, C. B. *Then Came Oil: The Story of the Last Frontier*. Westport, Conn.: Hyperion Press, 1938.

Goble, Danney. *Progressive Oklahoma: The Making of a New Kind of State*. Norman: University of Oklahoma Press, 1980.

Goings, Kenneth W. *The "NAACP Comes of Age": The Defeat of Judge John J. Parker*. Bloomington: Indiana University Press, 1990.

Goldberg, Robert Alan. *Barry Goldwater*. New Haven, Conn.: Yale University Press, 1995.

Golden, Harry L. *The Right Time: An Autobiography*. New York: Putnam, 1969.

Goldfield, David R. *Black, White, and Southern: Race Relations and Southern Culture, 1940 to the Present*. Baton Rouge: Louisiana State University Press, 1990.

———. *Cotton Fields and Skyscrapers: Southern City and Region, 1607–1980*. Baton Rouge: Louisiana State University Press, 1982.

Goldwater, Barry. *The Conscience of a Conservative*. Shepardsville, Ky.: Victor, 1960.

Goldwin, Robert A., ed. *A Nation of States: Essays on the American Federal System*. Chicago: Rand McNally, 1974 (second printing).

Gottfried, Paul. *The Conservative Movement*. New York: Twayne, 1993.

Gottmann, Jean. *Virginia at Mid-Century*. New York: Henry Holt, 1955.

———. *Virginia in Our Century*. 2nd ed. Charlottesville: University Press of Virginia, 1969.

Grauer, Neil A. *Wits and Sages*. Baltimore: Johns Hopkins University Press, 1984.

Greenberg, David. *Nixon's Shadow: The History of an Image*. New York: W. W. Norton, 2003.

Gregory, James N. *American Exodus: The Dust Bowl Migration and Okie Culture in California*. New York: Oxford University Press, 1989.

———. *The Southern Diaspora: How the Great Migrations of Black and White Southerners Transformed America*. Chapel Hill: University of North Carolina Press, 2005.

Guild, June Purcell. *Black Laws of Virginia: A Summary of Legislative Acts of Virginia Concerning Negroes from the Earliest Times to the Present*. Richmond, Va.: Whittet & Shepperson, 1936.

Hair, William Ivy. *Carnival of Fury: Robert Charles and the New Orleans Race Riot of 1900*. Baton Rouge: Louisiana State University Press, 1976.

Hamilton, Alexander, James Madison, and John Jay. *The Federalist Papers*. Edited by Charles Kesler. New York: Signet Classics, 2003.

Harbaugh, William H. *Lawyer's Lawyer: The Life of John W. Davis*. New York: Oxford University Press, 1973.

Hatch, Alden. *The Byrds of Virginia: An American Dynasty: 1670 to the Present*. New York: Holt, Rinehart, and Winston, 1969.

Havard, William C., ed. *The Changing Politics of the South*. Baton Rouge: Louisiana State University Press, 1972.

Heinemann, Ronald L. *Depression and New Deal in Virginia: The Enduring Dominion*. Charlottesville: University Press of Virginia, 1983.

———. *Harry Byrd of Virginia*. Charlottesville: University Press of Virginia, 1996.

Helms, Jesse. *When Free Men Shall Stand*. Grand Rapids, Mich.: Zondervan Publishing House, 1976.

Heymann, C. David. *Ezra Pound: The Last Rower*. New York: Seaver Books, 1976.

Hill, Oliver W., Sr. *The Big Bang "Brown vs. Board of Education," and Beyond: The Autobiography of Oliver W. Hill, Sr.* Winter Park, Fla.: FOUR-G, 2000.

Himmelstein, Jerome L. *To the Right: The Transformation of American Conservatism*. Berkeley: University of California Press, 1990.

Hirsch, Alan. *Talking Heads: Political Talk Shows and Their Star Pundits*. New York: St. Martin's, 1991.

Hirsch, Arnold R. *Making the Second Ghetto: Race and Housing in Chicago, 1940–1960*. Chicago: University of Chicago Press, 1998.

Hirsch, James S. *Riot and Remembrance: The Tulsa Race War and Its Legacy*. Boston: Houghton Mifflin, 2002.

Hixson, William B., Jr. *Search for the American Right Wing: An Analysis of the Social Science Record, 1955–1987*. Princeton, N.J.: Princeton University Press, 1992.

Hobson, Fred C., Jr. *Serpent in Eden: H. L. Mencken and the South*. Baton Rouge: Louisiana State University Press, 1974.

Hodgson, Godfrey. *The World Turned Right Side Up: A History of the Conservative Ascendancy in America*. New York: Houghton Mifflin, 1996.

Hofstadter, Richard. *The Paranoid Style in American Politics and Other Essays*. New York: Vintage Books, 1967.

Hollandsworth, James G. *An Absolute Massacre: The New Orleans Race Riot of July 30, 1866*. Baton Rouge: Louisiana State University Press, 2001.

Hunt, Lynn, ed. *The New Cultural History*. Berkeley: University of California Press, 1989.

Hyneman, Charles S. *The Supreme Court on Trial*. New York: Atherton/Prentice-Hall, 1964.

Jackson, John P., Jr. *Science for Segregation: Race, Law, and the Case against "Brown v. Board of Education."* New York: New York University Press, 2005.

Jackson, Joy T. *New Orleans in the Gilded Age: Politics and Urban Progress, 1880–1896*. Baton Rouge: Louisiana State University Press, 1969.

Jefferson, Thomas. *Notes on the State of Virginia*. Edited by William Peden. Chapel Hill: University of North Carolina Press, 1954.

Jeffries, John C., Jr. *Justice Lewis F. Powell, Jr.* New York: Charles Scribner's Sons, 1994.

Johnson, David E. *Douglas Southall Freeman*. Gretna, La.: Pelican, 2002.

Johnson, Hannibal B. *Black Wall Street: From Riot to Renaissance in Tulsa's Historic Greenwood District*. Austin, Tex.: Eakin Press, 1998.

Johnston, James Hugo. *Race Relations in Virginia and Miscegenation in the South, 1776–1860*. Amherst: University of Massachusetts Press, 1970.

Judis, John B. *William F. Buckley, Jr.: Patron Saint of the Conservatives*. New York: Simon and Schuster, 1988.

Katagiri, Yasuhiro. *The Mississippi State Sovereignty Commission: Civil Rights and States' Rights*. Jackson: University Press of Mississippi, 2001.

Keeler, Robert F. *"Newsday": A Candid History of the Respectable Tabloid*. New York: William Morrow, 1990.

Kendall, Willmoore. *Conservative Affirmation*. Chicago: Henry Regnery, 1963.

Key, V. O., Jr. *Southern Politics in State and Nation*. New York: Alfred A. Knopf, 1949.

Kilpatrick, James J. *Fine Print: Reflections on the Writing Art*. Kansas City: Andrews and McMeel, 1993.

———. *The Foxes' Union: And Other Stretchers, Tall Tales, and Discursive Reminiscences of Happy Years in Scrabble, Virginia*. McLean, Va.: EPM Publications, 1977.

———. *The Smut Peddlers*. Garden City, N.Y.: Doubleday, 1960.

———. *The Southern Case for School Segregation*. New York: Crowell-Collier Press, 1962.

———. *The Sovereign States: Notes of a Citizen of Virginia*. Chicago: Henry Regnery, 1957.

———. *The Writer's Art*. New York: Andrews, McMeel & Parker, 1984.

Kilpatrick, James J., and Eugene J. McCarthy. *A Political Bestiary: Viable Alternatives, Impressive Mandates, and Other Fables*. New York: Avon, 1979.

King, Martin Luther, Jr. *Why We Can't Wait*. New York: New American Library, 1964.

King, Richard H. *A Southern Renaissance: The Cultural Awakening of the American South, 1930–1955*. New York: Oxford University Press, 1980.

Kirk, Russell. *The Conservative Mind: From Burke to Eliot*. 6th ed. South Bend, Ind.: Gateway Editions, 1978.

Klarman, Michael J. *From Jim Crow to Civil Rights: The Supreme Court and the Struggle for Racial Equality*. New York: Oxford University Press, 2004.

Kluger, Richard. *Simple Justice: The History of "Brown v. Board of Education" and Black America's Struggle for Equality*. New York: Vintage Books, 2004.

Kneebone, John T. *Southern Liberal Journalists and the Issue of Race, 1920–1944*. Chapel Hill: University of North Carolina Press, 1985.

Kousser, J. Morgan. *Colorblind Injustice: Minority Voting Rights and the Undoing of the Second Reconstruction*. Chapel Hill: University of North Carolina Press, 1999.

Kruse, Kevin M. *White Flight: Atlanta and the Making of Modern Conservatism*. Princeton, N.J.: Princeton University Press, 2005.

Kurtz, Howard. *Hot Air: All Talk, All the Time*. New York: Times Books, 1996.

Larson, Edward J. *Sex, Race, and Science: Eugenics in the Deep South*. Baltimore: Johns Hopkins University Press, 1995.

Lassiter, Matthew D. *The Silent Majority: Suburban Politics in the Sunbelt South*. Princeton, N.J.: Princeton University Press, 2006.

Lassiter, Matthew D., and Joseph Crespino, eds. *The Myth of Southern Exceptionalism*. New York: Oxford University Press, 2010.

Lassiter, Matthew D., and Andrew B. Lewis, eds. *The Moderates' Dilemma: Massive Resistance to School Desegregation in Virginia*. Charlottesville: University Press of Virginia, 1998.

Lawrence, David. *The Editorials of David Lawrence*. Vol. 5. Washington, D.C.: U.S. News and World Report, 1970.

Leidholdt, Alexander. *Standing Before the Shouting Mob: Lenoir Chambers and Virginia's Massive Resistance to Public-School Integration*. Tuscaloosa: University of Alabama Press, 1997.

Lentz, Richard. *Symbols, the News Magazines, and Martin Luther King*. Baton Rouge: Louisiana State University Press, 1990.

Lewis, George. *Massive Resistance: The White Response to the Civil Rights Movement*. London: Hodder Arnold, 2006.

———. *The White South and the Red Menace: Segregationists, Anticommunism, and Massive Resistance, 1945–1965*. Gainesville: University Press of Florida, 2004.

Lichtman, Allan J. *White Protestant Nation: The Rise of the American Conservative Movement*. New York: Atlantic Monthly Press, 2008.

Lind, Michael. *Made in Texas: George W. Bush and the Southern Takeover of American Politics*. New York: Basic Books, 2008.

Link, William A. *Righteous Warrior: Jesse Helms and the Rise of Modern Conservatism*. New York: St. Martin's Press, 2008.

Lipset, Seymour Martin, and Earl Raab. *The Politics of Unreason: Right-Wing Extremism in America, 1790–1977*. New York: Harper and Row, 1978.

Lokos, Lionel. *House Divided: The Life and Legacy of Martin Luther King*. New Rochelle, N.Y.: Arlington House, 1968.

———. *The New Racism: Reverse Discrimination in America*. New Rochelle, N.Y.: Arlington House, 1971.

Lora, Ronald, and William Henry Longton, eds. *The Conservative Press in Twentieth-Century America*. Westport, Conn.: Greenwood Press, 1999.

Lowndes, Joseph E. *From the New Deal to the New Right: Race and the Southern Origins of Modern Conservatism*. New Haven, Conn.: Yale University Press, 2008.

Lublin, David. *The Republican South: Democratization and Partisan Change*. Princeton, N.J.: Princeton University Press, 2004.

Ludington, Townsend. *John Dos Passos: A Twentieth Century Odyssey*. New York: E. P. Dutton, 1980.

MacLean, Nancy. *Freedom Is Not Enough: The Opening of the American Workplace*. Cambridge, Mass.: Harvard University Press, 2006.

Maltz, Earl A. *Rethinking Constitutional Law: Originalism, Interventionism, and the Politics of Judicial Review*. Lawrence: University Press of Kansas, 1994.

Manis, Andrew. *A Fire You Can't Put Out: The Civil Rights Life of Birmingham's Reverend Fred Shuttlesworth*. Tuscaloosa: University of Alabama Press, 2001.

Mann, Robert. *The Walls of Jericho: Lyndon Johnson, Hubert Humphrey, Richard Russell, and the Struggle for Civil Rights*. New York: Harcourt Brace, 1996.

Margolis, Jon. *The Last Innocent Year: America in 1964: The Beginning of the "Sixties."* New York: Morrow, 1999.

Marsh, Charles. *God's Long Summer: Stories of Faith and Civil Rights*. Princeton, N.J.: Princeton University Press, 1997.

Massey, William A. *The New Fanatics*. Washington, D.C.: National Putnam Letters Committee, 1963.

Mayer, Jeremy D. *Running on Race: Racial Politics in Presidential Campaigns, 1960–2000*. New York: Random House, 2002.

McAdam, Doug. *Political Process and the Development of the Black Insurgency,*
1930–1970. Chicago: University of Chicago Press, 1982.

McGill, Ralph. *The South and the Southerner*. Boston: Little, Brown, 1963.

McGirr, Lisa. *Suburban Warriors: The Origins of the New American Right.*
Princeton, N.J.: Princeton University Press, 2001.

McMillen, Neil R. *The Citizens' Council: Organized Resistance to the Second*
Reconstruction, 1954–64. Urbana: University of Illinois Press, 1971.

McPherson, James Brian. *The Conservative Resurgence and the Press: The*
Media's Role in the Rise of the Right. Evanston, Ill.: Northwestern University
Press, 2008.

McReynolds, Edwin, Alice Marriott, and Estelle Faulconer. *Oklahoma: The*
Story of Its Past and Present. Norman: University of Oklahoma Press,
1985.

Meese, Edwin. *With Reagan: The Inside Story*. Washington, D.C.: Regnery
Gateway, 1992.

Mencken, H. L. *Prejudices: Second Series*. New York: Alfred A. Knopf, 1920.

Meyer, Frank S., ed. *What Is Conservatism?* New York: Holt, Rinehart, and
Winston, 1964.

Miles, Michael W. *The Odyssey of the American Right*. New York: Oxford
University Press, 1980.

Miller, James. *"Democracy Is in the Streets": From Port Huron to the Siege of*
Chicago. New York: Simon and Schuster, 1987.

Miner, Brad. *The Concise Conservative Encyclopedia: 200 of the Most Important*
Ideas, Individuals, Incitements, and Institutions That Have Shaped the
Movement. New York: Free Press, 1996.

Mintz, Frank P. *The Liberty Lobby and the American Right: Race, Conspiracy,*
and Culture. Westport, Conn.: Greenwood Press, 1985.

Moeser, John V., ed. *A Virginia Profile, 1960–2000: Assessing Current Trends*
and Problems. Palisades Park, N.J.: Commonwealth Books, 1981.

Moeser, John V., and Rutledge M. Dennis. *The Politics of Annexation:*
Oligarchic Power in a Southern City. Cambridge, Mass.: Schenkman
Publishing Company, 1982.

Morgan, H. Wayne, and Anne Hodges Morgan. *Oklahoma: A Bicentennial*
History. New York: W. W. Norton, 1977.

———, eds. *Oklahoma: New Views of the Forty-Sixth State*. Norman: University
of Oklahoma Press, 1982.

Morley, Felix. *Freedom and Federalism*. Chicago: Henry Regner, 1959.

Morris, Willie. *The Courting of Marcus Dupree*. New York: Doubleday, 1983.

Morton, Richard Lee. *Virginia Lives: The Old Dominion Who's Who.*
Hopkinsville, Ky.: Historical Record Association, 1964.

Mowry, George E. *Another Look at the Twentieth-Century South*. Baton Rouge:
Louisiana State University Press, 1973.

Mudd, Roger. *The Place to Be: Washington, CBS, and the Glory Days of*
Television News. New York: Public Affairs, 2008.

Murphy, Paul V. *The Rebuke of History: The Southern Agrarians and American Conservative Thought*. Chapel Hill: University of North Carolina Press, 2001.

Murphy, Walter F. *Congress and the Court: A Case Study in the American Political Process*. Chicago: University of Chicago Press, 1962.

Murray, Charles A. *Losing Ground: American Social Policy, 1950–1980*. New York: Basic Books, 1984.

Murray, Michael D., ed. *Encyclopedia of Television News*. Phoenix: Oryx Press, 1999.

Murray, William H. *The Negro's Place in Call of Race*. Tishomingo, Okla.: William H. Murray (privately printed), 1948.

Muse, Benjamin. *Virginia's Massive Resistance*. Bloomington: Indiana University Press, 1961.

Myrdal, Gunnar. *An American Dilemma: The Negro Problem and Modern Democracy*. New York: Harper and Brothers, 1944.

Nash, George H. *The Conservative Intellectual Movement in America: Since 1945*. New York: Basic Books, 1976.

Newby, I. A. *Challenge to the Court: Social Scientists and the Defense of Segregation, 1954–1966*. Baton Rouge: Louisiana State University Press, 1969 (second printing).

———. *Jim Crow's Defense: Anti-Negro Thought in America, 1900–1930*. Baton Rouge: Louisiana State University Press, 1965.

———. *The South: A History*. New York: Holt, Rinehart, and Winston, 1981.

Nickerson, Michelle, and Darren Dochuk, eds. *Sunbelt Rising: The Politics of Space, Place, and Region*. Philadelphia: University of Pennsylvania Press, 2011.

Nimmo, Dan, and Chevelle Newsome. *Political Commentators in the United States in the Twentieth Century: A Bio-Critical Sourcebook*. Westport, Conn.: Greenwood Press, 1997.

Novak, Michael. *The Joy of Sports: End Zones, Bases, Baskets, Balls, and the Consecration of the American Spirit*. New York: Hamilton Press, 1988.

Novak, Robert D. *The Agony of the G.O.P., 1964*. New York: MacMillan, 1965.

Nystrom, Justin A. *New Orleans After the Civil War: Race, Politics, and a New Birth of Freedom*. Baltimore: Johns Hopkins University Press, 2010.

Olds, William. *The Segregation Issue: Suggestions Regarding the Maintenance of State Autonomy*. Richmond, Va.: Press of Lawyers, 1955.

Olson, James, and Vera Olson. *The University of Missouri: An Illustrated History*. Columbia: University of Missouri Press, 1988.

O'Neill, Johnathan. *Originalism in American Law and Politics: A Constitutional History*. Baltimore: Johns Hopkins University Press, 2005.

O'Reilly, Kenneth. *Nixon's Piano: Presidents and Racial Politics from Washington to Clinton*. New York: Free Press, 1995.

Patterson, James T. *"Brown v. Board of Education": A Civil Rights Milestone and Its Troubled Legacy*. New York: Oxford University Press, 2001.

Peirce, Neal R. *The Border South States: People, Politics, and Power in the Five Border South States*. New York: W. W. Norton, 1975.

———. *The Great Plains States of America: People, Politics, and Power in the Nine Great Plains States*. New York: W. W. Norton, 1973.

Percy, William Alexander. *Lanterns on the Levee: Recollections of a Planter's Son*. Baton Rouge: Louisiana State University, 1977 (third printing).

Perlstein, Rick. *Before the Storm: Barry Goldwater and the Unmaking of the American Consensus*. New York: Hill and Wang, 2001.

———. *Nixonland: The Rise of a President and the Fracturing of America*. New York: Scribner, 2008.

Perry, Michael J. *The Constitution in the Courts: Law or Politics?* New York: Oxford University Press, 1994.

Phillips, Kevin P. *The Emerging Republican Majority*. New Rochelle, N.Y.: Arlington House, 1969.

Phillips-Fein, Kim. *Invisible Hands: The Making of the Conservative Movement from the New Deal to Reagan*. New York: W. W. Norton, 2009.

Philpot, Tasha S. *Race, Republicans, and the Return of the Party of Lincoln*. Ann Arbor: University of Michigan, 2007.

Posner, Richard A. *Public Intellectuals: A Study of Decline*. Cambridge, Mass.: Harvard University Press, 2001.

Powdermaker, Hortense. *After Freedom: A Cultural Study in the Deep South*. New York: Viking Press, 1939.

Pratt, Robert A. *The Color of Their Skin: Education and Race in Richmond, Virginia, 1954–1989*. Charlottesville: University Press of Virginia, 1992.

Proceedings of the Twenty-Eighth Republican National Convention. Washington, D.C.: Republican National Committee, 1964.

Purcell, Edward A., Jr. *Originalism, Federalism, and the American Constitutional Enterprise: A Historical Inquiry*. New Haven, Conn.: Yale University Press, 2007.

Putnam, Carleton. *Race and Reason: A Yankee View*. Washington, D.C.: Public Affairs Press, 1961.

Rakove, Jack N. *Original Meanings: Politics and Ideas in the Making of the Constitution*. New York: Vintage Books, 1996.

Randolph, Lewis A., and Gayle T. Tate. *Rights for a Season: The Politics of Race, Class, and Gender in Richmond, Virginia*. Knoxville: University of Tennessee Press, 2003.

Reed, John Shelton. *The Enduring South: Subcultural Persistence in Mass Society*. Chapel Hill: University of North Carolina Press, 1974.

Reed, Roy. *Faubus: The Life and Times of an American Prodigal*. Fayetteville: University of Arkansas Press, 1997.

Regnery, Alfred S. *Upstream: The Ascendance of American Conservatism*. New York: Threshold Editions, 2008.

Regnery, Henry. *Memoirs of a Dissident Publisher*. New York: Harcourt Brace Jovanovich, 1979.

Reinhard, David W. *The Republican Right Since 1945*. Lexington, Ky.: University Press of Kentucky, 1983.

Reps, John W. *Cities of the American West: A History of Frontier Urban Planning*. Princeton, N.J.: Princeton University Press, 1979.

Riley, Sam G. *Biographical Dictionary of American Newspaper Columnists*. Westport, Conn.: Greenwood Press, 1995.

Rising, George. *Clean for Gene: Eugene McCarthy's 1968 Presidential Campaign*. Westport, Conn.: Praeger, 1997.

Ritchie, Donald A. *Reporting from Washington: The History of the Washington Press Corps*. New York: Oxford University Press, 2005.

Roberts, Gene, and Hank Klibanoff. *The Race Beat: The Press, the Civil Rights Struggle, and the Awakening of a Nation*. New York: Alfred A. Knopf, 2006.

Roche, Jeff. *The Political Culture of the New West*. Lawrence: University Press of Kansas, 2008.

———. *Restructured Resistance: The Sibley Commission and the Politics of Desegregation in Georgia*. Athens: University of Georgia Press, 1998.

Rosengarten, Theodore. *All God's Dangers: The Life of Nate Shaw*. New York: Avon Books, 1974.

Rouse, Parke, Jr. *We Happy WASPs: Virginia in the Days of Jim Crow and Harry Byrd*. Richmond, Va.: Dietz Press, 1996.

Rubin, Louis D., Jr. *The Faraway Country: Writers of the Modern South*. Seattle: University of Washington Press, 1963.

———. *An Honorable Estate: My Time in the Working Press*. Baton Rouge: Louisiana State University Press, 2001.

———. *Virginia: A History*. New York: W. W. Norton, 1984.

Rubin, Louis D., Jr., and James J. Kilpatrick, eds. *The Lasting South: Fourteen Southerners Look at Their Home*. Chicago: Henry Regnery, 1957.

Ryan, Mary P. *Civic Wars: Democracy and Public Life in the American City During the Nineteenth Century*. Berkeley: University of California Press, 1997.

Sandbrook, Dominic. *Eugene McCarthy: The Rise and Fall of Postwar Liberalism*. New York: Alfred A. Knopf, 2004.

Sansing, David G. *The University of Mississippi: A Sesquicentennial History*. Jackson: University Press of Mississippi, 1999.

Savage, David G. *Turning Right: The Making of the Rehnquist Court*. New York: John Wiley & Sons, 1992.

The Savitar. Vols. 42–47. Columbia: University of Missouri, 1936–41.

Scales, James R., and Danney Goble. *Oklahoma Politics: A History*. Norman: University of Oklahoma Press, 1982.

Scalia, Antonin. *A Matter of Interpretation: Federal Courts and the Law*. Princeton, N.J.: Princeton University Press, 1998.

Schlesinger, Arthur Meier, Sr. *New Viewpoints in American History*. Westport, Conn.: Greenwood Press, 1977 (second printing).

Schwarz, Bernard. *The New Right and the Constitution: Turning Back the Legal Clock*. Boston: Northeastern University Press, 1990.

Schulman, Bruce J. *Lyndon B. Johnson and American Liberalism: A Brief Biography with Documents*. Boston: Bedford St. Martin's, 1995.

———. *The Seventies: The Great Shift in American Culture, Society, and Politics*. Cambridge, Mass.: Da Capo Press, 2002.

Schwartz, Lita Linzer, and Florence W. Kaslow. *Painful Partings: Divorce and Its Aftermath*. New York: John Wiley & Sons, 1997.

Scotchie, Joseph. *Barbarians in the Saddle: An Intellectual Biography of Richard M. Weaver*. New Brunswick, N.J.: Transaction, 1997.

Shafer, Byron E., and Richard Johnston. *The End of Southern Exceptionalism: Class, Race, and Partisan Change in the Postwar South*. Cambridge, Mass.: Harvard University Press, 2006.

Sherrill, Robert. *Gothic Politics in the Deep South: Stars of the New Confederacy*. New York: Grossman Publishers, 1968.

Silver, Christopher. *Twentieth-Century Richmond: Planning, Politics, and Race*. Knoxville: University of Tennessee Press, 1984.

Silver, Christopher, and John V. Moeser. *The Separate City: Black Communities in the Urban South, 1940–1968*. Lexington: University Press of Kentucky, 1995.

Sitkoff, Harvard. *The Struggle for Black Equality, 1954–1992*. New York: Hill and Wang, 1981.

Skocpol, Theda, Peter B. Evans, and Dietrich Rueschemeyer, eds. *Bringing the State Back In*. Cambridge: Cambridge University Press, 1985.

Skrentny, John D. *The Minority Rights Revolution*. Cambridge, Mass.: Harvard University Press, 2002.

Sleeper, Jim. *Liberal Racism*. New York: Viking, 1997.

Smith, Bob. *They Closed Their Schools: Prince Edward County, Virginia, 1951–1964*. Chapel Hill: University of North Carolina Press, 1965.

Smith, J. Douglas. *Managing White Supremacy: Race, Politics, and Citizenship in Jim Crow Virginia*. Chapel Hill: University of North Carolina Press, 2002.

Smith, Stephen A. *Myth, Media, and the Southern Mind*. Fayetteville: University of Arkansas Press, 1985.

Sobel, Mechal. *The World They Made Together: Black and White Values in Eighteenth-Century Virginia*. Princeton, N.J.: Princeton University Press, 1987.

Sokol, Jason. *There Goes My Everything: White Southerners in the Age of Civil Rights, 1945–1975*. New York: Alfred A. Knopf, 2006.

Sosna, Morton. *In Search of the Silent South: Southern Liberals and the Race Issue*. New York: Columbia University Press, 1977.

Southern, David W. *Gunnar Myrdal and Black-White Relations: The Use and Abuse of "An American Dilemma," 1944–1969*. Baton Rouge: Louisiana State University Press, 1987.

Sowell, Thomas. *Civil Rights: Rhetoric or Reality?* New York: William Morrow, 1984.

Stacks, Carol B. *All Our Kin: Strategies for Survival in a Black Community*. New York: Harper and Row, 1974.

Stein, Ben. *The View from Hollywood Boulevard: America as Brought to You by the People Who Make Television*. New York: Basic Books, 1979.

Steinberg, Stephen. *Turning Back: The Retreat from Racial Justice in American Thought and Policy*. Boston: Beacon Press, 1996.

Stephens, Frank F. *A History of the University of Missouri*. Columbia: University of Missouri Press, 1962.

Stock, Noel. *The Life of Ezra Pound*. San Francisco: North Point Press, 1982.

Stowe, Harriet Beecher. *Uncle Tom's Cabin*. 1852. New York: Barnes & Noble, 1995.

Sugrue, Thomas J. *The Origins of the Urban Crisis: Race and Inequality in Postwar Detroit*. Princeton, N.J.: Princeton University Press, 1996.

Sunstein, Cass R. *Radicals in Robes: Why Extreme Right-Wing Courts Are Wrong for America*. New York: Basic Books, 2005.

Sweeney, James R. *Race, Reason, and Massive Resistance: The Diary of David J. Mays, 1954–1959*. Athens: University of Georgia Press, 2008.

Synon, John J. *George Wallace: Profile of a Presidential Candidate*. Kilmarnock, Va.: Ms, 1968

Talmadge, Herman. *You and Segregation*. Birmingham, Ala.: Vulcan Press, 1955.

Tanenhaus, Sam. *The Death of Conservatism*. New York: Random House, 2009.

Teles, Steven M. *The Rise of the Conservative Legal Movement: The Battle for Control of the Law*. Princeton, N.J.: Princeton University Press, 2008.

Thelen, David. *Becoming Citizens in the Age of Television: How Americans Challenged the Media and Seized Political Initiative during the Iran-Contra Debate*. Chicago: University of Chicago Press, 1996.

Thernstrom, Stephan, and Abigail Thernstrom. *America in Black and White: One Nation Indivisible*. New York: Simon and Schuster, 1997.

Thomas, Emory M. *The Confederate State of Richmond: A Biography of the Capital*. Baton Rouge: Louisiana State University Press, 1971.

Thompson, Hunter S. *Fear and Loathing: On the Campaign Trail '72*. New York: Grand Central Publishing, 1973.

Thompson, John. *Closing the Frontier: Radical Response in Oklahoma, 1889–1923*. Norman: University of Oklahoma Press, 1986.

Tindall, George B. *The Emergence of the New South, 1913–1945*. Baton Rouge: Louisiana State University Press, 1967.

Toobin, Jeffrey. *The Nine: Inside the Secret World of the Supreme Court*. New York: Doubleday, 2007.

Tucker, William H. *The Funding of Scientific Racism: Wickliffe Draper and the Pioneer Fund*. Urbana: University of Illinois Press, 2002.

Tushnet, Mark V. *Making Civil Rights Law*. New York: Oxford University Press, 1994.

———. *Making Constitutional Law: Thurgood Marshall and the Supreme Court, 1961–1991*. New York: Oxford University Press, 1997.

Twelve Southerners. *I'll Take My Stand: The South and the Agrarian Tradition*. New York: Harper & Brothers, 1930.

Tyler-McGraw, Marie. *At the Falls: Richmond, Virginia, and Its People*. Chapel Hill: University of North Carolina Press, 1994.

Veblen, Eric P. *The "Manchester Union Leader" in New Hampshire Elections*. Hanover, N.H.: University Press of New England, 1975.

Viguerie, Richard A. *America's Right Turn: How Conservatives Used New and Alternative Media to Take Power*. Chicago: Bonus Books, 2004.

Viles, Jonas. *The University of Missouri: A Centennial History*. Columbia: E. W. Stephens, 1939.

Walker, David B. *The Rebirth of Federalism: Slouching Toward Washington*. New York: Seven Bridges Press, 2000.

Wallace, David Foster. *Consider the Lobster and Other Essays*. New York: Little, Brown, 2005.

Wallenstein, Peter. *Tell the Court I Love My Wife: Race, Marriage, and Law—An American History*. New York: Palgrave MacMillan, 2002.

Weaver, Richard M. *Ideas Have Consequences*. Chicago: University Press of Chicago, 1948.

———. *The Southern Tradition at Bay: A History of Postbellum Thought*. New Rochelle, N.Y.: Arlington House, 1968.

Webb, Clive. *Fight against Fear: Southern Jews and Black Civil Rights*. Athens: University of Georgia Press, 2001.

———. *Massive Resistance: Southern Opposition to the Second Reconstruction*. Edited by Clive Webb. New York: Oxford University Press, 2005.

Whalen, Charles, and Barbara Whalen. *The Longest Debate: A Legislative History of the 1964 Civil Rights Act*. Cabin John, Md.: Seven Locks Press, 1985.

Whittington, Keith E. *Constitutional Interpretation: Textual Meaning, Original Intent, and Judicial Review*. Lawrence: University Press of Kansas, 1999.

Wilhoit, Francis M. *The Politics of Massive Resistance*. New York: George Brazillier, 1973.

Wilkins, Roy. *Standing Fast: The Autobiography of Roy Wilkins*. New York: Da Capo Press, 1994.

Wilkinson, J. Harvie, III. *From "Brown" to "Bakke": The Supreme Court and School Integration, 1954–1978*. New York: Oxford University Press, 1979.

———. *Harry Byrd and the Changing Face of Virginia Politics, 1945–1966*. Charlottesville: University Press of Virginia, 1968.

Williams, Sara Lockwood. *Twenty Years of Education for Journalism: A History of the School of Journalism of the University of Missouri Columbia, Missouri, U. S. A*. Columbia: E. W. Stephens, 1929.

Williams, William Appleman. *The Tragedy of American Diplomacy*. 2nd ed. New York: Dell, 1972.

Williamson, Joel. *A Rage for Order: Black/White Relations in the American South Since Emancipation*. New York: Oxford University Press, 1986.

Wills, Garry. *Confessions of a Conservative*. Garden City, N.Y.: Doubleday, 1979.

———. *A Necessary Evil: A History of American Distrust of Government*. New York: Simon and Schuster, 1999.

————. *Reagan's America*. New York: Doubleday, 1987.

Wilson, Clyde N. *A Defender of Southern Conservatism: M. E. Bradford and His Achievements*. Columbia: University of Missouri Press, 1999.

Wolters, Raymond. *The Burden of Brown: Thirty Years of School Desegregation*. Knoxville: University of Tennessee Press, 1984.

————. *Race and Education, 1954–2007*. Columbia: University of Missouri Press, 2008.

————. *Right Turn: William Bradford Reynolds, the Reagan Administration, and Black Civil Rights*. New Brunswick, N.J.: Transaction, 1996.

Woods, Thomas E., Jr. *The Politically Incorrect Guide to American History*. New York: Regnery, 2004.

Woodward, C. Vann. *The Strange Career of Jim Crow*. 2nd ed. New York: Oxford University Press, 1957.

Workman, William D., Jr. *The Case for the South*. New York: Devin-Adair, 1960.

Wynes, Charles E. *Race Relations in Virginia, 1870–1902*. Charlottesville: University of Virginia Press, 1961.

Yarbrough, Tinsley E. *The Rehnquist Court and the Constitution*. New York: Oxford University Press, 2000.

Younger, Edward, and James Tice Moore, eds. *The Governors of Virginia: 1860–1978*. Charlottesville: University Press of Virginia, 1982.

Unpublished Works

Banks, Samuel Lee. "The Educational Views of James Jackson Kilpatrick Relative to Negroes and School Desegregation as Reflected in *The Richmond News Leader* Newspaper: 1954–1960." Master's thesis, Howard University, 1970.

Boyce, Bret. "Originalism and the Fourteenth Amendment." Senior research paper, Northwestern University School of Law, 1995.

Bramlett, Sharon A. "Southern vs. Northern Newspaper Coverage of a Race Crisis—The Lunch Counter Sit-In Movement, 1960–1964: An Assessment of Social Responsibility." Ph.D. diss., Indiana University, 1987.

Burnette, Ann Elizabeth. "Tradition and Circumstance: James Jackson Kilpatrick and Massive Resistance." Master's thesis, University of Virginia, 1985.

Corley, Robert Gaines. "James Jackson Kilpatrick: The Evolution of a Southern Conservative, 1955–1965." Master's thesis, University of Virginia, 1971.

Cronin, Morton John. "Four American Columnists: A Study in the Partisan Anatomy of David Lawrence, Walter Lippmann, Drew Pearson, and George Sokolsky." Ph.D. diss., University of Minnesota, 1953.

Dickinson, A. J. "Myth and Manipulation: The Story of the Crusade for Voters in Richmond, Virginia: A Case Study of Black Power in A Southern Urban Area." Senior thesis, Yale University, 1967.

Dochuk, Darren. "From Bible Belt to Sunbelt: Plain Folk Religion, Grassroots Politics, and the Southernization of Southern California, 1939–1969." Ph.D. diss., University of Notre Dame, 2005.

Edmonds, Bill. "Civil Rights and Southern Editors: Richmond, Little Rock, Tallahassee." Master's thesis, Florida State University, 1996.

Eischen, Kenneth. "An Analysis of the States' Rights Position of James J. Kilpatrick." Master's thesis, Mankato State College, 1969.

Endres, Kathleen L. "James J. Kilpatrick: A Conservative at Work." Spring 1973. James J. Kilpatrick Papers, Special Collections, University of Virginia.

Heidrick, John L. "James Jackson Kilpatrick: A Study in Contemporary American Conservatism." Master's thesis, Emporia State University, 1978.

Hershman, James Howard, Jr. "A Rumbling in the Museum: The Opponents of Virginia's Massive Resistance." Ph.D. diss., University of Virginia, 1978.

Holton, Dwight Carter. "Power to the People: The Struggle for Black Political Power in Richmond, Virginia." Senior thesis, Brown University, 1987.

Kilpatrick, James J. "The Hell He Is Equal: A Virginia Editor Defends the South's 'Prejudice' against the Negro." Unpublished article for the *Saturday Evening Post*, 1963. Box 6, 6626-c, James J. Kilpatrick Papers, Special Collections, University of Virginia.

Maxwell, Angela Christine. "A Heritage of Inferiority: Public Criticism and the American South." Ph.D. diss., University of Texas, 2008.

Nitschke, Marie Morris. "Virginius Dabney of Virginia: Portrait of a Southern Journalist in the Twentieth Century." Ph.D. diss., Emory University, 1987.

Peeples, Edward H. "Virginia Race History Notes." Work in progress.

Remick, Robert W. "J. Lindsay Almond, Harry F. Byrd, Sr., and the Demise of Massive Resistance, 1956–1959." Senior thesis, Hampden-Sydney College, 1982.

Shelly, Michael Bert. "David Lawrence and Ralph McGill on the Problems of Negro Civil Rights." Master's thesis, University of Illinois, 1963.

Spees, Lisa P. "James J. Kilpatrick: The Changing Views of a Southern Newspaper Editor on School Desegregation." Master's thesis, Emory University, 2009.

Thompson, John Walton, Jr. "Massive Resistance in Virginia." Senior thesis, Princeton University, 1961.

Walker, Anders. "'A Horrible Fascination': Sex, Segregation, & the Lost Politics of Obscenity." No. 2011-06. Saint Louis University School of Law Legal Studies Research Paper Series (February 7, 2011).

Williams, Oscar R. "The Civil Rights Movement in Richmond and Petersburg Virginia during 1960." Master's thesis, Virginia State University, 1990.

INDEX

Byrd, Harry F., Jr., 22, 44

Byrd, Harry F., Sr., 21, 26, 32, 54, 57–62, 64–65, 90, 105–6, 132; background of, 22; political activity, 22; refuses to abandon massive resistance, 85–86; death of, 155

Byrd, William, II, 19

Byrd machine/organization, 22–23, 26, 40, 44–45, 47, 61–62, 65, 84, 90, 105, 203

Cable News Network (CNN), 205

Calhoun, John C., 32, 41, 49–51, 55, 67, 71, 76, 92–93, 97, 205, 234 (n. 24)

Carlson, Frank, 130

Carmichael, Stokely, 156–57

Carter, Jimmy, 186, 205

Central Virginia Education Television Corporation, 102

Chambers, Lenoir, 65, 107

Charlottesville, Va., 28, 65, 79, 83

Chicago, 67, 104, 129, 131

Chodorov, Frank, 69, 73

Church, Frank, 130

The Citizen (journal), 75, 178–79

Citizens' Council, 58, 65, 75, 101, 117, 123, 147, 179, 184, 241 (n. 38); in Virginia, 99–100

Civil rights legislation, federal: 1957 Civil Rights Act, 76, 79; 1964 Civil Rights Act, 96, 99, 121–33, 135, 138–39, 149, 162, 164–65, 175–76, 178, 185, 213, 219; 1965 Voting Rights Act, 99, 105, 149, 162, 185–86; 1965 Immigration Act, 180; Equal Rights Amendment (ERA), 206, 259–60 (n. 13)

Civil rights movement, 4–6, 41–42, 63, 72, 77, 97–99, 101, 105–10, 112–13, 118–23, 152–57, 163, 185, 216, 243 (n. 6)

Civil War, 4, 8, 24, 40, 50, 54, 57, 61, 69, 71, 99

Clendinen, James A., 54

Coleman, Clarence, 83

Coleman, J. P., 63

Columbia Broadcasting System (CBS), 174, 205–6, 210

Communism, fears of, 35, 39, 72, 81, 99, 103, 123–25 (n. 42), 137, 145, 159, 164, 243 (n. 58), 245 (n. 42)

Confederacy, 4, 8, 19–20, 24, 35, 41, 55, 77, 144, 182, 240 (n. 15)

Congdon, Thomas B., Jr., 122

Connor, Eugene, 119–20

Conservatism: as a political and intellectual movement, 2–6, 40–42, 66–76, 92–93, 130–42, 155–56, 164–81, 184; historiography of, 3–4, 171, 226 (nn. 5, 7), 249 (n. 83), 250 (n. 89), 254 (n. 51), 255 (n. 68); in the 1970s, 4, 67, 166–81 passim, 203–5, 209–10, 219; and the CCG, 93, 102–6, 131; and the Goldwater campaign, 133–42; and neoconservatism, 165–66; and agrarianism, 181–95 passim

Coolidge, Calvin, 13, 36

Coordinating Committee for Fundamental American Freedoms (CCFAF), 136, 162; created, 123–25; publicity campaign of, 126, 129–33; funding of, 129–30; end of, 132–33

Crenna, Richard, 206

Crowell-Collier (publisher), 150, 251 (n. 19)

Crossfire, 205

Curtin, Jane, 211

Dabney, Virginius, 30, 65, 118; as editor, 23, 36; racial attitudes of, 36–37, 43, 233 (n. 3); and massive resistance, 65, 84, 86. See also *Richmond Times-Dispatch*

Daniels, Jonathan, 26, 230 (n. 51)

Darden, Colgate W., 27

Davidson, Donald, 75, 184, 187

133–34, 140; political views of, 133, 135 (n. 70)

Gravatt, J. Segar, 100

Graves, John Temple, 101

Gray, Garland, 45, 47

Gray Commission (Gray plan), 45–49, 58–60, 62, 64–65, 86, 90–92

Gray, James H., 110

Great Depression, 4–5, 10, 13, 16–18, 162, 222

Greensboro, N.C., 79; sit-in protests, 108

Green v. County School Board of New Kent County, 179

Griffin, Marvin, 63

Guggenheim, Daniel, 151

Guggenheim, Harry, 151

Guild, June Purcell, 44

Haley, J. Evetts, 59

Hall, Grover, 257 (n. 95)

Hamilton, Alexander, 55

Hamilton, Charles Henry, 18–19, 24, 84

Hamilton, John A., 84, 257 (n. 95)

Hanighen, Frank, 75

Harrigan, Anthony, 74

Harrison, Albertis, 241 (n. 31)

Harrison, Walter M., 11

Hartford Convention, 67, 237 (n. 64)

Hawley, Franklin, 9, 10

Hayden, Carl, 130

Hazlitt, Henry, 151

Helm, W. Stuart, 104

Helms, Jesse, 159, 246 (n. 40)

Henry, Patrick, 28

Hewitt, Don, 205

Hill, Oliver S., Sr., 215

Hilts, Philip, 204

Hiss, Alger, 202

Hodges, Luther, 63

Hoffman, K. V., 65

Holmes, Oliver Wendell, 25

Hoover, J. Edgar, 123

Houston, Mike, 30

Human Events (magazine), 68, 73, 75

Hunt, John, 161–63

Ickes, Harold, 26, 230 (n. 51)

Ingraham, Page L., 124

Integration, 42–43, 82, 160–61, 195; and affirmative action, 163–81 passim, 220–21, 262 (n. 45)

Interposition, 41–42, 49–66 passim, 86, 105, 113, 148, 212, 222

Jackson, Mississippi, 75, 116, 173, 179

Jackson, Thomas Jonathan, 8, 20

Jefferson, Thomas, 14, 20, 32, 36, 41, 49–51, 55–58, 67, 70–71, 92–93, 184, 187; *Notes on the State of Virginia*, 70

John Birch Society, 76, 99, 126, 140, 242 (n. 46)

Johnson, Albert W., 104

Johnson, James, 77

Johnson, Lyndon B., 122, 128, 133, 138, 140–42, 156, 159, 168, 203

Johnston, Erle E., Jr., 124, 256 (n. 86)

Jordan, Len B., 130

Jordan, Winthrop, 5

Kelly Ingram Park, 119

Kendall, Willmoore, 72

Kennedy, John F., 110, 116–17, 119, 122–23, 128, 139, 164, 173, 176

Kennedy, Randall, 150

Kennedy, Robert F., 116–17, 173

Key, V. O., 13, 21

Kilpatrick, Alma Hawley, 9, 10, 12, 17, 228 (n. 31)

Kilpatrick, Blanche, 9, 17

Kilpatrick, Christopher, 27

Kilpatrick, Douglas Mitchell, 8, 9, 13, 218

Kilpatrick, Hawley, 9, 17

Kilpatrick, James J., Jr.: racial attitudes of, 1–2, 33, 46, 52, 57, 68–70, 75, 93–94, 97, 111–12,

Stagg, Tom, Jr., 136–38; and "Operation Dixie," 137
Stanley, Thomas B., 43–45, 47, 49, 61
States' rights and state sovereignty, 1, 14–15, 26, 32, 40–78 passim, 90, 92–96, 103–4, 139, 185, 262 (n. 41)
Stein, Ben, 206
Steingold, Israel, 25
Stephens College, 18
Stuart, J. E. B., 20
Student Non-Violent Coordinating Committee (SNCC), 109, 112
Sturm, George, 11
Susskind, David, 110
Synon, John James, 124–26, 130–32, 246 (n. 49), 247–48 (n. 68); background of, 125

Taft Junior High School, 10, 11, 158
Talmadge, Herman, 234 (n. 21)
Tate, Allen, 183
Taylor, John, 187
Thompson, Hunter S., 207
Thucydides, 144
Thurmond, Strom, 26, 98, 140, 218, 235 (n. 37); endorses interposition, 76
Time, 39, 70, 120, 186, 214
Timmerman, George Bell, 63
Tindall, George Brown, 149
Tocqueville, Alexis de, 31–32, 51
Truman, Harry, 27, 32, 37, 127
Tuck, William, 26, 45, 64, 230 (n. 51)
Tucker, Samuel W., 215
Tucker, Tanya, 186
Tulsa, 15; and 1921 race riot, 15

U.S. Chamber of Commerce, 102, 124, 168–70
U.S. Congress, 14–15, 35, 41–42, 55, 71, 94, 102, 123, 132–33
U.S. Constitution, 14–5, 41–78 passim; Tenth Amendment, 48, 63, 71, 98, 113; Eleventh Amendment, 64; Thirteenth Amendment, 53,

98; Fourteenth Amendment, 46, 53, 63–64, 69, 94, 97–98, 129, 133; Fifteenth Amendment, 98, 133
U.S. News & World Report, 2, 73, 75, 99. *See also* Lawrence, David
U.S. Steelworkers v. Weber, 170
U.S. Supreme Court, 25, 41–65, 69, 71–75, 77, 79, 81–82, 113, 170–72, 213, 215, 220–21
University of Mississippi, 113–14, 116, 118–19, 121, 123, 144, 215
University of Missouri, 16–18, 28, 30
University of Richmond, 43, 55, 182
University of Virginia, 23, 28, 36

Van den Haag, Ernest, 176
Vanderbilt University, 75, 182–84, 187
Viguerie, Richard, 207, 219
Virginia, 3, 9, 40; James River, 19, 21; Southside, 21, 26, 44–45, 58, 83, 92, 125, 132, 151; political and social culture of, 21–22, 28, 187; Shenandoah Valley, 22; voter registration, 22; Black Belt, 45, 47; Chesterfield County, 49
Virginia Commission on Constitutional Government (CCG or VaCCG), 124, 126; created, 90–93, 241 (n. 31); publicity campaign, 94–96, 98, 100–106, 131, 241 (n. 38), 248 (n. 72); failures of, 105–6; publishes *Every Man His Own Law*, 106
Virginia Department of Education, 103
Virginia General Assembly, 50–52, 62–64, 69; legislation of, 20, 90, 92, 178
Virginia Industrialization Group, 87
Virginia and Kentucky Resolutions, 49–50, 54, 60, 63, 67, 94
Virginia Supreme Court of Appeals, 28, 39; invalidates school closings, 88